BOOK 3 – FINANCIAL REPORTING AND ANALYSIS

D1406972

LEVEL 1 BOOK 3: FINANCIAL REPORTING AND ANALYSIS

©2008 Kaplan Schweser. All rights reserved.

Published in 2008 by Kaplan Schweser.

Printed in the United States of America.

ISBN: 1-60373-235-7 / 978-1-60373-235-2

PPN: 45541CFA

READINGS AND LEARNING OUTCOME STATEMENTS

READINGS

The following material is a review of the Financial Reporting and Analysis principles designed to address the learning outcome statements set forth by CFA Institute.

STUDY SESSION 7

Reading Assignments
Financial Reporting and Analysis, CFA Program Curriculum, Volume 3
(CFA Institute, 2009)

STUDY SESSION 8

Reading Assignments
Financial Reporting and Analysis, CFA Program Curriculum, Volume 3
(CFA Institute, 2009)

STUDY SESSION 9

Reading Assignments
Financial Reporting and Analysis, CFA Program Curriculum, Volume 3
(CFA Institute, 2009)

STUDY SESSION 10

Reading Assignments
Financial Reporting and Analysis, CFA Program Curriculum, Volume 3
(CFA Institute, 2009)

LEARNING OUTCOME STATEMENTS (LOS)

The following material is a review of the Financial Reporting and Analysis principles designed to address the learning outcome statements set forth by CFA Institute.

STUDY SESSION 7

The topical coverage corresponds with the following CFA Institute assigned reading:

29. Financial Statement Analysis: An Introduction

The candidate should be able to:
a. discuss the roles of financial reporting and financial statement analysis. (page 11)
b. discuss the role of key financial statements (income statement, balance sheet, cash flow statement and statement of changes in owners' equity) in evaluating a company's performance and financial position. (page 11)
c. discuss the importance of financial statement notes and supplementary information (including disclosures of accounting methods, estimates and assumptions) and management's discussion and analysis. (page 12)
d. discuss the objective of audits of financial statements, the types of audit reports, and the importance of effective internal controls. (page 13)
e. identify and explain information sources other than annual financial statements and supplementary information that analysts use in financial statement analysis. (page 14)
f. describe the steps in the financial statement analysis framework. (page 15)

The topical coverage corresponds with the following CFA Institute assigned reading:

30. Financial Reporting Mechanics

The candidate should be able to:
a. identify the groups (operating, investing, and financing activities) into which business activities are categorized for financial reporting purposes and classify any business activity into the appropriate group. (page 20)
b. explain the relationship of financial statement elements and accounts, and classify accounts into the financial statement elements. (page 21)
c. explain the accounting equation in its basic and expanded forms. (page 22)
d. explain the process of recording business transactions using an accounting system based on the accounting equations. (page 23)
e. explain the need for accruals and other adjustments in preparing financial statements. (page 23)
f. prepare financial statements, given account balances or other elements in the relevant accounting equation, and explain the relationships among the income statement, balance sheet, statement of cash flows, and statement of owners' equity. (page 24)
g. describe the flow of information in an accounting system. (page 27)
h. explain the use of the results of the accounting process in security analysis. (page 27)

The topical coverage corresponds with the following CFA Institute assigned reading:

31. Financial Reporting Standards

The candidate should be able to:
a. explain the objective of financial statements and the importance of reporting standards in security analysis and valuation. (page 35)

b. explain the role of standard-setting bodies, such as the International Accounting Standards Board and the U.S. Financial Accounting Standards Board, and regulatory authorities such as the International Organization of Securities Commissions, the U.K. Financial Services Authority, and the U.S. Securities and Exchange Commission in establishing and enforcing financial reporting standards. (page 35)

c. discuss the ongoing barriers to developing one universally accepted set of financial reporting standards. (page 37)

d. describe the International Financial Reporting Standards (IFRS) framework, including the objective of financial statements, their qualitative characteristics, required reporting elements, and the constraints and assumptions in preparing financial statements. (page 37)

e. explain the general requirements for financial statements. (page 39)

f. compare and contrast key concepts of financial reporting standards under IFRS and alternative reporting systems, and discuss the implications for financial analysis of differing financial reporting systems. (page 40)

g. identify the characteristics of a coherent financial reporting framework and barriers to creating a coherent financial reporting network. (page 41)

h. discuss the importance of monitoring developments in financial reporting standards and evaluate company disclosures of significant accounting policies. (page 42)

STUDY SESSION 8

The topical coverage corresponds with the following CFA Institute assigned reading:

32. Understanding the Income Statement

The candidate should be able to:

a. describe the components of the income statement and construct an income statement using the alternative presentation formats of that statement. (page 48)

b. explain the general principles of revenue recognition and accrual accounting, demonstrate specific revenue recognition applications (including accounting for long-term contracts, installment sales, barter transactions, and gross and net reporting of revenue), and discuss the implications of revenue recognition principles for financial analysis. (page 50)

c. discuss the general principles of expense recognition, such as the matching principle, specific expense recognition applications (including depreciation of long-term assets and inventory methods), and the implications of expense recognition principles for financial analysis. (page 55)

d. determine which method of depreciation, accounting for inventory, or amortizing intangibles is appropriate, based on facts that might influence the decision. (page 56)

e. demonstrate the depreciation of long-term assets using each approved method, accounting for inventory using each approved method, and amortization of intangibles. (page 58)

f. distinguish between the operating and nonoperating components of the income statement. (page 61)

g. discuss the financial reporting treatment and analysis of nonrecurring items (including discontinued operations, extraordinary items, and unusual or infrequent items), and changes in accounting standards. (page 61)

   h. describe the components of earnings per share and calculate a company's earnings per share (both basic and diluted earnings per share) for both a simple and complex capital structure. (page 64)

   i. differentiate between dilutive and antidilutive securities, and discuss the implications of each for the earnings per share calculation. (page 64)

   j. evaluate a company's financial performance using common-size income statements and financial ratios based on the income statement. (page 72)

   k. state the accounting classification for items that are excluded from the income statement but affect owners' equity, and list the major types of items receiving that treatment. (page 74)

   l. describe and calculate comprehensive income. (page 75)

The topical coverage corresponds with the following CFA Institute assigned reading:

33. Understanding the Balance Sheet

The candidate should be able to:

   a. illustrate and interpret the components of the assets, liabilities, and equity sections of the balance sheet, and discuss the uses of the balance sheet in financial analysis. (page 86)

   b. describe the various formats of balance sheet presentation. (page 87)

   c. explain how assets and liabilities arise from the accrual process. (page 88)

   d. compare and contrast current and noncurrent assets and liabilities. (page 88)

   e. explain the measurement bases (e.g., historical cost and fair value) of assets and liabilities, including current assets, current liabilities, tangible assets, and intangible assets. (page 89)

   f. discuss off-balance sheet disclosures. (page 94)

   g. demonstrate the appropriate classifications and related accounting treatments for marketable and non-marketable financial instruments held as assets or owed by the company as liabilities. (page 94)

   h. list and explain the components of owners' equity. (page 96)

   i. interpret balance sheets, common-size balance sheets, the statement of changes in equity, and commonly used balance sheet ratios. (page 97)

The topical coverage corresponds with the following CFA Institute assigned reading:

34. Understanding the Cash Flow Statement

The candidate should be able to:

   a. compare and contrast cash flows from operating, investing, and financing activities, and classify cash flow items as relating to one of these three categories, given a description of the items. (page 109)

   b. describe how noncash investing and financing activities are reported. (page 111)

   c. compare and contrast the key differences in cash flow statements prepared under international financial reporting standards and U.S. generally accepted accounting principles. (page 111)

   d. demonstrate the difference between the direct and indirect methods of presenting cash from operating activities and explain the arguments in favor of each. (page 112)

   e. demonstrate how the cash flow statement is linked to the income statement and balance sheet. (page 114)

   f. demonstrate the steps in the preparation of direct and indirect cash flow statements, including how cash flows can be computed using income statement and balance sheet data. (page 115)

g. describe the process of converting a statement of cash flows from the indirect to the direct method of presentation. (page 121)

h. analyze and interpret a cash flow statement using both total currency amounts and common-size cash flow statements. (page 124)

i. explain and calculate free cash flow to the firm, free cash flow to equity, and other cash flow ratios. (page 126)

STUDY SESSION 9

The topical coverage corresponds with the following CFA Institute assigned reading:

35. Inventories

The candidate should be able to:

a. explain IFRS and U.S. GAAP rules for determining inventory cost including which costs are capitalized and methods of allocating costs between cost of goods sold and inventory. (page 141)

b. discuss how inventories are reported in the financial statements and how the lower of cost or net realizable value is used and applied. (page 142)

c. compute ending inventory balances and cost of goods sold using the FIFO, weighted average cost, and LIFO methods to account for product inventory and explain the relationship among and the usefulness of inventory and cost of goods sold data provided by the FIFO, weighted average cost, and LIFO methods when prices are 1) stable, 2) decreasing, or 3) increasing. (page 144)

d. discuss ratios useful for evaluating inventory management. (page 149)

e. analyze the financial statements of companies using different inventory accounting methods to compare and describe the effect of the different methods on cost of goods sold, inventory balances, and other financial statement items; and compute and describe the effects of the choice of inventory method on profitability, liquidity, activity, and solvency ratios. (page 150)

f. calculate adjustments to reported financial statements related to inventory assumptions in order to aid in comparing and evaluating companies. (page 151)

g. discuss the reasons that a LIFO reserve might rise or decline during a given period and discuss the implications for financial analysis. (page 156)

The topical coverage corresponds with the following CFA Institute assigned reading:

36. Long-Lived Assets

The candidate should be able to:

a. explain the accounting standards related to the capitalization of expenditures as part of long-lived assets, including interest costs. (page 165)

b. compute and describe the effects of capitalizing versus expensing on net income, shareholders' equity, cash flow from operations, and financial ratios including the effect on the interest coverage ratio of capitalizing interest costs. (page 166)

c. explain the circumstances in which software development costs and research and development costs are capitalized. (page 171)

d. identify the different depreciation methods for long-lived tangible assets and discuss how the choice of method, useful lives, and salvage values affect a company's financial statements, ratios, and taxes. (page 173)

e. discuss the use of fixed asset disclosures to compare companies' average age of depreciable assets, and calculate, using such disclosures, the average age and average depreciable life of fixed assets. (page 177)

    f.   describe amortization of intangible assets with finite useful lives, and the estimates that affect the amortization calculations. (page 178)

    g.   discuss the liability for closure, removal, and environmental effects of long-lived operating assets, and discuss the financial statement impact and ratio effects of that liability. (page 179)

    h.   discuss the impact of sales or exchanges of long-lived assets on financial statements. (page 182)

    i.   define impairment of long-lived tangible and intangible assets and explain what effect such impairment has on a company's financial statements and ratios. (page 182)

    j.   calculate and describe both the initial and long-lived effects of asset revaluations on financial ratios. (page 186)

The topical coverage corresponds with the following CFA Institute assigned reading:

37. Income Taxes

The candidate should be able to:

    a.   explain the differences between accounting profit and taxable income, and define key terms including deferred tax assets, deferred tax liabilities, valuation allowance, taxes payable, and income tax expense. (page 195)

    b.   explain how deferred tax liabilities and assets are created and the factors that determine how a company's deferred tax liabilities and assets should be treated for the purposes of financial analysis. (page 196)

    c.   determine the tax base of a company's assets and liabilities. (page 197)

    d.   calculate income tax expense, income taxes payable, deferred tax assets and deferred tax liabilities, and calculate and interpret the adjustment to the financial statements related to a change in the income tax rate. (page 199)

    e.   evaluate the impact of tax rate changes on a company's financial statements and ratios. (page 202)

    f.   distinguish between temporary and permanent items in pretax financial income and taxable income. (page 203)

    g.   discuss the implications of a valuation allowance for deferred tax assets (i.e., when it is required, what impact it has on financial statements, and how it might affect an analyst's view of a company). (page 206)

    h.   compare and contrast a company's deferred tax items and effective tax rate reconciliation between reporting periods. (page 207)

    i.   analyze disclosures relating to deferred tax items and the effective tax rate reconciliation, and discuss how information included in these disclosures affects a company's financial statements and financial ratios. (page 209)

    j.   identify the key provisions of and differences between income tax accounting under IFRS and U.S. GAAP. (page 209)

The topical coverage corresponds with the following CFA Institute assigned reading:

38. Long-Term Liabilities and Leases

The candidate should be able to:

    a.   compute the effects of debt issuance and amortization of bond discounts and premiums on financial statements and ratios. (page 223)

    b.   explain the role of debt covenants in protecting creditors by restricting a company's ability to invest, pay dividends, or make other operating and strategic decisions. (page 231)

    c.   describe the presentation of, and disclosures relating to, financing liabilities. (page 232)

d. determine the effects of changing interest rates on the market value of debt and on financial statements and ratios. (page 232)

e. describe two types of debt with equity features (convertible debt and debt with warrants) and calculate the effect of issuance of such instruments on a company's debt ratios. (page 233)

f. discuss the motivations for leasing assets instead of purchasing them and the incentives for reporting the leases as operating leases rather than finance leases. (page 235)

g. determine the effects of finance and operating leases on the financial statements and ratios of the lessees and lessors. (page 235)

h. distinguish between a sales-type lease and a direct financing lease, and determine the effects on the financial statements and ratios of the lessors. (page 242)

i. describe the types and economic consequences of off-balance-sheet financing, and determine how take-or-pay contracts, throughput arrangements, and the sale of receivables affect financial statements and selected financial ratios. (page 245)

STUDY SESSION 10

The topical coverage corresponds with the following CFA Institute assigned reading:

39. Financial Analysis Techniques

The candidate should be able to:

a. evaluate and compare companies using ratio analysis, common-size financial statements, and charts in financial analysis. (page 255)

b. describe the limitations of ratio analysis. (page 260)

c. calculate, classify, and interpret activity, liquidity, solvency, profitability, and valuation ratios. (page 260)

d. demonstrate how ratios are related and how to evaluate a company using a combination of different ratios. (page 269)

e. demonstrate the application of and interpret changes in the component parts of the DuPont analysis (the decomposition of return on equity). (page 274)

f. calculate and interpret the ratios used in equity analysis, credit analysis, and segment analysis. (page 278)

g. describe how the results of common-size and ratio analysis can be used to model and forecast earnings. (page 283)

The topical coverage corresponds with the following CFA Institute assigned reading:

40. Financial Reporting Quality: Red Flags and Accounting Warning Signs

The candidate should be able to:

a. describe incentives that might induce a company management to overreport or underreport earnings. (page 294)

b. describe activities that will result in a low quality of earnings. (page 295)

c. describe the "fraud triangle." (page 295)

d. describe the risk factors related to incentives and pressures that may lead to fraudulent accounting. (page 296)

e. describe the risk factors related to opportunities that may lead to fraudulent accounting. (page 297)

f. describe the risk factors related to attitudes and rationalizations that may lead to fraudulent accounting. (page 297)

g. describe common accounting warning signs and methods of detecting each. (page 298)

h. describe the accounting warning signs related to the Enron accounting scandal. (page 300)

i. describe the accounting warning signs related to the Sunbeam accounting scandal. (page 301)

The topical coverage corresponds with the following CFA Institute assigned reading:

41. **Accounting Shenanigans on the Cash Flow Statement**

The candidate should be able to analyze and discuss the following ways to manipulate the cash flow statement:
- stretching out payables
- financing of payables
- securitization of receivables
- using stock buybacks to offset dilution of earnings. (page 308)

The topical coverage corresponds with the following CFA Institute assigned reading:

42. **Financial Statement Analysis: Applications**

The candidate should be able to:

a. evaluate a company's past financial performance and explain how a company's strategy is reflected in past financial performance. (page 314)

b. prepare a basic projection of a company's future net income and cash flow. (page 315)

c. describe the role of financial statement analysis in assessing the credit quality of a potential debt investment. (page 316)

d. discuss the use of financial statement analysis in screening for potential equity investments. (page 317)

e. determine and justify appropriate analyst adjustments to a company's financial statements to facilitate comparison with another company. (page 317)

The topical coverage corresponds with the following CFA Institute assigned reading:

43. **International Standards Convergence**

The candidate should be able to:

a. identify and explain the major international accounting standards for each asset and liability category on the balance sheet and the key differences from U.S. generally accepted accounting principles (GAAP). (page 322)

b. identify and explain the major international accounting standards for major revenue and expense categories on the income statement, and the key differences from U.S. GAAP. (page 327)

c. identify and explain the major differences between international and U.S. GAAP accounting standards concerning the treatment of interest and dividends on the cash flow statement. (page 329)

d. interpret the effect of differences between international and U.S. GAAP accounting standards on the balance sheet, income statement, and the statement of changes in equity for some commonly used financial ratios. (page 329)

FINANCIAL STATEMENT ANALYSIS: AN INTRODUCTION

Study Session 7

EXAM FOCUS

This introduction may be useful to those with no previous experience with financial statements. While the income statement, balance sheet, and statement of cash flows are covered in detail in subsequent readings, candidates should pay special attention here to the other sources of information for financial analysis. The nature of the audit report is important, as is the information that is contained in the footnotes to financial statements, proxy statements, Management's Discussion and Analysis, and the supplementary schedules. A useful framework enumerating the steps in financial statement analysis is presented.

LOS 29.a: Discuss the roles of financial reporting and financial statement analysis.

Financial reporting refers to the way companies show their financial performance to investors, creditors, and other interested parties by preparing and presenting financial statements. The role of financial reporting is described by the International Accounting Standards Board (IASB) in its "Framework for the Preparation and Presentation of Financial Statements":

> "The objective of financial statements is to provide information about the financial position, performance and changes in financial position of an entity that is useful to a wide range of users in making economic decisions."

The role of **financial statement analysis** is to use the information in a company's financial statements, along with other relevant information, to make economic decisions. Examples of such decisions include whether to invest in the company's securities or recommend them to investors, and whether to extend trade or bank credit to the company. Analysts use financial statement data to evaluate a company's past performance and current financial position in order to form opinions about the company's ability to earn profits and generate cash flow in the future.

LOS 29.b: Discuss the role of key financial statements (income statement, balance sheet, cash flow statement and statement of changes in owners' equity) in evaluating a company's performance and financial position.

The **income statement** reports on the financial performance of the firm over a period of time. The elements of the income statement include revenues, expenses, and gains and losses.

- *Revenues* are inflows from delivering or producing goods, rendering services, or other activities that constitute the entity's ongoing major or central operations.

- *Expenses* are outflows from delivering or producing goods or services that constitute the entity's ongoing major or central operations.
- *Gains and losses* are increases and decreases in equity or net assets from peripheral or incidental transactions.

The **balance sheet** reports the firm's financial position at a point in time. The balance sheet consists of three elements:

1. *Assets* are probable current and future economic benefits obtained or controlled by a particular entity as a result of past transactions or events. Assets are a firm's economic resources.

2. *Liabilities* are probable future economic costs. They arise from present obligations of a particular entity to transfer assets or provide services to other entities in the future as a result of past transactions or events.

3. *Owners' equity* is the residual interest in the net assets of an entity that remains after deducting its liabilities.

Transactions are measured so that the fundamental **accounting equation** holds:

assets = liabilities + owners' equity

The **cash flow statement** reports the company's cash receipts and payments. These cash flows are classified as follows:

- *Operating cash flows* include the cash effects of transactions that involve the normal business of the firm.
- *Investing cash flows* are those resulting from the acquisition or sale of property, plant, and equipment, of a subsidiary or segment, of securities, and of investments in other firms.
- *Financing cash flows* are those resulting from issuance or retirement of the firm's debt and equity securities and include dividends paid to stockholders.

The **statement of changes in owners' equity** reports the amounts and sources of changes in equity investors' investment in the firm over a period of time.

LOS 29.c: Discuss the importance of financial statement notes and supplementary information (including disclosures of accounting methods, estimates and assumptions), and management's discussion and analysis.

Financial statement notes (footnotes) include disclosures that provide further details about the information summarized in the financial statements. Footnotes allow users to improve their assessments of the amount, timing, and uncertainty of the estimates reported in the financial statements. Footnotes:

- Provide information about accounting methods, assumptions, and estimates used by management.
- Are audited, whereas other disclosures, such as supplementary schedules, are not audited.

- Provide additional information on items such as business acquisitions or disposals, legal actions, employee benefit plans, contingencies and commitments, significant customers, sales to related parties, and segments of the firm.

Supplementary schedules contain additional information. Examples of such disclosures include:

- Operating income or sales by region or business segment.
- Reserves for an oil and gas company.
- Information about hedging activities and financial instruments.

Management's Discussion and Analysis (MD&A) provides an assessment of the financial performance and condition of a company from the perspective of its management. For publicly held companies in the United States, the MD&A is required to discuss:

- Results from operations, with a discussion of trends in sales and expenses.
- Capital resources and liquidity, with a discussion of trends in cash flows.
- A general business overview based on known trends.

Management's Discussion and Analysis can also include:

- Discussion of accounting policies that require significant judgements by management.
- Discussion of significant effects of currently known trends, events, and uncertainties (may voluntarily disclose forward-looking data).
- Liquidity and capital resource issues, and transactions or events with liquidity implications.
- Discontinued operations, extraordinary items, and other unusual or infrequent events.
- Extensive disclosures in interim financial statements.
- Disclosures of a segment's need for cash flows or its contribution to revenues or profit.

LOS 29.d: Discuss the objective of audits of financial statements, the types of audit reports, and the importance of effective internal controls.

An **audit** is an independent review of an entity's financial statements. Public accountants conduct audits and examine the financial reports and supporting records. The objective of an audit is to enable the auditor to provide an opinion on the fairness and reliability of the financial statements.

The independent certified public accounting firm employed by the board of directors is responsible for seeing that the financial statements conform to the applicable accounting standards. The auditor examines the company's accounting and internal control systems, confirms assets and liabilities, and generally tries to determine that there are no material errors in the financial statements. The auditor's report is an important source of information.

The **standard auditor's opinion** contains three parts and states that:

1. Whereas the financial statements are prepared by management and are its responsibility, the auditor has performed an independent review.

2. Generally accepted auditing standards were followed, thus providing *reasonable assurance* that the financial statements contain no material errors.

3. The auditor is satisfied that the statements were prepared in accordance with accepted accounting principles, and that the principles chosen and estimates made are reasonable. The auditor's report must also contain additional explanation when accounting methods have not been used consistently between periods.

An *unqualified opinion* indicates that the auditor believes the statements are free from material omissions and errors. If the statements make any exceptions to the accounting principles, the auditor may issue a *qualified opinion* and explain these exceptions in the audit report. The auditor can issue an *adverse opinion* if the statements are not presented fairly or are materially nonconforming with accounting standards.

The auditor's opinion will also contain an explanatory paragraph when a material loss is probable but the amount cannot be reasonably estimated. These "uncertainties" may relate to the *going concern assumption* (the assumption that the firm will continue to operate for the foreseeable future), the valuation or realization of asset values, or to litigation. This type of disclosure may be a signal of serious problems and may call for close examination by the analyst.

Under U.S. Generally Accepted Accounting Principles (GAAP), the auditor must state its opinion on the company's **internal controls**, which are the processes by which the company ensures that it presents accurate financial statements. The auditor can provide this opinion separately or as the fourth element of the standard auditor's opinion.

Internal controls are the responsibility of the firm's management. Under the Sarbanes-Oxley Act, management is required to provide a report on the company's internal control system that includes the following elements:

*   A statement that the firm's management is responsible for implementing and maintaining effective internal controls.
*   A description of how management evaluates the internal control system.
*   An assessment by management of the effectiveness over the most recent year of the firm's internal controls.
*   A statement that the firm's auditors have assessed management's report on internal controls.
*   A statement certifying that the firm's financial statements are presented fairly.

LOS 29.e: Identify and explain information sources other than annual financial statements and supplementary information that analysts use in financial statement analysis.

Besides the annual financial statements, an analyst should examine a company's *quarterly or semiannual reports*. These interim reports typically update the major financial statements and footnotes but are not necessarily audited.

Securities and Exchange Commission (SEC) filings are available from EDGAR (Electronic Data Gathering, Analysis, and Retrieval System, www.sec.gov). These include Form 8-K, which a company must file to report events such as acquisitions and disposals of major assets or changes in its management or corporate governance. Companies' annual and quarterly financial statements are also filed with the SEC (Form 10-K and Form 10-Q, respectively).

Proxy statements are issued to shareholders when there are matters that require a shareholder vote. These statements, which are also filed with the SEC and available from EDGAR, are a good source of information about the election of (and qualifications of) board members, compensation, management qualifications, and the issuance of stock options.

Corporate reports and press releases are written by management and are often viewed as public relations or sales materials. Not all of the material is independently reviewed by outside auditors. Such information can often be found on the company's web site.

An analyst should also review pertinent information on economic conditions and the company's industry and compare the company to its competitors. The necessary information can be acquired from trade journals, statistical reporting services, and government agencies.

LOS 29.f: Describe the steps in the financial statement analysis framework.

The **financial statement analysis framework**[1] consists of six steps:

1. *State the objective and context.* Determine what questions the analysis seeks to answer, the form in which this information needs to be presented, and what resources and how much time are available to perform the analysis.

2. *Gather data.* Acquire the company's financial statements and other relevant data on its industry and the economy. Ask questions of the company's management, suppliers, and customers, and visit company sites.

3. *Process the data.* Make any appropriate adjustments to the financial statements. Calculate ratios. Prepare exhibits such as graphs and common-size balance sheets.

4. *Analyze and interpret the data.* Use the data to answer the questions stated in the first step. Decide what conclusions or recommendations the information supports.

5. *Report the conclusions or recommendations.* Prepare a report and communicate it to its intended audience. Be sure the report and its dissemination comply with the Code and Standards that relate to investment analysis and recommendations.

6. *Update the analysis.* Repeat these steps periodically and change the conclusions or recommendations when necessary.

---

1. Hennie van Greuning and Sonja Brajovic Bratanovic, *Analyzing and Managing Banking Risk: Framework for Assessing Corporate Governance and Financial Risk*, International Bank for Reconstruction and Development, April 2003, p. 300.

KEY CONCEPTS

LOS 29.a

The role of financial reporting is to provide a variety of users with useful information about a company's performance and financial position.

The role of financial statement analysis is to use the data from financial statements to support economic decisions.

LOS 29.b

The income statement shows the results of a firm's business activities over the period. Revenues, the cost of generating those revenues, and the resulting profit or loss are presented on the income statement.

The balance sheet shows assets, liabilities, and owners' equity at a point in time.

The cash flow statement shows the sources and uses of cash over the period.

The statement of changes in owners' equity reports the amount and sources of changes in the equity owners' investment in the firm.

LOS 29.c

Important information about accounting methods, estimates, and assumptions is disclosed in the footnotes to the financial statements and supplementary schedules. These disclosures also contain information about segment results, commitments and contingencies, legal proceedings, acquisitions or divestitures, issuance of stock options, and details of employee benefit plans.

Management's Discussion and Analysis contains an overview of the company and important information about business trends, future capital needs, liquidity, significant events, and significant choices of accounting methods requiring management judgment.

LOS 29.d

The objective of audits of financial statements is to provide an opinion on the statements' fairness and reliability.

The auditor's opinion gives evidence of an independent review of the financial statements that verifies that appropriate accounting principles were used, that standard auditing procedures were used to establish reasonable assurance that the statements contain no material errors, and that management's report on the company's internal controls has been reviewed.

An auditor can issue an unqualified (clean) opinion if the statements are free from material omissions and errors, a qualified opinion that notes any exceptions to accounting principles, or an adverse opinion if the statements are not presented fairly in the auditor's opinion.

A company's management is responsible for maintaining an effective internal control system to ensure the accuracy of its financial statements. For public companies in the U.S., the Sarbanes-Oxley Act specifically requires a management report on the firm's internal controls, a description of the method used to evaluate their effectiveness, and a statement as to their effectiveness over the accounting period.

LOS 29.e

Along with the annual financial statements, important information sources for an analyst include a company's quarterly and semiannual reports, proxy statements, and press releases as well as information on the industry and peer companies from external sources.

LOS 29.f

The framework for financial analysis has six steps:
1. State the objective of the analysis.
2. Gather data.
3. Process the data.
4. Analyze and interpret the data.
5. Report the conclusions or recommendations.
6. Update the analysis. Follow up

CONCEPT CHECKERS

1. Which of the following statements *least accurately* describes a role of financial statement analysis?
    A. Use the information in financial statements to make economic decisions.
    B. Provide reasonable assurance that the financial statements are free of material errors.
    C. Evaluate an entity's financial position and past performance to form opinions about its future ability to earn profits and generate cash flow.

2. A firm's financial position at a specific point in time is reported in the:
    A. balance sheet.
    B. income statement.
    C. cash flow statement.

3. Information about accounting estimates, assumptions, and methods chosen for reporting is *most likely* found in:
    A. the auditor's opinion.
    B. financial statement notes.
    C. Management's Discussion and Analysis.

4. If an auditor finds that a company's financial statements have made a specific exception to applicable accounting principles, she is *most likely* to issue a:
    A. dissenting opinion.
    B. cautionary note.
    C. qualified opinion.

5. Information about elections of members to a company's Board of Directors is *most likely* found in:
    A. a 10-Q filing.
    B. a proxy statement.
    C. footnotes to the financial statements.

6. Which of these steps is *least likely* to be a part of the financial statement analysis framework?
    A. State the purpose and context of the analysis.
    B. Determine whether the company's securities are suitable for the client.
    C. Adjust the financial statement data and compare the company to its industry peers.

ANSWERS – CONCEPT CHECKERS

1. **B** This statement describes the role of an auditor, rather than the role of an analyst. The other responses describe the role of financial statement analysis.

2. **A** The balance sheet reports a company's financial position as of a specific date. The income statement, cash flow statement, and statement of changes in owners' equity show the company's performance during a specific period.

3. **B** Information about accounting methods and estimates is contained in the footnotes to the financial statements.

4. **C** An auditor will issue a qualified opinion if the financial statements make any exceptions to applicable accounting standards and will explain the effect of these exceptions in the auditor's report.

5. **B** Proxy statements contain information related to matters that come before shareholders for a vote, such as elections of board members.

6. **B** Determining the suitability of an investment for a client is not one of the six steps in the financial statement analysis framework. The analyst would only perform this function if he also had an advisory relationship with the client. Stating the objective and processing the data are two of the six steps in the framework. The others are gathering the data, analyzing the data, updating the analysis, and reporting the conclusions.

The following is a review of the Financial Reporting and Analysis principles designed to address the learning outcome statements set forth by CFA Institute®. This topic is also covered in:

FINANCIAL REPORTING MECHANICS

EXAM FOCUS

The analysis of financial statements requires an understanding of how a company's transactions are recorded in the various accounts. Candidates should focus on the financial statement elements (assets, liabilities, equity, revenues, and expenses) and be able to classify any account into its appropriate element. Candidates should also learn the basic and expanded accounting equations and why every transaction must be recorded in at least two accounts. Knowing the four types of accruals and when each of them is used, and understanding how changes in accounts affect the financial statements and the relationships among the financial statements, are all important topics.

LOS 30.a: Identify the groups (operating, investing, and financing activities) into which business activities are categorized for financial reporting purposes and classify any business activity into the appropriate group.

Business transactions can be classified for financial reporting as operating activities, investing activities, or financing activities.

Operating activities are transactions that involve the firm's primary activities of production and trade. Sales and their related costs are typically a firm's primary operating activities. Other examples of operating activities include paying taxes, buying short-term assets, and taking on short-term liabilities to support the firm's ordinary business.

Investing activities are transactions to acquire or dispose of long-term assets. Purchases and sales of property, plant, and equipment are investing activities, as are purchases and sales of securities issued by others.

Financing activities are transactions through which the firm raises or repays capital. These include issuing or repaying debt, issuing or repurchasing stock, and paying dividends to shareholders.

How a transaction is classified depends on the nature of the firm, rather than the nature of the transaction. For example, holding long-term securities is an investing activity for most firms but is an operating activity for a company whose primary business is making such investments.

LOS 30.b: Explain the relationship of financial statement elements and accounts, and classify accounts into the financial statement elements.

Financial statement elements are the major classifications of assets, liabilities, owners' equity, revenues, and expenses. **Accounts** are the specific records within each element where various transactions are entered. On the financial statements, accounts are typically presented in groups such as "inventory" or "accounts payable." A company's **chart of accounts** is a detailed list of the accounts that make up the five financial statement elements and the line items presented in the financial statements.

Contra accounts are used for entries that offset some part of the value of another account. For example, equipment is typically valued on the balance sheet at acquisition (historical) cost, and the estimated decrease in its value over time is recorded in a contra account titled "accumulated depreciation."

Classifying Accounts Into the Financial Statement Elements

Assets are the firm's economic resources. Examples of assets include:

- *Cash and cash equivalents.* Liquid securities with maturities of 90 days or less are considered cash equivalents.
- *Accounts receivable.* Accounts receivable often have an "allowance for bad debt expense" or "allowance for doubtful accounts" as a contra account.
- *Inventory.*
- *Financial assets* such as marketable securities.
- *Prepaid expenses.* Items that will be expenses on future income statements.
- *Property, plant, and equipment.* Includes a contra-asset account for accumulated depreciation.
- *Investment in affiliates* accounted for using the equity method.
- *Deferred tax assets.*
- *Intangible assets.* Economic resources of the firm that do not have a physical form, such as patents, trademarks, licenses, and goodwill. Except for goodwill, these values may be reduced by "accumulated amortization."

Liabilities are creditor claims on the company's resources. Examples of liabilities include:

- *Accounts payable* and *trade payables*.
- *Financial liabilities* such as short-term notes payable.
- *Unearned revenue.* Items that will show up on future income statements as revenues.
- *Income taxes payable.* The taxes accrued during the past year but not yet paid.
- *Long-term debt* such as bonds payable.
- *Deferred tax liabilities*.

Owners' equity is the owners' residual claim on a firm's resources, which is the amount by which assets exceed liabilities. Owners' equity includes:

- *Capital.* Par value of common stock.
- *Additional paid-in capital.* Proceeds from common stock sales in excess of par value. (Share repurchases that the company has made are represented in the contra account, *treasury stock*.)
- *Retained earnings.* Cumulative net income that has not been distributed as dividends.

- *Other comprehensive income.* Changes resulting from foreign currency translation, minimum pension liability adjustments, or unrealized gains and losses on investments.

Revenue represents inflows of economic resources and includes:

- *Sales.* Revenue from the firm's day-to-day activities.
- *Gains.* Increases in assets or equity from transactions incidental to the firm's day-to-day activities.
- *Investment income* such as interest and dividend income.

Expenses are outflows of economic resources and include:

- *Cost of goods sold.*
- *Selling, general, and administrative expenses.* These include such expenses as advertising, management salaries, rent, and utilities.
- *Depreciation* and *amortization.* To reflect the "using up" of tangible and intangible assets.
- *Tax expense.*
- *Interest expense.*
- *Losses.* Decreases in assets or equity from transactions incidental to the firm's day-to-day activities.

LOS 30.c: Explain the accounting equation in its basic and expanded forms.

The **basic accounting equation** is the relationship among the three balance sheet elements:

assets = liabilities + owners' equity

Owners' equity consists of capital contributed by the firm's owners and the cumulative earnings the firm has retained. With that in mind, we can state the **expanded accounting equation**:

assets = liabilities + contributed capital + ending retained earnings

Ending retained earnings for an accounting period is the result of adding that period's retained earnings (revenues minus expenses minus dividends) to beginning retained earnings. So the expanded accounting equation can also be stated as:

Assets =   Liabilities
            + Contributed Capital
            + Beginning Retained Earnings
            + Revenue
            – Expenses
            – Dividends

LOS 30.d: Explain the process of recording business transactions using an accounting system based on the accounting equations.

Keeping the accounting equation in balance requires **double-entry accounting**, in which a transaction has to be recorded in at least two accounts. An increase in an asset account, for example, must be balanced by a decrease in another asset account or by an increase in a liability or owners' equity account.

Some typical examples of double entry accounting include:

- *Purchase equipment for $10,000 cash.* Property, plant and equipment (an asset) increases by $10,000. Cash (an asset) decreases by $10,000.
- *Borrow $10,000 to purchase equipment.* PP&E increases by $10,000. Notes payable (a liability) increases by $10,000.
- *Buy office supplies for $100 cash.* Cash decreases by $100. Supply expense increases by $100. An expense reduces retained earnings, so owners' equity decreases by $100.
- *Buy inventory for $8,000 cash and sell it for $10,000 cash.* The purchase decreases cash by $8,000 and increases inventory (an asset) by $8,000. The sale increases cash by $10,000 and decreases inventory by $8,000, so assets increase by $2,000. At the same time, sales (a revenue account) increase by $10,000 and "cost of goods sold" (an expense) increases by the $8,000 cost of inventory. The $2,000 difference is an increase in net income and, therefore, in retained earnings and owners' equity (ignoring taxes).

LOS 30.e: Explain the need for accruals and other adjustments in preparing financial statements.

Revenues and expenses are not always recorded at the same time that cash receipts and payments are made. The principle of **accrual accounting** requires that revenue is recorded when the firm earns it and expenses are recorded as the firm incurs them, regardless of whether cash has actually been paid. Accruals fall into four categories:

1. *Unearned revenue.* The firm receives cash before it provides a good or service to customers. Cash increases and unearned revenue, a liability, increases by the same amount. When the firm provides the good or service, revenue increases and the liability decreases. For example, a newspaper or magazine subscription is typically paid in advance. The publisher records the cash received and increases the unearned revenue liability account. The firm recognizes revenues and decreases the liability as it fulfills the subscription obligation.

2. *Accrued revenue.* The firm provides goods or services before it receives cash payment. Revenue increases and accounts receivable (an asset) increases. When the customer pays cash, accounts receivable decreases. A typical example would be a manufacturer that sells goods to retail stores "on account." The manufacturer records revenue when it delivers the goods but does not receive cash until after the retailers sell the goods to consumers.

3. *Prepaid expenses.* The firm pays cash ahead of time for an anticipated expense. Cash (an asset) decreases and prepaid expense (also an asset) increases. Prepaid expense decreases and expenses increase when the expense is actually incurred. For example, a retail store that rents space in a shopping mall will often pay its rent in advance.

4. *Accrued expenses.* The firm owes cash for expenses it has incurred. Expenses increase and a liability for accrued expenses increases as well. The liability decreases when the firm pays cash to satisfy it. Wages payable are a common example of an accrued expense, as companies typically pay their employees at a later date for work they performed in the prior week or month.

Accruals require an accounting entry when the earliest event occurs (paying or receiving cash, providing a good or service, or incurring an expense) and require one or more offsetting entries as the exchange is completed. With unearned revenue and prepaid expenses, cash changes hands first and the revenue or expense is recorded later. With accrued revenue and accrued expenses, the revenue or expense is recorded first and cash is exchanged later. In all these cases, the effect of accrual accounting is to recognize revenues or expenses in the appropriate period.

Other Adjustments

Most assets are recorded on the financial statements at their historical costs. However, accounting standards require balance sheet values of certain assets to reflect their current market values. Accounting entries that update these assets' values are called **valuation adjustments**. To keep the accounting equation in balance, changes in asset values also change owners' equity, through gains or losses recorded on the income statement or in "other comprehensive income."

LOS 30.f: Prepare financial statements, given account balances or other elements in the relevant accounting equation, and explain the relationships among the income statement, balance sheet, statement of cash flows, and statement of owners' equity.

Figures 1 through 4 contain the financial statements for a sample corporation. The balance sheet summarizes the company's financial position at the end of the current accounting period (and in this example, it also shows the company's position at the end of the previous fiscal period). The income statement, cash flow statement, and statement of owners' equity show changes that occurred during the most recent accounting period.

Note these key relationships among the financial statements:

*   The income statement shows that net income was $37,500 in 20X8. The company declared $8,500 of that income as dividends to its shareholders. The remaining $29,000 is an increase in retained earnings. Retained earnings on the balance sheet increased by $29,000, from $30,000 in 20X7 to $59,000 in 20X8.
*   The cash flow statement shows a $24,000 net increase in cash. On the balance sheet, cash increased by $24,000, from $9,000 in 20X7 to $33,000 in 20X8.

- One of the uses of cash shown on the cash flow statement is a repurchase of stock for $10,000. The balance sheet shows this $10,000 repurchase as a decrease in common stock, from $50,000 in 20X7 to $40,000 in 20X8.
- The statement of owners' equity reflects the changes in retained earnings and contributed capital (common stock). Owners' equity increased by $19,000, from $80,000 in 20X7 to $99,000 in 20X8. This equals the $29,000 increase in retained earnings less the $10,000 decrease in common stock.

Figure 1: Income Statement for 20X8

Sales	$100,000
Expenses	
Cost of goods sold	40,000
Wages	5,000
Depreciation	7,000
Interest	500
Total expenses	$52,500
Income from continuing operations	47,500
Gain from sale of land	10,000
Pretax income	$57,500
Provision for taxes	20,000
Net income	$37,500
Common dividends declared	8,500

Figure 2: Balance Sheet for 20X7 and 20X8

	20X8	20X7
Assets		
Current assets		
Cash	$33,000	$9,000
Accounts receivable	10,000	9,000
Inventory	5,000	7,000
Noncurrent assets		
Land	$35,000	$40,000
Gross plant and equipment	85,000	60,000
less: Accumulated depreciation	(16,000)	(9,000)
Net plant and equipment	$69,000	$51,000
Goodwill	10,000	10,000
Total assets	$162,000	$126,000
Liabilities and Equity		
Current liabilities		
Accounts payable	$9,000	$5,000
Wages payable	4,500	8,000
Interest payable	3,500	3,000
Taxes payable	5,000	4,000
Dividends payable	6,000	1,000
Noncurrent liabilities		
Bonds	$15,000	$10,000
Deferred taxes	20,000	15,000
Stockholders' equity		
Common stock	$40,000	$50,000
Retained earnings	59,000	30,000
Total liabilities & stockholders' equity	$162,000	$126,000

Figure 3: Cash Flow Statement for 20X8

Cash collections	$99,000
cash inputs	(34,000)
cash expenses	(8,500)
cash interest	0
cash taxes	(14,000)
Cash flow from operations	$42,500
Cash from sale of land	$15,000
Purchase of plant and equipment	(25,000)
Cash flow from investments	($10,000)
Sale of bonds	$5,000
Repurchase of stock	(10,000)
Cash dividends	(3,500)
Cash flow from financing	($8,500)
Total cash flow	$24,000

Figure 4: Statement of Owners' Equity for 20X8

	Contributed Capital	Retained Earnings	Total
Balance, 12/31/20X7	$50,000	$30,000	$80,000
Repurchase of stock	($10,000)		($10,000)
Net income		$37,500	$37,500
Distributions		($8,500)	($8,500)
Balance, 12/31/20X8	$40,000	$59,000	$99,000

LOS 30.g: Describe the flow of information in an accounting system.

Information flows through an accounting system in four steps:

1. *Journal entries* record every transaction, showing which accounts are changed and by what amounts. A listing of all the journal entries in order of their dates is called the "general journal."

2. The *general ledger* sorts the entries in the general journal by account.

3. At the end of the accounting period, an *initial trial balance* is prepared that shows the balances in each account. If any adjusting entries are needed, they will be recorded and reflected in an *adjusted trial balance.*

4. The account balances from the adjusted trial balance are presented in the *financial statements*.

LOS 30.h: Explain the use of the results of the accounting process in security analysis.

An analyst does not have access to the detailed information that flows through a company's accounting system, but sees only the end product, the financial statements. An analyst needs to understand the various accruals, adjustments, and management assumptions that go into the financial statements. Much of this detail is contained in the footnotes to the statements and Management's Discussion and Analysis, so it is crucial for an analyst to review these parts of the financial statements. With this information, the analyst can better judge how well the financial statements reflect the company's true performance and what adjustments to the data are necessary for appropriate analysis.

Because adjustments and assumptions within the financial statements are, at least to some extent, at the discretion of management, the possibility exists that management may attempt to manipulate or misrepresent the company's financial performance. A good understanding of the accounting process can help an analyst identify financial statement entries that appear to be out of line.

KEY CONCEPTS

LOS 30.a

Business transactions can be categorized as:
- Operating activities—the firm's ordinary business.
- Investing activities—purchasing, selling, and disposing of long-term assets.
- Financing activities—raising and repaying capital.

LOS 30.b

Transactions are recorded in accounts that form the financial statement elements:
- Assets—the firm's economic resources.
- Liabilities—creditors' claims on the firm's resources.
- Owners' equity—paid-in capital (common and preferred stock), retained earnings, and cumulative other comprehensive income.
- Revenues—sales, investment income, and gains.
- Expenses—cost of goods sold, selling and administrative expenses, depreciation, interest, taxes, and losses.

LOS 30.c

The basic accounting equation:

$$\text{assets} = \text{liabilities} + \text{owners' equity}$$

The expanded accounting equation:

$$\text{assets} = \text{liabilities} + \text{contributed capital} + \text{ending retained earnings}$$

The expanded accounting equation can also be stated as:

$$\text{assets} = \text{liabilities} + \text{contributed capital} + \text{beginning retained earnings} + \text{revenue} - \text{expenses} - \text{dividends}$$

LOS 30.d

To keep the accounting equation in balance, each transaction has to be recorded in at least two accounts.

LOS 30.e

A firm must recognize revenues when they are earned and expenses when they are incurred. Accruals are required when the timing of cash payments made and received does not match the timing of the revenue or expense recognition on the financial statements.

LOS 30.f

The balance sheet shows a company's financial position at a point in time.

Changes in balance sheet accounts during an accounting period are reflected in the income statement, the cash flow statement, and the statement of owners' equity.

LOS 30.g

Information enters an accounting system as journal entries, which are sorted by account into a general ledger. Trial balances are formed at the end of an accounting period. Accounts are then adjusted and presented in financial statements.

LOS 30.h

Since financial reporting requires choices of method, judgment, and estimates, an analyst must understand the accounting process used to produce the financial statements in order to understand the business and the results for the period. Analysts should be alert to the use of accruals, changes in valuations, and other notable changes that may indicate management judgment is incorrect or, worse, that the financial statements have been deliberately manipulated.

CONCEPT CHECKERS

1. Richland Paper is a manufacturer of folding cartons for packaging retail items. This year the company acquired a new cutting machine that it expects to use for the next eight years. This purchase should be classified as a(n):
   A. operating activity.
   B. investing activity.
   C. financing activity.

2. Sparta Distributors, a wholesaler, has obtained a $5 million 10-year loan from Stoddard National Bank. How should each firm *best* classify this transaction?

	Sparta Distributors	Stoddard Nat'l Bank
A.	Investing activity	Financing activity
B.	Financing activity	Financing activity
C.	Financing activity	Operating activity

3. Accounts receivable and accounts payable are *most likely* classified as which financial statement elements?

	Accounts receivable	Accounts payable
A.	Assets	Liabilities
B.	Revenues	Liabilities
C.	Revenues	Expenses

4. Annual depreciation and accumulated depreciation are *most likely* classified as which financial statement elements?

	Depreciation	Accumulated depreciation
A.	Expenses	Contra liabilities
B.	Expenses	Contra assets
C.	Liabilities	Contra assets

5. The accounting equation is *least accurately* stated as:
   A. owners' equity = liabilities − assets.
   B. ending retained earnings = assets − contributed capital − liabilities.
   C. assets = liabilities + contributed capital + beginning retained earnings + revenue − expenses − dividends.

6. A decrease in assets would *least likely* be consistent with a(n):
   A. increase in expenses.
   B. decrease in revenues.
   C. increase in contributed capital.

7. An electrician repaired the light fixtures in a retail shop on October 24 and sent the bill to the shop on November 3. If both the electrician and the shop prepare financial statements under the accrual method on October 31, how will they each record this transaction?

	Electrician	Retail shop
A.	Accrued revenue	Accrued expense
B.	Accrued revenue	Prepaid expense
C.	Unearned revenue	Accrued expense

8. If a firm raises $10 million by issuing new common stock, which of its financial statements will reflect the transaction?
    A. Income statement and statement of owners' equity.
    B. Balance sheet, income statement, and cash flow statement.
    C. Balance sheet, cash flow statement, and statement of owners' equity.

9. An auditor needs to review all of a company's transactions that took place between August 15 and August 17 of the current year. To find this information, she would *most likely* consult the company's:
    A. general ledger.
    B. general journal.
    C. financial statements.

10. Paul Schmidt, a representative for Westby Investments, is explaining how security analysts use the results of the accounting process. He states, "Analysts do not have access to all the entries that went into creating a company's financial statements. If the analyst carefully reviews the auditor's report for any instances where the financial statements deviate from the appropriate accounting principles, he can then be confident that management is not manipulating earnings." Schmidt is:
    A. correct.
    B. incorrect, because the entries that went into creating a company's financial statements are publicly available.
    C. incorrect, because management can manipulate earnings even within the confines of generally accepted accounting principles.

COMPREHENSIVE PROBLEMS

For each account listed, indicate whether the account should be classified as Assets (A), Liabilities (L), Owners' Equity (O), Revenues (R), or Expenses (X).

Account	Financial statement element				
Accounts payable	A	L	O	R	X
Accounts receivable	A	L	O	R	X
Accumulated depreciation	A	L	O	R	X
Additional paid-in capital	A	L	O	R	X
Allowance for bad debts	A	L	O	R	X
Bonds payable	A	L	O	R	X
Cash equivalents	A	L	O	R	X
Common stock	A	L	O	R	X
Cost of goods sold	A	L	O	R	X
Current portion of long-term debt	A	L	O	R	X
Deferred tax items	A	L	O	R	X
Depreciation	A	L	O	R	X
Dividends payable	A	L	O	R	X
Dividends received	A	L	O	R	X
Gain on sale of assets	A	L	O	R	X
Goodwill	A	L	O	R	X
Inventory	A	L	O	R	X
Investment securities	A	L	O	R	X
Loss on sale of assets	A	L	O	R	X
Notes payable	A	L	O	R	X
Other comprehensive income	A	L	O	R	X
Prepaid expenses	A	L	O	R	X
Property, plant and equipment	A	L	O	R	X
Retained earnings	A	L	O	R	X
Sales	A	L	O	R	X
Unearned revenue	A	L	O	R	X

ANSWERS – CONCEPT CHECKERS

1. **B**   Purchasing property, plant, and equipment is an investing activity.

2. **C**   Obtaining a long-term loan is a financing activity for the wholesaler. For a bank, however, providing loans is its primary business, so making the loan would be best classified as an operating activity.

3. **A**   Accounts receivable are an asset and accounts payable are a liability.

4. **B**   Annual depreciation is an expense. Accumulated depreciation is a contra asset account that typically offsets the historical cost of property, plant, and equipment.

5. **A**   Owners' equity is equal to assets minus liabilities.

6. **C**   The expanded accounting equation shows that assets = liabilities + contributed capital + beginning retained earnings + revenue – expenses – dividends. A decrease in assets is consistent with an increase in expenses or a decrease in revenues but not with an increase in contributed capital.

7. **A**   The service is performed before cash is paid. This transaction represents accrued revenue to the electrician and an accrued expense to the retail shop. Since the invoice has not been sent as of the statement date, it is not shown in accounts receivable or accounts payable.

8. **C**   The $10 million raised appears on the cash flow statement as a cash inflow from financing and on the statement of owners' equity as an increase in contributed capital. Both assets (cash) and equity (common stock) increase on the balance sheet. The income statement is unaffected by stock issuance.

9. **B**   The general journal lists all of the company's transactions by date. The general ledger lists them by account.

10. **C**   Schmidt is correct in stating that analysts do not have access to the detailed accounting entries that went into a company's financial statements. However, he is incorrect in stating that an analyst can be sure management is not manipulating earnings if the audit report does not list deviations from accounting principles. Because accruals and many valuations require management's judgment, there is considerable room within the accounting standards for management to manipulate earnings.

ANSWERS – COMPREHENSIVE PROBLEMS

Account	Financial statement element				
Accounts payable		L			
Accounts receivable	A				
Accumulated depreciation *Contra to the asset being depreciated.*	A				
Additional paid-in capital			O		
Allowance for bad debts *Contra to accounts receivable.*	A				
Bonds payable		L			
Cash equivalents	A				
Common stock			O		
Cost of goods sold					X
Current portion of long-term debt		L			
Deferred tax items *Both deferred tax assets and deferred tax liabilities are recorded.*	A	L			
Depreciation					X
Dividends payable		L			
Dividends received				R	
Gain on sale of assets				R	
Goodwill *Intangible asset.*	A				
Inventory	A				
Investment securities	A				
Loss on sale of assets					X
Notes payable		L			
Other comprehensive income			O		
Prepaid expenses *Accrual account.*	A				
Property, plant and equipment	A				
Retained earnings			O		
Sales				R	
Unearned revenue *Accrual account.*		L			

FINANCIAL REPORTING STANDARDS

EXAM FOCUS

This topic review covers accounting standards: why they exist, who issues them, and who enforces them. Know the difference between the roles of private standard-setting bodies and government regulatory authorities and be able to name the most important organizations of both kinds. Become familiar with the framework for International Financial Reporting Standards, including qualitative characteristics, constraints and assumptions, and principles for preparing and presenting financial statements. Be able to identify barriers to convergence of national accounting standards (such as U.S. GAAP) with IFRS, key differences between the IFRS and GAAP frameworks, and elements of and barriers to creating a coherent financial reporting network.

LOS 31.a: Explain the objective of financial statements and the importance of reporting standards in security analysis and valuation.

The objective of financial statements is to provide economic decision makers with useful information about a firm's financial performance and changes in financial position.

Given the variety and complexity of possible transactions and the estimates and assumptions a firm must make when presenting its performance, financial statements could potentially take any form if reporting standards didn't exist. Reporting standards ensure that the information is "useful to a wide range of users," including security analysts, by making financial statements comparable to one another and narrowing the range of management's "reasonable" estimates.

LOS 31.b: Explain the role of standard-setting bodies, such as the International Accounting Standards Board and the U.S. Financial Accounting Standards Board, and regulatory authorities such as the International Organization of Securities Commissions, the U.K. Financial Services Authority, and the U.S. Securities and Exchange Commission in establishing and enforcing financial reporting standards.

Standard-setting bodies are professional organizations of accountants and auditors that establish financial reporting standards. **Regulatory authorities** are government agencies that have the legal authority to enforce compliance with financial reporting standards.

The two primary standard-setting bodies are the *Financial Accounting Standards Board* (FASB) and the *International Accounting Standards Board* (IASB). In the United States, the FASB sets forth Generally Accepted Accounting Principles (GAAP). Outside the United States, the IASB establishes International Financial Reporting Standards (IFRS).

Other national standard-setting bodies exist as well. Many of them (including the FASB) are working toward convergence with IFRS. Some of the older IASB standards are referred to as International Accounting Standards (IAS).

The IASB has four stated goals:[1]

1. Develop global accounting standards requiring transparency, comparability, and high quality in financial statements.

2. Promote the use of global accounting standards.

3. Account for the needs of emerging markets and small firms when implementing global accounting standards.

4. Achieve convergence between various national accounting standards and global accounting standards.

Regulatory authorities, such as the *Securities and Exchange Commission* (SEC) in the U.S. and the *Financial Services Authority* (FSA) in the United Kingdom, are established by national governments. Figure 1 summarizes the SEC's filing requirements for publicly traded companies in the United States. These filings, which are available from the SEC web site (www.sec.gov), are arguably the most important source of information for the analysis of publicly traded firms.

Most national authorities belong to the *International Organization of Securities Commissions* (IOSCO). The three objectives of financial market regulation according to IOSCO[2] are to (1) protect investors, (2) ensure the fairness, efficiency, and transparency of markets, and (3) reduce systemic risk. Because of the increasing globalization of securities markets, the IOSCO has a goal of uniform financial regulations across countries.

Figure 1: Securities and Exchange Commission Required Filings

Form S-1. Registration statement filed prior to the sale of new securities to the public.

Form 10-K. Required annual filing that includes information about the business and its management, audited financial statements and disclosures, and disclosures about legal matters involving the firm. Information required in Form 10-K is similar to that which a firm typically provides in its annual report to shareholders. However, a firm's annual report is not a substitute for the required 10-K filing. Equivalent SEC forms for foreign issuers in the U.S. markets are Form 40-F for Canadian companies and Form 20-F for other foreign issuers.

Form 10-Q. U.S. firms are required to file this form quarterly, with updated financial statements (unlike Form 10-K, these statements do not have to be audited) and disclosures about certain events such as significant legal proceedings or

---

1. International Accounting Standards Committee Foundation Constitution, July 2005.
2. International Organization of Securities Commissions, "Objectives and Principles of Securities Regulation," May 2003.

changes in accounting policy. Non-U.S. companies are typically required to file the equivalent Form 6-K semiannually.

Form DEF-14A. When a company prepares a proxy statement for its shareholders prior to the annual meeting or other shareholder vote, it also files the statement with the SEC as Form DEF-14A.

Form 8-K. Companies must file this form to disclose material events including significant asset acquisitions and disposals, changes in management or corporate governance, or matters related to its accountants, its financial statements, or the markets in which its securities trade.

Form 144. A company can issue securities to certain qualified buyers without registering the securities with the SEC but must notify the SEC that it intends to do so.

Forms 3, 4, and 5 involve the beneficial ownership of securities by a company's officers and directors. Analysts can use these filings to learn about purchases and sales of company securities by corporate insiders.

LOS 31.c: Discuss the ongoing barriers to developing one universally accepted set of financial reporting standards.

One barrier to developing one universally accepted set of accounting standards (referred to as "convergence") is simply that different standard-setting bodies and the regulatory authorities of different countries can and do disagree on the best treatment of a particular item or issue. Other barriers result from the political pressures that regulatory bodies face from business groups and others who will be affected by changes in reporting standards.

LOS 31.d: Describe the International Financial Reporting Standards (IFRS) framework, including the objective of financial statements, their qualitative characteristics, required reporting elements, and the constraints and assumptions in preparing financial statements.

The ideas on which the IASB bases its standards are expressed in the IFRS "Framework for the Preparation and Presentation of Financial Statements" that the organization adopted in 2001. The IFRS framework details the objective of financial statements, defines the qualitative characteristics necessary to meet that objective, and specifies the required reporting elements. The framework also notes certain constraints and assumptions that are involved in financial statement preparation.

The objective of financial statements, according to the IFRS framework, is "to provide information about the financial position, performance, and changes in financial position of an entity; this information should be useful to a wide range of users for the purpose of making economic decisions." Stated another way, the objective of financial statements is the fair presentation of a company's financial performance.

Qualitative Characteristics

To meet the objectives of fairness and usefulness, financial statements should be understandable, relevant, reliable, and comparable. The IFRS framework describes each of these qualities.

Understandability. Users with a basic knowledge of business and accounting and who make a reasonable effort to study the financial statements should be able to readily understand the information the statements present.

Comparability. Financial statement presentation should be consistent among firms and across time periods.

Relevance. Financial statements are relevant if the information in them can influence users' economic decisions or affect users' evaluations of past events or forecasts of future events. To be relevant, information should be timely and sufficiently detailed (meaning no material omissions or misstatements).

Reliability. Information is reliable if it reflects economic reality, is unbiased, and is free of material errors. Specific factors that support reliability include:

- *Faithful representation* of transactions and events.
- *Substance over form,* presenting not only the legal form of a transaction or event, but its economic reality.
- *Neutrality,* an absence of bias.
- *Prudence* and conservatism in making estimates.
- *Completeness,* within the limits of cost and materiality.

Required Reporting Elements

The elements of financial statements are the by now familiar groupings of assets, liabilities, and owners' equity (for measuring financial position) and income and expenses (for measuring performance). The IFRS framework describes each of these elements:

- Assets are the resources the entity controls and from which it expects to derive economic benefits in the future.
- Liabilities are obligations that are expected to require an outflow of resources.
- Equity is the owners' residual interest in the assets after deducting the liabilities.
- Income is an increase in economic benefits, either increasing assets or decreasing liabilities in a way that increases owners' equity (but not including contributions by owners). Income includes revenues and gains.
- Expenses are decreases in economic benefits, either decreasing assets or increasing liabilities in a way that decreases owners' equity (but not including distributions to owners). Losses are included in expenses.

An item should be *recognized* in its financial statement element if a future economic benefit from the item (flowing to or from the firm) is probable and if the item's value or cost can be measured reliably. The amounts at which items are reported in the financial statement elements depend on their measurement base. Bases of measurement used in financial statements include *historical cost* (the amount originally paid for the asset), *current cost* (the amount the firm would have to pay today for the same asset), *realizable value* (the amount for which the firm could sell the asset), *present value* (the discounted value of the asset's expected future cash flows), and *fair value* (the amount at which two parties in an arm's-length transaction would exchange the asset).

 Professor's Note: In the next Study Session, we will discuss these measurement bases and the situations in which each is appropriate.

Constraints and Assumptions

Some of the qualitative characteristics of financial statements can be at cross-purposes. One of the constraints on financial statement preparation is the need to balance reliability, in the sense of being free of error, with the timeliness that makes the information relevant. Cost is also a constraint; the benefit that users gain from the information should be greater than the cost of presenting it. A third constraint is the fact that intangible and non-quantifiable information about a company (its reputation, brand loyalty, capacity for innovation, etc.) cannot be captured directly in financial statements.

· reliability w/ timeliness
· cost
· intangibles

The two primary assumptions that underlie financial statements are the *accrual basis* and the *going concern assumption*. The accrual basis means that financial statements should reflect transactions at the time they actually occur, not necessarily when cash is paid. The going concern assumption means there is an assumption that the company will continue to exist for the foreseeable future. If this is not the case, then presenting the company's financial position fairly requires a number of adjustments (for example, its inventory or other assets may only be worth their liquidation values).

accrual
going concern

LOS 31.e: Explain the general requirements for financial statements.

International Accounting Standard (IAS) No. 1 defines which financial statements are required and how they must be presented. The **required financial statements** are:

- Balance sheet.
- Income statement.
- Cash flow statement.
- Statement of changes in owners' equity.
- Explanatory notes, including a summary of accounting policies.

The fundamental **principles for preparing financial statements** are stated in IAS No. 1:

- *Fair presentation,* defined as faithfully representing the effects of the entity's transactions and events according to the standards for recognizing assets, liabilities, revenues, and expenses.
- *Going concern basis,* meaning the financial statements are based on the assumption that the firm will continue to exist unless its management intends to (or must) liquidate it.
- *Accrual basis* of accounting is used to prepare the financial statements other than the statement of cash flows.

- *Consistency* between periods in how items are presented and classified, with prior-period amounts disclosed for comparison.
- *Materiality,* meaning the financial statements should be free of misstatements or omissions that could influence the decisions of users of financial statements.

Also stated in IAS No. 1 are **principles for presenting financial statements:**

- *Aggregation* of similar items and separation of dissimilar items.
- *No offsetting* of assets against liabilities or income against expenses unless a specific standard permits or requires it.
- Most entities should present a *classified balance sheet* showing current and noncurrent assets and liabilities.
- *Minimum information* is required on the face of each financial statement and in the notes. For example, the face of the balance sheet must show specific items such as cash and cash equivalents, plant, property and equipment, and inventories. Items listed on the face of the income statement must include revenue, profit or loss, tax expense, and finance costs, among others.
- *Comparative information* for prior periods should be included unless a specific standard states otherwise.

LOS 31.f: Compare and contrast key concepts of financial reporting standards under IFRS and alternative reporting systems, and discuss the implications for financial analysis of differing financial reporting systems.

Professor's Note: The "alternative reporting system" this LOS refers to is U.S. GAAP.

U.S. GAAP consists of standards issued by the FASB, along with numerous other pronouncements and interpretations. Like the IASB, the FASB has a framework for preparing and presenting financial statements. The two organizations are working toward a common framework, but at present the two frameworks differ in several respects.

- *Purpose of the framework.* Both frameworks are meant to help develop and revise standards, but the FASB framework, unlike the IASB framework, is not at the top of the "GAAP hierarchy." The IASB requires management to consider the framework if no explicit standard exists on an issue, but the FASB does not.
- *Objectives of financial statements.* The FASB framework presents different objectives for business and non-business financial statement reporting; the IASB framework has one objective for both.
- *Assumptions.* The IASB framework places more emphasis on the going concern assumption.
- *Qualitative characteristics.* In the FASB framework, relevance and reliability are the primary characteristics, while the IASB framework also lists comparability and understandability as primary characteristics.

- *Financial statement elements.* Differences here include: (1) The IASB framework lists income and expenses as the elements related to performance, while the FASB framework uses revenues, expenses, gains, losses, and comprehensive income. (2) The FASB defines an asset as a future economic benefit, whereas the IASB defines it as a resource from which a future economic benefit is expected. (3) The word "probable" is used by the FASB to define assets and liabilities and by the IASB to define the criteria for recognition. (4) The FASB framework does not allow the values of most assets to be adjusted upward.

Until these frameworks converge, analysts will need to interpret financial statements that are prepared under different standards. In many cases, however, a company will present a **reconciliation statement** showing what its financial results would have been under an alternative reporting system. The SEC requires foreign firms that issue securities in the U.S. to include the information necessary to reconcile their financial statements to U.S. GAAP.

Even when a unified framework emerges, special reporting standards that apply to particular industries (e.g., insurance and banking) will continue to exist.

LOS 31.g: Identify the characteristics of a coherent financial reporting framework and barriers to creating a coherent financial reporting network.

A coherent financial reporting framework is one that fits together logically. Such a framework should be transparent, comprehensive, and consistent.

- *Transparency*—full disclosure and fair presentation reveal the underlying economics of the company to the financial statement user.
- *Comprehensiveness*—all types of transactions that have financial implications should be part of the framework, including new types of transactions that emerge.
- *Consistency*—similar transactions should be accounted for in similar ways across companies, geographic areas, and time periods.

Barriers to creating a coherent financial reporting framework include issues related to valuation, standard setting, and measurement.

- *Valuation*—The different measurement bases for valuation involve a trade-off between relevance and reliability. Bases that require little judgment, such as historical cost, tend to be more reliable, but may be less relevant than a basis like fair value that requires more judgment.
- *Standard setting*—Three approaches to standard setting are a "principles-based" approach that relies on a broad framework, a "rules-based" approach that gives specific guidance about how to classify transactions, and an "objectives oriented" approach that blends the other two approaches. IFRS is largely a principles-based approach. U.S. GAAP has traditionally been more rules-based, but FASB is moving toward an objectives oriented approach.
- *Measurement*—Another trade-off in financial reporting is between properly valuing the elements at one point in time (as on the balance sheet) and properly valuing the changes between points in time (as on the income statement). An "asset/liability" approach, which standard setters have largely used, focuses on balance sheet valuation. A "revenue/expense" approach would tend to place more significance on the income statement.

LOS 31.h: Discuss the importance of monitoring developments in financial reporting standards and evaluate company disclosures of significant accounting policies.

As financial reporting standards continue to evolve, analysts need to monitor how these developments will affect the financial statements they use. An analyst should be aware of new products and innovations in the financial markets that generate new types of transactions. These might not fall neatly into the existing financial reporting standards. The analyst can use the financial reporting framework as a guide for evaluating what effect new products or transactions might have on financial statements.

To keep up to date on the evolving standards, an analyst can monitor professional journals and other sources such as the IASB (www.iasb.org) and FASB (www.fasb.org) Web sites. CFA Institute produces position papers on financial reporting issues through the CFA Centre for Financial Market Integrity (www.cfainstitute.org/cfacentre).

Companies that prepare financial statements under IFRS or U.S. GAAP must disclose their accounting policies and estimates in the footnotes. Significant policies and estimates that require management judgement are also addressed in Management's Discussion and Analysis. An analyst should use these disclosures to evaluate what policies are discussed, whether they cover all the relevant data in the financial statements, which policies required management to make estimates, and whether the disclosures and estimates have changed since the prior period.

Another disclosure that is required for public companies is the likely impact of implementing recently issued accounting standards. Management can discuss the impact of adopting a new standard, conclude that the standard does not apply or will not affect the financial statements materially, or state that they are still evaluating the effects of the new standards. Analysts should be aware of the uncertainty this last statement implies.

KEY CONCEPTS

LOS 31.a
Reporting standards are designed to ensure that different firms' statements are comparable to one another and to narrow the range of reasonable estimates on which financial statements are based. This aids users of the financial statements who rely on them for information about the company's activities, profitability, and creditworthiness.

LOS 31.b
Standard-setting bodies are private sector organizations that establish financial reporting standards. The two primary standard-setting bodies are the International Accounting Standards Board (IASB) and, in the U.S., the Financial Accounting Standards Board (FASB).

Regulatory authorities are government agencies that enforce compliance with financial reporting standards. Regulatory authorities include the Securities and Exchange Commission (SEC) in the U.S. and the Financial Services Authority (FSA) in the United Kingdom. Many national regulatory authorities belong to the International Organization of Securities Commissions (IOSCO).

LOS 31.c
Barriers to developing one universally accepted set of financial reporting standards include differences of opinion among standard-setting bodies and regulatory authorities from different countries and political pressure within countries from groups affected by changes in reporting standards.

LOS 31.d
The IFRS "Framework for the Preparation and Presentation of Financial Statements" begins with the objective of financial statements, defines the qualitative characteristics they should have, specifies the required reporting elements, and notes the constraints and assumptions involved in preparing financial statements.

Qualitative characteristics of financial statements include understandability, relevance, reliability, and comparability.

URRC

Elements of financial statements are assets, liabilities, and owners' equity (for measuring financial position) and income and expenses (for measuring performance).

Constraints on financial statement preparation include cost, the need to balance reliability with timeliness, and the difficulty of capturing non-quantifiable information in financial statements.

The two primary assumptions that underlie the preparation of financial statements are the accrual basis and the going concern assumption.

LOS 31.e
Required financial statements are the balance sheet, income statement, cash flow statement, statement of changes in owners' equity, and explanatory notes.

Principles for preparing financial statements stated in IAS No. 1 are:

Failing Evades Are commonly Made

- Fair presentation.
- Going concern basis.
- Accrual basis.
- Consistency between periods.
- Materiality.

Principles for presenting financial statements stated in IAS No. 1 are:

Aunt Nell call My Cat

- Aggregation.
- No offsetting.
- Classified balance sheet.
- Minimum required information.
- Comparative information.

LOS 31.f
IFRS and U.S. GAAP generally agree in their overall framework and purpose and are working toward convergence. However, IFRS requires users to consider the framework in the absence of a specific standard, U.S. GAAP distinguishes between objectives for business and non-business entities, the IASB framework gives more emphasis to the importance of the accrual and going concern assumptions than the FASB framework does, the U.S. GAAP framework establishes a hierarchy of qualitative financial statement characteristics, and some differences still exist in how each defines, recognizes, and measures the individual elements of financial statements.

Companies reporting under standards other than U.S. GAAP that trade in U.S. markets must reconcile their statements with U.S. GAAP, but the analyst must reconcile differences in other cases.

LOS 31.g
A coherent financial reporting framework should exhibit transparency, comprehensiveness, and consistency.

Barriers to creating a coherent framework include issues of valuation, standard setting, and measurement.

LOS 31.h
An analyst should be aware of evolving financial reporting standards and new products and innovations that generate new types of transactions.

Under IFRS and U.S. GAAP, companies must disclose their accounting policies and estimates in the footnotes and MD&A. Public companies are also required to disclose the likely impact of recently issued accounting standards on their financial statements.

CONCEPT CHECKERS

1. Standard-setting bodies are responsible for:
    A. establishing financial reporting standards only.
    B. establishing and enforcing standards for financial reporting.
    C. enforcing compliance with financial reporting standards only.

2. Which of the following organizations is *least likely* involved with enforcing compliance with financial reporting standards?
    A. Financial Services Authority (FSA).
    B. Securities and Exchange Commission (SEC).
    C. International Accounting Standards Board (IASB).

3. Dawn Czerniak is writing an article about international financial reporting standards. In her article she states, "Despite strong support from business groups for a universally accepted set of financial reporting standards, disagreements among the standard-setting bodies and regulatory authorities of various countries remain a barrier to developing one." Czerniak's statement is:
    A. correct.
    B. incorrect, because business groups have not supported a uniform set of financial reporting standards.
    C. incorrect, because disagreements among national standard-setting bodies and regulatory agencies have not been a barrier to developing a universal set of standards.

4. Which of the following characteristics *least likely* contributes to the reliability of financial statements?
    A. Neutrality.
    B. Timeliness.
    C. Completeness.

5. Which of the following *most accurately* lists a required reporting element that is used to measure a company's financial position, and one that is used to measure a company's performance?

	Position	Performance
A.	Assets	Liabilities
B.	Income	Expenses
C.	Liabilities	Income

6. International Accounting Standard (IAS) No. 1 *least likely* requires which of the following?
    A. Neither assets and liabilities, nor income and expenses, may be offset unless required or permitted by a financial reporting standard.
    B. Audited financial statements and disclosures, along with updated information about the firm and its management, must be filed annually.
    C. Fair presentation of financial statements means faithfully representing the firm's events and transactions according to the financial reporting standards.

7. Compared to the International Financial Reporting Standards (IFRS) framework, does the Financial Accounting Standards Board (FASB) framework for U.S. GAAP place more emphasis on:

	Comparability and understandability?	The going concern assumption?
A.	Yes	Yes
B.	No	Yes
C.	No	No

8. Which is *least likely* one of the conclusions about the impact of a change in financial reporting standards that might appear in management's discussion and analysis?
   A. Management has chosen not to implement the new standard.
   B. Management is currently evaluating the impact of the new standard.
   C. The new standard will not have a material impact on the company's financial statements.

ANSWERS – CONCEPT CHECKERS

1. **A**   Standard-setting bodies are private sector organizations that establish financial reporting standards. Enforcement is the responsibility of regulatory authorities.

2. **C**   The IASB is a standard-setting body. The SEC (in the United States) and the FSA (in the United Kingdom) are regulatory authorities.

3. **B**   Political pressure from business groups and other interest groups who are affected by financial reporting standards has been a barrier to developing a universally accepted set of financial reporting standards. Disagreements among national standard-setting bodies and regulatory agencies have also been a barrier.

4. **B**   Timeliness contributes to the relevance of financial statements, but there is often a trade-off between timeliness and reliability.

5. **C**   Balance sheet reporting elements (assets, liabilities, and owners' equity) measure a company's financial position. Income statement reporting elements (income, expenses) measure its financial performance.

6. **B**   It is the Securities and Exchange Commission's requirement that companies whose securities are publicly traded in the U.S. file Form 10-K annually. Fair presentation is one of the IAS No. 1 principles for preparing financial statements. The ban against offsetting is one of the IAS No. 1 principles for presenting financial statements.

7. **C**   Comparability, understandability, reliability and relevance are qualitative characteristics of financial statements in the IFRS framework, but only reliability and relevance are primary qualitative characteristics in the FASB framework. The IFRS framework places more emphasis on the going concern assumption.

8. **A**   Management can discuss the impact of adopting the new standard, conclude that it does not apply or will have no material impact, or state that they are still evaluating the potential impact.

The following is a review of the Financial Reporting and Analysis principles designed to address the learning outcome statements set forth by CFA Institute®. This topic is also covered in:

UNDERSTANDING THE INCOME STATEMENT

EXAM FOCUS

Now we're getting to the heart of the matter. Since forecasts of future earnings, and therefore estimates of firm value, depend crucially on understanding a firm's income statement, everything in this topic review is important. At least some questions requiring calculation of depreciation, COGS, and inventory under different cash flow assumptions, as well as basic and diluted EPS, are very likely to be included in your exam. The separation of items into operating and non-operating categories is important when estimating recurring income, as a first step in forecasting future firm earnings. Note well that questions regarding the effect on financial ratios of the choice of accounting method and of accounting estimates are one common way to test your understanding of the material on those topics presented here.

INCOME STATEMENT COMPONENTS AND FORMAT

The income statement reports the revenues and expenses of the firm over a period of time. The income statement is sometimes referred to as the "statement of operations," the "statement of earnings," or the "profit and loss statement." The income statement equation is:

revenues – expenses = net income

Investors examine a firm's income statement for valuation purposes while lenders examine the income statement for information about the firm's ability to make the promised interest and principal payments on its debt.

LOS 32.a: Describe the components of the income statement and construct an income statement using the alternative presentation formats of that statement.

Revenues are the amounts reported from the sale of goods and services in the normal course of business. Revenue less adjustments for estimated returns and allowances is known as **net revenue**.

Professor's Note: The terms "revenue" and "sales" are sometimes used synonymously. However, sales is just one component of revenue in many firms. In some countries, revenues are referred to as "turnover."

Expenses are the amounts incurred to generate revenue and include cost of goods sold, operating expenses, interest, and taxes. Expenses are grouped together by their nature or function. Presenting all depreciation expense from manufacturing and administration together in one line of the income statement is an example of grouping by nature of the expense. Combining all costs associated with manufacturing (e.g., raw materials, depreciation, labor, etc.) as cost of goods sold is an example of grouping by function.

> *Professor's Note: Some firms present expenses as negative numbers while other firms use parentheses to signify expenses. Still other firms present expenses as positive numbers with the assumption that users know that expenses are subtracted in the income statement.*

The income statement also includes **gains and losses,** which result from incidental transactions outside the firm's primary business activities. For example, a firm might sell surplus equipment used in its manufacturing operation that is no longer needed. The difference between the sales price and book value is reported as a gain or loss on the income statement.

Presentation formats

A firm can present its income statement using a single-step or multi-step format. In a single-step statement, all revenues are grouped together and all expenses are grouped together. A multi-step format includes *gross profit*, revenues minus cost of goods sold.

Figure 1 is an example of a multi-step income statement format for the BHG Company.

Figure 1: Multi-step Income Statement

BHG Company Income Statement *For the year ended December 31, 20X7*	
Revenue	$579,312
Cost of goods sold	(362,520)
Gross profit	216,792
Selling, general, and administrative expense	(109,560)
Depreciation expense	(69,008)
Operating profit	38,224
Interest expense	(2,462)
Income before tax	35,762
Provision for income taxes	(14,305)
Income from continuing operations	21,457
Earnings (losses) from discontinued operations, net of tax	1,106
Net income	$22,563

Gross profit is the amount that remains after the direct costs of producing a product or service are subtracted from revenue. Subtracting operating expenses, such as selling, general, and administrative expenses, from gross profit results in another subtotal known as **operating profit** or operating income. For nonfinancial firms, operating profit is profit before financing costs and income taxes are considered and before non-operating items are considered. Subtracting interest expense and income taxes from operating profit results in the firm's net income, sometimes referred to as "earnings" or the "bottom line."

 Professor's Note: Interest expense is usually considered an operating expense for financial firms.

If a firm has a controlling interest in a subsidiary, the pro-rata share of the subsidiary's income for the portion of the subsidiary that the firm does not own is reported in the parent's income statement as the **minority owners' interest**. This is subtracted since a controlling interest means the subsidiary's entire net income is included in the firm's income statement.

LOS 32.b: Explain the general principles of revenue recognition and accrual accounting, demonstrate specific revenue recognition applications (including accounting for long-term contracts, installment sales, barter transactions, and gross and net reporting of revenue), and discuss the implications of revenue recognition principles for financial analysis.

Under the accrual method of accounting, revenue is recognized when earned and expenses are recognized when incurred. The important point to remember is that accrual accounting does not necessarily coincide with the receipt or payment of cash. Consequently, firms can manipulate net income by recognizing revenue earlier or later or by delaying or accelerating the recognition of expenses.

According to the International Accounting Standards Board (IASB), the term "income" includes revenue and gains. Specifically, income is defined as increases in economic benefits during the accounting period in the form of inflows or enhancements of assets or decreases of liabilities that result in increases in equity, other than those relating to contributions from equity participants.[1]

According to the Financial Accounting Standards Board (FASB), revenue is recognized in the income statement when (a) realized or realizable and (b) earned.[2] The Securities and Exchange Commission (SEC) provides additional guidance by listing four criteria to determine whether revenue should be recognized:[3]

1. There is evidence of an arrangement between the buyer and seller.

2. The product has been delivered or the service has been rendered.

3. The price is determined or determinable.

4. The seller is reasonably sure of collecting money.

---

1. IASB, *Framework for the Preparation and Presentation of Financial Statements*, paragraph 69.
2. Statement of Financial Accounting Concepts No. 5, paragraph 83(b).
3. SEC Staff Accounting Bulletin 101.

If a firm receives cash before revenue recognition is complete, the firm reports it as *unearned revenue*. Unearned revenue is reported on the balance sheet as a liability. The liability is reduced in the future as the revenue is earned. For example, a magazine publisher typically receives subscription payments in advance of delivery. When payments are received, both assets (cash) and liabilities (unearned revenue) increase. As the magazines are delivered, the publisher recognizes revenue on the income statement and the liability is reduced.

Specific Revenue Recognition Applications

Revenue is usually recognized at delivery using the revenue recognition criteria previously discussed. However, in some cases, revenue may be recognized before delivery occurs or even after delivery takes place.

Long-term Contracts

The percentage-of-completion method and the completed-contract method are used for contracts that extend beyond one accounting period, often contracts related to construction projects.

In certain cases involving service contracts or licensing agreements, the firm may simply recognize revenue equally over the term of the contract or agreement.

The **percentage-of-completion method** is appropriate when the project's cost and revenue can be reliably estimated. Accordingly, revenue, expense, and therefore profit, are recognized as the work is performed. The percentage of completion is measured by the total cost incurred to date divided by the total expected cost of the project.

The **completed-contract method** is used when the outcome of a project cannot be reliably measured or the project is short-term. Accordingly, revenue, expense, and profit are recognized only when the contract is complete. Under either method, if a loss is expected, the loss must be recognized immediately.

Under International Financial Reporting Standards (IFRS), if the firm cannot reliably measure the outcome of the project, revenue is recognized to the extent of contract costs, costs are expensed when incurred, and profit is recognized only at completion.

The effect of using these different revenue recognition methods for long-term contracts on the income statement is illustrated in the following example.

Example: Revenue recognition for long-term contracts

Assume that AAA Construction Corp. has a contract to build a ship for $1,000 and a reliable estimate of the contract's total cost is $800. Project costs incurred by AAA are as follows:

AAA Project Costs

Year	20X5	20X6	20X7	Total
Cost incurred	$400	$300	$100	$800

Determine AAA's net income from this project for each year using the percentage-of-completion and completed contract methods.

Answer:

Since one-half of the total contract cost [$400 / $800] was incurred during 20X5, the project was 50% complete at year-end. Under the *percentage-of-completion method,* 20X5 revenue is $500 [$1,000 × 50%]. Expenses (cost incurred) were $400; thus, net income for 20X5 was $100 [$500 revenue – $400 expense].

At the end of 20X6, the project is 87.5% complete [($400 + $300) / $800]. Revenue to date should total $875 [$1,000 × 87.5%]. Since AAA already recognized $500 of revenue in 20X5, 20X6 revenue is $375 [$875 – $500]. 20X6 expenses were $300 so 20X6 net income was $75 [$375 revenue – $300 expense].

At the end of 20X7, the project is 100% complete [($400 + $300 +$100) / $800]. Revenue to date should total $1,000 [$1,000 × 100%]. Since AAA already recognized $875 of revenue in 20X5 and 20X6, 20X7 revenue is $125 [$1,000 – $875]. 20X7 expenses were $100 so 20X7 net income was $25 [$125 revenue – $100 expense].

The table below summarizes the AAA's revenue, expense, and net income over the term of project under the percentage-of-completion method.

AAA Income Statements

	20X5	20X6	20X7	Total
Revenue	$500	$375	$125	$1,000
Expense	400	300	100	800
Net income	$100	$75	$25	$200

Under the *completed contract method,* revenue, expenses, and profit are not recognized until the contract is complete. Therefore, at the end of 20X7, AAA reports revenue of $1,000, expense of $800, and net income of $200.

As compared to the completed contract method, the percentage-of-completion method is more aggressive since revenue is reported sooner. Also, the percentage-of-completion method is more subjective because it involves cost estimates. However, the percentage-of-completion method provides smoother earnings and results in better matching of revenues and expenses over time. Cash flow is the same under both methods.

Installment Sales

An **installment sale** occurs when a firm finances a sale and payments are expected to be received over an extended period. If collectibility is certain, revenue is recognized at the time of sale using the normal revenue recognition criteria. If collectibility cannot be reasonably estimated, the installment method is used. If collectibility is highly uncertain, the cost recovery method is used.

Under the **installment method**, profit is recognized as cash is collected. Profit is equal to the cash collected during the period multiplied by the total expected profit as a percentage of sales. The installment method is used in limited circumstances, usually involving the sale of real estate or other firm assets.

Under the **cost recovery method**, profit is recognized only when cash collected exceeds costs incurred.

The effects of using the installment and the cost recovery methods are illustrated in the following example.

Example: Revenue recognition for installment sales

Assume that BBB Property Corp. sells a piece of land for $1,000. The original cost of the land was $800. Collections received by BBB for the sale are as follows:

BBB Installment Collections

Year	20X5	20X6	20X7	Total
Collections	$400	$400	$200	$1,000

Determine BBB's profit under the installment and cost recovery methods.

Answer:

Total expected profit as a percentage of sales is 20% [($1,000 − $800) / $1,000]. Under the installment method, BBB will report profit in 20X5 and 20X6 of $80 [$400 × 20%] each year. In 20X7, BBB will report profit of $40 [$200 × 20%].

Under the cost recovery method, the collections received during 20X5 and 20X6 are applied to the recovery of costs. In 20X7, BBB will report $200 of profit.

IFRS addresses when installment sale treatment is appropriate for certain real estate transactions. Specifically, the date when title to the property is transferred and the date when the buyer acquires a vested interest may differ. Also, installment sale treatment may be required when the risks and rewards of ownership are not transferred because the seller remains involved in the property. Finally, significant uncertainty that the buyer can complete the transaction may require installment sale treatment.

Barter Transactions

In a **barter transaction**, two parties exchange goods or services without cash payment. A **round-trip transaction** involves the sale of goods to one party with the simultaneous purchase of almost identical goods from the same party. The underlying issue with these transactions is whether revenue should be recognized. In the late 1990s, several internet companies increased their revenue significantly by "buying" equal values of advertising space on each others' websites.

According to U.S. GAAP, revenue from a barter transaction can be recognized at fair value only if the firm has historically received cash payments for such goods and services and can use this historical experience to determine fair value.[4]

Under IFRS, revenue from barter transactions must be based on the fair value of revenue from similar nonbarter transactions with unrelated parties.[5]

Gross and Net Reporting of Revenue

Under **gross revenue reporting**, the selling firm reports sales revenue and cost of goods sold separately. Under **net revenue reporting**, only the difference in sales and cost is reported. While profit is the same, sales are higher using gross revenue reporting.

For example, consider a travel agent who arranges a first-class ticket for a customer flying to Singapore. The ticket price is $10,000, and the travel agent receives a $1,000 commission. Using gross reporting, the travel agent would report $10,000 of revenue, $9,000 of expense, and $1,000 of profit. Using net reporting, the travel agent would simply report $1,000 of revenue and no expense.

The following criteria must be met in order to use gross revenue reporting under U.S. GAAP. The firm must:

- Be the primary obligor under the contract.
- Bear the inventory risk and credit risk.
- Be able to choose its supplier.
- Have reasonable latitude to establish the price.

Implications for Financial Analysis

As noted previously, firms can recognize revenue before delivery, at the time of delivery, or after delivery takes place, as appropriate. Different revenue recognition methods can

---

4. Emerging Issues Task Force EITF 99-17, "Accounting for Advertising Barter Transactions."
5. IASB, SIC Interpretation 31, Revenue – Barter Transactions Involving Advertising Services, paragraph 5.

be used within the firm. Firms disclose their revenue recognition policies in the financial statement footnotes.

Users of financial information must consider two points when analyzing a firm's revenue: (1) how conservative are the firm's revenue recognition policies (recognizing revenue sooner rather than later is more aggressive), and (2) the extent to which the firm's policies rely on judgment and estimates.

LOS 32.c: Discuss the general principles of expense recognition, such as the matching principle, specific expense recognition applications (including depreciation of long-term assets and inventory methods), and the implications of expense recognition principles for financial analysis.

Expenses are subtracted from revenue to calculate net income. According to the IASB, expenses are decreases in economic benefits during the accounting period in the form of outflows or depletions of assets or incurrence of liabilities that result in decreases in equity other than those relating to distributions to equity participants.[6]

If the financial statements were prepared on a cash basis, neither revenue recognition nor expense recognition would be an issue. The firm would simply recognize cash received as revenue and cash payments as expense.

Under the accrual method of accounting, expense recognition is based on the **matching principle** whereby expenses to generate revenue are recognized in the same period as the revenue. Inventory provides a good example. Assume inventory is purchased during the fourth quarter of one year and sold during the first quarter of the following year. Using the matching principle, both the revenue and the expense (cost of goods sold) are recognized in the first quarter, when the inventory is sold, not the period in which the inventory was purchased.

Not all expenses can be directly tied to revenue generation. These costs are known as **period costs.** Period costs, such as administrative costs, are expensed in the period incurred.

The cost of long-lived assets must also be matched with revenues. Long-lived assets are expected to provide economic benefits beyond one accounting period. The allocation of cost over an asset's useful life is known as depreciation, depletion, or amortization expense.

If a firm sells goods or services on credit or provides a warranty to the customer, the matching principle requires the firm to estimate bad debt expense and/or warranty expense. By doing so, the firm is recognizing the expense in the period of the sale, rather than a later period.

---

6.   IASB *Framework for the Preparation and Presentation of Financial Statements,* paragraph 70.

Implications for Financial Analysis

Like revenue recognition, expense recognition requires a number of estimates. Since estimates are involved, it is possible for firms to delay or accelerate the recognition of expenses. Delayed expense recognition increases current net income and is therefore more aggressive.

Analysts must consider the underlying reasons for a change in an expense estimate. If a firm's bad debt expense has recently decreased, did the firm lower its expense estimate because its collection experience improved, or was the expense decreased to manipulate net income?

Analysts should also compare a firm's estimates to those of other firms within the firm's industry. If a firm's warranty expense is significantly less than that of a peer firm, is the lower warranty expense a result of higher quality products, or is the firm's expense recognition more aggressive than that of the peer firm?

Firms disclose their accounting policies and significant estimates in the financial statement footnotes and in the management discussion and analysis (MD&A) section of the annual report.

LOS 32.d: Determine which method of depreciation, accounting for inventory, or amortizing intangibles is appropriate, based on facts that might influence the decision.

Depreciation

If more benefits generated in early yrs, use ADR

Most firms use the *straight-line depreciation* method for financial reporting purposes. The straight-line method recognizes an equal amount of depreciation expense each period. However, most assets generate more benefits in the early years of their economic life and fewer benefits in the later years. In this case, an *accelerated depreciation method* is more appropriate for matching the expenses to revenues.

In the early years of an asset's life, the straight-line method will result in lower depreciation expense as compared to an accelerated method. Lower expense results in higher net income. In the later years of the asset's life, the effect is reversed, and straight-line depreciation results in higher expense and lower net income compared to accelerated methods.

Inventory

If a firm can identify exactly which items were sold and which items remain in inventory, it can use the *specific identification method*. For example, an auto dealer records each vehicle sold or in inventory by its identification number.

Under the *first-in, first-out* (FIFO) method, the first item purchased is assumed to be the first item sold. FIFO is appropriate for inventory that has a limited shelf life.

For example, a food products company will sell its oldest inventory first to keep the inventory on hand fresh.

Under the *last-in, first-out* (LIFO) method, the last item purchased is assumed to be the first item sold. LIFO is appropriate for inventory that does not deteriorate with age. For example, a coal mining company will sell coal off the top of the pile.

In the United States, LIFO is popular because of its income tax benefits. In an inflationary environment, LIFO results in higher cost of goods sold. Higher cost of goods sold results in lower taxable income and, therefore, lower income taxes.

The *weighted average cost* method is not affected by the physical flow of the inventory. It is popular because of its ease of use.

FIFO and average cost can be used under U.S. GAAP or IFRS. LIFO is allowed under U.S. GAAP but is prohibited under IFRS.

Figure 2 summarizes the effects of the inventory methods.

Figure 2: Inventory Method Comparison

Method	Assumption	Cost of goods sold consists of...	Ending inventory consists of...
FIFO (U.S. and IFRS)	The items first purchased are the first to be sold.	first purchased	most recent purchases
LIFO (U.S. only)	The items last purchased are the first to be sold.	last purchased	earliest purchases
Weighted average cost (U.S. and IFRS)	Items sold are a mix of purchases.	average cost of all items	average cost of all items

Intangible assets

Amortization expense for intangible assets with limited lives is similar to depreciation. The expense should match the proportion of the asset's economic benefits used during the period. Most firms use the straight-line method for financial reporting. Goodwill and other intangible assets with indefinite lives are not amortized.

LOS 32.e: Demonstrate the depreciation of long-term assets using each approved method, accounting for inventory using each approved method, and amortization of intangibles.

Depreciation expense can be computed under a number of different methods.

Straight-line depreciation (SL) allocates an equal amount of depreciation each year over the asset's useful life as follows:

$$\text{SL Depreciation expense} = \frac{\text{Cost} - \text{Residual value}}{\text{Useful life}}$$

Example: Calculating straight-line depreciation expense

Littlefield Company recently purchased a machine at a cost of $12,000. The machine is expected to have a residual value of $2,000 at the end of its useful life in 5 years. Calculate depreciation expense using the straight-line method.

Answer:

The annual depreciation expense each year will be:

$$\frac{\text{Cost} - \text{Residual value}}{\text{Useful life}} = \frac{(\$12,000 - \$2,000)}{5} = \$2,000$$

Accelerated depreciation speeds up the recognition of depreciation expense in a systematic way to recognize more depreciation expense in the early years of the asset's useful life and less depreciation expense in the later years of its life. Total depreciation expense over the life of the asset will be the same as it would be if straight-line depreciation were used.

The **declining balance method** (DB) applies a constant rate of depreciation to a declining book value.

The most common form of the declining balance method is *double-declining balance* (DDB), which uses 200% of the straight-line rate as the percentage rate applied to the declining balance. If an asset's life is ten years, the straight-line rate is 1/10 or 10%. The DDB rate for this asset is 2/10 or 20%.

$$\text{DDB depreciation} = \left(\frac{2}{\text{useful life}}\right)(\text{cost} - \text{accumulated depreciation})$$

DB does not explicitly use the asset's residual value in the calculations, but depreciation ends once the estimated residual value has been reached. If the asset is expected to have no residual value, the DB method will never fully depreciate it, so the method has to change (typically to straight-line) at some point in the asset's life.

Example: Calculating double-declining balance depreciation expense

Littlefield Company recently purchased a machine at a cost of $12,000. The machine is expected to have a residual value of $2,000 at the end of its useful life in five years. Calculate depreciation expense for all five years using the double-declining balance method.

Answer:

The depreciation expense using the double declining balance method is:

- Year 1: $(2 / 5)(\$12,000) = \$4,800$
- Year 2: $(2 / 5)(\$12,000 - \$4,800) = \$2,880$
- Year 3: $(2 / 5)(\$12,000 - \$7,680) = \$1,728$

In years 1 through 3, the company has recognized cumulative depreciation expense of $9,408. Since the total depreciation expense is limited to $10,000 ($12,000 – $2,000 salvage value), the depreciation in year 4 is limited to $592, rather than the $(2 / 5)(\$12,000 - \$9,408) = \$1,036.80$ using the DDB formula.

Year 5: Depreciation expense is $0, since the asset is fully depreciated.

Note that the rate of depreciation is doubled (2/5) from straight-line, and the only thing that changes from year to year is the base amount (book value) used to calculate annual depreciation.

 Professor's Note: We've been discussing the "double" declining balance method, which uses a factor of two times the straight-line rate. You can compute declining balance depreciation based on any factor (e.g., 1.5, double, triple).

Inventory Accounting Methods

Three methods of inventory accounting are:

1. **First In, First Out** (FIFO)
   - The cost of inventory first acquired (beginning inventory and early purchases) is assigned to the cost of goods sold for the period.
   - The cost of the most recent purchases is assigned to ending inventory.

2. **Last In, First Out** (LIFO)
   - The cost of inventory most recently purchased is assigned to the cost of goods sold for the period.
   - The costs of beginning inventory and earlier purchases are assigned to ending inventory.

3. **Average cost**
   - The cost per unit is calculated by dividing cost of goods available by total units available.
   - This average cost is used to determine both cost of goods sold and ending inventory.
   - Average cost results in cost of goods sold and ending inventory values between LIFO and FIFO.

Example: Inventory costing

Use the inventory data in the table below to calculate the cost of goods sold and ending inventory under each of the three methods.

Inventory Data

January 1 (beginning inventory)	2 units @ $2 per unit =	$4
January 7 purchase	3 units @ $3 per unit =	$9
January 19 purchase	5 units @ $5 per unit =	$25
Cost of goods available	10 units	$38
Units sold during January	7 units	

Answer:

FIFO cost of goods sold: Value the seven units sold using the unit cost of first units purchased. Start with the beginning inventory and the earliest units purchased and work down, as illustrated in the following table.

FIFO COGS Calculation

From beginning inventory	2 units @ $2 per unit	$4
From first purchase	3 units @ $3 per unit	$9
From second purchase	2 units @ $5 per unit	$10
FIFO cost of goods sold	7 units	$23
Ending inventory	3 units @ $5 per unit	$15

LIFO cost of goods sold: Value the seven units sold at unit cost of last units purchased. Start with the most recently purchased units and work up, as illustrated in the following table.

LIFO COGS Calculation

From second purchase	5 units @ $5 per unit	$25
From first purchase	2 units @ $3 per unit	$6
LIFO cost of goods sold	7 units	$31
Ending inventory	2 units @ $2 + 1 unit @ $3	$7

Average cost of goods sold: Value the seven units sold at the average unit cost of goods available.

Weighted Average COGS Calculation

Average unit cost	$38 / 10 units	$3.80 per unit
Weighted average cost of goods sold	7 units @ $3.80 per unit	$26.60
Ending inventory	3 units @ $3.80 per unit	$11.40

The following table summarizes the calculations of COGS and ending inventory for each method.

Summary:

Inventory system	COGS	Ending Inventory
FIFO	$23.00	$15.00
LIFO	$31.00	$7.00
Average Cost	$26.60	$11.40

Amortization of Intangible Assets

Amortization expense is the allocation of the cost of an intangible asset (such as a franchise agreement) over its useful life. Straight-line amortization is calculated exactly like straight-line depreciation.

Intangible assets with indefinite lives (e.g., goodwill) are not amortized. However, they must be tested for impairment at least annually. If the asset value is impaired, an expense equal to the impairment amount is recognized on the income statement.

LOS 32.f: Distinguish between the operating and nonoperating components of the income statement.

Operating and nonoperating transactions are usually reported separately in the income statement. For a nonfinancial firm, nonoperating transactions may result from investment income and financing expenses. For example, a nonfinancial firm may receive dividends and interest from investments in other firms. The investment income and any gains and losses from the sale of these securities are not a part of the firm's normal business operations. Interest expense is based on the firm's capital structure, which is also independent of the firm's operations.

LOS 32.g: Discuss the financial reporting treatment and analysis of nonrecurring items (including discontinued operations, extraordinary items, and unusual or infrequent items), and changes in accounting standards.

Discontinued operations. A *discontinued operation* is one that management has decided to dispose of, but either has not yet done so, or has disposed of in the current year after the operation had generated income or losses. To be accounted for as a discontinued operation, the business—in terms of assets, operations, and investing and financing activities—must be physically and operationally distinct from the rest of the firm.

The date when the company develops a formal plan for disposing of an operation is referred to as the *measurement date*, and the time between the measurement period and the actual disposal date is referred to as the *phaseout period*. Any income or loss from discontinued operations is reported separately in the income statement, net of tax, after income from continuing operations. Any past income statements presented must be restated, separating the income or loss from the discontinued operations. On the measurement date, the company will accrue any estimated loss during the phaseout period and any estimated loss on the sale of the business. Any expected gain on the disposal cannot be reported until after the sale is completed.

Analytical implications: The analysis is straightforward. Discontinued operations do not affect net income from continuing operations. The actual event of discontinuing a business segment or selling assets may provide information about the future cash flows of the firm, however.

Unusual or infrequent items. The definition of these items is obvious—these events are either unusual in nature *or* infrequent in occurrence, but *not* both. Examples of unusual or infrequent items include:

- Gains or losses from the sale of assets or part of a business.
- Impairments, write-offs, write-downs, and restructuring costs.

Unusual or infrequent items are included in income from continuing operations and are reported before tax.

Analytical implications: Even though unusual or infrequent items affect net income from continuing operations, an analyst may want to review them to determine whether they truly should be included when forecasting future firm earnings.

Extraordinary items. Under U.S. GAAP, an extraordinary item is a material transaction or event that is *both* unusual *and* infrequent in occurrence. Examples of these include:

- Losses from an expropriation of assets.
- Gains or losses from early retirement of debt (when it is judged to be both unusual and infrequent).
- Uninsured losses from natural disasters that are both unusual and infrequent.

Extraordinary items are reported separately in the income statement, net of tax, after income from continuing operations.

IFRS does not allow extraordinary items to be separated from operating results in the income statement.

Analytical implications: Judgment is required in determining whether a transaction or event is extraordinary. Although extraordinary items do not affect income from continuing operations, an analyst may want to review them to determine whether some portion should be included when forecasting future income. Some companies appear to be accident-prone and have "extraordinary" losses every year or every few years.

Changes in Accounting Standards

Accounting changes include changes in accounting principles, changes in accounting estimates, and prior-period adjustments.

A **change in accounting principle** refers to a change from one GAAP or IFRS method to another (e.g., a change in inventory accounting from LIFO to FIFO). A change in accounting principle requires *retrospective application*. Accordingly, all of the prior-period financial statements currently presented are restated to reflect the change. Retrospective application enhances the comparability of the financial statements over time.

principle-retro

 Professor's Note: The treatment of a change in accounting principle for U.S. firms is now covered by SFAS No. 154, "Accounting Changes and Error Corrections." The old standard, APB No. 20, provided for the cumulative effect of the accounting change to be reported in the income statement, below the line, net of tax. For the exam, you are responsible for the new standard, which requires retrospective application.

Generally, a **change in accounting estimate** is the result of a change in management's judgment, usually due to new information. For example, management may change the estimated useful life of an asset because new information indicates the asset has a longer or shorter life than originally expected. A change in estimate is applied prospectively and does not require the restatement of prior financial statements.

estimate — prospective

Analytical implications: Accounting estimate changes typically do not affect cash flow. An analyst should review changes in accounting estimates to determine the impact on future operating results.

A change from an incorrect accounting method to one that is acceptable under GAAP or IFRS or the correction of an accounting error made in previous financial statements is reported as a **prior-period adjustment.** Prior-period adjustments are made by restating results for all prior periods presented in the current financial statements. Disclosure of the nature of the adjustment and its effect on net income is also required.

incorrect— prior period adj + disclosure

Analytical implications: Prior-period adjustments usually involve errors or new accounting standards and do not typically affect cash flow. Analysts should review adjustments carefully because errors may indicate weaknesses in the firm's internal controls.

LOS 32.h: Describe the components of earnings per share and calculate a company's earnings per share (both basic and diluted earnings per share) for both a simple and complex capital structure.

LOS 32.i: Distinguish between dilutive and antidilutive securities, and discuss the implications of each for the earnings per share calculation.

Earnings per share (EPS) is one of the most commonly used corporate profitability performance measures for publicly-traded firms (nonpublic companies are not required to report EPS data). EPS is reported only for shares of common stock.

A company may have either a simple or complex capital structure:

- A **simple capital structure** is one that contains *no* potentially dilutive securities. A simple capital structure contains only common stock, nonconvertible debt, and nonconvertible preferred stock.
- A **complex capital structure** contains *potentially dilutive securities* such as options, warrants, or convertible securities.

All firms with complex capital structures must report both *basic* and *diluted* EPS. Firms with simple capital structures report only basic EPS.

BASIC EPS

The basic EPS calculation does not consider the effects of any dilutive securities in the computation of EPS.

$$\text{basic EPS} = \frac{\text{net income} - \text{preferred dividends}}{\text{weighted average number of common shares outstanding}}$$

The current year's preferred dividends are subtracted from net income because EPS refers to the per-share earnings *available to common shareholders*. Net income minus preferred dividends is the income available to common stockholders. Common stock dividends are *not* subtracted from net income because they are a part of the net income available to common shareholders.

The **weighted average number of common shares** is the number of shares outstanding during the year, weighted by the portion of the year they were outstanding.

Example: Weighted average shares and basic EPS

Johnson Company has net income of $10,000 and paid $1,000 cash dividends to its preferred shareholders and $1,750 cash dividends to its common shareholders. At the beginning of the year, there were 10,000 shares of common stock outstanding. 2,000 new shares were issued on July 1. Assuming a simple capital structure, what is Johnson's basic EPS?

Answer:

Calculate Johnson's weighted average number of shares.

Shares outstanding all year = 10,000(12) = 120,000

Shares outstanding 1/2 year = 2,000(6) = 12,000

Weighted average shares = 132,000 / 12 = 11,000 shares

$$\text{Basic EPS} = \frac{\text{net income} - \text{pref. div.}}{\text{wt. avg. shares of common}} = \frac{\$10,000 - \$1,000}{11,000} = \$0.82$$

> *Professor's Note: Remember, the payment of a cash dividend on common shares is not considered in the calculation of EPS.*

Effect of Stock Dividends and Stock Splits

A **stock dividend** is the distribution of additional shares to each shareholder in an amount proportional to their current number of shares. If a 10% stock dividend is paid, the holder of 100 shares of stock would receive 10 additional shares.

A **stock split** refers to the division of each "old" share into a specific number of "new" (post-split) shares. The holder of 100 shares will have 200 shares after a 2-for-1 split or 150 shares after a 3-for-2 split.

The important thing to remember is that each shareholder's proportional ownership in the company is unchanged by either of these events. Each shareholder has more shares but the same percentage of the total shares outstanding.

The effect of a stock dividend or a stock split on the weighted average number of common shares is illustrated in the following example.

Example: Effect of stock dividends

During the past year, R & J, Inc. had net income of $100,000, paid dividends of $50,000 to its preferred stockholders, and paid $30,000 in dividends to its common shareholders. R & J's common stock account showed the following:

January 1	Shares issued and outstanding at the beginning of the year	10,000
April 1	Shares issued	4,000
July 1	10% stock dividend	
September 1	Shares repurchased for the treasury	3,000

Compute the weighted average number of common shares outstanding during the year, and compute EPS.

Answer:

Step 1: Adjust the number of pre-stock-dividend shares to post-stock-dividend units (to reflect the 10% stock dividend) by multiplying all share numbers prior to the stock dividend by 1.1. Shares issued or retired after the stock dividend are not affected.

January 1	Initial shares adjusted for the 10% dividend	11,000
April 1	Shares issued adjusted for the 10% dividend	4,400
September 1	Shares of treasury stock repurchased (no adjustment)	–3,000

Step 2: Compute the weighted average number of post-stock dividend shares:

Initial shares	11,000 × 12 months outstanding	132,000
Issued shares	4,400 × 9 months outstanding	39,600
Retired treasury shares	–3,000 × 4 months retired	–12,000
Total share-month		159,600
Average shares	159,600 / 12	13,300

Step 3: Compute basic EPS:

$$\text{basic EPS} = \frac{\text{net income} - \text{pref. div.}}{\text{wt. avg. shares of common}} = \frac{\$100,000 - \$50,000}{13,300} = \$3.76$$

Things to know about the weighted average shares outstanding calculation:

- The weighting system is days outstanding divided by the number of days in a year, but on the exam, the monthly approximation method will probably be used.
- Shares issued enter into the computation from the date of issuance.
- Reacquired shares are excluded from the computation from the date of reacquisition.
- Shares sold or issued in a purchase of assets are included from the date of issuance.
- A stock split or stock dividend is applied to all shares outstanding prior to the split or dividend and to the beginning-of-period weighted average shares. A stock split or stock dividend adjustment is not applied to any shares issued or repurchased after the split or dividend date.

DILUTED EPS

Before calculating diluted EPS, it is necessary to understand the following terms:

- **Dilutive securities** are stock options, warrants, convertible debt, or convertible preferred stock that would *decrease EPS* if exercised or converted to common stock.
- **Antidilutive securities** are stock options, warrants, convertible debt, or convertible preferred stock that would *increase EPS* if exercised or converted to common stock.

The numerator of the basic EPS equation contains income available to common shareholders (net income less preferred dividends). In the case of diluted EPS, if there are dilutive securities, then the numerator must be adjusted as follows:

- If convertible preferred stock is dilutive (meaning EPS will fall if it is converted to common stock), the convertible preferred dividends must be added to earnings available to common shareholders.
- If convertible bonds are dilutive, then the bonds' after-tax interest expense is not considered an interest expense for diluted EPS. Hence, interest expense multiplied by (1 – the tax rate) must be added back to the numerator.

 Professor's Note: Interest paid on bonds is typically tax deductible for the firm. If convertible bonds are converted to stock, the firm saves the interest cost but loses the tax deduction. Thus, only the after-tax interest savings are added back to income available to common shareholders.

The basic EPS denominator is the weighted average number of shares. When the firm has dilutive securities outstanding, the denominator is the basic EPS denominator adjusted for the equivalent number of common shares that would be created by the conversion of all dilutive securities outstanding (convertible bonds, convertible preferred shares, warrants, and options), with each one considered separately to determine if it is dilutive.

If a dilutive security was issued during the year, the increase in the weighted average number of shares for diluted EPS is based on only the portion of the year the dilutive security was outstanding.

Dilutive stock options or warrants increase the number of common shares outstanding in the denominator for diluted EPS. There is no adjustment to the numerator.

Stock options and warrants are dilutive only when their exercise prices are less than the average market price of the stock over the year. If the options or warrants are dilutive, use the *treasury stock method* to calculate the number of shares used in the denominator.

The Treasury Stock Method

- The treasury stock method assumes that the hypothetical funds received by the company from the exercise of the options would be used to purchase shares of the company's common stock in the market at the average market price.
- The net increase in the number of shares outstanding (the adjustment to the denominator) is the number of shares created by exercising the options less the number of shares hypothetically repurchased with the proceeds of exercise.

Example: Treasury stock method

Baxter Company has 5,000 shares outstanding all year. Baxter had 2,000 outstanding warrants all year, convertible into one share each at $20 per share. The year-end price of Baxter stock was $40, and the average stock price was $30. What effect will these warrants have on the weighted average number of shares?

Answer:

If the warrants are exercised, the company will receive 2,000 × $20 = $40,000 and issue 2,000 new shares. The treasury stock method assumes the company uses these funds to repurchase shares at the average market price of $30. The company would repurchase $40,000 / $30 = 1,333 shares. Net shares issued would be 2,000 − 1,333 = 667 shares.

The **diluted EPS equation** is:

$$\text{diluted EPS} = \frac{\text{adjusted income available for common shares}}{\text{weighted-average common and potential common shares outstanding}}$$

where *adjusted income available for common shares* is:

    Net income − preferred dividends
 + Dividends on convertible preferred stock
 + After-tax interest on convertible debt

Therefore, diluted EPS is:

$$\text{diluted EPS} = \frac{\left[\begin{array}{c}\text{net income} - \text{preferred} \\ \text{dividends}\end{array}\right] + \left[\begin{array}{c}\text{convertible} \\ \text{preferred} \\ \text{dividends}\end{array}\right] + \left[\begin{array}{c}\text{convertible} \\ \text{debt} \\ \text{interest}\end{array}\right](1-t)}{\left(\begin{array}{c}\text{weighted} \\ \text{average} \\ \text{shares}\end{array}\right) + \left(\begin{array}{c}\text{shares from} \\ \text{conversion of} \\ \text{conv. pfd. shares}\end{array}\right) + \left(\begin{array}{c}\text{shares from} \\ \text{conversion of} \\ \text{conv. debt}\end{array}\right) + \left(\begin{array}{c}\text{shares} \\ \text{issuable from} \\ \text{stock options}\end{array}\right)}$$

check for dilution

Remember, each potentially dilutive security must be examined separately to determine if it is actually dilutive (i.e., would reduce EPS if converted to common stock). The effect of conversion to common is included in the calculation of diluted EPS for a given security only if it is, in fact, dilutive.

Sometimes in an acquisition there will be a provision that the shareholders of the acquired company will receive additional shares of the acquiring firm's stock if certain performance targets are met. These *contingent shares* should be included in the calculation of diluted EPS if the target has been met as of the end of the reporting period.

Example 1: EPS with convertible debt

During 20X6, ZZZ Corp. reported net income of $115,600 and had 200,000 shares of common stock outstanding for the entire year. ZZZ also had 1,000 shares of 10%, $100 par, preferred stock outstanding during 20X6. During 20X5, ZZZ issued 600, $1,000 par, 7% bonds for $600,000 (issued at par). Each of these bonds is convertible to 100 shares of common stock. The tax rate is 40%. Compute the 20X6 basic and diluted EPS.

Answer:

Step 1: Compute 20X6 basic EPS:

$$\text{basic EPS} = \frac{\$115,600 - \$10,000}{200,000} = \$0.53$$

Step 2: Calculate diluted EPS:

- Compute the increase in common stock outstanding if the convertible debt is converted to common stock at the beginning of 20X6:

    shares issuable for debt conversion = (600)(100) = 60,000 shares

- If the convertible debt is considered converted to common stock at the beginning of 20X6, then there would be no interest expense related to the convertible debt. Therefore, it is necessary to increase ZZZ's after-tax net income for the after-tax effect of the decrease in interest expense:

    increase in income = [(600)($1,000)(0.07)] (1 − 0.40) = $25,200

- Compute diluted EPS as if the convertible debt were common stock:

    $$\text{diluted EPS} = \frac{\text{net. inc.} - \text{pref. div.} + \text{convert. int. } (1-t)}{\text{wt. avg. shares} + \text{convertible debt shares}}$$

    $$\text{diluted EPS} = \frac{\$115,600 - \$10,000 + \$25,200}{200,000 + 60,000} = \$0.50$$

- Check to make sure that *diluted EPS is less than basic EPS* [$0.50 < $0.53]. If diluted EPS is more than the basic EPS, the convertible bonds are *antidilutive* and should not be treated as common stock in computing diluted EPS.

A quick way to determine whether the convertible debt is antidilutive is to calculate its per share impact by:

$$\frac{\text{convertible debt interest } (1-t)}{\text{convertible debt shares}}$$

If this per share amount is greater than basic EPS, the convertible debt is antidilutive, and the effects of conversion should not be included when calculating diluted EPS.

If this per share amount is less than basic EPS, the convertible debt is dilutive, and the effects of conversion should be included in the calculation of diluted EPS.

For ZZZ:

$$\frac{\$25,200}{60,000} = \$0.42$$

The company's basic EPS is $0.53, so the convertible debt is dilutive, and the effects of conversion should be included in the calculation of diluted EPS.

Example 2: EPS with convertible preferred stock

During 20X6, ZZZ reported net income of $115,600 and had 200,000 shares of common stock and 1,000 shares of preferred stock outstanding for the entire year. ZZZ's 10%, $100 par value preferred shares are each convertible into 40 shares of common stock. The tax rate is 40%. Compute basic and diluted EPS.

Answer:

Step 1: Calculate 20X6 basic EPS:

$$\text{basic EPS} = \frac{\$115,600 - \$10,000}{200,000} = \$0.53$$

Step 2: Calculate diluted EPS:

- Compute the increase in common stock outstanding if the preferred stock is converted to common stock at the beginning of 20X6: (1,000)(40) = 40,000 shares.
- If the convertible preferred shares were converted to common stock, there would be no preferred dividends paid. Therefore, you should add back the convertible preferred dividends that had previously been subtracted from net income in the numerator.

- Compute diluted EPS as if the convertible preferred stock were converted into common stock:

$$\text{diluted EPS} = \frac{\text{net. inc.} - \text{pref. div.} + \text{convert. pref. dividends}}{\text{wt. avg. shares} + \text{convert. pref. common shares}}$$

$$\text{diluted EPS} = \frac{\$115,600 - \$10,000 + \$10,000}{200,000 + 40,000} = \$0.48$$

- Check to see if diluted EPS is less than basic EPS ($0.48 < $0.53). If the answer is yes, the preferred stock is dilutive and must be included in diluted EPS as computed above. If the answer is no, the preferred stock is antidilutive and conversion effects are not included in diluted EPS.

Example 3: EPS with stock options

During 20X6, ZZZ reported net income of $115,600 and had 200,000 shares of common stock outstanding for the entire year. ZZZ also had 1,000 shares of 10%, $100 par, preferred stock outstanding during 20X6. ZZZ has 10,000 stock options (or warrants) outstanding the entire year. Each option allows its holder to purchase one share of common stock at $15 per share. The average market price of ZZZ's common stock during 20X6 is $20 per share. Compute the diluted EPS.

Answer:

Number of common shares created if the options are exercised:	10,000 shares
Cash inflow if the options are exercised ($15/share)(10,000):	$150,000
Number of shares that can be purchased with these funds is: $150,000 / $20	7,500 shares
Net increase in common shares outstanding from the exercise of the stock options (10,000 − 7,500)	2,500 shares

$$\text{diluted EPS} = \frac{\$115,600 - \$10,000}{200,000 + 2,500} = \$0.52$$

A quick way to calculate the net increase in common shares from the potential exercise of stock options or warrants when the exercise price is less than the average market price is:

$$\left[\frac{AMP - EP}{AMP}\right] \times N$$

where :
AMP = average market price over the year
EP = exercise price of the options or warrants
N   = number of common shares that the options
        and warrants can be converted into

For ZZZ: $\dfrac{\$20 - \$15}{\$20} \times 10,000 \text{ shares} = 2,500 \text{ shares}$

Example 4: EPS with convertible bonds, convertible preferred, and options

During 20X6, ZZZ reported net income of $115,600 and had 200,000 shares of common stock outstanding for the entire year. ZZZ had 1,000 shares of 10%, $100 par convertible preferred stock, convertible into 40 shares each, outstanding for the entire year. ZZZ also had 600, 7%, $1,000 par value convertible bonds, convertible into 100 shares each, outstanding for the entire year. Finally, ZZZ had 10,000 stock options outstanding during the year. Each option is convertible into one share of stock at $15 per share. The average market price of the stock for the year was $20. What are ZZZ's basic and diluted EPS? (Assume a 40% tax rate.)

Answer:

Step 1: From Examples 1, 2, and 3, we know that the convertible preferred stock, convertible bonds, and stock options are all dilutive. Recall that basic EPS was calculated as:

$$\text{basic EPS} = \frac{\$115,600 - \$10,000}{200,000} = \$0.53$$

Step 2: Review the number of shares created by converting the convertible securities and options (the denominator):

Converting the convertible preferred shares	40,000 shares
Converting the convertible bonds	60,000 shares
Exercising the options	2,500 shares

Step 3: Review the adjustments to net income (the numerator):

Converting the convertible preferred shares	$10,000
Converting the convertible bonds	$25,200
Exercising the options	$0

Step 4: Compute ZZZ's diluted EPS:

$$\text{diluted EPS} = \frac{115,600 - 10,000 + 10,000 + 25,200}{200,000 + 40,000 + 60,000 + 2,500} = \$0.47$$

LOS 32.j: Evaluate a company's financial performance using common-size income statements and financial ratios based on the income statement.

Common-size statements and ratios are tools used to facilitate analysis of the financial statements.

A **common-size income statement** expresses each income statement item as a percentage of sales. This format is known as *vertical common-size analysis* and allows the analyst to evaluate firm performance over time (time-series), as well as compare performance across firms, industries, or sectors (cross-sectional).

Example: Common-size income statements

The table below presents the income statements for Company A, Company B, and Company C. Also presented are the income statements in (vertical) common-size format. All three companies are involved in the same industry. Evaluate the financial performance of the three firms.

Income Statements – In Dollars and Common Size

	Company A		Company B		Company C	
Revenue	$1,000	100%	$5,000	100%	$5,000	100%
COGS	400	40%	2,500	50%	2,000	40%
Gross profit	600	60%	2,500	50%	3,000	60%
SG&A	150	15%	750	15%	750	15%
Production R&D	100	10%	250	5%	500	10%
Operating profit	350	35%	1,500	30%	1,750	35%
Interest expense	50	5%	250	5%	250	5%
Pre-tax income	300	30%	1,250	25%	1,500	30%
Income taxes	120	12%	500	10%	600	12%
Net income	$180	18%	$750	15%	$900	18%

Answer:

As compared to Company B, Company A is smaller in terms of sales and net income when stated in dollars. However, in common-size terms, Company A's net income is higher than Company B's net income (18% versus 15%). By presenting the income statements in common-size format, the analyst is able to compare the firms without regard to size.

Common size analysis also provides information about a firm's business strategies. Revenues are the same at Company B and Company C. However, Company C reports higher gross profit, higher operating profit, and higher net income. The higher profit can be traced to lower cost of goods sold. Notice that Company C spends more on production research and development (R&D) than Company B. As a result, Company C has been able to lower its production costs.

Presenting income tax expense as an effective rate is usually more meaningful than the common-size percentage. The effective rate is equal to income tax expense divided by pre-tax income. In the above example, the effective tax rate for all three companies is 40%.

Financial Ratios Based on the Income Statement

Profitability ratios examine how good management is at turning their efforts into profits. Ratios such as gross profit margin, operating profit margin, and net profit margin compare the first value at the top of the income statement (sales) to various profit measures. The different ratios are designed to isolate specific costs and identify specific measures of performance. Generally, higher margin ratios are more desirable.

Gross profit margin is the ratio of gross profit (sales less cost of goods sold) to sales:

$$\text{Gross profit margin} = \frac{\text{Gross profit}}{\text{Revenue}}$$

Gross profit margin can be increased by raising sales prices or lowering per-unit cost.

Net profit margin is the ratio of net income to sales:

$$\text{Net profit margin} = \frac{\text{Net income}}{\text{Revenue}}$$

Any subtotal presented in the income statement can be expressed in terms of a margin ratio. For example, operating profit margin is equal to operating income divided by revenue. Pre-tax margin is equal to pre-tax earnings divided by revenue.

 Professor's Note: Ratios are discussed in detail in the topic review on "Financial Analysis Techniques."

LOS 32.k: State the accounting classification for items that are excluded from the income statement but affect owners' equity, and list the major types of items receiving that treatment.

At the end of each accounting period, the net income of the firm is added to stockholders' equity through an account known as **retained earnings**. Therefore, any transaction that affects the income statement (net income) will also affect stockholders' equity. However, not all accounting transactions are reported in the income statement. For example, issuing stock and reacquiring stock are transactions that affect stockholders' equity but not net income. Dividends paid reduce stockholders' equity, but they do not reduce in net income. Finally, transactions included in **other comprehensive income** affect equity but not net income. Other comprehensive income includes:

1. Foreign currency translation gains and losses.

2. Adjustments for minimum pension liability.

3. Unrealized gains and losses from cash flow hedging derivatives.

4. Unrealized gains and losses from available-for-sale securities.

Available-for-sale securities are investment securities that are not expected to be held to maturity or sold in the near term. Available-for-sale securities are reported on the balance sheet at fair value. The unrealized gains and losses (the changes in fair value before the securities are sold) are not reported in the income statement but are reported directly in stockholders' equity as a component of other comprehensive income.

LOS 32.l: Describe and calculate comprehensive income.

Comprehensive income is a measure that includes all changes to equity other than owner contributions and distributions. That is, comprehensive income aggregates net income and other comprehensive income (foreign currency translation gains and losses, minimum pension liability adjustments, and unrealized gains and losses on cash flow hedging derivatives and available-for-sale securities).

(handwritten margin note: Fx trans G/L, Min pension liab, Unrealized G/L on hedging, Avail for sale)

Example: Calculating comprehensive income

Calculate comprehensive income for Triple C Corporation using the selected financial statement data found in the following table.

Triple C Corporation – Selected Financial Statement Data	
Net income	$1,000
Dividends received from available-for-sale securities	60
Unrealized loss from foreign currency translation	(15)
Dividends paid	(110)
Reacquire common stock	(400)
Unrealized gain from cash flow hedge	30
Unrealized loss from available-for-sale securities	(10)
Realized gain on sale of land	65

Answer:

Net income	$1,000
Unrealized loss from foreign currency translation	(15)
Unrealized gain from cash flow hedge	30
Unrealized loss from available-for-sale securities	(10)
Comprehensive income	$1,005

The dividends received for available-for-sale securities and the realized gain on the sale of land are already included in net income. Dividends paid and the reacquisition of common stock are transactions with shareholders, so they are not included in comprehensive income.

KEY CONCEPTS

LOS 32.a

The income statement shows an entity's revenues, expenses, gains and losses during a reporting period.

A multi-step income statement provides a subtotal for gross profit and a single step income statement does not. Expenses on the income statement can be grouped by the nature of the expense items or by their function, such as with expenses grouped into cost of goods sold.

LOS 32.b

Revenue is recognized when earned and expenses are recognized when incurred.

Methods for accounting for long-term contracts include:
• Percentage-of-completion—recognizes revenue in proportion to costs incurred.
• Completed-contract—recognizes revenue only when the contract is complete.

Revenue recognition methods for installment sales are:
• Normal revenue recognition at time of sale if collectability is reasonably assured.
• Installment sales method if collectability cannot be reasonably estimated.
• Cost recovery method if collectability is highly uncertain.

Revenue from barter transactions can only be recognized if its fair value can be estimated from historical data on similar non-barter transactions.

Gross revenue reporting shows sales and cost of goods sold, while net revenue reporting shows only the difference between sales and cost of goods sold and should be used when the firm is acting essentially as a selling agent and does not stock inventory, take credit risk, or have control over supplier and price.

A firm using a revenue recognition method that is aggressive will inflate current period earnings at a minimum and perhaps inflate overall earnings.

LOS 32.c

The matching principle requires that firms match revenues recognized in a period with the expenses required to generate them. One application of the matching principle is seen in accounting for inventory, with cost of goods sold as the cost of units sold from inventory that are included in current-period revenue. Other costs, such as straight-line depreciation of fixed assets or administrative overhead, are period costs and are taken without regard to revenues generated during the period.

Users of financial data should analyze the reasons for any changes in estimates of expenses and compare these estimates with those of peer companies.

LOS 32.d

An accelerated depreciation method is appropriate if a long-term asset generates proportionally more of its economic benefits in the early years of its life. Straight-line depreciation is appropriate when an asset's economic value decreases at an approximately constant rate over time.

Inventory that can be tracked by individual unit can be valued by specific identification. First-in-first-out inventory valuation is appropriate for goods with a limited shelf life. Last-in-first-out is widely used in the U.S. because of its tax advantages but is not allowed under IFRS. The weighted average cost method averages the cost of all units purchased or manufactured and currently available for sale.

Intangible assets with limited lives should be amortized using a method that reflects the flow over time of their economic benefits. Intangible assets with indefinite lives (e.g., goodwill) are not amortized.

LOS 32.e

Depreciation methods:
- Straight-line: Equal amount of depreciation expense in each year of the asset's useful life.
- Declining balance: Apply a constant rate of depreciation to the declining book value until book value equals residual value.

Inventory valuation methods:
- FIFO: Inventory reflects cost of most recent purchases, COGS reflects cost of oldest purchases.
- LIFO: COGS reflects cost of most recent purchases, inventory reflects cost of oldest purchases.
- Average cost: Unit cost equals cost of goods available for sale divided by total units available and is used for both COGS and inventory.
- Specific identification: each item in inventory is identified and its historical cost is used for calculating COGS when the item is sold.

Amortization methods for identifiable intangible assets should also approximate the pattern of decrease in their economic values, but intangible assets with indefinite lives are not amortized.

LOS 32.f

Operating income is generated from the firm's normal business operations. For a nonfinancial firm, income that results from investing or financing transactions is classified as non-operating income, while it is operating income for a financial firm since its business operations include investing in and financing securities.

LOS 32.g

Results of discontinued operations are reported below income from continuing operations, net of tax, from the date the decision to dispose of the operations is made. These results are segregated because they likely are non-recurring and do not affect future net income.

Unusual or infrequent items are reported before tax and above income from continuing operations. An analyst should determine how "unusual" or "infrequent" these items really are for the company when estimating future earnings and/or firm value.

Extraordinary items (both unusual and infrequent) are reported below income from continuing operations, net of tax under U.S. GAAP, but this treatment is not allowed under IFRS. Extraordinary items are not expected to continue in future periods.

Changes in accounting standards, changes in accounting methods applied, and corrections of accounting errors require retrospective restatement of all prior-period financial statements included in the current statement. A change in an accounting estimate, however, is applied prospectively (to subsequent periods) with no restatement of prior-period results.

LOS 32.h

$$\text{basic EPS} = \frac{\text{net income} - \text{preferred dividends}}{\text{weighted average number of common shares outstanding}}$$

When a company has potentially dilutive securities it must report diluted EPS.

For any convertible preferred stock, convertible debt, warrants, or stock options that are dilutive, the calculation of diluted EPS is:

$$\text{diluted EPS} = \frac{\left[\begin{array}{c}\text{net income} - \text{preferred}\\ \text{dividends}\end{array}\right] + \left[\begin{array}{c}\text{convertible}\\ \text{preferred}\\ \text{dividends}\end{array}\right] + \left[\begin{array}{c}\text{convertible}\\ \text{debt}\\ \text{interest}\end{array}\right](1-t)}{\left(\begin{array}{c}\text{weighted}\\ \text{average}\\ \text{shares}\end{array}\right) + \left(\begin{array}{c}\text{shares from}\\ \text{conversion of}\\ \text{conv. pfd. shares}\end{array}\right) + \left(\begin{array}{c}\text{shares from}\\ \text{conversion of}\\ \text{conv. debt}\end{array}\right) + \left(\begin{array}{c}\text{shares}\\ \text{issuable from}\\ \text{stock options}\end{array}\right)}$$

LOS 32.i

A dilutive security is one that, if converted to its common stock equivalent, would decrease EPS. An antidilutive security is one that would not reduce EPS if converted to its common stock equivalent.

LOS 32.j

A vertical common-size income statement expresses each line item as a percentage of sales. Gross profit margin and net profit margin are profitability ratios that can be read directly from a vertical common-size income statement. An analyst should examine changes in items on a vertical common-size income statement over time and compare values to those for peer companies or to industry averages.

LOS 32.k

Transactions with shareholders, such as dividends paid and shares issued or repurchased, are not reported on the income statement.

"Other comprehensive income" includes other transactions that affect equity but do not affect net income, including:

- Gains and losses from foreign currency translation.
- Pension obligation adjustments.
- Unrealized gains and losses from cash flow hedging derivatives.
- Unrealized gains and losses on available-for-sale securities.

LOS 32.l

Comprehensive income is the sum of net income and other comprehensive income.

CONCEPT CHECKERS

1. For a nonfinancial firm, are depreciation expense and interest expense included or excluded from operating expenses in the income statement?

	Depreciation expense	Interest expense
A.	Included	Included
B.	Included	Excluded
C.	Excluded	Included

2. Are income taxes and cost of goods sold examples of expenses classified by nature or classified by function in the income statement?

	Income taxes	Cost of goods sold
A.	Nature	Function
B.	Function	Nature
C.	Function	Function

3. Which of the following is *least likely* a condition necessary for revenue recognition?
    A. Cash has been collected.
    B. The goods have been delivered.
    C. The price has been determined.

4. AAA has a contract to build a building for $100,000 with an estimated time to completion of three years. A reliable cost estimate for the project is $60,000. In the first year of the project, AAA incurred costs totaling $24,000. How much profit should AAA report at the end of the first year under the percentage-of-completion method and the completed-contract method?

	Percentage-of-completion	Completed-contract
A.	$16,000	$0
B.	$16,000	$40,000
C.	$40,000	$0

5. Which principle requires that cost of goods sold be recognized in the same period in which the sale of the related inventory is recorded?
    A. Going concern.
    B. Certainty.
    C. Matching.

6. Which of the following would *least likely* increase pretax income?
    A. Decreasing the bad debt expense estimate.
    B. Increasing the useful life of an intangible asset.
    C. Decreasing the residual value of a depreciable tangible asset.

7. When accounting for inventory, are the first-in, first-out (FIFO) and last-in, first-out (LIFO) cost flow assumptions permitted under U.S. GAAP?

	FIFO	LIFO
A.	Yes	Yes
B.	Yes	No
C.	No	Yes

8.   Which of the following *best* describes the impact of depreciating equipment with a useful life of 6 years using the declining balance method as compared to the straight-line method?
       A. Total depreciation expense will be higher over the life of the equipment.
       B. Depreciation expense will be higher in the first year.
       C. Scrapping the equipment after five years will result in a larger loss.

9.   CC Corporation reported the following inventory transactions (in chronological order) for the year:

Purchase	Sales
40 units at $30	13 units at $35
20 units at $40	35 units at $45
90 units at $50	60 units at $60

       Assuming inventory at the beginning of the year was zero, calculate the year-end inventory using FIFO and LIFO.

       FIFO   LIFO
       A. $5,220 $1,040
       B. $2,100 $1,280
       C. $2,100 $1,040

10.   At the beginning of the year, Triple W Corporation purchased a new piece of equipment to be used in its manufacturing operation. The cost of the equipment was $25,000. The equipment is expected to be used for 4 years and then sold for $4,000. Depreciation expense to be reported for the second year using the double-declining-balance method is *closest to*:
       A. $5,250.
       B. $6,250.
       C. $7,000.

11.   Which of the following is *least likely* considered a nonoperating transaction from the perspective of a manufacturing firm?
       A. Dividends received from available-for-sale securities.
       B. Interest expense on subordinated debentures.
       C. Accruing bad debt expense for goods sold on credit.

12.   Changing an accounting estimate:
       A. is reported prospectively.
       B. requires restatement of all prior-period statements presented in the current financial statements.
       C. is reported by adjusting the beginning balance of retained earnings for the cumulative effect of the change.

13. Which of the following transactions would *most likely* be reported below income from continuing operations, net of tax?
    A. Gain or loss from the sale of equipment used in a firm's manufacturing operation.
    B. A change from the accelerated method of depreciation to the straight-line method.
    C. The operating income of a physically and operationally distinct division that is currently for sale, but not yet sold.

14. Which of the following statements about nonrecurring items is *least accurate*?
    A. Gains from extraordinary items are reported net of taxes at the bottom of the income statement before net income.
    B. Unusual or infrequent items are reported before taxes above net income from continuing operations.
    C. A change in accounting principle is reported in the income statement net of taxes after extraordinary items and before net income.

15. The Hall Corporation had 100,000 shares of common stock outstanding at the beginning of the year. Hall issued 30,000 shares of common stock on May 1. On July 1, the company issued a 10% stock dividend. On September 1, Hall issued 1,000, 10% bonds, each convertible into 21 shares of common stock. What is the weighted average number of shares to be used in computing basic and diluted EPS, assuming the convertible bonds are dilutive?

	Average shares, basic	Average shares, dilutive
A.	132,000	139,000
B.	132,000	146,000
C.	139,000	146,000

16. Given the following information, how many shares should be used in computing diluted EPS?
    - 300,000 shares outstanding.
    - 100,000 warrants exercisable at $50 per share.
    - Average share price is $55.
    - Year-end share price is $60.
    A. 9,091.
    B. 90,909.
    C. 309,091.

17. An analyst gathered the following information about a company:
    - 100,000 common shares outstanding from the beginning of the year.
    - Earnings of $125,000.
    - 1,000, 7% $1,000 par bonds convertible into 25 shares each, outstanding as of the beginning of the year.
    - The tax rate is 40%.

    The company's diluted EPS is *closest* to:
    A. $1.22.
    B. $1.25.
    C. $1.34.

18. An analyst has gathered the following information about a company:
    - 50,000 common shares outstanding from the beginning of the year.
    - Warrants outstanding all year on 50,000 shares, exercisable at $20 per share.
    - Stock is selling at year end for $25.
    - The average price of the company's stock for the year was $15.

    How many shares should be used in calculating the company's diluted EPS?
    A. 16,667.
    B. 50,000.
    C. 66,667.

19. To study trends in a firm's cost of goods sold (COGS), the analyst should standardize cost of goods sold by dividing it by:
    A. sales.
    B. net income.
    C. prior year COGS.

20. Which of the following ratios is a measure of profitability?
    A. Current ratio.
    B. Fixed asset turnover ratio.
    C. Pre-tax margin ratio.

21. Which of the following transactions affects owners' equity but does not affect net income?
    A. Foreign currency translation gain.
    B. Repaying the face amount on a bond issued at par.
    C. Dividends received from available-for-sale securities.

22. Which of the following is *least likely* to be included when calculating comprehensive income?
    A. Unrealized loss from cash flow hedging derivatives.
    B. Unrealized gain from available-for-sale securities.
    C. Dividends paid to common shareholders.

ANSWERS – CONCEPT CHECKERS

1. **B** Depreciation is included in the computation of operating expenses. Interest expense is a financing cost. Thus, it is excluded from operating expenses.

2. **A** Income taxes are expenses grouped together by their nature. Cost of goods sold includes a number of expenses related to the same function, the production of inventory.

3. **A** In order to recognize revenue, the seller must know the sales price and be reasonably sure of collection, and must have delivered the goods or rendered the service. Actual collection of cash is not required.

4. **A** $24,000/$60,000 = 40% of the project completed. 40% of $100,000 = $40,000 revenue. $40,000 revenue – $24,000 cost = $16,000 profit for the period. No profit would be reported in the first year using the completed contract method.

5. **C** The matching principle requires that the expenses incurred to generate the revenue be recognized in the same accounting period as the revenue.

6. **C** Decreasing the residual (salvage) value of a depreciable long-lived asset will result in higher depreciation expense and, thus, lower pretax income.

7. **A** LIFO and FIFO are both permitted under U.S. GAAP. LIFO is prohibited under IFRS.

8. **B** Accelerated depreciation will result in higher depreciation in the early years and lower depreciation in the later years compared to the straight-line method. Total depreciation expense will be the same under both methods. The book value would be higher in the later years using straight-line depreciation, so the loss from scrapping the equipment under an accelerated method is less compared the straight-line method.

9. **B** 108 units were sold (13 + 35 + 60) and 150 units were available for sale (beginning inventory of 0 plus purchases of 40 + 20 + 90), so there are 150 – 108 = 42 units in ending inventory. Under FIFO, units from the last batch purchased would remain in inventory: 42 × $50 = $2,100. Under LIFO, the first 42 units purchased would be in inventory: (40 × $30) + (2 × $40) = $1,280.

10. **B** Year 1: (2/4) × 25,000 = $12,500. Year 2: (2/4) × (25,000 – 12,500) = $6,250.

11. **C** Bad debt expense is an operating expense. The other choices are nonoperating items from the perspective of a manufacturing firm.

12. **A** A change in an accounting estimate is reported prospectively. No restatement of prior period statements is necessary.

13. **C** A physically and operationally distinct division that is currently for sale is treated as a discontinued operation. The income from the division is reported net of tax below income from continuing operations. Changing a depreciation method is a change of accounting principle, which is applied retrospectively and will change operating income.

14. **C** A change in accounting principle requires retrospective application; that is, all prior period financial statements currently presented are restated to reflect the change.

15. **A** The new stock is weighted by 8 / 12. The bonds are weighted by 4 / 12 and are not affected by the stock dividend.

Basic shares = {[100,000 × (12 / 12)] + [30,000 × (8 / 12)]} × 1.10 = 132,000

Diluted shares = 132,000 + [21,000 × (4 / 12)] = 139,000

16. **C** Since the exercise price of the warrants is less than the average share price, the warrants are dilutive. Using the treasury stock method to determine the denominator impact:

$$\frac{\$55 - \$50}{\$55} \times 100,000 \text{ shares} = 9,091 \text{ shares}$$

Thus, the denominator will increase by 9,091 shares to 309,091 shares. The question asks for the total, not just the impact of the warrants.

17. **B** First, calculate basic EPS = $\dfrac{\$125,000}{100,000} = \$1.25$

Next, check if the convertible bonds are dilutive:

numerator impact = (1,000 × 1,000 × 0.07) × (1 − 0.4) = $42,000

denominator impact = (1,000 × 25) = 25,000 shares

$$\text{per share impact} = \frac{\$42,000}{25,000 \text{ shares}} = \$1.68$$

Since $1.68 is greater than the basic EPS of $1.25, the bonds are antidilutive. Thus, diluted EPS = basic EPS = $1.25.

18. **B** The warrants in this case are antidilutive. The average price per share of $15 is less than the exercise price of $20. The year-end price per share is not relevant. The denominator consists of only the common stock for basic EPS.

19. **A** In a common-size income statement, each income statement account is divided by sales. COGS is then production costs as a percentage of price.

20. **C** Pre-tax margin (pre-tax earnings / revenue) measures profitability.

21. **A** A foreign currency translation gain is not included in net income but the gain increases owners' equity. Dividends received are reported in the income statement. The repayment of principal does not affect owners' equity.

22. **C** Comprehensive income includes all changes in equity except transactions with shareholders. Therefore, dividends paid to common shareholders are not included in comprehensive income.

The following is a review of the Financial Reporting and Analysis principles designed to address the learning outcome statements set forth by CFA Institute®. This topic is also covered in:

UNDERSTANDING THE BALANCE SHEET

EXAM FOCUS

While the income statement presents a picture of a firm's economic activities over a period of time, its balance sheet is a snapshot of its financial and physical assets and its liabilities at a point in time. Just as with the income statement, understanding balance sheet accounts, how they are valued, and what they represent, is also crucial to the financial analysis of a firm. Again, different choices of accounting methods and different accounting estimates will affect a firm's financial ratios, and an analyst must be careful to make the necessary adjustments in order to compare two or more firms. Special attention should be paid to the method by which each balance sheet item is calculated and how changes in balance sheet values relate to the income statement, to the statement of other comprehensive income, and to shareholders' equity. The next Study Session includes more detailed information on several balance sheet accounts, including inventories, long-term assets, deferred taxes, debt liabilities, and off-balance-sheet financing.

LOS 33.a: Illustrate and interpret the components of the assets, liabilities, and equity sections of the balance sheet, and discuss the uses of the balance sheet in financial analysis.

Assets provide probable future economic benefits controlled by an entity as a result of previous transactions.

Assets can be created by operating activities (e.g., generating net income), investing activities (e.g., purchasing manufacturing equipment), and financing activities (e.g., issuing debt). Figure 1 lists some of the more common asset accounts found on the balance sheet.

Figure 1: Common Balance Sheet Asset Accounts

Cash and equivalents

Accounts receivable (trade receivables)

Inventory

Prepaid expenses

Investments

Property, plant, and equipment

Intangible assets

Deferred tax assets

Pension assets

Liabilities are obligations owed by an entity from previous transactions that are expected to result in an outflow of economic benefits in the future.

Liabilities are created by financing activities (e.g., issuing debt) and operating activities (e.g., recognizing expense before payment is made). Figure 2 lists some of the more common liability accounts found in the balance sheet.

Figure 2: Common Balance Sheet Liability Accounts

Accounts payable (trade payables)

Accrued expenses

Unearned revenue

Notes payable

Bonds payable

Capital (financial) lease obligations

Pension liabilities

Deferred tax liabilities

Inherent in the definition of both assets and liabilities is that a future economic impact is probable and can be reliably measured.

• probable
• reliably measured

Stockholders' equity is the residual interest in assets that remains after subtracting a firm's liabilities. Stockholders' equity is also referred to as "shareholders' equity" and "owners' equity," or sometimes just "equity" or "net assets."

Equity is created by financing activities (e.g., issuing capital stock) and by operating activities (e.g., generating net income). Figure 3 lists some of the more common equity accounts found in the balance sheet.

Figure 3: Common Balance Sheet Equity Accounts

Capital stock

Additional paid-in-capital (capital in excess of par)

Treasury stock

Retained earnings

Accumulated other comprehensive income

The balance sheet is important to investors and lenders alike. However, the analyst must understand its limitations. Not all assets and liabilities are reported on the balance sheet, and those that are not necessarily reported at fair value.

LOS 33.b: Describe the various formats of balance sheet presentation.

There is no standardized balance sheet format. However, two common formats are the account format and the report format.

Just like the balance sheet equation, an **account format** is a layout in which assets are presented on the left hand side of the page and liabilities and equity are presented on the right hand side. In a **report format**, the assets, liabilities, and equity are presented in one column.

A **classified balance sheet** groups together similar items to arrive at significant subtotals. For example, current assets are grouped together and current liabilities are grouped together. Similarly, noncurrent assets are grouped together, as are noncurrent liabilities.

LOS 33.c: Explain how assets and liabilities arise from the accrual process.

Assets and liabilities are created by business transactions. For example, if a firm issues bonds in exchange for cash, assets (cash) increase and liabilities (bonds payable) increase by the same amount.

The accrual method of accounting also creates assets and liabilities. Under accrual accounting, revenue recognition and expense recognition do not necessarily coincide with cash receipts and cash payments. In particular:

- Cash received in advance of recognizing revenue results in an increase in assets (cash) and an increase in liabilities (unearned revenue). Once the revenue is earned, liabilities (unearned revenue) decrease and equity (retained earnings) increases.
- Recognizing revenue before cash is received results in an increase in assets (accounts receivable) and an increase in equity (retained earnings). Once the cash is collected, an asset (cash) increases and another asset (accounts receivable) decreases by the same amount.
- Cash paid in advance of recognizing an expense results in a decrease in one asset (cash) and an increase in another asset (prepaid expenses) by the same amount. Once the expense is recognized, assets (prepaid expenses) decrease and equity (retained earnings) decreases by an equal amount.
- Recognizing an expense before cash is paid results in an increase in liabilities (accrued expenses) and a decrease in equity (retained earnings). Once the expense is paid, assets (cash) decrease and liabilities (accrued expenses) decrease by an equal amount.

LOS 33.d: Compare and contrast current and noncurrent assets and liabilities.

---

*operating cycle –
produce/purchase inv
sell product
collect cash*

Current assets include cash and other assets that will likely be converted into cash or used up within one year or one operating cycle, whichever is greater. The **operating cycle** is the time it takes to produce or purchase inventory, sell the product, and collect the cash. Current assets are usually presented in the order of their liquidity, with cash being the most liquid. Current assets reveal information about the operating activities of the firm.

Current liabilities are obligations that will be satisfied within one year or one operating cycle, whichever is greater. More specifically, a liability that meets any of the following criteria is considered current:

- Settlement is expected during the normal operating cycle.
- Settlement is expected within one year.
- There is not an unconditional right to defer settlement for more than one year.

Current assets minus current liabilities equals **working capital**. Not enough working capital may indicate liquidity problems. Too much working capital may be an indication of inefficient use of assets.

Noncurrent assets do not meet the definition of current assets because they will not be converted into cash or used up within one year or operating cycle. Noncurrent assets provide information about the firm's investing activities, which form the foundation upon which the firm operates.

Noncurrent liabilities do not meet the criteria of current liabilities. Noncurrent liabilities provide information about the firm's long-term financing activities.

International Financial Reporting Standards (IFRS) requires the current/noncurrent format unless a **liquidity-based presentation** is more relevant, as in the banking industry.

IFRS req classified B/S

If a firm has a controlling interest in a subsidiary that is not 100% owned, the parent reports a minority (noncontrolling) interest in its consolidated balance sheet. The **minority interest** is the pro-rata share of the subsidiary's net assets (equity) not owned by the parent company.

Under IFRS, the minority interest is reported in the equity section of the consolidated balance sheet. Under U.S. GAAP, the minority interest can be reported in the liabilities section, the equity section, or the "mezzanine section" of the balance sheet. The mezzanine section is located between liabilities and equity.

IFRS minority—equity section GAAP liab equity mezzanine

LOS 33.e: Explain the measurement bases (e.g., historical cost and fair value) of assets and liabilities, including current assets, current liabilities, tangible assets, and intangible assets.

Under current accounting standards, the balance sheet contains a mixture of historical costs and fair values. In addition, sometimes replacement cost and the present value of future cash flows are used to measure assets and liabilities.

Historical cost is the value that was exchanged at the acquisition date. Historical cost is verifiable and objective; however, its relevance to investment analysis declines over time as prices change.

Fair value is the amount at which an asset can be bought or sold, or a liability can be incurred or settled, between knowledgeable, willing parties in an arm's-length transaction. Fair value is subjective to a significant extent.

Because of this mixture of measurement bases, the balance sheet value of total assets should not be interpreted as the value of the firm. Analysts must adjust the balance sheet to better assess a firm's investment potential or creditworthiness.

Specific assets and their related liabilities are not usually offset (netted) on the balance sheet. For example, if a firm purchases manufacturing equipment for $3 million that is subject to a loan of $2 million, the asset and liability are shown separately on the balance sheet rather than reporting a net asset value of $1 million.

The financial statement footnotes should include the following information about the measurement of the firm's assets and liabilities:

- Basis for measurement.
- Carrying value of inventory by category.
- Amount of inventory carried at fair value less costs to sell.
- Write-downs and reversals, with a discussion of the circumstances that led to them.
- Inventories pledged as collateral for liabilities.
- Inventories recognized as an expense.

Current Assets

Current assets include cash and other assets that will be converted into cash or used up within one year or the firm's operating cycle, whichever is greater. Some of the more common current assets include the following:

- Cash and cash equivalents (liquid low-risk securities with maturities less than 90 days).
- Accounts receivable (trade receivables)—amounts expected to be collected from the sale of goods and services. Receivables are typically reported net of an allowance for bad debt (net receivables). This is not considered offsetting because of the nature of the allowance.
- Inventories—items held for sale or used in the manufacturing of goods to be sold. Manufacturing firms separately report inventories of raw materials, work-in-process, and finished goods.
- Marketable securities—debt or equity securities that are traded in a public market (e.g., Treasury securities, certain equity securities, and mutual funds).
- Other current assets including prepaid expenses.

Inventory is reported at the lower of cost or net realizable value. **Net realizable value** is the selling price of the inventory less the estimated cost of completion and disposal costs. For a manufacturer, inventory cost includes direct materials, direct labor, and overhead. Inventory cost excludes the following:

- Abnormal amounts of wasted materials, labor, and overhead.
- Storage costs beyond the production process.
- Administrative overhead.
- Disposal (selling) costs.

As discussed in the topic review on understanding the income statement, the cost flow assumption (i.e., FIFO, LIFO, average cost, or specific identification) affects the carrying (book) value of the inventory.

Standard costing and the retail method are used by some firms to measure inventory. **Standard costing**, often used by manufacturing firms, involves assigning predetermined costs to goods produced. Firms that use the **retail method** measure inventory at retail prices and then subtract gross profit in order to reflect cost.

Prepaid expenses are operating costs that have been paid in advance. As the costs are actually incurred, an expense is recognized in the income statement and prepaid expenses (an asset) decrease. For example, if a firm makes an annual rent payment of $400,000 at the beginning of the year, an asset (cash) decreases and another asset (prepaid rent) increases by the amount of the payment. At the end of three months, one-quarter of the prepaid rent has been used. At this point, the firm may recognize $100,000 of rent expense in its income statement and reduce assets (prepaid rent) by $100,000 to $300,000.

Current Liabilities

Current liabilities are obligations that will be satisfied within one year or operating cycle, whichever is greater.

Accounts payable (trade payables) are amounts owed to suppliers for goods or services purchased on credit.

Notes payable are obligations in the form of promissory notes owed to creditors. Notes payable can also be included in noncurrent liabilities, if their maturities are greater than one year.

The **current portion of long-term debt** is the principal portion of debt due within one year or the firm's operating cycle, whichever is greater.

Taxes payable are current taxes that have been recognized in the income statement but have not yet been paid.

Accrued liabilities (accrued expenses) are expenses that have been recognized in the income statement but are not yet contractually due. Accrued expenses result from the accrual method of accounting, under which expenses are recognized as incurred. For example, consider a firm that is required to make annual year-end interest payments of $100,000 on an outstanding bank loan. At the end of March, the firm would recognize one-quarter ($25,000) of the total interest expense in its income statement and an accrued liability would be increased by the same amount, even though the liability is not actually due until the end of the year.   → liabilities

Unearned revenue (unearned income) is cash collected in advance of providing goods and services. For example, a magazine publisher receives subscription payments in advance of delivery. When payment is received, both assets (cash) and liabilities (unearned revenue) increase by the same amount. As the magazines are delivered, the publisher recognizes revenue in the income statement and the liability is reduced.   → liabilities

Tangible Assets

Long-term assets with physical substance are known as **tangible assets.** Tangible assets, such as plant, equipment, and natural resources, are reported on the balance sheet at historical cost less accumulated depreciation or depletion. Historical cost includes the original cost of the asset plus all costs necessary to get the asset ready for use (e.g., freight and installation).

Land is also a tangible asset that is reported at historical cost. However, land is not depreciated.

Tangible assets not used in the operations of the firm should be classified as investment assets.

Intangible Assets

Intangible assets are long-term assets that lack physical substance. Financial securities are not considered intangible assets. The value of an *identifiable intangible asset* is based on the rights or privileges conveyed to its owner over a finite period. Accordingly, the cost of an identifiable intangible asset is amortized over its useful life. Examples of identifiable intangibles include patents, trademarks, and copyrights. Note, however, that the value of internally produced intangible assets may not be recorded on the balance sheet.

An intangible asset that is *unidentifiable* cannot be purchased separately and may have an infinite life. Intangible assets with infinite lives are not amortized, but are tested for impairment at least annually. The best example of an unidentifiable intangible asset is goodwill.

Intangible assets that are purchased are reported on the balance sheet at historical cost less accumulated amortization. Except for certain legal costs, intangible assets that are created internally, including research and development costs, are expensed as incurred under U.S. GAAP. Under IFRS, a firm must identify the research stage and the development stage. Accordingly, the firm must expense costs during the research stage but can capitalize costs during the development stage.

All of the following should be expensed as incurred:

- Start-up and training costs.
- Administrative overhead.
- Advertising and promotion.
- Relocation and reorganization costs.
- Termination costs.

Some analysts completely eliminate intangible assets, particularly unidentifiable intangibles, for analytical purposes. Analysts should, however, consider the value to the firm of each intangible asset before making any adjustments.

Goodwill is the excess of purchase price over the fair value of the identifiable assets and liabilities acquired in a business acquisition. Let's look at an example of calculating goodwill.

[handwritten margin note: GAAP → internally created expensed; IFRS – can capitalize development stage]

Example: Goodwill

Wood Corporation paid $600 million for the outstanding stock of Pine Corporation. At the acquisition date, Pine reported the following condensed balance sheet.

Pine Corporation – Condensed Balance Sheet

	Book value (millions)
Current assets	$80
Plant and equipment, net	760
Goodwill	30
Liabilities	400
Stockholders' equity	470

The fair value of the plant and equipment was $120 million more than its recorded book value. The fair values of all other identifiable assets and liabilities were equal to their recorded book values. Calculate the amount of goodwill Wood should report on its consolidated balance sheet.

Answer:

	Book value (millions)
Current assets	$80
Plant and equipment, net	880 = 760 + 120
Liabilities	(400)
Fair value of net assets	560
Purchase price	600
Less: Fair value of net assets	(560)
Acquisition goodwill	40

Goodwill is equal to the excess of purchase price over the fair value of identifiable assets and liabilities acquired. The plant and equipment was "written-up" by $120 million to reflect fair value. The goodwill reported on Pine's balance sheet is an unidentifiable asset and is thus ignored in the calculation of Wood's goodwill.

Accounting goodwill should not be confused with economic goodwill. Economic goodwill derives from the expected future performance of the firm, while accounting goodwill is the result of past acquisitions.

Goodwill is created in a purchase acquisition. Internally generated goodwill is expensed as incurred. Goodwill is not amortized but must be tested for impairment at least annually. If impaired, goodwill is reduced and a loss is recognized in the income statement. The impairment loss does not affect cash flow. As long as goodwill is not impaired, it can remain on the balance sheet indefinitely.

Since goodwill is not amortized, firms can manipulate net income upward by allocating more of the acquisition price to goodwill and less to the identifiable assets. The result is less depreciation and amortization expense, resulting in higher net income.

When computing ratios, analysts should eliminate goodwill from the balance sheet and goodwill impairment charges from the income statement for comparability. Also, analysts should evaluate future acquisitions in terms of the price paid relative to the earning power of the acquired assets.

LOS 33.f: Discuss off-balance-sheet disclosures.

The financial statement footnotes should disclose information about the firm's:

- Accounting policies, including revenue recognition, other accounting methods, and judgments used.
- Estimation of uncertainty, including key assumptions that pose a significant risk.
- Debt agreement terms.
- Leases and off-balance-sheet financing.
- Business segments.
- Contingent assets and liabilities.
- Pension plans.

The footnotes should include a description of the firm and its legal identification details.

LOS 33.g: Demonstrate the appropriate classifications and related accounting treatments for marketable and non-marketable financial instruments held as assets or owed by the company as liabilities.

Financial instruments can be found on both the asset side and liability side of the balance sheet. **Financial assets** include investment securities (stocks and bonds), derivatives, loans, and receivables. **Financial liabilities** include derivatives, notes payable, and bonds payable.

Some financial assets and liabilities are reported on the balance sheet at fair value, while others are reported at cost or present value. Reporting assets and liabilities at fair value is known as **marking-to-market**. Certain marketable investment securities and derivatives (both assets and liabilities) are subject to mark-to-market adjustments.

 Professor's Note: The Financial Accounting Standards Board recently issued SFAS No. 159, "The Fair Value Option for Financial Assets and Financial Liabilities." This new standard extends the ability to report almost all financial assets and liabilities at fair value if a firm chooses to do so.

Marketable investment securities are classified as either held-to-maturity, trading, or available-for-sale.

Held-to-maturity securities are debt securities acquired with the intent that they will be held to maturity. Held-to-maturity securities are reported on the balance sheet at amortized cost. Amortized cost is equal to the face (par) value less any unamortized discount or plus any unamortized premium. Subsequent changes in market value are ignored.

Trading securities are debt and equity securities acquired with the intent to profit over the near term. Trading securities are reported on the balance sheet at fair value. Unrealized gains and losses, that is, changes in market value before the securities are sold, are reported in the income statement.

Available-for-sale securities are debt and equity securities that are not expected to be held to maturity or traded in the near term. Like trading securities, available-for-sale securities are reported on the balance sheet at fair value. However, any unrealized gains and losses are not recognized in the income statement but are reported in other comprehensive income as a part of stockholders' equity.

Dividend and interest income and realized gains and losses (actual gains or losses when the securities are sold) are recognized in the income statement for all three classifications of securities.

Figure 4 summarizes the different classifications of investment securities.

Figure 4: Summary of Investment Security Classifications

	Trading	*Available-for-sale*	*Held-to-maturity*
Balance sheet	Fair value	Fair value	Amortized cost
Income statement	Dividends Interest Realized gains/losses Unrealized gains/losses	Dividends Interest Realized gains/losses	Interest Realized gains/losses

Example: Classification of investment securities

Triple D Corporation purchased a 6% bond, at par, for $1,000,000 at the beginning of the year. Interest rates have recently increased and the market value of the bond declined $20,000. Determine the bond's effect on Triple D's financial statements under each classification of securities.

Answer:

If the bond is classified as a *held-to-maturity* security, the bond is reported on the balance sheet at $1,000,000. Interest income of $60,000 [$1,000,000 × 6%] is reported in the income statement.

If the bond is classified as a *trading* security, the bond is reported on the balance sheet at $980,000. The $20,000 unrealized loss and $60,000 of interest income are both recognized in the income statement.

If the bond is classified as an *available-for-sale* security, the bond is reported on the balance sheet at $980,000. Interest income of $60,000 is recognized in the income statement. The $20,000 unrealized loss is not recognized in the income statement. Rather, it is reported as a change in stockholders' equity.

Most financial liabilities, such as bonds and notes payable, are reported at their amortized cost. Derivatives, as well as non-derivative financial instruments with exposures hedged by derivatives, are reported at fair value. Financial liabilities classified as held-for-trading, such as a short position in a stock taken to earn a near-term profit, are also reported at fair value.

LOS 33.h: List and explain the components of owners' equity.

Owners' equity is the residual interest in assets that remains after subtracting an entity's liabilities. The owners' equity section of the balance sheet includes contributed capital, any minority (noncontrolling) interest, retained earnings, treasury stock, and accumulated other comprehensive income.

Contributed capital is the total amount paid in by the common and preferred shareholders. Preferred shareholders have certain rights and privileges not possessed by the common shareholders. For example, preferred shareholders are paid dividends at a specified rate, usually expressed as a percentage of their par values, and have priority over the claims of the common shareholders in the event of liquidation.

The par value of common stock and preferred stock is a "stated" or "legal" value. Par value has no relationship to fair value. Some common shares are even issued without a par value. When par value exists, it is reported separately in stockholders' equity.

Also disclosed is the number of common shares that are authorized, issued, and outstanding. **Authorized shares** are the number of shares that may be sold under the firm's articles of incorporation. **Issued shares** are the number of shares that have actually been sold to shareholders. The number of **outstanding shares** is equal to the issued shares less shares that have been reacquired by the firm (i.e., treasury stock).

Minority interest (noncontrolling interest) is the minority shareholders' pro-rata share of the net assets (equity) of a subsidiary that is not wholly owned by the parent.

Retained earnings are the undistributed earnings (net income) of the firm since inception, the cumulative earnings that have not been paid out to shareholders as dividends.

Treasury stock is stock that has been reacquired by the issuing firm but not yet retired. Treasury stock reduces stockholders' equity. It does not represent an investment in the firm. Treasury stock has no voting rights and does not receive dividends.

Accumulated other comprehensive income includes all changes in stockholders' equity except for transactions recognized in the income statement (net income) and transactions with shareholders, such as issuing stock, reacquiring stock, and paying dividends.

As discussed in the topic review on understanding the income statement, comprehensive income aggregates net income and certain special transactions that are not reported in the income statement but that affect stockholders' equity. These special transactions comprise what is known as "other comprehensive income." Comprehensive income is equal to net income plus other comprehensive income.

> *Professor's Note: It is easy to confuse the two terms "comprehensive income" and "accumulated other comprehensive income." Comprehensive income is an income measure over a period of time. It includes net income and other comprehensive income for the period. Accumulated other comprehensive income does not include net income but is a component of stockholders' equity at a point in time.*

IFRS – no comp income required

Under U.S. GAAP, the firm can report comprehensive income in the income statement (below net income), in a separate statement of comprehensive income, or in the statement of changes in stockholders' equity. Firms are not required to report comprehensive income under IFRS.

LOS 33.i: Interpret balance sheets, common-size balance sheets, the statement of changes in equity, and commonly used balance sheet ratios.

The statement of changes in stockholders' equity summarizes all transactions that increase or decrease the equity accounts for the period. The statement includes transactions with shareholders, and a reconciliation of the beginning and ending balance of each equity account, including capital stock, additional paid-in-capital, retained earnings, and accumulated other comprehensive income. In addition, the components of accumulated other comprehensive income are disclosed (i.e., unrealized gains and losses from available-for-sale securities, cash flow hedging derivatives, foreign currency translation, and adjustments for minimum pension liability).

A statement of changes in stockholders' equity is illustrated in Figure 5.

Figure 5: Sample Statement of Changes in Stockholders' Equity

	Common Stock	Retained Earnings (in thousands)	Accumulated Other Comprehensive Income (loss)	Total
Beginning balance	$49,234	$26,664	($406)	$75,492
Net income		6,994		6,994
Net unrealized loss on available-for-sale securities			(40)	(40)
Net unrealized loss on cash flow hedges			(56)	(56)
Minimum pension liability			(26)	(26)
Cumulative translation adjustment			42	42
Comprehensive income				6,914
Issuance of common stock	1,282			1,282
Repurchases of common stock	(6,200)			(6,200)
Dividends		(2,360)		(2,360)
Ending balance	$44,316	$31,298	($486)	$75,128

Common-Size Balance Sheets

As with the income statement, common-size balance sheets and ratios can facilitate analysis of a firm.

A **common-size balance sheet** expresses each balance sheet account as a percentage of total assets. This format is known as *vertical common-size analysis* and allows the analyst to evaluate the balance sheet items over time (time-series analysis), as well as to compare a firm's balance sheet items to those of other firms, industry averages, and sector data (cross-sectional analysis). Several commercial services provide data for comparison.

Commonly Used Balance Sheet Ratios

Liquidity ratios and solvency ratios are considered pure balance sheet ratios since both the numerator and denominator are from the balance sheet. **Liquidity ratios** measure the firm's ability to satisfy short-term obligations when due. **Solvency ratios** measure the firm's ability to satisfy long-term obligations.

Liquidity ratios

The **current ratio** is the best known measure of liquidity.

$$\text{current ratio} = \frac{\text{current assets}}{\text{current liabilities}}$$

A current ratio of less than one means that the firm has negative working capital and may be facing a liquidity crisis. Working capital is equal to current assets minus current liabilities.

The **quick ratio** (acid test ratio) is a more conservative measure of liquidity because it excludes inventories and less liquid current assets from the numerator.

$$\text{quick ratio} = \frac{\text{cash} + \text{marketable securities} + \text{receivables}}{\text{current liabilities}}$$

The **cash ratio** is the most conservative measure of liquidity.

$$\text{cash ratio} = \frac{\text{cash} + \text{marketable securities}}{\text{current liabilities}}$$

The higher the liquidity ratios, the more likely the firm will be able to pay its short-term bills when they are due. The ratios differ only in the assumed liquidity of the current assets.

Solvency ratios

The following ratios measure financial risk and leverage. With all four ratios, the higher the ratio, the greater the leverage and the greater the risk.

The **long-term debt-to-equity ratio** measures long-term financing sources relative to the equity base.

$$\text{long-term debt-to-equity} = \frac{\text{total long-term debt}}{\text{total equity}}$$

The **debt-to-equity ratio** measures total debt relative to the equity base.

$$\text{debt-to-equity} = \frac{\text{total debt}}{\text{total equity}}$$

The **total debt ratio** measures the extent to which assets are financed by creditors.

$$\text{total debt ratio} = \frac{\text{total debt}}{\text{total assets}}$$

The **financial leverage ratio** is a variation of the debt-to-equity ratio that is used as a component of the DuPont model.

$$\text{financial leverage} = \frac{\text{total assets}}{\text{total equity}}$$

Financial Leverage $=\dfrac{Assets}{Equity}$

 Professor's Note: More detail on the precise definitions and calculation of commonly used financial ratios is presented in a subsequent topic review.

Usefulness and limitations of ratio analysis

Even in forward-looking "efficient markets" (where securities prices reflect all available information), financial ratios based on backward-looking data provide useful information to analysts. Specifically, ratios provide the following:

- Insights into the financial relationships that are useful in forecasting future earnings and cash flows.
- Information about the financial flexibility of the firm.
- A means of evaluating management's performance.

Financial ratios are not without limitations:

- Ratios are not useful when viewed in isolation.
- Comparisons with other companies are made more difficult because of different accounting methods. Some of the more common differences include inventory methods (FIFO and LIFO), depreciation methods (accelerated and straight-line), and lease accounting (capital and operating).
- There may be difficulty in locating comparable ratios when analyzing companies that operate in multiple industries.
- Conclusions cannot be made from viewing one set of ratios. Ratios must be viewed relative to one another over time, between companies or relative to benchmark values.
- Judgment is required. Determining the target or comparison value for a ratio is difficult and may actually be some range of acceptable values rather than a single target value.

KEY CONCEPTS

LOS 33.a

Assets are probable future economic benefits owned or controlled by an entity as a result of previous transactions.

Liabilities are obligations owed by an entity from previous transactions that are expected to result in an outflow of economic benefits in the future.

Stockholders' equity is the residual interest in assets that remains after subtracting an entity's liabilities. Equity = assets – liabilities.

The balance sheet provides information about a company's assets, how it raises capital, probable cash flows from inventory and receivables, its liabilities, its short-term liquidity, and use of financial leverage.

LOS 33.b

A balance sheet in an account format lists assets on the left side and liabilities and equity on the right side. A report format balance sheet lists assets, liabilities, and equity in a single column. A classified balance sheet groups accounts into subtotals such as current assets and current liabilities.

LOS 33.c

Under accrual accounting, sales in excess of cash collected will create balance sheet assets, and expenditures in excess of cash paid for them will result in balance sheet liabilities.

LOS 33.d

Current (noncurrent) assets are those expected to be used up or converted to cash in less than (more than) one year or the firm's operating cycle, whichever is greater. Current (noncurrent) liabilities are those the firm expects to pay in less than (more than) one year or the firm's operating cycle, whichever is greater.

LOS 33.e

Balance sheet values are a mixture of historical costs and fair values.

Accounts receivable are reported at net realizable value (based on management's estimates of collectability).

Inventory is reported at the lower of cost or net realizable value.

Tangible noncurrent assets are reported at their historical costs less accumulated depreciation.

Identifiable intangible assets with definite lives are reported at their historical costs when purchased or, under some circumstances, when created, less accumulated amortization.

Goodwill, the difference between the purchase price of a business and the fair value of its identifiable assets less liabilities, is an intangible asset that is not amortized but must be tested for impairment at least annually.

LOS 33.f

Notes to the financial statements should disclose information about:

- The firm's accounting policies.
- Estimates and assumptions that pose significant risk.
- Terms of debt agreements.
- Obligations from off-balance-sheet financing such as operating leases.
- Business segments.
- Contingent assets and liabilities.
- Pension plans.

LOS 33.g

Held-to-maturity securities are reported at amortized cost.

Trading securities are reported at fair value, and any unrealized gains and losses are reported in net income.

Available-for-sale securities are reported at fair value, and any unrealized gains and losses are reported as a component of stockholders' equity.

Bonds and notes payable are reported at their amortized cost (proceeds). Derivatives, instruments with exposures hedged by derivatives, and financial liabilities held for trading are reported at fair value.

LOS 33.h

Owners' equity includes:

- Contributed capital—the amount paid in by common and preferred shareholders.
- Minority interest—the portion of a subsidiary that is not owned by the parent.
- Retained earnings—the cumulative undistributed earnings of the firm since inception.
- Treasury stock—common stock that the firm has repurchased.
- Accumulated other comprehensive income—includes all changes to equity from sources other than net income and transactions with shareholders.

LOS 33.i

The statement of changes in equity summarizes the transactions during a period that increase or decrease equity, including transactions with shareholders.

A vertical common-size balance sheet expresses each balance sheet item as a percentage of total assets.

Liquidity ratios that can be read from a common-size balance sheet include the current ratio, the quick ratio, and the cash ratio.

Solvency ratios that can be read from a common-size balance sheet include the long-term debt-to-equity ratio, the debt-to-equity ratio, the debt ratio, and the financial leverage ratio.

Comparisons of ratios among firms may be difficult because of different accounting methods and the judgment and estimates that are involved.

CONCEPT CHECKERS

1. Which of the following is *most likely* an essential characteristic of an asset?
   A. An asset is tangible.
   B. An asset is obtained at a cost.
   C. An asset provides future benefits.

2. Which of the following is *least likely* a satisfactory statement of the balance sheet equation?
   A. stockholders' equity = assets – liabilities.
   B. liabilities = assets – stockholders' equity.
   C. assets = liabilities – stockholders' equity.

3. Century Company's balance sheet follows:

Century Company Balance Sheet (in millions)	20X7	20X6
Current assets	$340	$280
Noncurrent assets	660	630
Total assets	$1,000	$910
Current liabilities	$170	$110
Noncurrent liabilities	50	50
Total liabilities	$220	$160
Equity	$780	$750
Total liabilities and equity	$1,000	$910

Is Century's balance sheet presentation an example of a report format, and is the balance sheet a classified presentation?

	Report format	Classified
A.	Yes	Yes
B.	No	No
C.	No	Yes

4. At the beginning of the year, Tenant Company paid its annual operating lease obligation in advance. What is the immediate impact of this transaction on Tenants' total assets and total liabilities?

	Assets	Liabilities
A.	No effect	No effect
B.	No effect	Decrease
C.	Increase	Decrease

5. How should the proceeds received from the advance sale of tickets to a sporting event be treated by the seller, assuming the tickets are nonrefundable?
    A. Unearned revenue is recognized to the extent that costs have been incurred.
    B. Revenue is recognized to the extent that costs have been incurred.
    C. Revenue is deferred until the sporting event is held.

6. Which of the following would *most likely* result in a current liability?
    A. Possible warranty claims.
    B. Future operating lease payments.
    C. Estimated income taxes for the current year.

7. Which of the following inventory valuation methods is required by the accounting standard-setting bodies?
    A. Lower of cost or net realizable value.
    B. Weighted average cost.
    C. First-in, first-out.

8. SF Corporation has created employee goodwill by reorganizing its retirement benefit package. An independent management consultant estimated the value of the goodwill at $2 million. In addition, SF recently purchased a patent that was developed by a competitor. The patent has an estimated useful life of five years. Should SF report the goodwill and patent on its balance sheet?

	Goodwill	Patent
A.	Yes	No
B.	No	Yes
C.	No	No

9. At the beginning of the year, Parent Company purchased all 500,000 shares of Sub Incorporated for $15 per share. Just before the acquisition date, Sub's balance sheet reported net assets of $6 million. Parent determined the fair value of Sub's property and equipment was $1 million higher than reported by Sub. What amount of goodwill should Parent report as a result of its acquisition of Sub?
    A. $0.
    B. $500,000.
    C. $1,500,000.

10. Which of the following is *least likely* to be disclosed in the financial statement footnotes?
    A. Off-balance-sheet financing.
    B. Contingencies and commitments.
    C. Fair value of noncurrent assets used in the production of income.

Use the following information to answer Questions 11 and 12.

At the beginning of the year, Company P purchased 1,000 shares of Company S for $80 per share. During the year, Company S paid a dividend of $4 per share. At the end of the year, Company S's share price was $75.

11. What amount should Company P report on its balance sheet at year-end if the investment in Company S is considered a trading security, and what amount should be reported if the investment is considered an available-for-sale security?

Trading	Available-for-sale
A. $75,000	$75,000
B. $75,000	$80,000
C. $80,000	$80,000

12. What amount of investment income should Company P recognize in its income statement if the investment in Company S is considered trading, and what amount should be recognized if the investment is considered available-for-sale?

Trading	Available-for-sale
A. ($1,000)	($1,000)
B. ($1,000)	$4,000
C. ($5,000)	$4,000

13. Miller Corporation has 160,000 shares of common stock authorized. There are 92,000 shares issued and 84,000 shares outstanding. How many shares of treasury stock does Miller own?
    A. 8,000.
    B. 68,000
    C. 76,000.

14. Selected data from Alpha Company's balance sheet at the end of the year follows:

Investment in Beta Company, at fair value	$150,000
Deferred taxes	$86,000
Common stock, $1 par value	$550,000
Preferred stock, $100 par value	$175,000
Retained earnings	$893,000
Accumulated other comprehensive income	$46,000

    The investment in Beta Company had an original cost of $120,000. Assuming the investment in Beta is classified as available-for-sale, Alpha's total owners' equity at year-end is *closest* to:
    A. $1,618,000.
    B. $1,664,000.
    C. $1,714,000.

15. How would the collection of accounts receivable *most likely* affect the current and cash ratios?

	Current ratio	Cash ratio
A.	Increase	Increase
B.	No effect	Increase
C.	No effect	No effect

16. Comparing a company's ratios with those of its competitors is known as:
    A. Longitudinal analysis.
    B. Common-size analysis.
    C. Cross-sectional analysis.

ANSWERS – CONCEPT CHECKERS

1. **C**   An asset is a future economic benefit obtained or controlled as a result of past transactions. Some assets are intangible (e.g., goodwill), and others may be donated.

2. **C**   Assets must equal liabilities plus stockholders' equity. Otherwise, the balance sheet would not balance.

3. **A**   In a report format, the assets, liabilities, and equity are presented in one column. A classified balance sheet groups together similar items (e.g., current and noncurrent assets and liabilities) to arrive at significant subtotals.

4. **A**   Tenant has simply prepaid its annual payment; rent expense has not yet been incurred. When cash is paid in advance of recognizing an expense, one asset (cash) decreases and another asset (prepaid expenses) increases by the same amount. Liabilities are not affected.

5. **C**   The ticket revenue should not be recognized until it is earned. Even though the tickets are nonrefundable, the seller is still obligated to hold the event.

6. **C**   Estimated income taxes for the current year are likely reported as a current liability. To recognize the warranty expense, it must be probable, not just possible. Future operating lease payments are not reported on the balance sheet.

7. **A**   Inventories are required to be valued at the lower of cost or net realizable value (or "market" under U.S. GAAP). FIFO and average cost are two of the inventory cost flow assumptions among which a firm has a choice.

8. **B**   Goodwill developed internally is expensed as incurred. The purchased patent is reported on the balance sheet.

9. **B**   Purchase price of $7,500,000 [$15 per share × 500,000 shares] – Fair value of net assets of $7,000,000 [$6,000,000 book value + $1,000,000 increase in property and equipment] = Goodwill of $500,000.

10. **C**   Property and equipment (i.e., noncurrent assets used in the production of income) is reported at original cost less accumulated depreciation. There is no requirement to disclose the fair value in the footnotes.

11. **A**   Both trading securities and available-for-sale securities are reported on the balance sheet at their fair values. At year-end, the fair value is $75,000 [$75 per share × 1,000 shares].

12. **B**   A loss of $1,000 is recognized if the securities are considered trading securities ($4 dividend × $1,000 shares) – ($5 unrealized loss × 1,000 shares). Income is $4,000 if the investment in Company S is considered available-for-sale [$4 dividend × $1,000].

13. **A**   The difference between the issued shares and the outstanding shares is the treasury shares.

14. **B**   Total stockholders' equity consists of common stock of $550,000, preferred stock of $175,000, retained earnings of $893,000, and accumulated other comprehensive income of $46,000, for a total of $1,664,000. The $30,000 unrealized gain from the investment in Beta is already included in accumulated other comprehensive income.

15. **B**   The collection of accounts receivable would increase cash and decrease accounts receivable. Thus, current assets would not change and the current ratio would remain the same. Since the numerator of the cash ratio only includes cash and marketable securities, the collection of receivables would increase the cash ratio.

16. **C**   Comparing ratios of a firm to those of its competitors is known as cross-sectional analysis.

The following is a review of the Financial Reporting and Analysis principles designed to address the learning outcome statements set forth by CFA Institute®. This topic is also covered in:

UNDERSTANDING THE CASH FLOW STATEMENT

Study Session 8

EXAM FOCUS

This topic review covers the third important required financial statement: the statement of cash flows. Since the income statement is based on the accrual method, net income may not represent cash generated from operations. A company may be generating positive and growing net income but may be headed for insolvency because insufficient cash is being generated from operating activities. Constructing a statement of cash flows, by either the direct or indirect method, is therefore very important in an analysis of a firm's activities and prospects. Make sure you understand the preparation of a statement of cash flows by either method, the classification of various cash flows as operating, financing, or investing cash flows, and the key differences in these classifications between U.S. GAAP and international accounting standards. This is very testable material, and you should expect several questions based on it.

THE CASH FLOW STATEMENT

The **cash flow statement** provides information beyond that available from the income statement, which is based on accrual, rather than cash, accounting. The cash flow statement provides the following:

- Information about a company's cash receipts and cash payments during an accounting period.
- Information about a company's operating, investing, and financing activities.
- An understanding of the impact of accrual accounting events on cash flows.

The cash flow statement provides information to assess the firm's liquidity, solvency, and financial flexibility. An analyst can use the statement of cash flows to determine whether:

- Regular operations generate enough cash to sustain the business.
- Enough cash is generated to pay off existing debts as they mature.
- The firm is likely to need additional financing.
- Unexpected obligations can be met.
- The firm can take advantage of new business opportunities as they arise.

LOS 34.a: Compare and contrast cash flows from operating, investing, and financing activities, and classify cash flow items as relating to one of these three categories, given a description of the items.

Items on the cash flow statement come from two sources: (1) income statement items and (2) changes in balance sheet accounts. A firm's cash receipts and payments are classified on the cash flow statement as either operating, investing, or financing activities.

Cash flow from operating activities (CFO), sometimes referred to as "cash flow from operations" or "operating cash flow," consists of the inflows and outflows of cash resulting from transactions that affect a firm's net income.

Cash flow from investing activities (CFI) consists of the inflows and outflows of cash resulting from the acquisition or disposal of long-term assets and certain investments.

Cash flow from financing activities (CFF) consists of the inflows and outflows of cash resulting from transactions affecting a firm's capital structure.

Examples of each cash flow classification, in accordance with U.S. GAAP, are presented in Figure 1.

Figure 1: U.S. GAAP Cash Flow Classifications

Operating Activities	
Inflows	*Outflows*
Cash collected from customers	Cash paid to employees and suppliers
Interest and dividends received	Cash paid for other expenses
Sale proceeds from trading securities	Acquisition of trading securities
	Interest paid
	Taxes paid

Investing Activities	
Inflows	*Outflows*
Sale proceeds from fixed assets	Acquisition of fixed assets
Sale proceeds from debt & equity investments	Acquisition of debt & equity investments
Principal received from loans made to others	Loans made to others

Financing Activities	
Inflows	*Outflows*
Principal amounts of debt issued	Principal paid on debt
Proceeds from issuing stock	Payments to reacquire stock
	Dividends paid to shareholders

Note that the acquisition of debt and equity investments (other than trading securities) and loans made to others are reported as investing activities; however, the income from these investments (interest and dividends received) is reported as an operating activity. Also, note that principal amounts borrowed from others are reported as financing activities; however, the interest paid is reported as an operating activity. Finally, note that dividends paid to the firm's shareholders are financing activities.

 Professor's Note: Don't confuse dividends received and dividends paid. Under U.S. GAAP, dividends received are operating activities and dividends paid are financing activities.

LOS 34.b: Describe how noncash investing and financing activities are reported.

Noncash investing and financing activities are not reported in the cash flow statement since they do not result in inflows or outflows of cash.

For example, if a firm acquires real estate with financing provided by the seller, the firm has made an investing and financing decision. This transaction is the equivalent of borrowing the purchase price. However, since no cash is involved in the transaction, it is not reported as an investing and financing activity in the cash flow statement.

Another example of a noncash transaction is an exchange of debt for equity. Such an exchange results in a reduction of debt and an increase in equity. However, since no cash is involved in the transaction, it is not reported as a financing activity in the cash flow statement.

Noncash transactions must be disclosed in either a footnote or supplemental schedule to the cash flow statement. Analysts should be aware of the firm's noncash transactions, incorporate them into analysis of past and current performance, and include their effects in estimating future cash flows.

LOS 34.c: Compare and contrast the key differences in cash flow statements prepared under international financial reporting standards and U.S. generally accepted accounting principles.

Recall from Figure 1 that under U.S. GAAP, dividends paid to the firm's shareholders are reported as financing activities while interest paid is reported in operating activities. Interest received and dividends received from investments are also reported as operating activities.

International Financial Reporting Standards (IFRS) allow more flexibility in the classification of cash flows. Under IFRS, interest and dividends received may be classified as either operating *or* investing activities. Dividends paid to the company's shareholders and interest paid on the company's debt may be classified as either operating *or* financing activities.

Another important difference relates to income taxes paid. Under U.S. GAAP, all taxes paid are reported as operating activities, even taxes related to investing and financing transactions. Under IFRS, income taxes are also reported as operating activities unless the expense is associated with an investing or financing transaction.

For example, consider a company that sells land that was held for investment for $1 million. Income taxes on the sale total $160,000. Under U.S. GAAP, the firm reports an inflow of cash from investing activities of $1 million and an outflow of cash from operating activities of $160,000. Under IFRS, the firm can report a net inflow of $840,000 from investing activities.

LOS 34.d: Demonstrate the difference between the direct and indirect methods of presenting cash from operating activities and explain the arguments in favor of each.

There are two methods of presenting the cash flow statement: the direct method and the indirect method. Both methods are permitted under U.S. GAAP and IFRS. The use of the direct method, however, is encouraged by both standard setters. The difference in the two methods relates to the presentation of cash flow from operating activities. The presentation of cash flows from investing activities and financing activities is exactly the same under both methods.

Direct Method

Under the **direct method**, each line item of the accrual-based income statement is converted into cash receipts or cash payments. Recall that under the accrual method of accounting, the timing of revenue and expense recognition may differ from the timing of the related cash flows. Under cash-basis accounting, revenue and expense recognition occur when cash is received or paid. Simply stated, the direct method converts an accrual-basis income statement into a cash-basis income statement.

Figure 2 contains an example of a presentation of operating cash flow for Seagraves Supply Company using the direct method.

Figure 2: Direct Method of Presenting Operating Cash Flow

Seagraves Supply Company	
Operating Cash Flow – Direct Method	
For the year ended December 31, 20X7	
Cash collections from customers	$429,980
Cash paid to suppliers	(265,866)
Cash paid for operating expenses	(124,784)
Cash paid for interest	(4,326)
Cash paid for taxes	(14,956)
Operating cash flow	$20,048

Notice the similarities of the direct method cash flow presentation and an income statement. The direct method begins with cash inflows from customers and then deducts cash outflows for purchases, operating expenses, interest, and taxes.

Indirect Method

Under the **indirect method**, net income is converted to operating cash flow by making adjustments for transactions that affect net income but are not cash transactions. These adjustments include eliminating noncash expenses (e.g., depreciation and amortization), nonoperating items (e.g., gains and losses), and changes in balance sheet accounts resulting from accrual accounting events.

Figure 3 contains an example of a presentation of operating cash flow for Seagraves Supply Company under the indirect method.

Figure 3: Indirect Method of Presenting Operating Cash Flow

Seagraves Supply Company
Operating Cash Flow – Indirect Method
For the year ended December 31, 20X7

Net income	$18,788
Adjustments to reconcile net income to cash flow provided by operating activities:	
Depreciation and amortization	7,996
Deferred income taxes	416
Increase in accounts receivable	(1,220)
Increase in inventory	(20,544)
Decrease in prepaid expenses	494
Increase in accounts payable	13,406
Increase in accrued liabilities	712
Operating cash flow	$20,048

Notice that under the indirect method, the starting point is net income, the "bottom line" of the income statement. Under the direct method, the starting point is the top of the income statement, revenues, adjusted to show cash received from customers. Total cash flow from operating activities is exactly the same under both methods, only the presentation methods differ.

Arguments in Favor of Each Method

The primary advantage of the direct method is that it presents the firm's operating cash receipts and payments, while the indirect method only presents the net result of these receipts and payments. Therefore, the direct method provides more information than the indirect method. This knowledge of past receipts and payments is useful in estimating future operating cash flows.

The main advantage of the indirect method is that it focuses on the differences in net income and operating cash flow. This provides a useful link to the income statement when forecasting future operating cash flow. Analysts forecast net income and then derive operating cash flow by adjusting net income for the differences between accrual accounting and the cash basis of accounting.

Disclosure requirements

Under U.S. GAAP, a direct method presentation must also disclose the adjustments necessary to reconcile net income to cash flow from operating activities. This disclosure is the same information that is presented in an indirect method cash flow statement. This reconciliation is not required under IFRS.

Under IFRS, payments for interest and taxes must be disclosed separately in the cash flow statement under either method (direct or indirect). Under U.S. GAAP, payments for interest and taxes can be reported in the cash flow statement or disclosed in the footnotes.

LOS 34.e: Demonstrate how the cash flow statement is linked to the income statement and balance sheet.

The cash flow statement reconciles the beginning and ending balances of cash over an accounting period. The change in cash is a result of the firm's operating, investing, and financing activities as follows:

$$
\begin{array}{rl}
 & \text{Operating cash flow} \\
+ & \text{Investing cash flow} \\
+ & \text{Financing cash flow} \\
\hline
= & \text{Change in cash balance} \\
+ & \text{Beginning cash balance} \\
\hline
= & \text{Ending cash balance}
\end{array}
$$

It is important to understand that net income, based on accrual accounting, is not the same thing as cash earnings. When the timing of revenue or expense recognition differs from the receipt or payment of cash, it is reflected in changes in balance sheet accounts.

For example, when revenues (sales) exceed cash collections, accounts receivable increase. The opposite occurs when cash collections exceed revenues; accounts receivable (an asset) decrease. When purchases from suppliers exceed cash payments, accounts payable (a liability) increase. When cash payments exceed purchases, payables decrease.

Investing activities typically relate to the firm's noncurrent assets, while financing activities typically relate to the firm's noncurrent liabilities and equity.

Each balance sheet account can be analyzed in terms of the transactions that increase or decrease the account over a period of time. For example, the following is a reconciliation of inventory:

$$
\begin{array}{rl}
 & \text{Beginning inventory balance} \\
+ & \text{Inventory purchases} \\
- & \text{Cost of goods sold} \\
\hline
= & \text{Ending inventory balance}
\end{array}
$$

Handwritten margin note: Beg + purchases | add − cost | minuses ending

Professor's Note: Given three of the four variables in the above reconciliation, it is easy to solve for the fourth. This type of analysis can be applied to any balance sheet account as long as you know which transactions increase and which transactions decrease the account.

The firm's balance sheet, income statement, and cash flow statement are all related. Understanding these relationships is important for analytical purposes, as well as for detecting possible aggressive accounting practices.

LOS 34.f: Demonstrate the steps in the preparation of direct and indirect cash flow statements, including how cash flows can be computed using income statement and balance sheet data.

Professor's Note: Throughout the discussion of the direct and indirect methods, remember the following points:

- *CFO is calculated differently, but the result is the same under both methods.*
- *The calculation of CFI and CFF is identical under both methods.*
- *There is an inverse relationship between changes in assets and changes in cash flows. In other words, an increase in an asset account is a use of cash, and a decrease in an asset account is a source of cash.*
- *There is a direct relationship between changes in liabilities and changes in cash flow. In other words, an increase in a liability account is a source of cash, and a decrease in a liability is a use of cash.*
- *Sources of cash are positive numbers (cash inflows) and uses of cash are negative numbers (cash outflows).*

Direct Method

The direct method of present a firm's statement of cash flows shows only cash payments and cash receipts over the period. The sum of these inflows and outflows is the company's CFO. The direct method gives the analyst more information than the indirect method. The analyst can see the actual amounts that went to each use of cash and that were received from each source of cash. This information can help the analyst to better understand the firm's performance over time and to forecast future cash flows.

The following are common components of cash flow that appear on a statement of cash flow presented under the direct method:

- Cash collected from customers, typically the main component of CFO.
- Cash used in the production of goods and services (cash inputs).
- Cash operating expenses.
- Cash paid for interest.
- Cash paid for taxes.

Professor's Note: A common "trick" in direct method questions is to provide information on depreciation expense along with other operating cash flow components. When using the direct method, ignore depreciation expense—it's a noncash charge. We'll see later that we do consider depreciation expense in indirect method computations, but we do this solely because depreciation expense and other noncash expenses have been subtracted in calculating net income (our starting point) and need to be added back to get cash flow.

Investing cash flows (CFI) are calculated by examining the change in the gross asset accounts that result from investing activities, such as property, plant, and equipment, intangible assets, and investment securities. Related accumulated depreciation or amortization accounts are ignored since they do not represent cash expenses.

 Professor's Note: In this context, "gross" simply means an amount that is presented on the balance sheet before deducting any accumulated depreciation or amortization.

When calculating cash paid for a new asset, it is necessary to determine whether old assets were sold. If assets were sold during the period, you must use the following formula:

cash paid for new asset = ending gross assets + gross cost of old assets sold – beginning gross assets

 Professor's Note: It may be easier to think in terms of the account reconciliation format discussed earlier. That is, beginning gross assets + cash paid for new assets – gross cost of assets sold = ending gross assets. Given three of the variables, simply solve for the fourth.

When calculating the cash flow from an asset that has been sold, it is necessary to consider any gain or loss from the sale using the following formula:

cash from asset sold = book value of the asset + gain (or – loss) on sale

Financing cash flows (CFF) are determined by measuring the cash flows occurring between the firm and its suppliers of capital. Cash flows between the firm and its creditors result from new borrowings (positive CFF) and debt principal repayments (negative CFF). Note that interest paid is technically a cash flow to creditors, but it is included in CFO under U.S. GAAP. Cash flows between the firm and its shareholders occur when equity is issued, shares are repurchased, or dividends are paid. CFF is the sum of these two measures:

net cash flows from creditors = new borrowings – principal amounts repaid

net cash flows from shareholders = new equity issued – share repurchases – cash dividends paid

Cash dividends paid can be calculated from dividends declared and any changes in dividends payable.

Finally, total cash flow is equal to the sum of CFO, CFI, and CFF. If calculated correctly, the total cash flow will equal the change in cash from one balance sheet to the next.

Indirect Method

Cash flow from operations is presented differently under the indirect method, but the amount of CFO is the same under either method. Cash flow from financing and cash flow from investing are presented in the same way on cash flow statements prepared under both the direct and indirect methods of presenting the statement of cash flows.

Under the indirect method of presenting CFO, we begin with net income and adjust it for differences between accounting items and actual cash receipts and cash disbursements. Depreciation, for example, is deducted in calculating net income, but requires no cash outlay in the current period. Therefore, we must add depreciation (and amortization) to net income for the period in calculating CFO.

Another adjustment to net income on an indirect statement of cash flows is to subtract gains on the disposal of assets. Proceeds from the sale of fixed assets are an investing cash flow. Since gains are a portion of such proceeds, we need to subtract them from net income in calculating CFO under the indirect method.

Under the indirect method, we also need to adjust net income for change in balance sheet accounts. If, for example, accounts receivable went up during the period, we know that sales during the period were greater than the cash collected from customers. Since sales were used to calculate net income under the accrual method, we need to reduce net income to reflect the fact that credit sales, rather than cash collected were used in calculating net income.

A change in accounts payable indicates a difference between purchases and the amount paid to suppliers. An increase in accounts payable, for example, results when purchases are greater than cash paid to suppliers. Since purchases were subtracted in calculating net income, we need to add any increase in accounts payable to net income so that CFO reflects the actual cash disbursements for purchases (rather than total purchases).

The steps in calculating CFO under the indirect method can be summarized as follows:

Step 1: Begin with net income.

Step 2: Subtract gains or add losses that resulted from financing or investing cash flows (such as gains from sale of land).

Step 3: Add back all noncash charges to income (such as depreciation and amortization) and subtract all noncash components of revenue.

Step 4: Add or subtract changes to balance sheet operating accounts as follows:
- Increases in the operating asset accounts (uses of cash) are subtracted, while decreases (sources of cash) are added.
- Increases in the operating liability accounts (sources of cash) are added, while decreases (uses of cash) are subtracted.

Example: Statement of cash flows using the indirect method

Use the following balance sheet and income statement to prepare a statement of cash flows under the indirect method.

Income Statement for 20X7

Sales	$100,000
Expense	
Cost of goods sold	40,000
Wages	5,000
Depreciation	7,000
Interest	500
Total expenses	$52,500
Income from continuing operations	$47,500
Gain from sale of land	10,000
Pretax income	57,500
Provision for taxes	20,000
Net income	$37,500
Common dividends declared	$8,500

Balance Sheets for 20X7 and 20X6

	20X7	20X6
Assets		
Current assets		
Cash	$33,000	$9,000
Accounts receivable	10,000	9,000
Inventory	5,000	7,000
Noncurrent assets		
Land	$35,000	$40,000
Gross plant and equipment	85,000	60,000
less: Accumulated depreciation	(16,000)	(9,000)
Net plant and equipment	$69,000	$51,000
Goodwill	10,000	10,000
Total assets	$162,000	$126,000

Liabilities

Current liabilities

Accounts payable	$9,000	$5,000
Wages payable	4,500	8,000
Interest payable	3,500	3,000
Taxes payable	5,000	4,000
Dividends payable	6,000	1,000
Total current liabilities	28,000	21,000
Noncurrent liabilities		
Bonds	$15,000	$10,000
Deferred tax liability	20,000	15,000
Total liabilities	$63,000	$46,000

Stockholders' equity

Common stock	$40,000	$50,000
Retained earnings	59,000	30,000
Total equity	$99,000	$80,000
Total liabilities & stockholders' equity	$162,000	$126,000

Any discrepancies between the changes in accounts reported on the balance sheet and those reported in the statement of cash flows are typically due to business combinations and changes in exchange rates.

Answer:

Operating Cash Flow:

Step 1: Start with net income of $37,500.
Step 2: Subtract gain from sale of land of $10,000.
Step 3: Add back noncash charges of depreciation of $7,000.
Step 4: Subtract increases in receivables and inventories and add increases of payables and deferred taxes.

Net income	$37,500
Gain from sale of land	(10,000)
Depreciation	7,000
Subtotal	$34,500
Changes in operating accounts	
Increase in receivables	($1,000)
Decrease in inventories	2,000
Increase in accounts payable	4,000
Decrease in wages payable	(3,500)
Increase in interest payable	500
Increase in taxes payable	1,000
Increase in deferred taxes	5,000
Cash flow from operations	$42,500

Investing cash flow:

In this example, we have two components of investing cash flow: the sale of land and the change in gross plant and equipment (P&E).

cash from sale of land = decrease in asset + gain on sale = $5,000 + $10,000 = $15,000 (source)

> beginning land + land purchased – gross cost of land sold = ending land = $40,000 + $0 – $5,000 = $35,000

Note: If the land had been sold at a loss, we would have subtracted the loss amount from the decrease in land.

P&E purchased = ending gross P&E + gross cost of P&E sold – beginning gross P&E
= $85,000 + $0 – $60,000 = $25,000 (use)

> beginning gross P&E + P&E purchased – gross cost of P&E sold = ending P&E = $60,000 + $25,000 – $0 = $85,000

Cash from sale of land	$15,000
Purchase of plant and equipment	(25,000)
Cash flow from investments	($10,000)

Financing cash flow:

cash from bond issue = ending bonds payable + bonds repaid – beginning bonds payable = $15,000 + $0 – $10,000 = $5,000 (source)

> beginning bonds payable + bonds issued – bonds repaid = ending bonds payable = $10,000 + $5,000 – $0 = $15,000

cash to reacquire stock = beginning common stock + stock issued – ending common stock = $50,000 + $0 – $40,000 = $10,000 (use, or a net share repurchase of $10,000)

> beginning common stock + stock issued – stock reacquired = ending common stock = $50,000 + $0 – $10,000 = $40,000

cash dividends = – dividend declared + increase in dividends payable
= –$8,500* + $5,000 = –$3,500 (use)

> beginning dividends payable + dividends declared – dividends paid = ending dividends payable = $1,000 + $8,500 – $3,500 = $6,000

Note: If the dividend declared amount is not provided, you can calculate the amount as follows: dividends declared = beginning retained earnings + net income – ending retained earnings. Here, $30,000 + $37,500 – $59,000 = $8,500.

Sale of bonds	$5,000
Repurchase of stock	(10,000)
Cash dividends	(3,500)
Cash flow from financing	($8,500)

Total cash flow:

Cash flow from operations	$42,500
Cash flow from investments	(10,000)
Cash flow from financing	(8,500)
Total cash flow	$24,000

The total cash flow of $24,000 is equal to the increase in the cash account. The difference between beginning cash and ending cash should be used as a check figure to ensure that the total cash flow calculation is correct.

Both IFRS and U.S. GAAP encourage the use of a statement of cash flows in the direct format. Under U.S. GAAP, a statement of cash flows under the direct method must include footnote disclosure of the indirect method. Most companies however, report cash flows using the indirect method, which requires no additional disclosure. The next LOS illustrates the method an analyst will use to create a statement of cash flows in the direct method format when the company reports using the indirect method.

LOS 34.g: Describe the process of converting a statement of cash flows from the indirect to the direct method of presentation.

The only difference between the indirect and direct methods of presentation is in the cash flow from operations (CFO) section. CFO under the direct method can be computed using a combination of the income statement and a statement of cash flows prepared under the indirect method.

There are two major sections in CFO under the direct method: cash inflows (receipts) and cash outflows (payments). We will illustrate the conversion process using some frequently used accounts. Please note that the list below is for illustrative purposes only and is far from all-inclusive of what may be encountered in practice. The general principle here is to adjust each income statement item for its corresponding balance sheet accounts and to eliminate noncash and nonoperating transactions.

Cash collections from customers:

1. Begin with net sales from the income statement.

2. Subtract (add) any increase (decrease) in the accounts receivable balance as reported in the indirect method. If the company has sold more on credit than has been collected from customers, accounts receivable will increase and cash collections will be less than net sales.

3. Add (subtract) an increase (decrease) in unearned revenue. Unearned revenue includes cash advances from customers. Cash received from customers when the goods or services have yet to be delivered is not included in net sales, so the advances must be added to net sales in order to calculate cash collections.

Cash payments to suppliers:

1. Begin with cost of goods sold (COGS) as reported in the income statement.

2. If depreciation and/or amortization have been included in COGS (they increase COGS), these items must be added back to COGS when computing the cash paid to suppliers.

3. Reduce (increase) COGS by any increase (decrease) in the accounts payable balance as reported in the indirect method. If payables have increased, then more was spent on credit purchases during the period than was paid on existing payables, so cash payments are reduced by the amount of the increase in payables.

4. Add (subtract) any increase (decrease) in the inventory balance as disclosed in the indirect method. Increases in inventory are not included in COGS for the period but still represent the purchase of inputs, so they increase cash paid to suppliers.

5. Subtract an inventory write-off that occurred during the period. An inventory write-off, as a result of applying the lower of cost or market rule, will reduce ending inventory and increase COGS for the period. However, no cash flow is associated with the write-off.

Other items in a direct method cash flow statement follow the same principles. Cash taxes paid, for example, can be derived by starting with income tax expense on the income statement. Adjustment must be made for changes in related balance sheet accounts (deferred tax assets and liabilities, and income taxes payable).

Cash operating expense is equal to selling, general, and administrative expense (SG&A) from the income statement, increased (decreased) for any increase (decrease) in prepaid expenses. Any increase in prepaid expenses is a cash outflow that is not included in SG&A for the current period.

Example: Direct method for computing CFO

Prepare a cash flow statement using the direct method using the indirect statement of cash flows, balance sheet and income statement from the previous example.

Answer:

Professor's Note: There are many ways to think about these calculations and lots of sources and uses and pluses and minuses to keep track of. It's easier if you use a "+" sign for net sales and a "−" sign for cost of goods sold and other cash expenses used as the starting points. Doing so will allow you to consistently follow the rule that an increase in assets or decrease in liabilities is a use of cash and a decrease in assets or an increase in liabilities is a source. We'll use this approach in the answer to the example. Remember, sources are always + and uses are always −.

The calculations that follow include a reconciliation of each account, analyzing the transactions that increase and decrease the account for the period. As previously discussed, this reconciliation is useful in understanding the interrelationships between the balance sheet, income statement, and cash flow statement.

Cash from operations:

Keep track of the balance sheet items used to calculate CFO by marking them off the balance sheet. They will not be needed again when determining CFI and CFF.

cash collections = sales − increase in accounts receivable = $100,000 − $1,000 = $99,000

> beginning receivables + sales − cash collections = ending receivables = $9,000 + $100,000 − $99,000 = $10,000

cash paid to suppliers = − COGS + decrease in inventory + increase in accounts payable = −$40,000 + $2,000 + $4,000 = −$34,000

> beginning inventory + purchases − COGS = ending inventory = $7,000 + $38,000 (not provided) − $40,000 = $5,000

> beginning accounts payable + purchases − cash paid to suppliers = ending accounts payable = $5,000 + $38,000 (not provided) − $34,000 = $9,000

cash wages = − wages − decrease in wages payable = −$5,000 − $3,500 = −$8,500

> beginning wages payable + wages expense − wages paid = ending wages payable = $8,000 + $5,000 − $8,500 = $4,500

cash interest = − interest expense + increase in interest payable = −$500 + $500 = 0

> beginning interest payable + interest expense − interest paid = ending interest payable = $3,000 + $500 − $0 = $3,500

cash taxes = –tax expense + increase in taxes payable + increase in deferred tax liability

= –$20,000 + $1,000 + $5,000 = –$14,000

beginning taxes payable + beginning deferred tax liability + tax expense – taxes paid = ending taxes payable + ending deferred tax liability = $4,000 + $15,000 + $20,000 – $14,000 = $5,000 + $20,000

Cash collections	$99,000
Cash to suppliers	(34,000)
Cash wages	(8,500)
Cash interest	0
Cash taxes	(14,000)
Cash flow from operations	$42,500

LOS 34.h: Analyze and interpret a cash flow statement using both total currency amounts and common-size cash flow statements.

Major Sources and Uses of Cash

Cash flow analysis begins with an evaluation of the firm's sources and uses of cash from operating, investing, and financing activities. Sources and uses of cash change as the firm moves through its life cycle. For example, when a firm is in the early stages of growth, it may experience negative operating cash flow as it uses cash to finance increases in inventory and receivables. This negative operating cash flow is usually financed externally by issuing debt or equity securities. These sources of financing are not sustainable. Eventually, the firm must begin generating positive operating cash flow or the sources of external capital may no longer be available. Over the long term, successful firms must be able to generate operating cash flows that exceed capital expenditures and provide a return to debt and equity holders.

Operating Cash Flow

An analyst should identify the major determinants of operating cash flow. Positive operating cash flow can be generated by the firm's earning-related activities. However, positive operating cash flow can also be generated by decreasing noncash working capital, such as liquidating inventory and receivables or increasing payables. Decreasing noncash working capital is not sustainable, since inventories and receivables cannot fall below zero and creditors will not extend credit indefinitely unless payments are made when due.

Operating cash flow also provides a check of the quality of a firm's earnings. A stable relationship of operating cash flow and net income is an indication of quality earnings. (This relationship can also be affected by the business cycle and the firm's life cycle.) Earnings that significantly exceed operating cash flow may be an indication of aggressive (or even improper) accounting choices such as recognizing revenues too soon or delaying the recognition of expenses. The variability of net income and operating cash flow should also be considered.

Investing Cash Flow

The sources and uses of cash from investing activities should be examined. Increasing capital expenditures, a use of cash, is usually an indication of growth. Conversely, a firm may reduce capital expenditures or even sell capital assets in order to save or generate cash. This may result in higher cash outflows in the future as older assets are replaced or growth resumes. As mentioned above, generating operating cash flow that exceeds capital expenditures is a desirable trait.

Financing Cash Flow

The financing activities section of the cash flow statement reveals information about whether the firm is generating cash flow by issuing debt or equity. It also provides information about whether the firm is using cash to repay debt, reacquire stock, or pay dividends. For example, an analyst would certainly want to know if a firm issued debt and used the proceeds to reacquire stock or pay dividends to shareholders.

Common-Size Cash Flow Statement

Like the income statement and balance sheet, common-size analysis can be used to analyze the cash flow statement.

The cash flow statement can be converted to common-size format by expressing each line item as a percentage of revenue. Alternatively, each inflow of cash can be expressed as a percentage of total cash inflows, and each outflow of cash can be expressed as a percentage of total cash outflows.

Example: Common-size cash flow statement analysis

Triple Y Corporation's common-size cash flow statement is shown in the table below. Explain the decrease in Triple Y's total cash flow as a percentage of revenues.

Triple Y Corporation

Cash Flow Statement (Percent of Revenues)

Year	20X9	20X8	20X7
Net income	13.4%	13.4%	13.5%
Depreciation	4.0%	3.9%	3.9%
Accounts receivable	−0.6%	−0.6%	−0.5%
Inventory	−10.3%	−9.2%	−8.8%
Prepaid expenses	0.2%	−0.2%	0.1%
Accrued liabilities	5.5%	5.5%	5.6%
Operating cash flow	12.2%	12.8%	13.8%
Cash from sale of fixed assets	0.7%	0.7%	0.7%
Purchase of plant and equipment	−12.3%	−12.0%	−11.7%
Investing cash flow	−11.6%	−11.3%	−11.0%
Sale of bonds	2.6%	2.5%	2.6%
Cash dividends	−2.1%	−2.1%	−2.1%
Financing cash flow	0.5%	0.4%	0.5%
Total cash flow	1.1%	1.9%	3.3%

Answer:

Operating cash flow has decreased as a percentage of revenues. This appears to be due largely to accumulating inventories. Investing activities, specifically purchases of plant and equipment, have also required an increasing percentage of the firm's cash flow.

LOS 34.i: Explain and calculate free cash flow to the firm, free cash flow to equity, and other cash flow ratios.

Free cash flow is a measure of cash that is available for discretionary purposes. This is the cash flow that is available once the firm has covered its capital expenditures. This is a fundamental cash flow measure and is often used for valuation. There are measures of free cash flow. Two of the more common measures are free cash flow to the firm and free cash flow to equity.

Free Cash Flow to the Firm

Free cash flow to the firm (FCFF) is the cash available to all investors, both equity owners and debt holders. FCFF can be calculated by starting with either net income or operating cash flow.

FCFF is calculated from net income as:

$$FCFF = NI + NCC + [Int \times (1 - tax\ rate)] - FCInv - WCInv$$

where:
NI = net income
NCC = noncash charges (depreciation and amortization)
Int = interest expense
FCInv = fixed capital investment (net capital expenditures)
WCInv = working capital investment

Note that interest expense, net of tax, is added back to net income. This is because FCFF is the cash flow available to stockholders and debt holders. Since interest is paid to (and therefore "available to") the debt holders, it must be included in FCFF.

FCFF can also be calculated from operating cash flow as:

$$FCFF = CFO + [Int \times (1 - tax\ rate)] - FCInv$$

where:
CFO = cash flow from operations
Int = interest expense
FCInv = fixed capital investment (net capital expenditures)

It is not necessary to adjust for noncash charges and changes in working capital when starting with CFO, since they are already reflected in the calculation of CFO. For firms that follow IFRS, it is not necessary to adjust for interest expense that is included as a part of financing activities. Additionally, firms that follow IFRS can report dividends paid as operating activities. In this case, the dividends paid would be added back to CFO. Again, the goal is to calculate the cash flow that is available to the shareholders and debt holders. It is not necessary to adjust dividends for taxes since dividends paid are not tax deductible.

Free Cash Flow to Equity

Free cash flow to equity (FCFE) is the cash flow that would be available for distribution to common shareholders. FCFE can be calculated as follows:

$$FCFE = CFO - FCInv + \text{Net borrowing}$$

where:
CFO   = cash flow from operations
FCInv   = fixed capital investment (net capital expenditures)
Net borrowing = debt issued – debt repaid

If firms that follow IFRS have subtracted dividends paid in calculating CFO, dividends must be added back when calculating FCFE.

Other Cash Flow Ratios

Just as with the income statement and balance sheet, the cash flow statement can be analyzed by comparing the cash flows either over time or to those of other firms. Cash flow ratios can be categorized as performance ratios and coverage ratios.

Performance Ratios

The **cash flow-to-revenue ratio** measures the amount of operating cash flow generated for each dollar of revenue.

$$\text{Cash flow-to-revenue} = \frac{CFO}{\text{net revenue}}$$

The **cash return-on-assets ratio** measures the return of operating cash flow attributed to all providers of capital.

$$\text{Cash return-on-assets} = \frac{CFO}{\text{average total assets}}$$

The **cash return-on-equity ratio** measures the return of operating cash flow attributed to shareholders.

$$\text{Cash return-on-equity} = \frac{CFO}{\text{average total equity}}$$

The **cash-to-income ratio** measures the ability to generate cash from firm operations.

$$\text{Cash-to-income} = \frac{CFO}{\text{operating income}}$$

Cash flow per share is a variation of basic earnings per share measured by using CFO instead of net income.

$$\text{Cash flow per share} = \frac{\text{CFO} - \text{preferred dividends}}{\text{weighted average number of common shares}}$$

Coverage Ratios

The **debt coverage ratio** measures financial risk and leverage.

$$\text{Debt coverage} = \frac{\text{CFO}}{\text{total debt}}$$

The **interest coverage ratio** measures the firm's ability to meet its interest obligations.

$$\text{Interest coverage} = \frac{\text{CFO} + \text{interest paid} + \text{taxes paid}}{\text{interest paid}}$$

The **reinvestment ratio** measures the firm's ability to acquire long-term assets with operating cash flow.

$$\text{Reinvestment} = \frac{\text{CFO}}{\text{cash paid for long-term assets}}$$

The **debt payment ratio** measures the firm's ability to satisfy long-term debt with operating cash flow.

$$\text{Debt payment} = \frac{\text{CFO}}{\text{cash long-term debt repayment}}$$

The **dividend payment ratio** measures the firm's ability to make dividend payments from operating cash flow.

$$\text{Dividend payment} = \frac{\text{CFO}}{\text{dividends paid}}$$

The **investing and financing ratio** measures the firm's ability to purchase assets, satisfy debts, and pay dividends.

$$\text{Investing and financing} = \frac{\text{CFO}}{\text{cash outflows from investing and financing activities}}$$

KEY CONCEPTS

LOS 34.a

Cash flow from operating activities (CFO) consists of the inflows and outflows of cash resulting from transactions that affect a firm's net income.

Cash flow from investing activities (CFI) consists of the inflows and outflows of cash resulting from the acquisition or disposal of long-term assets and certain investments.

Cash flow from financing activities (CFF) consists of the inflows and outflows of cash resulting from transactions affecting a firm's capital structure, such as issuing or repaying debt and issuing or repurchasing stock.

LOS 34.b

Noncash investing and financing activities, such as taking on debt to the seller of a purchased asset, are not reported in the cash flow statement but must be disclosed in the footnotes or a supplemental schedule.

LOS 34.c

Under U.S. GAAP, dividends paid are financing activities. Interest paid, interest received, and dividends received are operating activities.

Under IFRS, dividends paid and interest paid can be reported as either operating activities or financing activities. Interest received and dividends received can be reported as either operating activities or investing activities.

LOS 34.d

Under the direct method of presenting CFO, each line item of the accrual-based income statement is adjusted to get cash receipts or cash payments.

Under the indirect method of presenting CFO, net income is adjusted for transactions that affect net income but do not affect operating cash flow, such as depreciation and gains or losses on asset sales.

LOS 34.e

The cash flow statement reconciles the beginning and ending values of cash on the balance sheet.

Differences between transactions reported on an accrual basis (on the income statement) and their effect on cash flows (reported on the statement of cash flows) result in increases or decreases in balance sheet items.

LOS 34.f

The direct method of calculating CFO is to sum cash inflows and cash outflows for operating activities.
- Cash collections from customers—sales adjusted for changes in receivables and unearned revenue.

- Cash paid for inputs—COGS adjusted for changes in inventory and accounts payable.
- Cash operating expenses—SG&A adjusted for changes in related accrued liabilities or prepaid expenses.
- Cash interest paid—interest expense adjusted for the change in interest payable.
- Cash taxes paid—income tax expense adjusted for changes in taxes payable and changes in deferred tax assets and liabilities.

The indirect method of calculating CFO begins with net income and adjusts it for gains or losses related to investing or financing cash flows, noncash charges to income, and changes in balance sheet operating items.

CFI is calculated by determining the changes in asset accounts that result from investing activities. The cash flow from selling an asset is its book value plus any gain on the sale (or minus any loss on the sale).

CFF is the sum of net cash flows from creditors (new borrowings minus principal repaid) and net cash flows from shareholders (new equity issued minus share repurchases minus cash dividends paid).

LOS 34.g
An indirect cash flow statement can be converted to a direct cash flow statement by adjusting each income statement account for changes in associated balance sheet accounts and by eliminating noncash and non-operating items.

LOS 34.h
An analyst should determine whether a company is generating positive operating cash flow over time that is greater than its capital spending needs and whether the company's accounting policies are causing reported earnings to diverge from operating cash flow.

A common-size cash flow statement shows each item as a percentage of revenue or shows each cash inflow as a percentage of total inflows and each outflow as a percentage of total outflows.

LOS 34.i
Free cash flow to the firm (FCFF) is the cash available to all investors, both equity owners and debt holders.
- FCFF = net income + noncash charges + [interest expense × (1 – tax rate)] – fixed capital investment – working capital investment.
- FCFF = CFO + [interest expense × (1 – tax rate)] – fixed capital investment.

Free cash flow to equity (FCFE) is the cash flow that is available for distribution to the common shareholders after all obligations have been paid.

FCFE = CFO – fixed capital investment + net borrowing.

Cash flow performance ratios, such as cash return on equity or on assets, and cash coverage ratios, such as debt coverage or cash interest coverage, provide information about the firm's operating performance and financial strength.

CONCEPT CHECKERS

1.   Using the following information, what is the firm's cash flow from operations?

Net income	$120
Decrease in accounts receivable	20
Depreciation	25
Increase in inventory	10
Increase in accounts payable	7
Decrease in wages payable	5
Increase in deferred tax liabilities	15
Profit from the sale of land	2

  A. $158.
  B. $170.
  C. $174.

Use the following data to answer Questions 2 through 4.

Net income	$45
Depreciation	75
Taxes paid	25
Interest paid	5
Dividends paid	10
Cash received from sale of company building	40
Sale of preferred stock	35
Repurchase of common stock	30
Purchase of machinery	20
Issuance of bonds	50
Debt retired through issuance of common stock	45
Paid off long-term bank borrowings	15
Profit on sale of building	20

2.   The cash flow from *operations* is:
  A. $70.
  B. $100.
  C. $120.

3. The cash flow from *investing activities* is:
    A. –$30.
    B. $20.
    C. 50.

4. The cash flow from *financing activities* is:
    A. $30.
    B. $55.
    C. $75.

5. Given the following:

Sales	$1,500
Increase in inventory	100
Depreciation	150
Increase in accounts receivable	50
Decrease in accounts payable	70
After-tax profit margin	25%
Gain on sale of machinery	$30

    The cash flow from *operations* is:
    A. $115.
    B. $275.
    C. $375.

6. Which of the following items is *least likely* considered a cash flow from financing activity under U.S. GAAP?
    A. Receipt of cash from the sale of bonds.
    B. Payment of cash for dividends.
    C. Payment of interest on debt.

7. Which of the following would be *least likely* to cause a change in investing cash flow?
    A. The sale of a division of the company.
    B. The purchase of new machinery.
    C. An increase in depreciation expense.

8. Which of the following is *least likely* a change in cash flow from operations under U.S. GAAP?
    A. A decrease in notes payable.
    B. An increase in interest expense.
    C. An increase in accounts payable.

9. Where are dividends paid to shareholders reported in the cash flow statement under U.S. GAAP and IFRS?

    <u>U.S. GAAP</u>   <u>IFRS</u>
    A. Operating or financing activities   Operating or financing activities
    B. Financing activities   Operating or financing activities
    C. Operating activities   Financing activities

10. Sales of inventory would be classified as:
    A. operating cash flow.
    B. investing cash flow.
    C. financing cash flow.

11. Issuing bonds would be classified as:
    A. investing cash flow.
    B. financing cash flow.
    C. no cash flow impact.

12. Sale of land would be classified as:
    A. operating cash flow.
    B. investing cash flow.
    C. financing cash flow.

13. An increase in taxes payable would be classified as:
    A. operating cash flow.
    B. financing cash flow.
    C. no cash flow impact.

14. An increase in notes payable would be classified as:
    A. investing cash flow.
    B. financing cash flow.
    C. no cash flow impact.

15. Under U.S. GAAP, an increase in interest payable would be classified as:
    A. operating cash flow.
    B. financing cash flow.
    C. no cash flow impact.

16. Under U.S. GAAP, an increase in dividends payable would be classified as:
    A. operating cash flow.
    B. investing cash flow.
    C. financing cash flow.

17. The write-off of obsolete equipment would be classified as:
    A. operating cash flow.
    B. investing cash flow.
    C. no cash flow impact.

18. Sale of obsolete equipment would be classified as:
    A. operating cash flow.
    B. investing cash flow.
    C. financing cash flow.

19.   Under IFRS, interest expense would be classified as:
       A. either operating cash flow or financing cash flow.
       B. operating cash flow only.
       C. financing cash flow only.

20.   Depreciation expense would be classified as:
       A. operating cash flow.
       B. investing cash flow.
       C. no cash flow impact.

21.   Under U.S. GAAP, dividends received from investments would be classified as:
       A. operating cash flow.
       B. investing cash flow.
       C. financing cash flow.

22.   Torval Inc. retires debt securities by issuing equity securities. This is considered
       a:
       A. cash flow from investing.
       B. cash flow from financing.
       C. noncash transaction.

23.   Net income for Monique Inc. for the year ended December 31, 20X7 was
       $78,000. Its accounts receivable balance at December 31, 20X7 was $121,000,
       and this balance was $69,000 at December 31, 20X6. The accounts payable
       balance at December 31, 20X7 was $72,000 and was $43,000 at December
       31, 20X6. Depreciation for 20X7 was $12,000, and there was an unrealized
       gain of $15,000 included in 20X7 income from the change in value of trading
       securities. Which of the following amounts represents Monique's cash flow from
       operations for 20X7?
       A. $52,000.
       B. $67,000.
       C. $82,000.

24.   Martin Inc. had the following transactions during 20X7:
       • Purchased new fixed assets for $75,000.
       • Converted $70,000 worth of preferred shares to common shares.
       • Received cash dividends of $12,000. Paid cash dividends of $21,000.
       • Repaid mortgage principal of $17,000.

       Assuming Martin follows U.S. GAAP, which of the following amounts represents
       Martin's cash flows from investing and cash flows from financing in 20X7,
       respectively?

	Cash flows from investing	Cash flows from financing
A.	($5,000)	($21,000)
B.	($75,000)	($21,000)
C.	($75,000)	($38,000)

25. In preparing a common-size cash flow statement, each cash flow is expressed as a percentage of:
    A. total assets.
    B. total revenues.
    C. the change in cash.

COMPREHENSIVE PROBLEMS

Use the following data to answer Questions A through F.

Balance Sheet Data

Assets	20X7	20X6
Cash	$290	$100
Accounts receivable	250	200
Inventory	740	800
Property, plant, & equipment	920	900
Accumulated depreciation	(290)	(250)
Total Assets	$1,910	$1,750
Liabilities and Equity		
Accounts payable	$470	$450
Interest payable	15	10
Dividends payable	10	5
Mortgage	535	585
Bank note	100	0
Common stock	430	400
Retained earnings	350	300
Total Liabilities and Equity	$1,910	$1,750

Income Statement for the Year 20X7	20X7
Sales	$1,425
Cost of goods sold	1,200
Depreciation	100
Interest Expense	30
Gain on sale of old machine	10
Taxes	45
Net income	$60

Notes:

- Dividends declared to shareholders were $10.
- New common shares were sold at par for $30.
- Fixed assets were sold for $30. Original cost of these assets was $80, and $60 of accumulated depreciation has been charged to their original cost.
- The firm borrowed $100 on a 10-year bank note—the proceeds of the loan were used to pay for new fixed assets.
- Depreciation for the year was $100 (accumulated depreciation up $40 and depreciation on sold assets $60).

A.   Calculate cash flow from operations, using the *indirect* method.

B.   Calculate total cash collections, cash paid to suppliers, and other cash expenses.

C.   Calculate cash flow from operations using the *direct* method.

D.   Calculate cash flow from financing, cash flow from investing, and total cash flow.

E.   Calculate free cash flow to equity owners.

F.   What would the impact on investing cash flow and financing cash flow have been if the company leased the new fixed assets instead of borrowing the money and purchasing the equipment?

ANSWERS – CONCEPT CHECKERS

1. **B** Net income – profits from sale of land + depreciation + decrease in receivables – increase in inventories + increase in accounts payable – decrease in wages payable + increase in deferred tax liabilities = 120 – 2 + 25 + 20 – 10 + 7 – 5 + 15 = $170. Note that the profit on the sale of land should be subtracted from net income to avoid double counting the gain in net income and investing activities.

2. **B** Net income – profit on sale of building + depreciation = 45 – 20 + 75 = $100. Note that taxes and interest are already deducted in calculating net income, and that the profit on the sale of the building should be subtracted from net income.

3. **B** Cash from sale of building – purchase of machinery = 40 – 20 = $20.

4. **A** Sale of preferred stock + issuance of bonds – principal payments on bank borrowings – repurchase of common stock – dividends paid = 35 + 50 – 15 – 30 – 10 = $30. Note that we did not include $45 of debt retired through issuance of common stock since this was a noncash transaction. Knowing how to handle noncash transactions is important.

5. **B** Net income = $1,500 × 0.25 = $375, and cash flow from operations = net income – gain on sale of machinery + depreciation – increase in accounts receivable – increase in inventory – decrease in accounts payable = 375 – 30 + 150 – 50 – 100 – 70 = $275.

6. **C** The payment of interest on debt is an *operating* cash flow under U.S. GAAP.

7. **C** Depreciation does not represent a cash flow. To the extent that it affects the firm's taxes, an increase in depreciation changes operating cash flows, but not investing cash flows.

8. **A** A change in notes payable is a financing cash flow.

9. **B** Under U.S. GAAP, dividends paid are reported as financing activities. Under IFRS, dividends paid can be reported as either operating or financing activities.

10. **A** Sales of inventory would be classified as operating cash flow.

11. **B** Issuing bonds would be classified as financing cash flow.

12. **B** Sale of land would be classified as investing cash flow.

13. **A** Increase in taxes payable would be classified as operating cash flow.

14. **B** Increase in notes payable would be classified as financing cash flow.

15. **A** Increase in interest payable would be classified as operating cash flow under U.S. GAAP.

16. **C** Increase in dividends payable would be classified as financing cash flow under U.S. GAAP.

17. **C** Write-off of obsolete equipment has no cash flow impact.

18. **B** Sale of obsolete equipment would be classified as investing cash flow.

19. **A** Under IFRS, interest expense can be classified as either an operating cash flow or financing cash flow.

20. **C**   Depreciation expense would be classified as no cash flow impact.

21. **A**   Dividends received from investments would be classified as operating cash flow under U.S. GAAP.

22. **C**   The exchange of debt securities for equity securities is a noncash transaction.

23. **A**

Net income	$78,000
Depreciation	12,000
Unrealized gain	(15,000)
Increase in accounts receivable	(52,000)
Increase in accounts payable	29,000
Cash flow from operations	$52,000

24. **C**   Purchased new fixed assets for $75,000 – cash <u>outflow</u> from investing
Converted $70,000 of preferred shares to common shares – noncash transaction
Received dividends of $12,000 – cash <u>inflow</u> from operations
Paid dividends of $21,000 – cash <u>outflow</u> from financing
Mortgage repayment of $17,000 – cash <u>outflow</u> from financing
CFI = –75,000
CFF = –21,000 – 17,000 = –$38,000

25. **B**   The cash flow statement can be converted to common-size format by expressing each line item as a percentage of revenue.

ANSWERS – COMPREHENSIVE PROBLEMS

A.   Net income – gain on sale of machinery + depreciation – increase in receivables + decrease in inventories + increase in accounts payable + increase in interest payable = 60 – 10 + 100 – 50 + 60 + 20 + 5 = $185.

B.   Cash collections = sales – increase in receivables = 1,425 – 50 = $1,375.

Cash paid to suppliers = –cost of goods sold + decrease in inventory + increase in accounts payable = –1,200 + 60 + 20 = –$1,120. (Note that the question asks for cash paid to suppliers, so no negative sign is needed in the answer.)

Other cash expenses = –interest expense + increase in interest payable – tax expense = –30 + 5 – 45 = –$70. (Note that the question asks for cash expenses so no negative sign is needed in the answer.)

C.   CFO cash collections – cash to suppliers – other cash expenses = 1,375 – 1,120 – 70 = $185. This must match the answer to Question A, because CFO using the direct method will be the same as CFO under the indirect method.

D.   CFF = sale of stock + new bank note – payment of mortgage – dividends + increase in dividends payable = 30 + 100 – 50 – 10 + 5 = $75.

CFI = sale of fixed assets – new fixed assets = 30 – 100 = –$70. Don't make this difficult. We sold assets for 30 and bought assets for 100. Assets sold had an original cost of 80, so (gross) PP&E only went up by 20.

The easiest way to determine total cash flow is to simply take the change in cash from the balance sheet. However, adding the three components of cash flow will yield $185 - 70 + 75 = \$190$.

E.   FCFE = cash flow from operations – capital spending + sale of fixed assets + debt issued – debt repaid = $\$185 - 100 + 30 + 100 - 50 = \$165$. No adjustment is necessary for interest since FCFE includes debt service.

F.   Investing cash flow would be higher and financing cash flow would be lower. The company would spend less on investments but would not have inflows from the borrowing.

The following is a review of the Financial Reporting and Analysis principles designed to address the learning outcome statements set forth by CFA Institute®. This topic is also covered in:

INVENTORIES

EXAM FOCUS

This topic review discusses specific analytical processes for inventory. The complication in analyzing inventory is that firms can choose among different cost flow methods—FIFO, LIFO, and weighted average cost. You should know how to calculate inventory balances and COGS using all three methods and how to convert LIFO inventory and LIFO COGS to a FIFO basis for comparison. You must understand how the different cost flow methods affect the firm's liquidity, profitability, activity and solvency ratios.

INVENTORY ACCOUNTING

Merchandising firms, such as wholesalers and retailers, purchase inventory that is ready for sale. In this case, inventory is reported in one account on the balance sheet. On the other hand, manufacturing firms normally report inventory using three separate accounts: raw materials, work-in-process, and finished goods.

The choice of **inventory cost flow method** affects the firm's income statement, balance sheet, and several important financial ratios. Additionally, the cost flow method can affect the firm's income taxes and, thus, the firm's cash flow.

The inventory cost flow method should not be confused with the **inventory valuation method** as required by IFRS and U.S. GAAP. Generally, inventory is reported on the balance sheet at cost and a writedown (loss) is recognized if the market value of inventory declines below cost. The valuation method (lower of cost or net realizable value for firms reporting under IFRS, and lower of cost or market for firms reporting under U.S. GAAP) is applied regardless of the cost flow method.

Cost of goods sold is related to the beginning balance of inventory, purchases, and the ending balance of inventory. The relationship is summarized in the following equation:

COGS = beginning inventory + purchases − ending inventory

This equation can be rearranged to solve for any of the four variables:

Purchases = ending inventory − beginning inventory + COGS

Beginning inventory = COGS − purchases + ending inventory

Ending inventory = beginning inventory + purchases − COGS

Professor's Note: Many candidates find the inventory equation easiest to remember in this last form. If you start with beginning inventory, add the goods that came in (purchases), and subtract the goods that went out (COGS), the result must be ending inventory.

LOS 35.a: Explain IFRS and U.S. GAAP rules for determining inventory cost including which costs are capitalized and methods of allocating costs between cost of goods sold and inventory.

Cost is the basis for most inventory valuation. The main issue involves determining the amounts that should be included in cost.

The costs included in inventory are similar under IFRS and U.S. GAAP. These costs, known as "product costs," are capitalized in the "Inventories" account on the balance sheet and include:

- Purchase cost.
- Conversion costs.
- Allocation of fixed production overhead based on normal capacity levels.
- Other costs necessary to bring the inventory to its present location and condition.

By capitalizing inventory cost as an asset, expense recognition is delayed until the inventory is sold.

Not all inventory costs are capitalized; some are expensed in the period incurred. These costs, known as **period costs**, include:

- Unallocated portion of fixed production overhead.
- Abnormal waste of materials, labor, or overhead.
- Storage costs (unless required as part of the production process).
- Administrative overhead.
- Selling costs.

Example: Costs included in inventory

Vindaloo Company manufactures a single product. The following information has been taken from the company's production and cost records for last year:

Normal production capacity	5,000,000 units
Units produced	4,000,000 units
Conversion cost for finished goods	$20,000,000
Raw materials	$15,000,000
Fixed overhead	$6,000,000
Freight-in	$800,000
Storage cost for finished goods	$500,000
Abnormal waste	$100,000

Assuming no units remain unfinished at year-end, calculate the capitalized cost of one unit.

Answer:

Capitalized inventory cost includes the conversion cost, raw materials cost, freight-in, and the allocated fixed overhead. The allocation of fixed overhead is based on the units produced relative to normal production capacity. Since Vindaloo operated at 80% of normal production capacity last year (4,000,000 units produced / 5,000,000 units normal capacity), 80% of the fixed overhead is capitalized. The remaining 20% of fixed overhead is expensed.

Conversion cost for finished goods	$20,000,000	
Raw materials	$15,000,000	
Allocated fixed overhead	$4,800,000	($6,000,000 fixed overhead × 80%)
Freight-in	$800,000	
Total capitalized cost	$40,600,000	
Units produced	4,000,000	
Capitalized cost per unit	$10.15	($40,600,000 / 4,000,000 units produced)

Storage costs, abnormal waste, and the remaining unallocated fixed overhead are expensed in the period incurred.

LOS 35.b: Discuss how inventories are reported in the financial statements and how the lower of cost or net realizable value is used and applied.

Under IFRS, inventory is reported on the balance sheet at the lower of cost or **net realizable value**. Net realizable value is equal to the estimated sales price less the estimated selling costs. If net realizable value is less than the balance sheet cost, the inventory is "written down" to net realizable value and a loss is recognized in the income statement. If there is a subsequent recovery in value, the inventory can be "written up" and a gain is recognized in the income statement. However, the amount of any such gain is limited to the amount previously recognized as a loss. In other words, inventory cannot be reported on the balance sheet at an amount that exceeds original cost.

Under U.S. GAAP, inventories are reported on the balance sheet at the lower of cost or market. Market is usually equal to replacement cost; however, market cannot be greater than net realizable value (NRV) or less than NRV minus a normal profit margin. If replacement cost exceeds NRV, then market is NRV. If replacement cost is less than NRV minus a normal profit margin, then market is NRV minus a normal profit margin.

> *Professor's Note: Think of lower of cost or market, where "market" cannot be outside a range of values. The range is from net realizable value minus a normal profit margin to net realizable value. So the size of the range is the normal profit margin. "Net" means net of selling costs.*

If cost exceeds market, the inventory is written down to market on the balance sheet and a loss is recognized in the income statement. If there is a subsequent recovery in value, no write-up is allowed under U.S. GAAP. In this case, the market value becomes the new cost basis.

no writeups allowed under GAAP

Example: Inventory writedown

Zoom Incorporated sells digital cameras. Per-unit cost information pertaining to Zoom's inventory is as follows:

Original cost $210
Estimated selling price $225
Estimated selling costs $22
Net realizable value $203
Replacement cost $197
Normal profit margin $12

What are the per-unit carrying values of Zoom's inventory under IFRS and under U.S. GAAP?

Answer:

Under IFRS, inventory is reported on the balance sheet at the lower of cost or net realizable value. Since original cost of $210 exceeds net realizable value ($225 – $22 = $203), the inventory is written down to the net realizable value of $203 and a $7 loss ($203 net realizable value – $210 original cost) is reported in the income statement.

Under U.S. GAAP, inventory is reported at the lower of cost or market. In this case, market is equal to replacement cost of $197, since net realizable value of $203 is greater than replacement cost, and net realizable value minus a normal profit margin ($203 – $12 = $191) is less than replacement cost. Since original cost exceeds market (replacement cost), the inventory is written down to $197 and a $13 loss ($197 replacement cost – $210 original cost) is reported in the income statement.

Example: Inventory write-up

Assume that in the year after the writedown in the previous example, net realizable value and replacement cost both increase by $10. What is the impact of the recovery under IFRS and under U.S. GAAP?

Answer:

Under IFRS, Zoom will write up inventory to $210 per unit and recognize a $7 gain in its income statement. The write-up (gain) is limited to the original writedown of $7. The carrying value cannot exceed original cost.

Under U.S. GAAP, no write-up is allowed. The per-unit carrying value will remain at $197. Zoom will simply recognize higher profit when the inventory is sold.

Reporting inventory above historical cost is permitted under IFRS and U.S. GAAP in certain industries. This exception applies mainly to producers and dealers of commodity-like products, such as agricultural and forest products, mineral ores, and precious metals. Under this exception, inventory is reported at net realizable value and the unrealized gains and losses from changing market prices are recognized in the income statement. If an active market exists for the commodity, the quoted market price is used to value the inventory. Otherwise, recent market transactions are used.

LOS 35.c: Compute ending inventory balances and cost of goods sold using the FIFO, weighted average cost, and LIFO methods to account for product inventory and explain the relationship among and the usefulness of inventory and cost of goods sold data provided by the FIFO, weighted average cost, and LIFO methods when prices are 1) stable, 2) decreasing, or 3) increasing.

If the cost of inventory remains constant over time, determining the firm's COGS and ending inventory is simple. To compute COGS, simply multiply the number of units sold by the cost per unit. Similarly, to compute ending inventory, multiply the number of units remaining by the cost per unit.

However, it is likely that, over time, the cost of purchasing or producing inventory will change. As a result, firms must select a cost flow method to allocate inventory cost for the period to the income statement (COGS) and the balance sheet (ending inventory).

Under IFRS, the permissible cost flow methods are:

handwritten note in margin: no LIFO under IFRS

- Specific identification.
- First-in, first-out (FIFO).
- Weighted average cost.

The same cost flow methods are also permissible under U.S. GAAP. However, U.S. GAAP also permits the use of the last-in, first-out (LIFO) method. LIFO is *not* allowed under IFRS.

> *Professor's Note: FIFO, LIFO and weighted average cost are sometimes referred to as "cost flow assumptions." Since it may be impractical to specifically identify the actual cost of each unit of inventory, firms make assumptions about how inventory cost flows through the system.*

Within the firm, one or more cost flow methods may be used. However, the firm must employ the same cost flow method for inventories of a similar nature and use.

Specific Identification Method

Under the specific identification method, each unit sold is matched with the unit's actual cost. Specific identification is appropriate when inventory items are not interchangeable. It is commonly used by firms with a small number of costly and easily distinguishable items in inventory, such as jewelry and automobiles. Specific identification is also appropriate for special orders or projects outside a firm's normal course of business.

FIFO Method

Under the FIFO method, the first item purchased (the oldest inventory) is assumed to be the first item sold. The advantage of FIFO is that ending inventory is valued based on the most recent purchases, arguably the best approximation of current replacement cost. FIFO COGS is based on the earliest purchase costs. When prices are rising, COGS will be understated compared to current replacement cost and, as a result, earnings will be overstated.

LIFO Method

Under the LIFO method, the item purchased most recently is assumed to be the first item sold. LIFO produces better matching in the income statement since COGS and sales revenue are both measured using recent prices. When prices are rising, LIFO COGS will be higher than FIFO COGS, and earnings will be lower. Lower earnings translate into lower income taxes, which increase cash flow. Under LIFO, ending inventory on the balance sheet is valued using the earliest costs. Therefore, when prices are rising, LIFO ending inventory is less than replacement value.

As discussed previously, LIFO is permitted under U.S. GAAP but is not allowed under IFRS. The **LIFO conformity rule** of the U.S. tax code requires firms that use LIFO for tax purposes to also use LIFO for financial reporting purposes. This is one area where conformity between financial reporting and tax reporting standards is required.

The income tax advantages of using LIFO explain its popularity among U.S. firms. Because of generally rising prices, using LIFO for tax reporting generates tax savings since LIFO earnings are lower than FIFO earnings. This results in the peculiar situation where *lower reported income is associated with higher cash flow from operations.*

Weighted Average Cost Method

Weighted-average cost is a simple and objective method. The average cost per unit of inventory is computed by dividing the total cost of goods available for sale (beginning inventory + purchases) by the total quantity available for sale. To compute COGS, the average cost per unit is multiplied by the number of units sold. Similarly, to compute ending inventory, the average cost per unit is multiplied by the number of units that remain.

When prices are either increasing or decreasing over time, the weighted average cost method will produce an inventory value between those produced by FIFO and LIFO.

Figure 1: Inventory Cost Flow Method Comparison

Method	Assumption	Cost of goods sold consists of...	Ending inventory consists of...
FIFO (U.S. and IFRS)	The items first purchased are the first to be sold.	first purchased	most recent purchases
LIFO (U.S. only)	The items last purchased are the first to be sold.	last purchased	earliest purchases
Weighted average cost (U.S. and IFRS)	Items sold are a mix of purchases.	average cost of all items	average cost of all items

Let's look at an example of how to calculate COGS and ending inventory using the FIFO, LIFO, and average cost inventory valuation methods.

Example: Inventory Cost Flow Methods

Use the inventory data in the following figure to calculate the cost of goods sold and ending inventory under the FIFO, LIFO, and weighted average cost methods.

Inventory Data

January 1 (beginning inventory)	2 units @ $2 per unit =	$4
January 7 purchase	3 units @ $3 per unit =	$9
January 19 purchase	5 units @ $5 per unit =	$25
Cost of goods available	10 units	$38
Units sold during January	7 units	

Answer:

FIFO cost of goods sold. Value the seven units sold at the unit cost of the first units purchased. Start with the earliest units purchased and work down, as illustrated in the following figure.

FIFO COGS Calculation

From beginning inventory	2 units @ $2 per unit =	$4
From first purchase	3 units @ $3 per unit =	$9
From second purchase	2 units @ $5 per unit =	$10
FIFO cost of goods sold	7 units	$23
Ending inventory	3 units @$5 =	$15

LIFO cost of goods sold. Value the seven units sold at the unit cost of the last units purchased. Start with the most recently purchased units and work up, as illustrated in the following figure.

LIFO COGS Calculation

From second purchase	5 units @ $5 per unit =	$25
From first purchase	2 units @ $3 per unit =	$6
LIFO cost of goods sold	7 units	$31
Ending inventory	2 units @$2 + 1 unit @$3 =	$7

Average cost of goods sold. Value the seven units sold at the average unit cost of goods available.

Weighted Average COGS Calculation

Average unit cost	$38 / 10 =	$3.80 per unit
Weighted average cost of goods sold	7 units @ $3.80 per unit =	$26.60
Ending inventory	3 units @ $3.80 per unit =	$11.40

Summary

Inventory system	COGS	Ending Inventory
FIFO	$23.00	$15.00
LIFO	$31.00	$7.00
Average Cost	$26.60	$11.40

Note that prices and inventory levels were rising over the period and that purchases during the period were the same for all cost flow methods.

During periods of rising prices and stable or increasing inventory quantities, LIFO COGS is higher than FIFO COGS. This is because the last units purchased have a higher cost than the first units purchased. Under LIFO, the more costly last units in are the first units out (to COGS). Of course, higher COGS will result in lower net income.

Using similar logic, we can see that LIFO ending inventory is lower than FIFO ending inventory. Under LIFO, ending inventory is valued using older, lower costs.

During periods of falling prices and stable or increasing inventory quantities, the cost flow effects of using LIFO and FIFO will be reversed; that is, LIFO COGS will be lower and LIFO ending inventory will be higher. This makes sense because the most recent lower-cost purchases are sold first under LIFO, and the units in ending inventory are assumed to be the earliest purchases with higher costs.

Consider the diagram in Figure 2 to help visualize the FIFO-LIFO difference during periods of rising prices and growing inventory levels.

Remember, it's not the older or newer physical inventory units that are reported in the income statement and balance sheet; rather, it is the *costs* that are assigned to the units sold and to the units remaining in inventory.

Figure 2: LIFO and FIFO Diagram—Rising Prices and Growing Inventory Balances

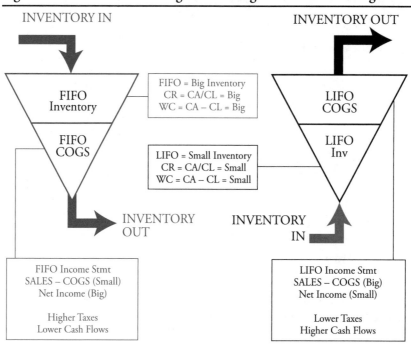

During periods of rising prices, the LIFO assumption results in higher COGS, lower net income, and lower inventory levels. This decreases the current ratio (current assets / current liabilities) and increases inventory turnover (COGS / average inventory).

LIFO
lower CR
higher inv turn

> *Professor's Note: Be able to describe the effects of LIFO and FIFO, assuming inflation, in your sleep. When prices are falling, the effects are simply reversed. When you are finished with this review, take the time to look at these graphs and relationships again to solidify the concepts in your mind.*

Usefulness of Inventory and Cost of Goods Sold Data Provided by the LIFO, FIFO, and Average Cost Methods

> *Professor's Note: The presumption in this section is that inventory quantities are stable or increasing.*

During periods of stable prices, all three cost flow methods will yield the same results for inventory, COGS, and earnings. During periods of trending prices (up or down), the cost flow methods may result in significant differences. It is necessary to adjust for the differences when comparing firms that use different cost flow methods.

Ending Inventory

When prices are trending up or down, FIFO provides the most useful measure of ending inventory. This is a critical point. Recall that FIFO inventory is made up of the most recent purchases. These purchases can be viewed as an approximation of replacement cost, which represents economic value.

On the other hand, LIFO inventory is made up of outdated costs that may have no relationship to today's economic value. For analytical and comparative purposes, it is necessary to adjust LIFO inventory by converting it to a FIFO basis. This adjustment will be demonstrated later in this topic review.

> *Professor's Note: Remember that FIFO is always preferred from a balance sheet perspective since FIFO inventory is based on the most recent costs. LIFO provides better income statement information (COGS).*

The lower costs associated with LIFO inventory are less likely to exceed market value, thereby making inventory writedowns less likely under LIFO.

Cost of Goods Sold

Changing prices can also result in significant differences in COGS under LIFO and FIFO. Recall that LIFO COGS is based on the most recent purchases. As a result, when prices are rising, LIFO COGS will be higher than FIFO COGS. When prices are falling, LIFO COGS will be lower than FIFO COGS.

When prices are trending, the weighted-average cost method will produce values of COGS and ending inventory between those of FIFO and LIFO.

Disclosure of a firm's cost flow method is found in the financial footnotes. This information allows the analyst to make adjustments to the financial statements as necessary for analytical and comparative purposes.

LOS 35.d: Discuss ratios useful for evaluating inventory management.

Inventory turnover and the **number of days in inventory** are popular inventory metrics. These ratios can be used to evaluate the age of a firm's inventory as well as the effectiveness of inventory management.

$$\text{inventory turnover} = \frac{\text{cost of goods sold}}{\text{average inventory}}$$

$$\text{number of days of inventory} = \frac{365}{\text{inventory turnover}}$$

 # days b/t receiving raw materials and selling finished goods

Inventory ratios should not be viewed in isolation but, rather, should be compared to industry norms.

Low inventory turnover (high number of days in inventory), coupled with low or declining revenue growth compared to the industry, may be a sign of slow-moving or obsolete inventory. This may necessitate a downward revaluation (writedown) of inventory.

High inventory turnover (low number of days in inventory) is usually preferred as it reduces the risk of obsolescence and minimizes carrying costs such as storage, insurance, and handling. However, high inventory turnover may also be an indication of inadequate inventory levels. Too little inventory may result in lost revenue when orders cannot be filled.

High turnover, coupled with high or increasing revenue growth compared to the industry, is an indication of inventory management efficiency. High turnover and slower revenue growth may indicate insufficient inventory levels.

Inventory ratios are directly affected by the firm's choice of cost flow method, as are other ratios such as the current ratio, the debt-to-equity ratio, and return on assets. When evaluating a firm's performance or when comparing the firm to industry peers, the analyst must understand the differences that result from the different cost flow methods.

 Professor's Note: Calculating and interpreting the inventory turnover ratio and the number of days of inventory will be discussed in the topic review on Financial Analysis Techniques in the next Study Session and again in the Study Session on Corporate Finance.

LOS 35.e: Analyze the financial statements of companies using different inventory accounting methods to compare and describe the effect of the different methods on cost of goods sold, inventory balances, and other financial statement items; and compute and describe the effects of the choice of inventory method on profitability, liquidity, activity, and solvency ratios.

 Professor's Note: The presumption in this section is that prices are rising and inventory quantities are stable or increasing.

The differences among LIFO and FIFO COGS, ending inventory, and other financial statement items are summarized in Figure 3. Values and ratios using the weighted average cost method will fall between the LIFO and FIFO values and ratios.

Figure 3: LIFO and FIFO Comparison—Rising Prices and Stable or Increasing Inventories

LIFO results in...	*FIFO results in...*
higher COGS	lower COGS
lower taxes	higher taxes
lower net income (EBT and EAT)	higher net income (EBT and EAT)
lower inventory balances	higher inventory balances
lower working capital (CA – CL)	higher working capital (CA – CL)
higher cash flows (less taxes paid out)	lower cash flows (more taxes paid out)

A firm's choice of inventory cost flow method can have a significant impact on profitability, liquidity, activity, and solvency. Later we will discuss the adjustments necessary to compare firms with different cost flow methods.

Profitability

As compared to FIFO, LIFO produces higher COGS in the income statement and will result in lower earnings. Any profitability measure that includes COGS will be lower under LIFO. For example, higher COGS will result in lower gross, operating, and net profit margins compared to FIFO.

LIFO profitability measure lower

Liquidity

As compared to FIFO, LIFO results in a lower inventory value on the balance sheet. Since inventory (a current asset) is lower under LIFO, the current ratio, a popular measure of liquidity, is also lower under LIFO than under FIFO. Working capital is lower under LIFO as well, also because current assets are lower.

The quick ratio is unaffected by the firm's inventory cost flow method since inventory is excluded from its numerator.

Activity

Inventory turnover (COGS/average inventory) is higher for firms that use LIFO compared to firms that use FIFO. Under LIFO, COGS is valued at more recent, higher prices, while inventory is valued at older, lower prices. Number of days of inventory (365/inventory turnover) is therefore lower under LIFO compared to FIFO.

LIFO higher inv turn lower days

Solvency

LIFO results in lower total assets compared to FIFO, since LIFO inventory is lower. Lower total assets under LIFO result in lower stockholders' equity (assets – liabilities). Since total assets and stockholders' equity are lower under LIFO, the debt ratio and the debt-to-equity ratio are higher under LIFO compared to FIFO.

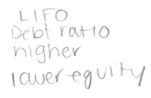

LIFO Debt ratio higher lower equity

 Professor's Note: Another way of thinking about the impact of LIFO on stockholders' equity is that since LIFO COGS is higher, net income is lower. Lower net income will result in lower stockholders' equity (retained earnings) compared to FIFO stockholders' equity.

LOS 35.f: Calculate adjustments to reported financial statements related to inventory assumptions in order to aid in comparing and evaluating companies.

When prices are changing, LIFO and FIFO can result in significant differences in ending inventories and COGS, thereby making it difficult to make comparisons across different firms. As previously discussed, there are also valuation problems with LIFO (understates inventory when prices are rising) that necessitate adjustment. Thus, for analytical and comparison purposes, it is necessary to convert the LIFO values to FIFO values.

Professor's Note: Usually, it is not necessary to convert from weighted average cost to FIFO because the differences in COGS and ending inventory under these two methods are usually immaterial.

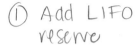

① Add LIFO reserve

The LIFO to FIFO conversion is relatively simple because a firm using LIFO is required to disclose the **LIFO reserve** in the footnotes. The LIFO reserve is the difference between LIFO inventory and FIFO inventory:

$$\text{LIFO reserve} = \text{FIFO inventory} - \text{LIFO inventory}$$

$$\text{FIFO inventory} = \text{LIFO inventory} + \text{LIFO reserve}$$

Figure 4 illustrates that adding the LIFO reserve to the LIFO inventory yields FIFO inventory. Remember, FIFO inventory is a better representation of the economic value of inventory.

Figure 4: LIFO Reserve

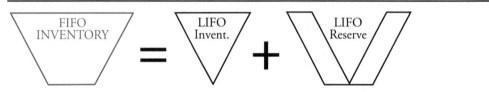

② Add taxes for liabilities + taxes

Once the LIFO inventory is converted to FIFO inventory, the accounting equation (assets = liabilities + equity) will be out of balance. To make the accounting equation balance, it is necessary to adjust liabilities for the difference in taxes created by the conversion and to adjust stockholders' equity by the LIFO reserve, net of tax. The income tax adjustment is necessary because the LIFO firm pays lower taxes than the FIFO firm (when prices are rising). Stated differently, had the firm been using FIFO instead of LIFO, income taxes would have been higher. So, upon conversion, we include the taxes.

For example, say the LIFO reserve is $150 and the tax rate is 40%. To convert the balance sheet to FIFO, increase assets (inventory) by the $150 LIFO reserve. In addition, increase liabilities (taxes) by $60 ($150 LIFO reserve × 40% tax rate) and increase stockholders' equity (retained earnings) by $90 [$150 reserve × (1 − 40% tax rate)]. This will bring the accounting equation back into balance.

③ convert COGS to LIFO

For comparison purposes it is also necessary to convert the LIFO firm's COGS to FIFO COGS. The difference between LIFO COGS and FIFO COGS is equal to the *change* in the LIFO reserve. So, to convert COGS from LIFO to FIFO, simply subtract the change in the LIFO reserve:

$$\text{FIFO COGS} = \text{LIFO COGS} - (\text{ending LIFO reserve} - \text{beginning LIFO reserve})$$

When prices are rising, FIFO COGS is lower than LIFO COGS, so subtracting the change in the LIFO reserve (the difference in COGS under the two methods) from

LIFO COGS makes intuitive sense. When prices are falling, we still subtract the change in the LIFO reserve to convert from LIFO COGS to FIFO COGS. In this case, however, the change in the LIFO reserve is negative and subtracting it will result in higher COGS. When prices are falling, FIFO COGS are greater than LIFO COGS.

 Professor's Note: Ideally, we would prefer to convert from FIFO COGS to LIFO COGS for analytical purposes. LIFO COGS is a better representation of economic costs since it is based on the most recent purchases. However, the FIFO to LIFO conversion of COGS is beyond the scope of this topic review.

Example: Converting ending inventory and COGS from LIFO to FIFO

Sipowitz Company, which uses LIFO, reported end-of-year inventory balances of $500 in 20X5 and $700 in 20X6. The LIFO reserve was $200 for 20X5 and $300 for 20X6. COGS during 20X6 was $3,000. Convert 20X6 ending inventory and COGS to a FIFO basis.

Answer:

Inventory:

$$\text{Inv}_F = \text{Inv}_L + \text{LIFO reserve} = \$700 + \$300 = \$1,000$$

COGS:

$$\text{COGS}_F = \text{COGS}_L - (\text{ending LIFO reserve} - \text{beginning LIFO reserve})$$

$$= \$3,000 - (\$300 - \$200) = \$2,900$$

We are now ready to use the results from the conversion of LIFO to FIFO for analytical purposes. Let's take a look at a more comprehensive example.

Example: Converting from LIFO to FIFO

Sample balance sheets for 20X5 and 20X6 and an income statement for 20X6 are shown below. The sample balance sheets and income statement were prepared using the LIFO inventory cost flow method. Calculate the current ratio, inventory turnover, long-term debt-to-equity ratio, and operating profit margin for 20X6 for LIFO and FIFO inventory valuation methods.

Sample Balance Sheet

Year	20X6	20X5
Assets		
Cash	$105	$95
Receivables	205	195
Inventories	310	290
Total current assets	620	580
Gross property, plant, and equipment	$1,800	$1,700
Accumulated depreciation	360	340
Net property, plant, and equipment	1,440	1,360
Total assets	$2,060	$1,940
Liabilities and equity		
Payables	$110	$90
Short-term debt	160	140
Current portion of long-term debt	55	45
Current liabilities	$325	$275
Long-term debt	$610	$690
Deferred taxes	105	95
Common stock	300	300
Additional paid in capital	400	400
Retained earnings	320	180
Common shareholders equity	1,020	880
Total liabilities and equity	$2,060	$1,940

Sample Income Statement

Year	20X6
Sales	$4,000
Cost of goods sold	3,000
Gross profit	$1,000
Operating expenses	650
Operating profit	350
Interest expense	50
Earnings before taxes	300
Taxes	100
Net income	200
Common dividends	$60

Footnote: The company uses the LIFO inventory cost flow assumption to account for inventories. As compared to FIFO, inventories would have been $100 higher in 20X6 and $90 higher in 20X5.

Answer:

The firm's effective tax rate is necessary for several of the adjustments. The tax rate can be derived from the income statement by dividing tax expense by earnings before tax. The tax rate is $100 / $300 = 33%.

Current ratio

The current ratio (current assets / current liabilities) under LIFO is $620 / $325 = 1.9.

To convert to FIFO, the 20X6 LIFO reserve of $100 is added to current assets, and taxes on the LIFO reserve ($100 LIFO reserve × 33% tax rate = $33) are added to current liabilities. Thus, under FIFO, the current ratio is ($620 + $100 LIFO reserve) / ($325 + $33 tax liability) = 2.0. The current ratio is higher under FIFO as ending inventory now approximates replacement cost.

[handwritten: •add reserve to CA   add taxes to CL]

Inventory turnover

The inventory turnover ratio (COGS / average inventory) for 20X6 under LIFO is $3,000 / $300 = 10.0.

[handwritten: COGS − Ending LIFO reserve − Beg LIFO reserve]

To convert to FIFO COGS, it is necessary to subtract the change in the LIFO reserve from LIFO COGS. The change in the LIFO reserve is $100 ending reserve – $90 beginning reserve = $10. Also, the average LIFO reserve is added to average LIFO inventory: ($90 beginning reserve + $100 ending reserve) / 2 = $95. Alternatively, we can calculate average FIFO inventory by averaging the beginning and ending FIFO inventory: ($290 beginning LIFO inventory + $90 beginning LIFO reserve + $310 ending LIFO inventory + $100 ending LIFO reserve) / 2 = $395.

[handwritten: add reserve to inv]

Thus, under FIFO, inventory turnover is ($3,000 – $10 change in LIFO reserve) / ($300 + $95 average LIFO reserve) = 7.6. Inventory turnover is lower under FIFO due to higher average inventory in the denominator and lower COGS in the numerator (assuming rising prices).

Long-term debt to equity

The long-term debt to equity ratio (long-term debt / stockholders' equity) under LIFO is ($610 + $105) / $1,020 = 0.70.

[handwritten: add tax to equity]

To convert to FIFO, the 20X6 LIFO reserve, net of tax, is added to stockholders' equity: $100 × (1 – 33%) = $67. The adjustment to stockholders' equity is necessary to make the accounting equation balance. The 20X6 LIFO reserve of $100 was added to total assets and $33 of taxes was added to current liabilities, so $67 is added to stockholders' equity.

Thus, under FIFO, long-term debt to equity is ($610 + $105) / ($1,020 + $67 ending LIFO reserve, net of tax) = 0.66. Long-term debt-to-equity is lower under FIFO (assuming rising prices) because stockholders' equity is higher, since it reflects the effects of bringing the LIFO reserve onto the balance sheet.

Operating profit margin

The operating profit margin (operating profit / revenue) under LIFO is $350 / $4,000 = 8.8%.

To convert to FIFO operating profit margin, the analyst should subtract the $10 change in the LIFO reserve from LIFO COGS. Decreasing COGS by $10 increases operating profit by $10. Thus, under FIFO, operating profit margin is ($350 + $10 change in LIFO reserve) / $4,000 = 9.0%. Operating profit margin is higher under FIFO than under LIFO because COGS is lower under FIFO than under LIFO (assuming rising prices).

 Professor's Note: Had you been asked to adjust net profit margin, it would have been necessary to increase taxes by $3.30 ($10 change in reserve × 33% tax rate). Then, FIFO net income would have increased by $6.70 [$10 change in reserve × (1 – 33% tax rate)].

LOS 35.g: Discuss the reasons that a LIFO reserve might rise or decline during a given period and discuss the implications for financial analysis.

Recall that the LIFO reserve is equal to the difference between LIFO inventory and FIFO inventory. The LIFO reserve will increase each period when prices are rising and inventory quantities are stable or increasing. If the firm is liquidating its inventory, or if prices are falling, the LIFO reserve will decline.

A **LIFO liquidation** occurs when a LIFO firm's inventory quantities are declining. In this situation, the older, lower costs are now included in COGS. The result is higher profit margins and higher income taxes. Note, however, that the higher profit is artificial (phantom) because it is not sustainable. The firm cannot liquidate its inventory indefinitely, because it will eventually run out of goods to sell. You can think of a LIFO liquidation as recognizing previously unrecognized gains in inventory value in operating income.

phantom profit

Obviously, firms can increase earnings by simply liquidating the older, lower cost inventory rather than purchasing new inventory. However, LIFO liquidations can also result from strikes, recessions, or declining demand from customers.

If the firm classifies its inventories into narrow categories such as specific products, LIFO liquidations within some of these categories are more likely to occur. Firms can reduce the likelihood of LIFO liquidations and phantom profits by pooling inventory into broader categories for financial reporting. Within a pool, a decrease in the inventory of one item can be offset by increases in inventories of other items.

The analyst should adjust COGS for the decline in the LIFO reserve caused by a decline in inventory. Firms must disclose a LIFO liquidation in the financial statement footnotes to facilitate the adjustment.

Example: LIFO liquidation

At the beginning of 20X8, Big 4 Manufacturing Company had 560 units of inventory as follows:

Year Purchased	Number of Units	Cost Per Unit	Total Cost
20X4	120	$10	$1,200
20X5	140	11	1,540
20X6	140	12	1,680
20X7	160	13	2,080
	560		$6,500

Due to a strike, no units were produced during 20X8. During 20X8, Big 4 sold 440 units. Absent the strike, Big 4 would have had a cost of $14 for each unit produced. Compute the artificial (phantom) profit that resulted from the liquidation of inventory.

Answer:

Because of the LIFO liquidation, actual COGS was $5,300 as follows:

	Units	Cost	
Beginning Inventory	560	$6,500	
+ Purchases	-0-	-0-	
– Ending Inventory	120	1,200	($10 × 120 units)
= COGS (Actual)	440	$5,300	

Had Big 4 replaced the 440 units sold, COGS would have been $6,160 as follows:

	Units	Cost	
Beginning Inventory	560	$6,500	
+ Purchases	440	6,160	($14 × 440 units)
– Ending Inventory	560	6,500	
= COGS (If replaced)	440	$6,160	

Due to the LIFO liquidation, COGS was lower by $860 ($6,160 – $5,300); thus, pretax profit was higher by $860. The higher profit is unsustainable because Big 4 will eventually run out of inventory.

Falling prices. If prices are falling, the value of inventory under FIFO is lower compared to LIFO inventory since the most recent costs are lower than the costs of goods purchased earlier. In this case, FIFO still provides the more accurate estimate of the economic value of inventory. COGS under FIFO is higher than COGS under LIFO since the earlier, higher-cost purchases are reflected in FIFO COGS.

KEY CONCEPTS

LOS 35.a

Costs included in inventory on the balance sheet include purchase cost, conversion cost, allocation of fixed production overhead based on normal capacity levels, and other costs necessary to bring the inventory to its present location and condition. All of these costs for inventory acquired or produced in the current period are added to beginning inventory value and then allocated either to cost of goods sold for the period or to ending inventory.

Period costs, such as unallocated overhead, abnormal waste, most storage costs, administrative costs, and selling costs, are expensed.

LOS 35.b

Under IFRS, inventories are valued at the lower of cost or net realizable value. Inventory "write-up" is allowed, but only to the extent that a previous writedown to net realizable value was recorded.

Under U.S. GAAP, inventories are valued at the lower of cost or market. Market is usually equal to replacement cost but cannot exceed net realizable value or be less than net realizable value minus a normal profit margin. No subsequent "write-up" is allowed.

LOS 35.c

Inventory cost flow methods:

- FIFO – The cost of the first item purchased is the cost of the first item sold. Ending inventory is based on the cost of the most recent purchases, thereby approximating replacement cost.
- LIFO – The cost of the last item purchased is the cost of the first item sold. Ending inventory is based on the cost of the earliest items purchased. When prices are rising, ending inventory is lower and COGS is higher compared to FIFO. Higher COGS results in lower taxes and, thus, higher cash flow. LIFO is prohibited under IFRS.
- Weighted average cost – COGS and inventory values are between their FIFO and LIFO values.
- Specific identification – Each item of inventory is valued at cost and that is the cost when that item is sold.

LOS 35.d

Inventory ratios can be used to evaluate inventory management and should be viewed relative to industry norms. These inventory ratios are affected by the choice of inventory cost flow method (FIFO, LIFO, weighted average). High turnover (low days in inventory) is preferred, but if inventory turnover is too high, sales may be lost because inventory is too low. Low turnover (high days in inventory) may indicate inventory is too high and may be a sign of obsolescence and potential writedowns in future periods.

LOS 35.e

When prices are rising and inventory quantities are stable or increasing:

LIFO results in:	*FIFO results in:*
higher COGS	lower COGS
lower taxes	higher taxes
lower net income	higher net income
lower inventory balances	higher inventory balances
higher cash flows (less taxes paid out)	lower cash flows (more taxes paid out)
lower net and gross margins	higher net and gross margins
lower current ratio	higher current ratio
higher inventory turnover	lower inventory turnover
D/A and D/E higher	D/A and D/E lower

Weighted average cost provides results between LIFO and FIFO.

LOS 35.f

For analytical and comparison purposes, LIFO inventory should be converted to FIFO inventory by adding the LIFO reserve to current assets, adding income taxes on the LIFO reserve to current liabilities, and adding the LIFO reserve, net of tax, to stockholders' equity, so that the accounting equation balances. LIFO COGS can be converted to FIFO COGS by subtracting the change in the LIFO reserve over the period.

LOS 35.g

The LIFO reserve can decline because of either a LIFO liquidation or falling prices. A LIFO liquidation (inventory quantity decreases) will result in lower COGS and an increase in profit as older, lower-cost inventory is (assumed to be) sold. However, the increase in profit is artificial (phantom) because it is not sustainable once the current inventory is depleted. When prices are decreasing, inventory value is higher under LIFO than under FIFO, so the LIFO reserve declines.

CONCEPT CHECKERS

1. Which of the following is *most likely* included in a firm's ending inventory?
   A. Storage costs of finished goods.
   B. Fixed production overhead.
   C. Selling and administrative costs.

2. Which of the following statements *best* describes the treatment of inventory on the balance sheet?
   A. Inventory is carried at the lower of cost or net realizable value under IFRS and the lower of cost or market under U.S. GAAP.
   B. Once an inventory writedown occurs, a subsequent recovery in value is recognized under U.S. GAAP but is not recognized under IFRS.
   C. The carrying value of inventory can never exceed original cost under IFRS or U.S. GAAP.

3. Kamp, Inc. sells specialized bicycle shoes. At year-end, due to a sudden increase in manufacturing costs, the replacement cost per pair of shoes is $55. The historical cost is $43, and the current selling price is $50. The normal profit margin is 10% of the selling price, and the selling costs are $3 per pair. According to U.S. GAAP, which of the following amounts should each pair of shoes be recorded on Kamp's year-end balance sheet?
   A. $42.
   B. $43.
   C. $47.

4. From an analyst's perspective, inventory balances based on:
   A. LIFO are preferable since they reflect historical cost.
   B. FIFO are preferable since they reflect current cost.
   C. weighted averages are preferable since they reflect normal results.

5. During periods of rising prices and stable or increasing inventory levels:
   A. LIFO COGS > weighted average COGS > FIFO COGS.
   B. LIFO COGS < weighted average COGS < FIFO COGS.
   C. LIFO COGS = weighted average COGS = FIFO COGS.

6. During periods of falling prices:
   A. LIFO income > weighted average income > FIFO income.
   B. LIFO income < weighted average income < FIFO income.
   C. LIFO income = weighted average income = FIFO income.

7. In periods of rising prices and stable or increasing inventory quantities, LIFO (as compared to FIFO) results in:
   A. lower COGS, higher taxes, lower inventory, and lower cash flows.
   B. lower COGS, higher taxes, lower inventory, and higher cash flows.
   C. higher COGS, lower taxes, lower inventory, and higher cash flows.

8. In periods of falling prices, compared to using LIFO, firms using FIFO will
    report:
    A. higher earnings.
    B. lower earnings.
    C. identical earnings.

9. If prices are rising and two firms are identical except for inventory methods, the
    firm using FIFO will have:
    A. higher net income.
    B. lower inventory.
    C. higher total cash flow.

10. In periods of rising prices and stable or increasing inventory levels, compared to
     FIFO accounting for inventories, LIFO accounting will give:
     A. lower profitability ratios.
     B. higher inventory values.
     C. a higher current ratio.

11. All else equal, in periods of rising prices and inventory levels, which of the
     following statements is *most accurate*?
     A. FIFO firms have higher debt-to-equity ratios than otherwise identical LIFO
         firms.
     B. LIFO firms have higher gross profit margins than otherwise identical FIFO
         firms.
     C. FIFO firms will have greater stockholders' equity than otherwise identical
         LIFO firms.

12. A firm uses LIFO for inventory accounting and reports the following:
     *   COGS $125,000
     *   Beginning inventory $25,000
     *   Ending inventory $27,000
     *   Footnotes to the financial statements reveal a beginning LIFO reserve of
         $12,000 and an ending LIFO reserve of $15,000
     COGS on a FIFO basis is:
     A. $122,000.
     B. $125,000.
     C. $128,000.

13. A firm's financial statements are prepared using LIFO. Ignoring income taxes,
     which of the following accounts should an analyst *most likely* adjust before
     comparing this firm's financial statement ratios to those of a firm that uses
     FIFO?
     A. Stockholders' equity.
     B. Accounts receivable.
     C. Long-term debt.

14. A LIFO liquidation will *most likely* result in an increase in:
     A. gross profit margin.
     B. inventory.
     C. accounts payable.

15. Assuming no LIFO liquidation, a LIFO firm reports higher net income than an otherwise identical FIFO firm. Prices must be:
    A. steady.
    B. rising.
    C. falling.

COMPREHENSIVE PROBLEMS

1. A firm with a beginning inventory of zero made the following purchases and sales:

Quarter	Purchases	Sales
Q1	40 units at $30	13 units at $35
Q2	20 units at $40	35 units at $45
Q3	90 units at $50	60 units at $60

   A. Calculate the firm's inventory value at the end of the period using the FIFO, LIFO, and weighted average inventory cost flow assumptions.
   B. Calculate the firm's gross profit at the end of the period using FIFO, LIFO, and weighted average inventory cost flow assumptions.

2. A company's LIFO reserve is $50,000 at the beginning of a period and $60,000 at the end of the period. The firm's tax rate is 40%. What adjustments, if any, should an analyst make to the company's financial statements to:
   A. adjust end-of-period LIFO inventory to FIFO inventory?
   B. calculate the debt-to-equity ratio on a FIFO basis?
   C. adjust end-of-period accounts payable from a LIFO basis to a FIFO basis?
   D. adjust COGS from a LIFO basis to a FIFO basis?

ANSWERS – CONCEPT CHECKERS

1. **B** A portion of fixed production overhead based on normal capacity is capitalized as inventory. Storage costs not related to the production process, and selling and administrative costs, are expensed as incurred.

2. **A** Inventory is reported at the lower of cost or net realizable value under IFRS and the lower of cost or market under U.S. GAAP. In some cases, inventories can be carried at an amount that is greater than cost (e.g., precious metals, agricultural and forest products).

3. **B** Market is equal to the replacement cost subject to replacement cost being within a specific range. The upper bound is net realizable value (NRV), which is equal to selling price ($50) less selling costs ($3) for an NRV of $47. The lower bound is NRV ($47) less normal profit (10% of selling price = $5) for a net amount of $42. Since replacement cost ($55) is greater than NRV ($47), market equals NRV ($47). Additionally, we have to use the lower of cost ($43) or market ($47) principle, so the shoes should be recorded at the cost of $43.

4. **B** Under FIFO, older inventory is assumed to be sold first, so current inventory cost is a better indication of inventory replacement cost.

5. **A** Weighted average COGS will always be between FIFO and LIFO whether prices are rising or falling. If prices are rising, LIFO COGS will be the highest because the most recent production costs are included in COGS.

6. **A** LIFO COGS will be the lowest of the three methods when prices are falling. That means LIFO income will be the highest.

7. **C** With rising prices, LIFO results in higher COGS. Higher COGS means lower income, lower income means lower taxes, and lower taxes mean higher cash flow.

8. **B** Falling prices for a firm using FIFO mean older, more expensive goods are going to COGS, thus lowering net income compared to LIFO.

9. **A** Firms using FIFO will have lower COGS, which means they will have higher net income when compared to a firm using LIFO when prices are rising.

10. **A** With rising prices, LIFO will result in higher COGS. Higher COGS will result in lower profitability as compared to FIFO. Inventory values, and therefore the current ratio, are lower using LIFO than using FIFO.

11. **C** All else equal, the FIFO firm has a higher level of assets due to higher inventory. Since liabilities are assumed to be equal, the FIFO firm must have higher equity to finance those assets.

12. **A** FIFO COGS = LIFO COGS – (ending LIFO reserve – beginning LIFO reserve) = $125,000 – ($15,000 – $12,000) = $122,000.

13. **A** Restating LIFO inventory on a FIFO basis would increase inventory and therefore assets, which means equity would need to increase to keep the accounting equation in balance.

14. **A** COGS per unit decline and profit margins increase.

15. **C** If the LIFO firm is reporting higher net income, prices must be falling.

ANSWERS – COMPREHENSIVE PROBLEMS

1. A. 108 units were sold (13 + 35 + 60), and 150 units were available for sale (beginning inventory of 0 plus purchases of 40 + 20 + 90), so there are 150 – 108 = 42 units in ending inventory.

    Under FIFO, 42 units from the last purchase would remain in inventory:
    42 × $50 = $2,100.

    Under LIFO, the first 42 units purchased would remain in inventory:
    (40 × $30) + (2 × $40) = $1,280.

    The average cost of inventory is [(40 × $30) + (20 × $40) + (90 × $50)] / (40 + 20 + 90) = $43.33. Inventory value under the weighted average cost method is $43.33 × 42 units = $1,820.

    B. Revenue = (13 × $35) + (35 × $45) + (60 × $60) = $5,630.

    Purchases = (40 × $30) + (20 × $40) + (90 × $50) = $6,500.

    Under LIFO:
    COGS = purchases + beginning inventory – ending inventory
    = 6,500 + 0 – 1,280 = $5,220.
    Gross profit = $5,630 – $5,220 = $410.

    Under FIFO:
    COGS = purchases + beginning inventory – ending inventory
    = 6,500 + 0 – 2,100 = $4,400.
    Gross profit = $5,630 – $4,400 = $1,230.

    Under weighted average cost:
    COGS = 43.33 × 108 = 4,680.
    Gross profit = $5,630 – $4,680 = $950.

2. A. To adjust end-of-period LIFO inventory to FIFO inventory, the analyst should add the LIFO reserve of $60,000 to LIFO inventory.

    B. Retained earnings must be increased by the LIFO reserve net of tax, or $60,000 × (1 – 0.4) = $36,000.

    C. No adjustment is needed. Accounts payable are not affected by inventory accounting methods.

    D. To adjust COGS from a LIFO basis to a FIFO basis, the analyst should decrease LIFO COGS by the $10,000 change in the LIFO reserve.

LONG-LIVED ASSETS

EXAM FOCUS

Firms can either capitalize an expenditure on the balance sheet as an asset or expense it on the income statement in the current period. You should be familiar with the effects this decision has on financial statement components and ratios. In addition, you should understand the issues surrounding the capitalization of construction interest, research and development costs, and software development costs, and be able to make the necessary adjustments for analytical purposes. Be prepared to compute depreciation expense using all three methods and understand the ratio effects of the choice of method. Be able to identify when an asset is impaired and calculate the loss. Finally, be able to identify when a firm can revalue assets upward.

LOS 36.a: Explain the accounting standards related to the capitalization of expenditures as part of long-lived assets, including interest costs.

When a firm makes an expenditure, it can either capitalize the cost as an asset on the balance sheet or expense the cost in the income statement for the period. As a general rule, an expenditure that is expected to provide a future economic benefit over multiple accounting periods is capitalized, but if the future economic benefit is unlikely or highly uncertain, the expenditure is expensed.

An expenditure that is capitalized is initially recorded at cost, presumably its fair value at acquisition. The capitalized cost is reported on the balance sheet as an asset and is reported in the cash flow statement as an outflow from investing activities. Except for land and intangible assets with indefinite lives, the cost is then allocated to each subsequent income statement over the life of the asset, as depreciation expense (for tangible assets) or amortization expense (for intangible assets with finite lives).

Sometimes assets are acquired in a nonmonetary exchange. In this case, cost is based on the fair value of the asset exchanged, or on the fair value of the asset received if it can be determined more readily.

An expenditure that is expensed is reported in the cash flow statement as an outflow from operating activities. Although total cash flow is not affected by the choice, the cash flow classifications (CFI vs. CFO) are affected by the decision to capitalize or expense.

if expensed, op activity

Capitalized Interest

When a firm constructs an asset for its own use or, in limited circumstances, for resale, the interest that accrues during the construction period is capitalized as a part of the asset's cost. The objective of capitalizing interest is to accurately measure the cost of the asset and to better match the cost with the revenues generated by the constructed asset. This treatment is now required by both U.S. GAAP and IFRS.

The interest rate used to capitalize interest is based on debt specifically related to the construction of the asset. If no construction debt is outstanding, the interest rate is based on existing unrelated borrowings. Interest costs on general corporate debt in excess of project construction costs are expensed.

Capitalized interest is not reported in the income statement as interest expense. Once construction interest is capitalized, the interest cost is allocated to the income statement through depreciation expense (if the asset is held for use), or COGS (if the asset is held for sale).

Generally, capitalized interest is reported in the cash flow statement as an outflow from investing activities, while interest expense is reported as an outflow from operating activities.

LOS 36.b: Compute and describe the effects of capitalizing versus expensing on net income, shareholders' equity, cash flow from operations, and financial ratios including the effect on the interest coverage ratio of capitalizing interest costs.

Although it may make no operational difference, the choice between capitalizing and expensing will affect net income, shareholders' equity, total assets, cash flow from operations, cash flow from financing, and various financial ratios.

Net income. Capitalizing an expenditure delays the recognition of expense in the income statement. Thus, in the period that an expenditure is capitalized, the firm will report higher net income compared to expensing. In subsequent periods, the firm will report lower net income compared to expensing, as the capitalized expenditure is allocated to the income statement through depreciation expense. This allocation process reduces the variability of net income by spreading the expense over time.

Conversely, if a firm expenses the expenditure in the current period, net income is reduced by the total amount of the expenditure (assuming no tax effects). In subsequent periods, no allocation of cost is necessary; thus, net income in future periods is higher than if the asset was capitalized.

Over the life of an asset, *total* net income will be identical. Timing of the expense recognition is the only difference.

Shareholders' equity. Because capitalization results in higher net income in the period of the expenditure as compared to expensing, it also results in higher shareholders' equity (retained earnings). As the cost is allocated to the income statement in subsequent periods, net income will be reduced along with shareholders' equity (retained earnings). Total assets are higher with capitalization and liabilities are unaffected, so that A − L = E holds.

If the expenditure is expensed, shareholders' equity (retained earnings) will reflect the entire reduction in net income in the period of the expenditure.

Cash flow from operations. A capitalized expenditure is usually reported in the cash flow statement as an outflow from investing activities. If expensed, the expenditure is reported as an outflow from operating activities. Thus, capitalizing an expenditure will result in lower investing cash flow and higher operating cash flow as compared to expensing. Assuming no tax effects, *total* cash flow will be exactly the same. The classification of the cash flow is the only difference.

Recall that when an expenditure is capitalized, depreciation expense is recognized in subsequent periods. Depreciation is a non-cash expense and, aside from any tax effects, does not affect operating cash flow.

Financial ratios. Capitalizing an expenditure results in higher assets and higher equity compared to expensing. Thus, both the debt-to-assets ratio and the debt-to-equity ratio are lower (they have larger denominators) with capitalization.

Capitalizing an expenditure will *initially* result in higher return on assets (ROA) and higher return on equity (ROE). This is the result of higher net income in the first year. In subsequent years, ROA and ROE will be lower for the capitalizing firm as net income is reduced by the depreciation expense.

Since the expensing firm recognizes the entire expense in the first year, ROA and ROE will be lower in the first year and higher in the subsequent years. After the first year, net income (numerator) is higher, and assets and equity (denominators) are lower, than they would be if the firm had capitalized the expenditure.

Interest coverage ratio. The interest coverage ratio (EBIT / interest expense) measures a firm's ability to make required interest payments on its debt.

Recall that construction interest is capitalized as an asset and then allocated to the income statement as the asset is depreciated over time. Thus, in the year of the expenditure, capitalizing results in lower interest expense and higher net income compared to expensing. The result is a higher interest coverage ratio (smaller denominator) when interest is capitalized.

In subsequent periods, the capitalized interest is allocated to the income statement as depreciation expense, not interest expense. Higher depreciation expense results in lower EBIT. Thus, in subsequent periods, the capitalized interest results in a lower interest coverage ratio (smaller numerator).

For firms in an expansion phase, capitalizing interest may result in earnings that are higher over many periods compared to an expensing firm because the amount of depreciation from previously capitalized interest is less than the amount of additional interest that is being newly capitalized.

Implications for Analysis

An analyst may want to reverse the effect of capitalized interest and restate the financial statements and related ratios. Many analysts consider interest coverage ratios based on total interest expense (including capitalized interest) to be a better measure of the solvency of the firm, since the interest is a required payment. Bond rating firms often make this adjustment. When there are debt covenants (provisions of the borrowing agreement) that specify a minimum interest coverage ratio, analysts should be aware of how the ratio is calculated for determining whether the covenant has been violated (which can mean immediate repayment is required). If the requirement is that the interest coverage ratio be calculated with capitalized interest included in interest expense, the analyst must adjust the ratio accordingly to determine how close the firm is to violating the debt covenant.

For analytical purposes, the effects of capitalizing interest costs can be reversed by making the following adjustments:

- Interest that was capitalized during the year should be added to interest expense. The amount of interest capitalized is disclosed in the financial statement footnotes.
- The allocation of interest capitalized in previous years should be removed from depreciation expense.
- Interest that was capitalized during the year is classified as a cash outflow from investing activities. For analysis, it should be added back to cash flow from investing activities and subtracted from cash flow from operating activities.
- Ratios such as interest coverage and profitability ratios should be recalculated with the restated figures. The interest coverage ratio and net profit margin will likely be lower without capitalization.

The financial effects of capitalizing versus expensing are summarized in Figure 1.

Figure 1: Financial Statement Effects of Capitalizing vs. Expensing

	Capitalizing	*Expensing*
Total assets	Higher	Lower
Shareholders' equity	Higher	Lower
Income variability	Lower	Higher
Net income (first year)	Higher	Lower
Net income (subsequent years)	Lower	Higher
Cash flow from operations	Higher	Lower
Cash flow from investing	Lower	Higher
Debt ratio & Debt-to-equity	Lower	Higher
Interest coverage (first year)	Higher	Lower
Interest coverage (subsequent years)	Lower	Higher

Let's work through an extended example of the financial statement effects of capitalizing interest.

Example: Effect of Capitalizing Interest

Soprano Company Balance Sheet

	20X6	20X5
Assets		
Current assets		
Cash	$105	$95
Receivables	205	195
Inventories	310	290
Total current assets	$620	$580
Noncurrent assets		
Gross property, plant, and equipment	$1,800	$1,700
Accumulated depreciation	(360)	(340)
Net property, plant, and equipment	$1,440	$1,360
Total assets	$2,060	$1,940
Liabilities and equity		
Current liabilities		
Payables	$110	$90
Short-term debt	160	140
Current portion of long-term debt	55	45
Total current liabilities	$325	$275
Noncurrent liabilities		
Long-term debt	$610	$690
Deferred taxes	105	95
Stockholders' equity		
Common stock	$300	$300
Additional paid in capital	400	400
Retained earnings	320	180
Common shareholders' equity	1,020	880
Total liabilities and equity	$2,060	$1,940

Soprano Company Income Statement

	20X6
Sales	$4,000
Cost of goods sold	$3,000
Gross profit	1,000
Operating expense	650
Operating profit	350
Interest expense	50
Earnings before taxes	300
Taxes	100
Net income	$200
Common dividends	$60

During 20X6, the company capitalized $20 of construction interest. The capitalized interest increased depreciation expense $5 for the year. For analytical purposes, you have decided to treat the capitalized interest as an immediate expense.

Complete the following table, ignoring any income tax effects:

Soprano Company Answer Template

	Interest Capitalized (Reported)	Interest Expensed (Adjusted)
Total assets	$2,060	
Interest coverage ratio	7.0	
Net profit margin	5.0%	
Cash flow from operations	$220	
Cash flow from investing	($100)	
Long-term debt-to-equity	59.8%	

Answer:

Adjusted total assets: The capitalized interest, net of the related depreciation, is removed from total assets (net property, plant, and equipment). Adjusted total assets are $2,045 ($2,060 total assets – $20 capitalized interest + $5 related depreciation).

Adjusted net profit margin: The capitalized interest is treated as interest expense and the related depreciation is eliminated from operating expense. Adjusted net profit margin is 4.6% [($200 net income – $20 interest expense + $5 related depreciation) / $4,000 revenue].

Adjusted interest coverage ratio: The capitalized interest is treated as interest expense and the related depreciation is eliminated from EBIT. The adjusted interest coverage ratio (EBIT / interest expense) is 5.1 [($350 EBIT + $5 related depreciation) / ($50 interest expense + $20 capitalized interest)].

Adjusted operating cash flow: The capitalized interest is subtracted from operating cash flow. Adjusted operating cash flow is $200 ($220 reported operating cash flow – $20 capitalized interest).

Adjusted investing cash flow: The capitalized interest is added back to investing cash flow. Adjusted investing cash flow is –$80 (–$100 reported investing cash flow + $20 capitalized interest).

Total cash flow does not change. We have simply reclassified the interest from an investing cash flow to an operating cash flow.

Note: We ignored the income tax effects in this example for simplicity.

Adjusted long-term debt-to-equity: The capitalized interest, net of the related depreciation expense, is subtracted from net income; thus, shareholders' equity (retained earnings) decreases by the same amount. Adjusted long-term debt-to-equity is 60.7% [$610 / ($1,020 reported equity – $20 capitalized interest + $5 related depreciation)].

LOS 36.c: Explain the circumstances in which software development costs and research and development costs are capitalized.

Intangible assets are long-term assets that lack physical substance, such as patents, brand names, copyrights, and franchises. The value of an identifiable intangible asset is based on the rights or privileges granted to the firm using the asset over a finite period. Consequently, the cost of an intangible asset is *amortized* over its useful life. Not all intangible assets are reported on the balance sheet.

An **unidentifiable intangible asset** is one that cannot be purchased separately and may have an infinite life. Intangible assets with infinite lives are not amortized but are tested for impairment at least annually. The most common example of an unidentifiable intangible asset is **goodwill**. Goodwill is the excess of purchase price over the fair value of the identifiable assets (net of liabilities) acquired in a business acquisition.

Intangible assets can be created internally, purchased externally, or obtained as a part of a business acquisition.

Created internally. With some exceptions, costs incurred by the firm to create intangible assets are expensed as incurred. Important exceptions are **research and development costs** and **software development costs**.

Under U.S. GAAP, research and development costs are generally expensed as incurred. Under IFRS, research costs (costs incurred during the research phase of an internal project) are expensed as incurred. However, development costs (costs incurred during the development phase of an internal project) are capitalized.

Costs incurred to develop software for sale to others are expensed as incurred until the product's technological feasibility has been established. Once technological feasibility occurs, U.S. GAAP requires subsequent costs to be capitalized. Of course, judgment is involved in determining technological feasibility. Costs incurred when a firm develops software for its own internal use are also capitalized.

Purchased externally. An intangible asset purchased from another party is initially recorded on the balance sheet at cost, presumably its fair value at acquisition.

Obtained in a business acquisition. The **purchase method** is used to account for business acquisitions. Under the purchase method, the purchase price is allocated to the "identifiable" assets and liabilities of the acquired firm on the basis of fair value. Any remaining amount of the purchase price is recorded as goodwill. Goodwill is said to be an "unidentifiable" asset that cannot be separated from the business itself.

Only goodwill created in a business acquisition is capitalized on the balance sheet. Internally generated goodwill is not.

Under U.S. GAAP, a fair value of the acquired firm's **in-process research and development (IPR&D)** must be estimated before computing goodwill. IPR&D is the amount related to a project that is incomplete at the acquisition date. IPR&D is expensed in the period when the acquisition takes place. By assigning a higher value to IPR&D, the firm will recognize less goodwill, higher expense, and lower earnings in the period of the acquisition, and higher earnings in the future. IPR&D is usually not considered a recurring item. Thus, analysts will often remove this expense from the income statement when forecasting future earnings.

Under IFRS, IPR&D is not immediately expensed. Rather, the acquiring firm may report IPR&D as a separate "finite-lived" asset. Alternatively, IPR&D may be included as a part of goodwill.

Professor's Note: Recently, the Financial Accounting Standards Board issued SFAS No. 141(R), effective December 15, 2008. Under the new standard, the treatment of IPR&D differs significantly. You are not expected to know the new standard for the exam.

LOS 36.d: Identify the different depreciation methods for long-lived tangible assets and discuss how the choice of method, useful lives, and salvage values affect a company's financial statements, ratios, and taxes.

Depreciation is the systematic allocation of the asset's cost over time. Two important terms are:

- *Carrying (book) value.* The net value of an asset or liability on the balance sheet. For property, plant, and equipment, carrying value equals historical cost minus accumulated depreciation.
- *Historical cost.* The original purchase price of the asset including installation and transportation costs. The gross investment in the asset is the same as its historical cost.

Depreciation is a real and significant operating expense. Even though depreciation doesn't require current cash expenditures (the cash outflow was made in the past when the asset was purchased), it is an expense nonetheless and cannot be ignored.

The analyst must decide whether the reported depreciation expense is more or less than *economic depreciation,* which is the actual decline in the value of the asset over the period. One chain of video rental stores was found to be overstating income by depreciating its stock of movies by equal amounts each year. In fact, a greater portion of the decrease in the value of newly released movies occurs in the first year. Depreciating the rental assets by a greater amount during the first year would have better approximated actual economic depreciation.

Review of Depreciation Methods

Depreciation may be reported using straight-line, accelerated, or units-of-production methods.

Straight-line (SL) depreciation is the dominant method of computing depreciation for financial reporting. Depreciation is the same amount each year over the asset's estimated life:

$$\text{depreciation expense} = \frac{\text{original cost} - \text{salvage value}}{\text{depreciable life}}$$

With an **accelerated depreciation method,** more depreciation expense is recognized in the early years of an asset's life and less depreciation expense in the later years of its life. Accelerated depreciation methods result in lower net income in the early years of an asset's life and greater net income in the later years of an asset's life, compared to straight-line depreciation. No additional depreciation expense is charged once the asset's book value reaches its estimated salvage value. Firms may use an accelerated method initially for an asset, and then switch to the straight-line method.

One often-used accelerated depreciation method is the **double-declining balance (DDB) method**:

$$\text{DDB depreciation in year } x = \frac{2}{\text{asset life in years}} \times \text{book value at beginning of year } x$$

Depreciation under the **units-of-production method** is based on usage rather than time. The depreciable cost of the asset (cost – estimated salvage value) is divided by the number of units the asset is expected to produce over its useful life to get depreciation per unit. Each year the number of units produced is multiplied by depreciation per unit to get the depreciation expense for the year. No additional depreciation expense is charged once the asset's book value reaches its estimated salvage value.

Choice of Method

Under U.S. GAAP, a firm may use different depreciation methods for financial reporting and for tax reporting. In many countries this is not the case. U.S. firms will often use straight-line depreciation for financial statements and an accelerated method for tax reporting in order to reduce taxable income (and taxes paid) in the early years of an asset's life, effectively deferring payment of some taxes until the later years of the asset's life. The U.S. income tax code allows the use of an accelerated method referred to as **Modified Accelerated Cost Recovery System (MACRS)** depreciation.

For a firm using straight-line depreciation for financial reporting, using an accelerated method for tax reporting does not change income tax expense reported on the income statement. The difference between income tax expense and income taxes payable in the early years is reported as an addition to the firm's **deferred tax liability** (on the balance sheet). In the later years, when depreciation for tax is less than depreciation reported on the income statement, the excess of taxes payable over income tax expense reduces the deferred tax liability.

Note that *total* depreciation expense over an asset's life is the same under all methods. The pattern of depreciation expense and of net income (or taxable income) is different, not their totals over the asset's life. The differences in depreciation, net income, and reported net profit margin for the three methods are illustrated in the following example.

Example: Effect of depreciation methods on net income

Sackett Laboratories purchases chemical processing machinery for $550,000. The equipment has an estimated useful life of five years and an estimated salvage value of $50,000. The company expects to produce 20,000 units of output using this machinery, with 6,000 units in each of the first two years, 3,000 units in the next two years, and 2,000 units in the fifth year. The company's effective tax rate is 30%. Revenues are $600,000 per year, and expenses other than depreciation are $300,000 in each year. Calculate Sackett's net income and net profit margin if the company depreciates the machinery using a.) the straight-line method, b.) the double declining balance method, changing to the straight-line method after two years, and c.) the units of production method.

Answer

Using the *straight-line method*, depreciation expense in each year is ($550,000 – $50,000)/5 = $100,000.

Using the *double declining balance method*, each year's depreciation is 2/5 of the book value. In year 1, depreciation expense is $550,000 × 2/5 = $220,000, and in year 2, depreciation expense is ($550,000 – $220,000) × 2/5 = $132,000. Straight-line depreciation expense for the remaining three years is ($550,000 – $220,000 – $132,000 – $50,000) / 3 = $49,333.

Using the *units of production method*, depreciation expense in the first two years is (6,000/20,000) × ($550,000 – $50,000) = $150,000, in the next two years is (3,000/20,000) × ($550,000 – $50,000) = $75,000, and in the fifth year is (2,000/20,000) × ($550,000 – $50,000) = $50,000.

Straight-line depreciation:

	Year 1	Year 2	Year 3	Year 4	Year 5	Total
Revenue	600,000	600,000	600,000	600,000	600,000	3,000,000
Other expenses	300,000	300,000	300,000	300,000	300,000	1,500,000
Depreciation expense	100,000	100,000	100,000	100,000	100,000	500,000
Pretax income	200,000	200,000	200,000	200,000	200,000	1,000,000
Tax expense	60,000	60,000	60,000	60,000	60,000	300,000
Net income	140,000	140,000	140,000	140,000	140,000	700,000
Net profit margin	23.3%	23.3%	23.3%	23.3%	23.3%	23.3%

Double-declining balance:

	Year 1	Year 2	Year 3	Year 4	Year 5	Total
Revenue	600,000	600,000	600,000	600,000	600,000	3,000,000
Other expenses	300,000	300,000	300,000	300,000	300,000	1,500,000
Depreciation expense	220,000	132,000	49,333	49,333	49,333	500,000
Pretax income	80,000	168,000	250,667	250,667	250,667	1,000,000
Tax expense	24,000	50,400	75,200	75,200	75,200	300,000
Net income	56,000	117,600	175,467	175,467	175,467	700,000
	9.3%	19.6%	29.2%	29.2%	29.2%	23.3%

Units of production:

	Year 1	Year 2	Year 3	Year 4	Year 5	Total
Revenue	600,000	600,000	600,000	600,000	600,000	3,000,000
Other expenses	300,000	300,000	300,000	300,000	300,000	1,500,000
Depreciation expense	150,000	150,000	75,000	75,000	50,000	500,000
Pretax income	150,000	150,000	225,000	225,000	250,000	1,000,000
Tax expense	45,000	45,000	67,500	67,500	75,000	300,000
Net income	105,000	105,000	157,500	157,500	175,000	700,000
	17.5%	17.5%	26.3%	26.3%	29.2%	23.3%

The accelerated depreciation methods result in pretax income, tax expense, net income, and net profit margins that are lower in the early years and higher in the later years, compared to straight-line depreciation. Over the entire period, however, depreciation expense, tax expense, pretax income, net income, and net profit margin are unaffected by the depreciation method chosen.

Useful Lives and Salvage Values

In general, a longer estimated useful life decreases annual depreciation and increases reported net income, while a shorter estimated useful life will have the opposite effect. A higher estimate of the residual (salvage) value will also decrease depreciation and increase net income, while a lower estimate of the salvage value will increase depreciation and decrease net income.

Although companies are required to disclose information on depreciable lives, such disclosures are often given as ranges and cover groups of assets rather than specific assets. The choice of estimated lives and residual values gives companies some ability to manage earnings, and an analyst should be alert to instances of excessively long depreciable life assumptions or excessively high salvage values, both of which will lead to an overstatement of net income.

- Management could estimate a useful life longer than warranted (thus reducing depreciation expense and increasing income) and then write down the overstated assets in a restructuring process.
- Management might also write down assets, taking an immediate charge against income, and then record less future depreciation expense based on the reduced carrying value. This results in higher future net income in exchange for a one-time charge to current income.

- The life of a depreciable asset or the residual value could be significantly overstated, thus understating depreciation expense during the life of the asset and increasing the loss when the asset is retired.

Under IFRS, a company may adjust the estimated residual value either up or down as new information is used to update this estimate. Under U.S. GAAP, the initial estimate of an asset's residual value may be revised downward, but may not be increased.

GAAP cant revise residual value UP

Depreciation expense may be allocated between COGS and SG&A expenses. While this allocation will not affect operating margins, it will affect the gross margin (which is computed before SG&A expense) and operating expenses (which are in addition to COGS).

LOS 36.e: Discuss the use of fixed asset disclosures to compare companies' average age of depreciable assets, and calculate, using such disclosures, the average age and average depreciable life of fixed assets.

The footnotes to the financial statements typically provide the analyst considerable information about the company's fixed assets and depreciation methods. An analyst can use this data to estimate the average age of the firm's assets. The average age is useful for two reasons:

- It helps identify older, less efficient assets, which may make the firm less competitive.
- An analyst can estimate when major capital expenditures will be required, which will help the analyst forecast when the firm will face significant financing requirements.

Different companies provide different levels of detail in their footnote disclosures regarding fixed assets and depreciation, and groupings of assets with different useful lives are common. As a result, the following methods of estimating average age of assets do not produce precise values, but can provide indications of areas that require more investigation by the analyst.

There are three useful calculations regarding a firm's fixed assets:

- **Average age** (in years) is approximated by:

$$\frac{\text{accumulated depreciation}}{\text{annual depreciation expense}}$$

$age = \dfrac{AD}{DExp}$

This calculation is more accurate with straight-line depreciation. The calculation can be significantly affected by the mix of assets.

- **Average depreciable life** is approximated by:

$$\frac{\text{ending gross investment}}{\text{annual depreciation expense}}$$

$Life = \dfrac{Gross\ Inv}{D\ Exp}$

Gross investment is the original cost of the asset. Gross investment excludes accumulated depreciation and any impairment charges.

*all divided by depr expens

- **Remaining useful life** is approximated by:

$$\frac{\text{ending net investment}}{\text{annual depreciation expense}}$$

Useful $\frac{NetInv}{DExp}$

Net investment is equal to original cost (gross investment) minus accumulated depreciation.

> *Professor's Note: The remaining useful life can also be approximated by subtracting the average age from the average depreciable life.*

Example: Calculating average age and average depreciable life

At the end of 20X8, a company has gross fixed assets of $3 million and accumulated depreciation of $1 million. During the year, depreciation expense was $500,000.

What is the average age, average depreciable life, and remaining useful life of the company's fixed assets?

Answer:

$$\text{average age} = \frac{\text{accumulated depreciation}}{\text{depreciation expense}} = \frac{\$1,000,000}{\$500,000} = 2 \text{ years}$$

$$\text{average depreciable life} = \frac{\text{ending gross investment}}{\text{depreciation expense}} = \frac{\$3,000,000}{\$500,000} = 6 \text{ years}$$

$$\text{remaining useful life} = \frac{\text{ending net investment}}{\text{depreciation expense}} = \frac{\$2,000,000}{\$500,000} = 4 \text{ years}$$

Another popular metric is to compare annual capital expenditures to depreciation expense. This gives an indication of whether the firm is replacing its PP&E at the same rate that its value is depreciating.

LOS 36.f: Describe amortization of intangible assets with finite useful lives, and the estimates that affect the amortization calculations.

The allocation of an intangible asset's cost to the income statement is known as **amortization expense**. Amortizing an intangible asset is the same concept as depreciating a tangible asset.

Intangible assets with finite lives are amortized over their expected useful lives. The expense should match the benefits of owning the asset as they are used up during the period. Examples of intangible assets with finite lives include franchise rights granted for a specific period, acquired patents or copyrights, and a license that the firm plans to stop using after a period of years.

Intangible assets with indefinite lives are not amortized, so no expense is reported on the income statement unless the asset is subject to an *impairment charge*. (Impairment is explained later in this review.) Examples of intangible assets without finite lives include goodwill, a trademark that can be renewed at minimal cost, and a license that can be renewed at little or no cost.

LOS 36.g: Discuss the liability for closure, removal, and environmental effects of long-lived operating assets, and discuss the financial statement impact and ratio effects of that liability.

Companies often own or operate assets that cause environmental damage, including strip mines, nuclear power plants, offshore oil platforms, and production plants that produce toxic waste as a by-product. Governments often require the company to clean up the site and/or return it to its original condition once the company ceases using the asset. These obligations are known as **asset retirement obligations (ARO)**.

The company initially measures the ARO at fair value using a discounted cash flow approach. The present value of the obligation, discounted at a rate based on the firm's credit standing, is reported on the balance sheet as a liability. The same amount is added to the carrying value of the specific asset. This keeps the accounting equation in balance without causing an immediate reduction in equity.

Subsequently, the ARO amount is depreciated on the income statement over the remaining life of the related asset. In addition, the company will recognize accretion expense on the liability. The accretion expense is equal to the increase in the liability due to the passage of time.

At maturity, the ARO liability is equal to the full amount of the obligation and the related asset is fully depreciated. At this point, the obligation has been fully recognized in the income statement.

> **Example: Accounting for an asset retirement obligation**
>
> An oil company is obligated to remediate a property once production is complete in 5 years. The future obligation is estimated at $1 million. Assuming a discount rate of 8%, discuss the financial statement impact of the ARO.
>
> **Answer:**
>
> At a discount rate of 8%, the present value of the obligation is $680,583. The present value of the obligation is added to the balance sheet value of the related asset and is also reported as a liability. The oil company will then depreciate the asset and recognize accretion expense (at 8%) on the liability.
>
> *Professor's Note: Adding an amount equal to the present value of the estimated future asset retirement costs to the purchase cost of the asset may seem a bit strange. This increase in asset value serves to perfectly offset the ARO liability at acquisition so that equity is not affected by the ARO liability.*

At the end of the first year, the oil company will recognize *additional* depreciation expense (above what it would have been without the ARO) of $136,117 ($680,583 / 5 years) because of the increase in asset value to offset the ARO liability. In addition, accretion expense of $54,447 is recognized in the income statement ($680,583 × 8%), which represents the movement of the ARO liability toward its estimated future value of $1 million. At the end of the first year, the ARO liability has a balance of $735,030 ($680,583 + $54,447 or $680,583 × 1.08). The liability has simply increased by 8%, the amount of the accretion expense.

 Professor's Note: We can also calculate the balance of the ARO liability at the end of the first year as the present value of $1 million discounted for the remaining 4 years at 8%.

The accounting equation balances, as assets decrease by the depreciation expense of $136,117, liabilities increase by the accretion expense of $54,447, and stockholders' equity decreases by the total expense of $190,564 ($136,117 depreciation expense + $54,447 accretion expense).

Over time, accretion expense increases as the liability increases toward its face amount. Hence, at the end of the second year, accretion expense is equal to $58,802 ($735,030 ARO balance × 8%).

At the end of the asset's life, the ARO liability will have a balance of $1 million and the value that was added to the asset initially will have been depreciated to zero.

Ratio Effects and Analytical Issues

Recognizing an ARO will increase both assets and liabilities by the same amount. Earnings will be lower as both additional depreciation expense and accretion expense on the ARO liability are recognized in the income statement.

For analytical purposes, it is recommended that the ARO be treated as debt on the balance sheet and when calculating solvency ratios, such as the debt ratio and debt-to-equity ratio. Note that any related offsetting amounts such as dedicated asset retirement funds, trust funds, escrow accounts, and the present value of any tax savings expected when the asset retirement costs are actually paid (tax rate times current ARO) should be subtracted from the liability to get the adjustment to debt. In any event, treating the net ARO as debt will increase the debt ratio and debt-to-equity ratio.

In addition, the accretion expense should be treated as interest when calculating the interest coverage ratio. This adjustment is accomplished by adding the accretion expense to both EBIT and interest expense, which will typically decrease the interest coverage ratio.

treat ARO like debt

accretion expense as interest

Example: ARO Adjustments

A manufacturing firm reports an ARO liability of $100,000. In addition, the firm has a dedicated fund of $35,000 that it expects to utilize for the obligation at retirement. The firm also expects to receive income tax benefits when the obligation is paid. The firm reports the accretion of the ARO as an operating expense in the income statement. Assuming the appropriate discount rate is 10% and the firm's tax rate is 40%, calculate the adjustments necessary to compute the debt-to-equity ratio and the interest coverage ratio for analytical purposes.

Answer:

For calculating the debt-to-equity ratio, the ARO liability, less the expected tax savings of $40,000 ($100,000 × 40% tax rate) and the retirement fund, is treated as debt.

Thus, debt is increased $25,000 ($100,000 ARO liability – $40,000 tax savings – $35,000 retirement fund). The result of the adjustment is an increase in the debt-to-equity ratio (higher numerator).

For calculating the interest coverage ratio, accretion expense of $10,000 ($100,000 ARO liability × 10%) is reclassified as interest expense. This is accomplished by adding $10,000 back to EBIT and adding $10,000 to interest expense. Assuming EBIT is greater than interest expense, the result is a lower interest coverage ratio.

Figure 2 summarizes the ratio effects of recognizing AROs.

Figure 2: Ratio effects of AROs

Ratio	Numerator	Denominator	Effect on Ratio
Asset turnover	Sales will not change.	Assets will increase by the amount of the ARO.	Decrease
Debt-to-equity	Debt is higher by the amount of the ARO.	Equity will decrease as depreciation and accretion expense are recognized.	Increase
Return on assets	Net income will decrease as depreciation and accretion expense are recognized.	Assets will increase by the amount of the ARO.	Decrease
Interest coverage	EBIT will decrease as depreciation expense is recognized.	Interest expense will increase from accretion of ARO.	Decrease

LOS 36.h: Discuss the impact of sales or exchanges of long-lived assets on financial statements.

Eventually, long-lived assets are sold, exchanged, or abandoned.

When a long-lived asset is *sold*, the difference between the sale proceeds and the carrying (book) value of the asset is reported as a gain or loss in the income statement. The carrying value is equal to original cost minus accumulated depreciation, adjusted for any impairment charges.

The gain or loss is usually reported in the income statement as a part of income from continuing operations. Also, if the firm presents its cash flow statement using the indirect method, the gain or loss is removed from net income to compute cash flow from operations (selling a long-lived asset is an investing cash inflow).

If the asset is considered a "component" of the business, the gain or loss is reported below income from continuing operations as a discontinued operation. A component is a subsidiary, segment, or asset group whose cash flows can be clearly distinguished from those of the rest of the firm. Recall that discontinued operations are reported in the income statement, net of tax, below income from continuing operations.

If a long-lived asset is *abandoned*, the treatment is similar to a sale, except there are no proceeds. In this case, the carrying value of asset is removed from the balance sheet and a loss of that amount is recognized in the income statement.

If a long-lived asset is *exchanged* for another asset, a gain or loss is computed by comparing the carrying value of the old asset with fair value of the new asset (or the fair value of the old asset if it is clearly more evident). The carrying value of the old asset is removed from the balance sheet and the new asset is recorded at its fair value.

For analytical and forecasting purposes, excluding gains and losses from asset dispositions is recommended.

LOS 36.i: Define impairment of long-lived tangible and intangible assets and explain what effect such impairment has on a company's financial statements and ratios.

Long-lived tangible assets that are held for use are tested for **impairment** when events and circumstances indicate the firm may not be able to recover the carrying value through future use. For example, there may have been a significant decline in the market value of the asset or a significant change in the asset's physical condition.

Under U.S. GAAP, impairment accounting involves two steps. In the first step, the asset is tested for impairment by applying a **recoverability test**. If the asset is impaired, the second step involves measuring the loss.

Recoverability. An asset is considered impaired if the carrying value (original cost less accumulated depreciation) is greater than the asset's future *undiscounted* cash flows.

Because the recoverability test is based on undiscounted cash flow, tests for impairment involve considerable management discretion.

Loss measurement. If the asset is impaired, the impairment loss is equal to the excess of carrying value over the fair value of the asset (or the *discounted* value of the future cash flows if the fair value is not known).

 Professor's Note: The difference in testing for impairment and measuring the impairment loss can be confusing. In testing for impairment, undiscounted cash flows are used. Once impairment has been detected, the loss is based on discounted expected future cash flows, or fair value.

Example: Asset impairment

Information related to equipment owned by Brownfield Company follows:

Original cost	$900,000
Accumulated depreciation to date	$100,000
Expected future cash flows	$700,000
Fair value	$580,000

Assuming Brownfield will continue to use the equipment in the future, test the asset for impairment and discuss the results.

Answer:

The carrying value of the equipment is $800,000 ($900,000 original cost – $100,000 accumulated depreciation). Since the carrying value exceeds the expected future cash flows ($800,000 carrying value > $700,000 expected future cash flows), the equipment is impaired.

The impairment loss is equal to $220,000 ($800,000 carrying value – $580,000 fair value). Thus, the carrying value of the equipment on the balance sheet is reduced to $580,000 and a $220,000 impairment loss is recognized in the income statement.

Impairment of Intangible Assets

Under U.S. GAAP, impairment accounting for finite-lived intangible assets is virtually the same as for tangible assets. They are tested for impairment when events or circumstances indicate the firm may not be able to recover the carrying value. For example, there may have been an adverse change as a result of litigation or a significant change in business conditions.

Goodwill and other infinite-lived intangible assets are not amortized. Instead, they are tested for impairment at least annually. Impairment occurs when the carrying value exceeds the fair value. However, measuring the fair value of goodwill is complicated by the fact that goodwill cannot be separated from the business. Because of its inseparability, goodwill is valued at the reporting unit level.

Goodwill impairment also potentially involves two steps. In the first step, if the carrying value of the reporting unit (including the goodwill) exceeds the fair value of the reporting unit, an impairment exists. Once it is determined the goodwill is impaired, the loss is measured as the difference between the carrying value of the goodwill and the *implied* fair value of the goodwill.

Professor's Note: Notice the impairment test for goodwill is based on the decline in value of the reporting unit, while the impairment loss is recorded as a decline in value of goodwill.

The implied fair value of goodwill is calculated in the same manner as goodwill at the acquisition date. That is, the fair value of the reporting unit is allocated to the identifiable assets and liabilities as if they were acquired on the impairment measurement date. Any excess is considered the implied fair value of goodwill. The following example illustrates the process.

Example: Impairment of goodwill

Last year, Parent Company acquired Sub Company for $1,000,000. On the date of acquisition, the fair value of Sub's net assets was $800,000. Thus, Parent reported acquisition goodwill of $200,000 ($1,000,000 purchase price – $800,000 fair value of Sub's net assets).

At the end of this year, the fair value of Sub is $950,000 and the fair value of Sub's net assets is $775,000. Assuming the carrying value of Sub is $980,000, determine whether goodwill is impaired and calculate the loss if applicable.

Answer:

Since the carrying value of Sub exceeds the fair value of Sub ($980,000 carrying value > $950,000 fair value), an impairment exists.

To measure the impairment loss, the implied goodwill must be compared to the carrying value of the goodwill. At the impairment measurement date, the implied value of goodwill is $175,000 ($950,000 fair value of Sub – $775,000 fair value of Sub's net assets). Since the carrying value of goodwill exceeds the implied value of goodwill, an impairment loss of $25,000 is recognized ($200,000 goodwill carrying value – $175,000 implied goodwill), thereby reducing goodwill to $175,000.

Testing for and recognizing impairment losses are similar under IFRS, except that testing and computation of any asset impairment is done in a single step. The carrying value of the asset is compared to the "recoverable amount" of the asset and if the recoverable amount is less than the carrying value, the difference is recorded as an asset impairment. The recoverable amount is the amount the asset would bring in a sale minus selling costs (net selling price) or fair value (discounted value of expected future cash flows and disposal proceeds at the end of its useful life), if the former cannot be determined. Under IFRS, goodwill impairment is tested and computed in the same way as for a tangible asset and the calculation is made at the level of a cash generating unit.

Long-lived assets held for sale

When a firm decides to sell a long-lived asset, the asset is no longer depreciated or amortized and the asset is immediately tested for impairment. If the asset's carrying value exceeds its fair value less the costs to sell, the asset is considered impaired and the difference is recognized as a loss.

Reversing an Impairment Loss

Once an impaired asset is written down, its value may rise in a subsequent period. Under U.S. GAAP, recoveries are allowed for assets held for sale, but not for assets held for use or goodwill.

Asset held for sale. If an impairment loss occurs, subsequent recoveries are allowed. Recoveries are reported as a component of continuing operations.

Assets held for use. When an asset that is held for use is impaired, the reduced carrying value of the asset becomes its new cost basis for calculating future depreciation or amortization. No recoveries are permitted.

Under IFRS, subsequent recoveries are allowed for both assets held for use and assets held for sale.

Impact of Impairment on Financial Statement and Ratios

Impairment reduces the carrying value of the asset on the balance sheet and is recognized as a loss in the income statement. Thus, an impairment will result in lower assets and lower equity (retained earnings).

In the year of impairment, ROA and ROE will decrease since earnings are lower. In subsequent periods, ROA and ROE will increase due to the higher earnings and lower assets and equity. Asset turnover will also increase because of the lower assets.

Just like depreciation, an impairment loss has no impact on cash flow. The cash flow occurred when the firm paid for the asset. Also, there are no tax savings from an impairment in asset value until the asset is sold or otherwise disposed of. This results in a decrease in deferred tax liabilities.

Analysis of Impairments

An impairment loss is an indication the firm has not recognized enough depreciation or amortization expense, thereby overstating earnings.

Because of the judgment involved in forecasting an asset's future cash flows, management has considerable discretion when recognizing an impairment loss. Thus, management can easily manipulate earnings upward or downward. For example, the firm may overstate an impairment loss in the current period in order to increase earnings in the future. Future earnings are higher since depreciation (or amortization) expense on the impaired asset is lower. Overstating a loss sometimes occurs during recession or when a firm hires a new management team. Alternatively, a firm may overstate its current period earnings by understating or even ignoring an impairment loss.

LOS 36.j: Calculate and describe both the initial and long-lived effects of asset revaluations on financial ratios.

Under U.S. GAAP, long-lived assets are reported on the balance sheet at depreciated cost (original cost minus accumulated depreciation) less any impairment losses. Increasing the carrying value is generally prohibited. One exception relates to long-lived assets held for sale. In this case, prior impairment losses can be reversed.

Likewise, firms that report under IFRS can report long-lived assets at depreciated cost. Alternatively, IFRS firms can choose to report long-lived assets at fair value. If the firm revalues an asset upward, a gain is recognized in the income statement to the extent that it reverses a previously recognized loss. Otherwise, the gain is reported as a direct adjustment to equity (other comprehensive income).

Revaluing an asset's value upward will result in:

- Higher total assets and higher stockholders' equity.
- Lower leverage ratios as measured by the debt ratio and the debt-to-equity ratio (higher denominators).
- Higher earnings in the period the revaluation occurs.
- Higher depreciation expense and thus lower profitability in periods after revaluation.
- Lower ROA and ROE in periods after revaluation (lower numerators and higher denominators). However, the increase in the asset value is likely the result of higher operating capacity. Higher capacity should result in higher revenues and, thus, higher earnings.

The analyst should be interested in the origin of the appraisal that supports the revaluation. Appraisals from independent sources are usually more reliable than appraisals from management.

KEY CONCEPTS

LOS 36.a

When a firm makes an expenditure, it can either capitalize the cost as an asset on the balance sheet or expense the cost in the income statement, depending on the nature of the expenditure.

An expenditure that is capitalized is classified as an investing cash flow. An operating expenditure that is not capitalized is classified as an operating cash flow.

Interest that accrues on amounts invested to construct an asset must be capitalized. Once construction interest is capitalized as part of the cost of the constructed asset, the interest is reported in the income statement as depreciation expense or COGS.

LOS 36.b

Financial statement effects of capitalizing vs. expensing:

	Capitalizing	*Expensing*
Total assets	Higher	Lower
Stockholders' equity	Higher	Lower
Income variability	Lower	Higher
Net income (first year)	Higher	Lower
Net income (subsequent years)	Lower	Higher
Cash flow from operations	Higher	Lower
Cash flow from investing	Lower	Higher
Debt ratio & Debt-to-equity ratio	Lower	Higher
Interest coverage ratio (first year)	Higher	Lower
Interest coverage ratio (subsequent years)	Lower	Higher

LOS 36.c

Under U.S. GAAP, research and development costs are expensed as incurred. Under IFRS, research costs are expensed as incurred and development costs are capitalized.

Costs incurred to develop software for sale to others are expensed as incurred until the product's technological feasibility has been established. Once technological feasibility has been established, subsequent costs are capitalized.

LOS 36.d

Depreciation methods:
- Straight-line—equal amount of expense each period.
- Accelerated (declining balance)—greater depreciation expense in the early years and less depreciation expense and greater taxes in the later years of an asset's life.
- Units-of-production—expense based on usage rather than time.

In the early years of an asset's life, accelerated depreciation will result in higher depreciation expense, lower net income, and lower ROA and ROE as compared to straight-line depreciation. Cash flow is the same assuming tax depreciation is unaffected by the choice of method for financial reporting.

LOS 36.e

An estimate of the average age of fixed assets can be compared to their average useful life to estimate the timing of a company's future capital expenditures.

- Average age (in years) = Accumulated depreciation / annual depreciation expense
- Average depreciable life = Ending gross investment / annual depreciation expense
- Remaining useful life = Ending net investment / annual depreciation expense

LOS 36.f

Amortization of an intangible asset's cost is the same process as depreciating the cost of a tangible asset. Finite-lived intangible assets are amortized over their useful lives. Infinite-lived intangible asset values are not amortized but are tested for impairment at least annually.

LOS 36.g

The present value of an asset retirement obligation is added to both assets and liabilities. The firm depreciates the asset and recognizes accretion expense on the liability each period.

For analytical purposes, the ARO liability (less any amounts dedicated to asset retirement costs and any expected tax savings) should be treated as debt and the accretion expense should be treated as interest expense. Adjusting for an ARO will result in lower profitability, a higher debt-to-equity ratio, and a lower interest coverage ratio.

LOS 36.h

When a long-lived asset is *sold*, the difference between the sale proceeds and the carrying (book) value of the asset is reported as a gain or loss and included in income from continuing operations. Gain or loss from the sale of a separable "component" of a firm is reported as a discontinued operation, net of tax.

When a long-lived asset is *abandoned*, the carrying (book) value is removed from the balance sheet and a loss is recognized in that amount.

If a long-lived asset is *exchanged* for another asset, gain or loss is computed by comparing the book value of the old asset with fair value of the new asset.

For analytical and forecasting purposes, gains and losses from asset sales or disposals should be excluded as they are typically not a recurring source of income or loss.

LOS 36.i

The recognition of asset impairments involves considerable management discretion. An asset is impaired when its carrying value exceeds the sum of its estimated future cash flows. The amount of an impairment loss is the difference between the carrying value and the discounted present value of its estimated future cash flows or its market value, if known.

Goodwill is impaired if the carrying value of the reporting unit (including goodwill) exceeds the fair value of the reporting unit. The amount of the impairment loss recognized is the difference between the balance sheet value of the goodwill and the implied fair value of the goodwill (carrying value of the unit minus fair value).

Under U.S. GAAP, subsequent recoveries are permitted for assets held for sale but not for assets held for use. Under IFRS, subsequent recoveries are allowed for both.

In the year an impairment charge is taken, ROA and ROE will decrease since earnings will decrease by a greater proportion than assets or equity. In subsequent periods, ROA and ROE will be greater as a result of the impairment charge as assets and equity have been reduced by the charge. Impairments have no impact on cash flow.

LOS 36.j
Upward revaluation of assets is generally prohibited under U.S. GAAP, but is permitted under IFRS.

An upward revaluation of assets will increase assets and stockholders' equity. It will decrease leverage ratios and increase profitability in the period the revaluation occurs. In subsequent periods, ROA and ROE are lower than without the revaluation, as assets and equity are increased.

CONCEPT CHECKERS

1. Interest costs incurred for construction of an asset for a firm's own use are:
   A. expensed as incurred.
   B. capitalized and then, once construction is completed, allocated to the income statement over the life of the constructed asset.
   C. capitalized and then, once construction is completed, allocated to the income statement over the life of the loan.

2. For analysis of firms, the amount of capitalized interest should be:
   A. added to fixed assets.
   B. added to cash flow from investing activities.
   C. subtracted from interest expense.

3. Firm A expenses costs while Firm B capitalizes them. All other things being equal, which of the following *best* describes the debt ratios of Firm A and Firm B?
   A. They will be equal.
   B. Firm B's will be higher.
   C. Firm A's will be higher.

4. Which of the following statements is *least accurate*? All other things being equal, firms that capitalize costs will:
   A. show smoother reported income than expensing firms.
   B. have higher operating cash flow and lower investment cash flow than expensing firms.
   C. have lower profitability ratios in the year costs are capitalized, compared to expensing firms.

5. Capitalizing construction interest costs leads to:
   A. a higher debt ratio.
   B. higher future depreciation expense.
   C. higher reported income after the first year.

6. U.S. generally accepted accounting principles (GAAP) require that costs incurred in establishing the technological feasibility of software be:
   A. capitalized and allocated over the estimated life of the software.
   B. expensed in the period incurred.
   C. capitalized if the firm intends to use the software internally.

7. Which of the following statements about research and development expenditures is *most accurate*?
   A. According to IFRS, research costs are expensed as incurred while development costs are capitalized.
   B. The costs associated with the creation of a brand name within a company are capitalized.
   C. According to U.S. GAAP, once technological feasibility is reached, development costs for software to be sold must be expensed as incurred.

8.   In the early years of an asset's life, compared to a firm using straight-line depreciation, a firm using the double-declining balance depreciation method will report:
     A. lower depreciation expense.
     B. higher asset turnover.
     C. higher retained earnings.

9.   Which of the following statements is *least likely* correct? Assuming the firm continues to invest in new assets, firms that choose accelerated depreciation over straight-line depreciation will tend to have lower:
     A. depreciation expense.
     B. net income.
     C. return on assets.

Use the following data to answer Questions 10 through 12.

Gross plant and equipment $1,500,000
Depreciation expense $225,000
Accumulated depreciation $675,000
The firm uses straight-line depreciation.

10. The average age of the plant and equipment is:
     A. 2.7 years.
     B. 3.0 years.
     C. 3.7 years.

11. The average depreciable life of the plant and equipment is:
     A. 3.0 years.
     B. 3.7 years.
     C. 6.7 years.

12. The remaining useful life of the plant and equipment is:
     A. 3.0 years.
     B. 3.7 years.
     C. 6.7 years.

13. Which of the following statements about intangible assets is *least accurate*?
     A. Intangible assets with unlimited lives are tested for impairment at least annually.
     B. The allocation of an intangible asset's cost to the income statement should match the benefits used up during the period.
     C. The income statement allocation of the cost of a finite-lived intangible asset is known as accretion expense.

14. Which of the following statements about an asset retirement obligation (ARO) is *least likely* correct?
     A. An ARO increases depreciation expense.
     B. Operating cash flow is lower as a result of ARO expense allocations in the income statement.
     C. The periodic accretion expense should be treated as interest expense for analytical purposes.

15.   A firm recently recognized a $15,000 loss on the sale of machinery used in its manufacturing operation. The original cost of the machinery was $100,000 and the accumulated depreciation at the date of sale was $60,000. What amount did the firm receive from the sale?
       A. $25,000.
       B. $45,000.
       C. $85,000.

16.   An asset is impaired when:
       A. the firm cannot fully recover the carrying amount of the asset through operations.
       B. accumulated depreciation plus salvage value exceeds acquisition cost.
       C. the present value of future cash flows from an asset exceeds its carrying amount.

17.   Which of the following accounts is *least likely* to be affected by recognizing an asset impairment?
       A. Cash.
       B. Fixed assets.
       C. Stockholders' equity.

18.   The fair value of equipment used by Slayton Corporation exceeds its carrying value. Which of the following statements is *least accurate*?
       A. Under IFRS, Slayton can choose to report the equipment at fair value.
       B. Under U.S. GAAP, Slayton can choose to report the equipment at fair value.
       C. Under IFRS, Slayton can choose to report the asset at its carrying value.

ANSWERS – CONCEPT CHECKERS

1. **B** Interest costs from construction are capitalized and allocated over the life of the asset.

2. **B** For analytical purposes, the amount of cash outflow for capitalized interest should be subtracted from operating cash flow and added to investing cash flow.

3. **C** Firm A, the expensing firm, will have a lower level of assets, making its debt ratio (total debt / total assets) higher.

4. **C** Firms that capitalize costs will show higher profitability ratios in the year of expenditure since the cost will be spread out over time.

5. **B** The higher future depreciation expense results from the allocation of the capitalized interest over the asset's life.

6. **B** Under U.S. GAAP, costs to establish technological feasibility of software must be expensed.

7. **A** According to IFRS, research costs are expensed while development costs are capitalized. Under U.S. GAAP, both research and development costs are expensed as incurred. Costs incurred to create intangible assets (other than R&D and software) are expensed. U.S. GAAP requires software development costs to be capitalized after feasability has been established.

8. **B** In the early years, accelerated depreciation will result in higher depreciation expense; thus, lower retained earnings. Assets are lower with accelerated depreciation; thus, asset turnover (sales / assets) is higher.

9. **A** A firm that continues to invest in new assets will have higher depreciation expense due to the use of accelerated methods.

10. **B** Average age $= \dfrac{\text{accumulated depreciation}}{\text{depreciation expense}} = \dfrac{675,000}{225,000} = 3.0$ years

11. **C** Average depreciable life $= \dfrac{\text{ending gross investment}}{\text{depreciation expense}} = \dfrac{1,500,000}{225,000} = 6.7$ years

12. **B** Remaining useful life $= \dfrac{\text{ending net investment}}{\text{depreciation expense}} = \dfrac{1,500,000 - 675,000}{225,000} = 3.7$ years

13. **C** The allocation of an intangible asset is known as amortization expense.

14. **B** Cash flow is not affected by the expense allocations of an ARO. Both depreciation expense and accretion expense are noncash charges.

15. **A** Gain or loss is equal to the sale proceeds minus the carrying value (cost minus accumulated depreciation) at the time of sale. Given the loss of $15,000 and carrying value of $40,000 ($100,000 – $60,000), we can solve for the proceeds of $25,000 (–15,000 +40,000).

16. **A** An asset is impaired when the firm cannot recover its carrying value. Recoverability is tested based on undiscounted future cash flows.

17. **A** Cash is not affected when an impairment loss is recognized.

18. **B**   Firms following IFRS can choose to report long-lived assets at fair value or cost less accumulated depreciation. Firms following U.S. GAAP are prohibited from revaluing equipment up to fair value.

INCOME TAXES

EXAM FOCUS

In many countries, financial reporting standards and tax reporting standards differ. Candidates should be aware of the terminology that relates to each set of standards, notably taxes payable, which are the taxes actually due to the government; and income tax expense, which is reported on the income statement and reflects taxes payable plus any deferred income tax expense. The timing of revenue and expense recognition in the income statement and the tax return may lead to the creation of deferred tax liabilities, which the company may have to pay in the future, or deferred tax assets, which may provide benefits in the future. For the exam, you should know that some differences between taxable and pretax income are temporary, while some are permanent and will never reverse. Be prepared to calculate taxes payable, tax expense, deferred tax liabilities and assets, and be able to make the necessary adjustments for analytical purposes.

LOS 37.a: Explain the differences between accounting profit and taxable income, and define key terms including deferred tax assets, deferred tax liabilities, valuation allowance, taxes payable, and income tax expense.

Financial accounting standards (IFRS and U.S. GAAP) are often different than income tax laws and regulations. As a result, the amount of income tax expense recognized in the income statement may differ from the actual taxes owed to the taxing authorities.

Tax Return Terminology

- **Taxable income.** Income subject to tax based on the tax return.
- **Taxes payable.** The tax liability on the balance sheet caused by *taxable income*. This is also known as current tax expense, but do not confuse this with *income tax expense* (see below).
- **Income tax paid.** The actual cash flow for income taxes including payments or refunds from other years.
- **Tax loss carryforward.** A current or past loss that can be used to reduce taxable income (thus, taxes payable) in the future. Can result in a deferred tax asset.
- **Tax base.** Net amount of an asset or liability used for tax reporting purposes.

Financial Reporting Terminology

- **Accounting profit.** Pretax financial income based on financial accounting standards. Also known as "income before tax" and "earnings before tax."

- **Income tax expense.** Expense recognized in the income statement that includes taxes payable and *changes* in deferred tax assets and liabilities (DTA and DTL). The income tax expense equation is:

$$\text{Income tax expense} = \text{taxes payable} + \Delta\text{DTL} - \Delta\text{DTA}$$

- **Deferred tax liabilities.** Balance sheet amounts that result from an excess of income tax expense over taxes payable that are expected to result in future cash outflows.
- **Deferred tax assets.** Balance sheet amounts that result from an excess of taxes payable over income tax expense that are expected to be recovered from future operations. Can also result from tax loss carryforwards.
- **Valuation allowance.** Reduction of deferred tax assets based on the likelihood the assets will not be realized.
- **Carrying value.** Net balance sheet value of an asset or liability.
- **Permanent difference.** A difference between taxable income (tax return) and pretax income (income statement) that will not reverse in the future.
- **Temporary difference.** A difference between the tax base and the carrying value of an asset or liability that will result in either taxable amounts or deductible amounts in the future. Several examples of how temporary differences arise are presented later in this review.

LOS 37.b: Explain how deferred tax liabilities and assets are created and the factors that determine how a company's deferred tax liabilities and assets should be treated for the purposes of financial analysis.

Differences between the treatment of an accounting item for tax reporting and for financial reporting can occur when:

- The timing of revenue and expense recognition in the income statement and the tax return differ.
- Certain revenues and expenses are recognized in the income statement but never on the tax return or vice-versa.
- Assets and/or liabilities have different carrying amounts and tax bases.
- Gain or loss recognition in the income statement differs from the tax return.
- Tax losses from prior periods may offset future taxable income.
- Financial statement adjustments may not affect the tax return or may be recognized in different periods.

Deferred Tax Liabilities

A **deferred tax liability** is created when income tax expense (income statement) is greater than taxes payable (tax return) due to temporary differences. Deferred tax liabilities occur when:

- Revenues (or gains) are recognized in the income statement before they are included on the tax return due to temporary differences.
- Expenses (or losses) are tax deductible before they are recognized in the income statement.

Deferred tax liabilities are expected to reverse (i.e., they are caused by temporary differences) and result in future cash outflows when the taxes are paid.

DTL =
income tax
expense >
taxes payable

depr methods

The most common way that deferred tax liabilities are created is when different depreciation methods are used on the tax return and the income statement.

Deferred Tax Assets

A **deferred tax asset** is created when taxes payable (tax return) are greater than income tax expense (income statement) due to temporary differences. Deferred tax assets occur when:

DTA = income tax expense < tax payable

- Revenues (or gains) are taxable before they are recognized in the income statement.
- Expenses (or losses) are recognized in the income statement before they are tax deductible.
- Tax loss carryforwards are available to reduce future taxable income.

Similar to deferred tax liabilities, deferred tax assets are expected to reverse through future operations. However, deferred tax assets are expected to provide future tax savings, while deferred tax liabilities are expected to result in future cash outflows.

Post-employment benefits, warranty expenses, and *tax loss carryforwards* are typical causes of deferred tax assets.

Treatment for Analytical Purposes

If deferred tax liabilities are expected to reverse in the future, they are best classified by an analyst as liabilities. If, however, they are not expected to reverse in the future, they are best classified as equity (DTL decreased and equity increased by the same amount). The key question is, "when or will the total deferred tax liability be reversed in the future?" In practice, the treatment of deferred taxes for analytical purposes varies. An analyst must decide on the appropriate treatment on a case-by-case basis.

Permanent DTL straight to equity (increases)

LOS 37.c: Determine the tax base of a company's assets and liabilities.

Tax Base of Assets

An asset's **tax base** is the amount that will be deducted (expensed) on the tax return in the future as the economic benefits of the asset are realized. If the economic benefit is not taxable, the tax base and the **carrying value** of the asset will be the same. The carrying value is the value of the asset reported on the financial statements, net of depreciation and amortization.

tax exempt. tax base = carrying value (net depr t amort)

Following are a few examples of calculating the tax bases of various assets.

Depreciable equipment. The cost of equipment is $100,000. In the income statement, depreciation expense of $10,000 is recognized each year for 10 years. On the tax return, the asset is depreciated at $20,000 per year for 5 years.

At the end of the first year, the tax base is $80,000 ($100,000 cost − $20,000 accumulated tax depreciation) and the carrying value is $90,000 ($100,000 cost − $10,000 accumulated financial depreciation).

Research and development. At the beginning of this year, $75,000 of R&D was expensed in the income statement. On the tax return, the R&D was capitalized and is amortized on a straight-line basis over 3 years.

At the end of the first year, the tax base is $50,000 ($75,000 cost − $25,000 accumulated tax amortization) and the asset has no carrying value (does not appear on the balance sheet) because the entire cost was expensed.

Accounts receivable. Gross receivables totaling $20,000 are outstanding at year-end. Because collection is uncertain, the firm recognizes bad debt expense of $1,500 in the income statement. For tax purposes, bad debt expense cannot be deducted until the receivables are deemed worthless.

At the end of the year, the tax base of the receivables is $20,000 since no bad debt expense has been deducted on the tax return. The carrying value is $18,500 ($20,000 − $1,500 bad debt expense).

Tax Base of Liabilities

A liability's tax base is the carrying value of the liability minus any amounts that will be deductible on the tax return in the future. The tax base of revenue received in advance is the carrying value minus the amount of revenue that will *not* be taxed in the future.

Following are a few examples of calculating the tax bases of various liabilities:

Customer advance. At year-end, $10,000 was received from a customer for goods that will be shipped next year. On the tax return, revenue received in advance is taxable when collected.

The carrying value of the liability is $10,000. The carrying value will be reduced when the goods are shipped next year. For revenue received in advance, the tax base is equal to the carrying value minus any amounts that will *not* be taxed in the future. Since the customer advance has already been taxed, $10,000 will not be taxed in the future. Thus, the customer advance liability has a tax base of zero ($10,000 carrying value − $10,000 revenue not taxed in the future).

Warranty liability. At year-end, a firm estimates that $5,000 of warranty expense will be required on goods already sold. On the tax return, warranty expense is not deductible until the warranty work is actually performed. The warranty work will be performed next year.

The carrying value of the warranty liability is $5,000. The tax base is equal to the carrying value minus the amount deductible in the future. Thus, the warranty liability has a tax base of zero ($5,000 carrying value − $5,000 warranty expense deductible in the future).

Note payable. The firm has an outstanding promissory note with a principal balance of $30,000. Interest accrues at 10% and is paid at the end of each quarter.

The promissory note is treated the same way on the tax return and in the financial statements. Thus, the carrying value and the tax base are both $30,000. Interest paid is included in both pre-tax income on the income statement and in taxable income on the tax return.

LOS 37.d: <u>Calculate</u> income tax expense, income taxes payable, deferred tax assets and <u>deferred tax</u> liabilities, and calculate and interpret the adjustment to the financial statements related to a change in the income tax rate.

 Professor's Note: The effects of changing tax rates on deferred tax assets and liabilities are explained in the next LOS.

Example: Deferred tax liabilities

Assume the original cost of an asset is $600,000. The asset has a 3-year life and no salvage value is expected. For tax purposes, the asset is depreciated using an accelerated depreciation method with tax return depreciation of $300,000 in Year 1, $200,000 in Year 2, and $100,000 in Year 3. The firm recognizes straight-line (SL) depreciation expense of $200,000 each year in its income statements. Earnings before interest, taxes, depreciation, and amortization (EBITDA) is $500,000 each year. The firm's tax rate is 40%. Calculate the firm's income tax expense, taxes payable, and deferred tax liability for each year of the asset's life.

Answer:

The tables below illustrate the calculation of taxes payable reported on the tax return and income tax expense reported in the income statement.

Tax Return (40% Tax Rate, Accelerated Depreciation)

	Year 1	Year 2	Year 3	Total 1-3
EBITDA	$500,000	$500,000	$500,000	$1,500,000
Depreciation	$300,000	$200,000	$100,000	$600,000
Taxable income	$200,000	$300,000	$400,000	$900,000
Tax Rate	× 0.40	× 0.40	× 0.40	× 0.40
Tax Payable	$80,000	$120,000	$160,000	$360,000

Income Statement (40% Tax Rate, SL Depreciation)

	Year 1	Year 2	Year 3	Total 1-3
EBITDA	$500,000	$500,000	$500,000	$1,500,000
Depreciation	$200,000	$200,000	$200,000	$600,000
Pre-Tax Income	$300,000	$300,000	$300,000	$900,000
Tax Rate	× 0.40	× 0.40	× 0.40	× 0.40
Income Tax Expense	$120,000	$120,000	$120,000	$360,000

In year 1, the firm recognizes $120,000 of income tax expense on the income statement but taxes payable (tax return) are only $80,000. So, income tax expense is *initially* higher than taxes payable. The $40,000 difference is deferred to a future period by using an accelerated depreciation method for tax purposes. The $40,000 is reported on the balance sheet by creating a DTL.

The tax base and the carrying value of the asset are used to calculate the *balance* of the DTL. At the end of year 1, the carrying value of the asset is $400,000 and the tax base of the asset is $300,000. By multiplying the $100,000 difference by the 40% tax rate, we get the *balance* of the DTL of $40,000.

We can reconcile income tax expense and taxes payable with the *change* in the DTL. In this example, the DTL increased $40,000 (from zero to $40,000) during year 1. Thus, income tax expense in year 1 is $120,000 ($80,000 taxes payable + $40,000 *change* in the DTL).

In year 2, depreciation expense is the same on the tax return and the income statement. Thus, taxable income is equal to pretax income and there is no change in the DTL. Income tax expense in year 2 is $120,000 ($120,000 taxes payable + $0 *change* in the DTL).

In year 3, the firm recognizes income tax expense of $120,000 on the income statement but $160,000 in taxes payable (tax return). The $40,000 deferred tax liability recognized at the end of year 1 has reversed as a result of lower depreciation expense using the accelerated method on the tax return. In year 3, income tax expense is $120,000 [$160,000 taxes payable + (–$40,000 *change* in DTL)].

Note that over the useful life of the asset, total depreciation, total taxable (and pretax) income, and total taxes payable (and income tax expense) are the same on the financial statements and the tax return. Also, at the end of year 3, both the tax base and the carrying value of the asset are equal to zero. By using accelerated depreciation for tax purposes, the firm *deferred* $40,000 of taxes from year 1 to year 3.

Example: Deferred tax assets

Consider warranty guarantees and associated expenses. Pretax income (financial reporting) includes an accrual for warranty expense, but warranty cost is not deductible for taxable income until the firm has made actual expenditures to meet warranty claims. Suppose:

- A firm has sales of $5,000 for each of two years.
- The firm estimates that warranty expense will be 2% of annual sales ($100).
- The actual expenditure of $200 to meet all warranty claims was not made until the second year.
- Assume a tax rate of 40%.

Calculate the firm's income tax expense, taxes payable, and deferred tax assets for Year 1 and Year 2.

Answer:

For tax reporting, taxable income and taxes payable for two years are:

Tax Reporting—Warranty Expense

	Year 1	Year 2
Revenue	$5,000	$5,000
Warranty expense	0	200
Taxable income	$5,000	$4,800
Taxes payable	2,000	1,920
Net income	$3,000	$2,880

For financial reporting, pretax income and tax expense are:

Financial Reporting—Warranty Expense

	Year 1	Year 2
Revenue	$5,000	$5,000
Warranty expense	100	100
Pretax Income	$4,900	$4,900
Tax expense	1,960	1,960
Net Income	$2,940	$2,940

(handwritten margin notes)

Taxes payable
– Tax expense
─────────
DTA balance

carrying val
– Tax base
─────────
* tax rate
= DTA

In year 1, the firm reports $1,960 of tax expense in the income statement, but $2,000 of taxes payable are reported on the tax return. In this example, taxes payable are *initially* higher than tax expense and the $40 difference is reported on the balance sheet by creating a DTA.

The tax base and the carrying value of the warranty liability are used to calculate the *balance* of the DTA. At the end of year 1, the carrying value of the warranty liability is $100 (the warranty expense has been recognized in the income statement but it has not been paid) and the tax base of the liability is $0 (the warranty expense has not been recognized on the tax return). By multiplying the $100 difference by the 40% tax rate, we get the *balance* of the DTA of $40 [($100 carrying value – $0 tax base) × 40%].

We can reconcile income tax expense and taxes payable with the *change* in the DTA. In this example, the DTA increased $40 (from zero to $40) during year 1. Thus, income tax expense in year 1 is $1,960 ($2,000 taxes payable – $40 *change* in the DTA).

In year 2, the firm recognizes $1,960 of tax expense in the income statement but only $1,920 is reported on the tax return (taxes payable). The $40 deferred tax asset recognized at the end of year 1 has reversed as a result of the warranty expense recognition on the tax return. So, in year 2, income tax expense is $1,960 [$1,920 taxes payable + (–$40 *change* in DTA)].

Professor's Note: To summarize, if taxable income (on the tax return) is less than pretax income (on the income statement) and the difference is expected to reverse in future years, a deferred tax liability is created. If taxable income is greater than pretax income and the difference is expected to reverse in future years, a deferred tax asset is created.

LOS 37.e: Evaluate the impact of tax rate changes on a company's financial statements and ratios.

(handwritten margin notes)

↑ in tax rate:
 ↑ DTA
  ↑ DTL

Decrease in
tax rate:
 ↓ DTA
 ↓ DTL

When the income tax rate changes, deferred tax assets and liabilities are adjusted to reflect the new rate. The adjustment can also affect income tax expense.

An increase in the tax rate will increase both deferred tax liabilities and deferred tax assets. A decrease in the tax rate will decrease both deferred tax liabilities and deferred tax assets.

DTL and DTA values on the balance sheet must be changed because the new tax rate is the rate expected to be in force when the associated reversals occur. If there is an increase (decrease) in the tax rate, when previously deferred income is recognized for tax, the tax due will be higher (lower), and when expense items previously reported in the financial statements are recognized for tax, the benefit will be greater (less).

Changes in the balance sheet values of DTLs and DTAs to account for a change in the tax rate will affect income tax expense in the current period.

income tax expense = taxes payable + ΔDTL – ΔDTA

If tax rates increase, the increase in the DTL is added to taxes payable and the increase in the DTA is subtracted from taxes payable to arrive at income tax expense.

If tax rates decrease, the decrease in the DTL would result in lower income tax expense and the decrease in the DTA would result in higher income tax expense. In the case of the DTL we are adding a negative change, and in the case of the DTA we are subtracting a negative change.

The following example illustrates the effects of a change in the tax rate.

Example: Accounting effects of a change in a firm's tax rate

A firm owns equipment with a carrying value of $200,000 and a tax base of $160,000 at year-end. The tax rate is 40%. In this case, the firm will report a DTL of $16,000 [($200,000 carrying value – $160,000 tax base) × 40%]. The firm also has a DTA of $10,000 that was created by bad debt that was recognized as an expense in the income statement but has not yet been deducted on the tax return. The bad debt expense created a DTA of $4,000 [($10,000 tax base– $0 carrying value) × 40%]. Calculate the effect on the firm's income tax expense if the tax rate decreases to 30%.

Answer:

As a result of the decrease in tax rate, the balance of the DTL is reduced to $12,000 [($200,000 carrying value – $160,000 tax base) × 30%]. Thus, due to the lower tax rate, the change in the DTL is –$4,000 ($16,000 reported DTL – $12,000 adjusted DTL).

The balance of the DTA is reduced to $3,000 [$10,000 tax base – $0 carrying value) × 30%]. Thus, due to the lower tax rate, the DTA decreases by $1,000 ($4,000 reported DTA – $3,000 adjusted DTA).

Using the income tax equation, we can see that income tax expense decreases by $3,000 (income tax expense = taxable income + ΔDTL – ΔDTA).

-4,000 – 1000
-3,000 decrease

LOS 37.f: Distinguish between temporary and permanent items in pretax financial income and taxable income.

A **permanent difference** is a difference between taxable income and pretax income that will not reverse in the future. Permanent differences do not create deferred tax assets or deferred tax liabilities. Permanent differences can be caused by revenue that is not taxable, expenses that are not deductible, or tax credits that result in a direct reduction of taxes.

Permanent differences will cause the firm's **effective tax rate** to differ from the **statutory tax rate**. The statutory rate is the tax rate of the jurisdiction where the firm operates. The effective tax rate is derived from the income statement.

$$\text{effective tax rate} = \frac{\text{income tax expense}}{\text{pretax income}}$$

The statutory rate and effective rate may also differ if the firm is operating in more than one tax jurisdiction.

A **temporary difference** refers to a difference between the tax base and the carrying value of an asset or liability that will result in taxable amounts or deductible amounts in the future. If the temporary difference is expected to reverse in the future and the balance sheet item is expected to provide future economic benefits, a DTA or DTL is created.

Temporary differences can result in either expected future taxable income or expected future tax deductions.

Example: Temporary and permanent differences between taxes payable and income tax expense

Using the following table and the examples of determining the tax base of assets and liabilities presented earlier, identify the type of difference (taxable temporary, deductible temporary, or permanent), and determine if the difference creates a DTA or a DTL.

	Tax Base	Carrying Value	Type of Difference	Result
Assets				
Depreciable equipment	$80,000 <	$90,000	Temporary	DTL
Research and development	50,000 >	0	Temporary	DTA
Accounts receivable	20,000 >	18,500	Temporary	DTA
Municipal bond interest	5,000	5,000	Permanent	
Liabilities				
Customer advance	$0 <	$10,000	Temporary	DTL
Warranty liability	0 <	5,000	Temporary	DTL
Officers' life insurance	0	0	Perm	
Note payable	30,000	30,000		
Interest paid	0	0		

Answer:

Depreciable equipment. Accelerating depreciation expense on the tax return will result in a taxable temporary difference. Taxable income will be higher in the future because accelerated depreciation will be lower when the reversal occurs. Since the carrying value of the asset > the tax base, a DTL is created.

Research and development. Capitalized R&D for tax purposes will result in a deductible temporary difference as taxable income will be lower in the future when the reversal occurs. Since the tax base of the asset > the carrying value, a DTA is created.

Accounts receivable. Delaying bad debt expense for tax purposes will result in a deductible temporary difference as taxable income will be lower in the future when the reversal occurs. Since the tax base of the asset > carrying value, a DTA is created.

Municipal bond interest. Since municipal bond interest is typically not taxable, it results in a permanent difference. No deferred taxes are recognized.

Customer advance. Recognizing the customer advance on the tax return will result in a deductible temporary difference as COGS is included in taxable income in the future when the goods are delivered. Since the carrying value of the liability > the tax base, a DTA is created.

Warranty liability. Delaying warranty expense for tax purposes will result in a deductible temporary difference as taxable income will be lower in the future when the reversal occurs. Since the carrying value of the liability > the tax base, a DTA is created.

Officers' life insurance. Since officers' life insurance is not tax deductible, it results in a permanent difference. No deferred taxes are recognized.

Note payable and interest paid. No temporary differences result from the note payable or the interest paid on the note. No deferred taxes are recognized.

Temporary differences leading to DTLs can arise from an investment in another firm (e.g., subsidiaries, affiliates, branches, and joint ventures) when the parent company recognizes earnings from the investment before dividends are received. However, if the parent company can control the timing of the future reversal and it is probable the temporary difference will not reverse, no DTL is reported.

A temporary difference from an investment will result in a DTA only if the temporary difference is expected to reverse in the future and sufficient taxable profits are expected to exist when the reversal occurs.

LOS 37.g: Discuss the implications of a valuation allowance for deferred tax assets (i.e., when it is required, what impact it has on financial statements, and how it might affect an analyst's view of a company).

Although deferred taxes are created from temporary differences that are expected to reverse in the future, neither deferred tax assets nor deferred tax liabilities are carried on the balance sheet at their discounted present value. However, deferred tax assets are assessed at each balance sheet date to determine the likelihood of sufficient future taxable income to recover the tax assets. Without future taxable income, a DTA is worthless.

According to U.S. GAAP, if it is more likely than not (> 50% probability) that some or all of a DTA will not be realized (insufficient future taxable income to recover the tax asset), then the DTA must be reduced by a **valuation allowance**. The valuation allowance is a contra account that reduces the net balance sheet value of the DTA. Increasing the valuation allowance will decrease the net balance sheet DTA, increasing income tax expense and decreasing net income.

If circumstances change, the net DTA can be increased by decreasing the valuation allowance. This would result in higher earnings.

It is up to management to defend the recognition of all deferred tax assets. If a company has order backlogs or existing contracts which are expected to generate future taxable income, a valuation allowance might not be necessary. However, if a company has cumulative losses over the past few years or a history of inability to use tax loss carryforwards, then the company would need to use a valuation allowance to reflect the likelihood that a deferred tax asset will never be realized.

Because an increase (decrease) in the valuation allowance will decrease (increase) earnings, management can manipulate earnings by changing the valuation allowance.

Whenever a company reports substantial deferred tax assets, an analyst should review the company's financial performance to determine the likelihood that those assets will be realized. Analysts should also scrutinize changes in the valuation allowance to determine whether those changes are economically justified.

Professor's Note: A valuation allowance account is only used for deferred tax assets. Deferred tax assets and deferred tax liabilities appear separately on the balance sheet, and they are not typically netted.

LOS 37.h: Compare and contrast a company's deferred tax items and effective tax rate reconciliation between reporting periods.

Companies are required to disclose details on the source of the temporary differences that cause the deferred tax assets and liabilities reported on the balance sheet. Changes in those balance sheet accounts are reflected in income tax expense on the income statement. Here are some common examples of temporary differences you may encounter.

- A deferred tax liability results from using accelerated *depreciation* for tax purposes and straight-line depreciation for the financial statements. The analyst should consider the firm's growth rate and capital spending levels when determining whether the difference will actually reverse.
- *Impairments* generally result in a deferred tax asset since the writedown is recognized immediately in the income statement, but the deduction on the tax return is generally not allowed until the asset is sold or disposed of.
- *Restructuring* generates a deferred tax asset because the costs are recognized for financial reporting purposes when the restructuring is announced, but not deducted for tax purposes until actually paid. Note that restructuring usually results in significant cash outflows (net of the tax savings) in the years after the restructuring costs are reported.
- In the United States, firms that use LIFO for their financial statements are required to use LIFO for tax purposes, so no temporary differences result. However, in countries where this is not a requirement, temporary differences can result from the *choice of inventory cost-flow method*.
- *Post-employment benefits* and *deferred compensation* are both recognized for financial reporting when earned by the employee but not deducted for tax purposes until actually paid. These can result in a deferred tax asset that will be reversed when the benefits or compensation are paid.
- A deferred tax adjustment is made to stockholder's equity to reflect the future tax impact of unrealized gains or losses on *available-for-sale marketable securities* that are taken directly to equity. No DTL is added to the balance sheet for the future tax liability when gains/losses are realized.

Example: Analyzing deferred tax item disclosures

WCCO Inc.'s income tax expense has consistently been larger than taxes payable over the last three years. WCCO disclosed in the footnotes to its 20X5 financial statements the major items recorded as deferred tax assets and liabilities (in millions of dollars), as shown in the following table.

Deferred Tax Disclosures in Footnotes to WCCO Inc. Financial Statements

	20X5	20X4	20X3
Employee benefits	$278	$310	$290
International tax loss carryforwards	101	93	115
Subtotal	379	403	405
Valuation allowance	(24)	(57)	(64)
Deferred tax asset	355	346	341
Property, plant and equipment	452	361	320
Unrealized gains on available-for-sale securities	67	44	23
Deferred tax liability	519	405	343
Deferred income taxes	$164	$59	$2

Use the table above to explain why income tax expense has exceeded taxes payable over the last three years. Also explain the effect of the change in the valuation allowance on WCCO's earnings for 20X5.

Answer:

The company's deferred tax asset balance results from international tax loss carryforwards and employee benefits (most likely pension and other post-retirement benefits), offset by a valuation allowance. The company's deferred tax liability balance results from property, plant, and equipment (most likely from using accelerated depreciation methods for tax purposes and straight-line on the financial statements) and unrealized gains on securities classified as available-for-sale (because the unrealized gain is not taxable until realized).

Income tax expense is equal to taxes payable plus deferred income tax expense. Because deferred tax liabilities have been growing faster than deferred tax assets, deferred income tax expense has been positive, resulting in income tax expense being higher than taxes payable.

Management decreased the valuation allowance by $33 million in 20X5. This resulted in a reduction in deferred income tax expense and an increase in reported earnings for 20X5.

LOS 37.i: Analyze disclosures relating to deferred tax items and the effective tax rate reconciliation, and discuss how information included in these disclosures affects a company's financial statements and financial ratios.

Typically, the following deferred tax information is disclosed:

- Deferred tax liabilities, deferred tax assets, any valuation allowance, and the net change in the valuation allowance over the period.
- Any unrecognized deferred tax liability for undistributed earnings of subsidiaries and joint ventures.
- Current-year tax effect of each type of temporary difference.
- Components of income tax expense.
- Reconciliation of reported income tax expense and the tax expense based on the statutory rate.
- Tax loss carryforwards and credits.

Analyzing the Effective Tax Rate Reconciliation

Some firms' reported income tax expense differs from the amount based on the statutory income tax rate. Recall that the statutory rate is the tax rate of the jurisdiction where the firm operates. The differences are generally the result of:

- Different tax rates in different tax jurisdictions (countries).
- Permanent tax differences: tax credits, tax-exempt income, nondeductible expenses, and tax differences between capital gains and operating income.
- Changes in tax rates and legislation.
- Deferred taxes provided on the reinvested earnings of foreign and unconsolidated domestic affiliates.
- Tax holidays in some countries (watch for special conditions such as termination dates for the holiday or a requirement to pay the accumulated taxes at some point in the future).

Understanding the differences between reported income tax expense and the amount based on the statutory income tax rate will enable the analyst to better estimate future earnings and cash flow.

When estimating future earnings and cash flows, the analyst should understand each element of the reconciliation, including its relative impact, how it has changed with time, and how it is likely to change in the future.

In analyzing trends in tax rates, it is important to only include reconciliation items that are continuous in nature rather than those that are sporadic. Items including different rates in different countries, tax-exempt income, and non-deductible expenses tend to be continuous. Other items are almost always sporadic, such as the occurrence of large asset sales and tax holiday savings. The disclosures of each financial statement should be reviewed based on the footnotes and management discussion and analysis.

Example: Analyzing the tax rate reconciliation

Novelty Distribution Company (NDC) does business in the United States and abroad. The company's reconciliation between effective and statutory tax rates for three years is provided in the following figure.

Statutory U.S. Federal Income Tax Rate Reconciliation

	20X3	20X4	20X5
Statutory U.S. federal income tax rate	35.0%	35.0%	35.0%
State income taxes, net of related federal income tax benefit	2.1%	2.2%	2.3%
Benefits and taxes related to foreign operations	(6.5%)	(6.3%)	(2.7%)
Tax rate changes	0.0%	0.0%	(2.0%)
Capital gains on sale of assets	0.0%	(3.0%)	0.0%
Special items	(1.6%)	8.7%	2.5%
Other, net	0.8%	0.7%	(1.4%)
Effective income tax rates	29.8%	37.3%	33.7%

	20X3	20X4	20X5
Taxable income	$2,330.00	$1,660.00	$2,350.00
Statutory U.S. federal income tax	815.50	581.00	822.50
State income taxes, net of related federal income tax benefit	48.93	36.52	54.05
Benefits and taxes related to foreign operations	(151.45)	(104.58)	(63.45)
Tax rate changes	–	–	(47.00)
Capital gains on sale of assets	–	(49.80)	–
Special items	(37.28)	144.42	58.75
Other, net	18.64	11.62	(32.90)
Effective income taxes	$694.34	$619.18	$791.95

Analyze the trend in effective tax rates over the three years shown.

Answer:

For some trend analysis, the analyst may want to convert the reconciliation from percentages to absolute numbers. However, for this example, the trends can be analyzed simply by using the percentages.

The effective tax rate is upward trending over the 3-year period. Contributing to the upward trend is an increase in the state income tax rate and the loss of benefits related to taxes on foreign income. In 20X4, a loss related to the sale of assets partially offset an increase in taxes created by special items. In 20X3 and 20X5, the special items and the other items also offset each other. The fact that the special items and other items are so volatile over the 3-year period suggests that it will be difficult for an analyst to forecast the effective tax rate for NDC for the foreseeable future without additional information. This volatility also reduces comparability with other firms.

LOS 37.j: Identify the key provisions of and differences between income tax accounting under IFRS and U.S. GAAP.

Accounting for income taxes under U.S. GAAP and IFRS is similar in most respects. However, there are some differences. Many differences relate to the different tax laws and regulations of the different countries. Figure 1 is a summary of a few of the more important differences.

Figure 1: Tax Accounting Differences, IFRS vs. U.S. GAAP

	U.S. GAAP	IFRS
Revaluation of fixed assets and intangible assets	Not applicable, no revaluation allowed.	Deferred taxes are recognized in equity.
Undistributed profit from an investment in a subsidiary	No deferred taxes for foreign subsidiaries that meet the indefinite reversal criterion. No deferred taxes for domestic subsidiaries if the amounts are tax free.	Deferred taxes are recognized unless the parent is able to control the distribution of profit and it is probable the temporary difference will not reverse in the future.
Undistributed profit from an investment in a joint venture (JV)	No deferred taxes for foreign corporate JVs that meet the indefinite reversal criterion.	Deferred taxes are recognized unless the venturer is able to control the sharing of profit and it is probable the temporary difference will not reverse in the future.
Undistributed profit from an investment in an associate firm.	Deferred taxes are recognized from temporary differences.	Deferred taxes are recognized unless the investor is able to control the sharing of profit and it is probable the temporary difference will not reverse in the future.
Deferred tax asset recognition	Recognized in full and then reduced if "more likely than not" that some or all of the tax asset will not be realized.	Recognized if "probable" that sufficient taxable profit will be available to recover the tax asset.
Tax rate used to measure deferred taxes	Enacted tax rate only.	Enacted or substantially enacted tax rate.
Presentation of deferred taxes on the balance sheet	Classified as current or non-current based on the classification of the underlying asset or liability.	Netted, and classified as noncurrent.

KEY CONCEPTS

LOS 37.a

Deferred tax terminology:

- **Taxable income.** Income subject to tax based on the tax return.
- **Accounting profit.** Pretax income from the income statement based on financial accounting standards.
- **Deferred tax assets.** Balance sheet asset value that results when taxes payable (tax return) are greater than income tax expense (income statement) and the difference is expected to reverse in future periods.
- **Deferred tax liabilities.** Balance sheet liability value that results when income tax expense (income statement) is greater than taxes payable (tax return) and the difference is expected to reverse in future periods.
- **Valuation allowance.** Reduction of deferred tax assets (contra account) based on the likelihood that the future tax benefit will not be realized.
- **Taxes payable.** The tax liability from the tax return. Note that this term also refers to a liability that appears on the balance sheet for taxes due but not yet paid.
- **Income tax expense.** Expense recognized in the income statement that includes taxes payable and changes in deferred tax assets and liabilities.

LOS 37.b

A *deferred tax liability* is created when income tax expense (income statement) is higher than taxes payable (tax return). Deferred tax liabilities occur when revenues (or gains) are recognized in the income statement before they are taxable on the tax return, or expenses (or losses) are tax deductible before they are recognized in the income statement.

A *deferred tax asset* is created when taxes payable (tax return) are higher than income tax expense (income statement). Deferred tax assets are recorded when revenues (or gains) are taxable before they are recognized in the income statement, expenses (or losses) are recognized in the income statement before they are tax deductible, or tax loss carryforwards are available to reduce future taxable income.

LOS 37.c

An asset's tax base is its value for tax purposes. The tax base for a depreciable fixed asset is its cost minus any depreciation or amortization previously taken on the tax return. When an asset is sold, the taxable gain or loss on the sale is equal to the sale price minus the asset's tax base.

A liability's tax base is its value for tax purposes. When there is a difference between the book value of a liability on a firm's financial statements and its tax base that will result in future taxable gains or losses when the liability is settled, the firm will recognize a deferred tax asset or liability to reflect this future tax or tax benefit.

LOS 37.d

If taxable income is less than pretax income and the cause of the difference is expected to reverse in future years, a DTL is created. If taxable income is greater than pretax income and the difference is expected to reverse in future years, a DTA is created.

The balance of the DTA or DTL is equal to the difference between the tax base and the carrying value of the asset or liability, multiplied by the tax rate.

Income tax expense and taxes payable are related through the change in the DTA and the change in the DTL: Income tax expense = taxes payable + ΔDTL − ΔDTA.

LOS 37.e

When a firm's income tax rate increases (decreases), deferred tax assets and deferred tax liabilities are both increased (decreased) to reflect the new rate. Changes in these values will also affect income tax expense.

An increase in the tax rate will increase both a firm's DTL and its income tax expense. A decrease in the tax rate will decrease both a firm's DTL and its income tax expense.

An increase in the tax rate will increase a firm's DTA and decrease its income tax expense. A decrease in the tax rate will decrease a firm's DTA and increase its income tax expense.

LOS 37.f

A temporary difference is a difference between the tax base and the carrying value of an asset or liability that will result in taxable amounts or deductible amounts in the future.

A permanent difference is a difference between taxable income and pretax income that will not reverse in the future. Permanent differences do not create DTAs or DTLs.

LOS 37.g

If it is more likely than not that some or all of a DTA will not be realized (because of insufficient future taxable income to recover the tax asset), then the DTA must be reduced by a valuation allowance. The valuation allowance is a contra account that reduces the DTA value on the balance sheet. Increasing the valuation allowance will increase income tax expense and reduce earnings. If circumstances change, the DTA can be revalued upward by decreasing the valuation allowance, which would increase earnings.

LOS 37.h

Firms are required to reconcile their effective income tax rate with the applicable statutory rate in the country where the business is domiciled. Analyzing the trend of the individual items of the reconciliation can aid in understanding past earnings trends and in predicting future effective tax rates. Where adequate data is provided, they can also be helpful in predicting future earnings or cash flows and for adjusting financial ratios.

LOS 37.i

Deferred tax liabilities that are never expected to reverse, typically because of expected growth in capital expenditures, should be treated for analytical purposes as equity. If deferred tax liabilities are expected to reverse, they should be treated for analytical purposes as liabilities.

LOS 37.j

The accounting treatment of income taxes under U.S. GAAP and their treatment under IFRS are similar in most respects. One major difference relates to the revaluation of fixed assets and intangible assets. U.S. GAAP prohibits upward revaluations, but they are permitted under IFRS and result in deferred tax assets that are recognized in equity.

CONCEPT CHECKERS

1. Which of the following statements is *most accurate*? The difference between taxes payable for the period and the tax expense recognized on the financial statements results from differences:
    A. in management control.
    B. between basic and diluted earnings.
    C. between financial and tax accounting.

2. Which of the following tax definitions is *least accurate*?
    A. Taxable income is income based on the rules of the tax authorities.
    B. Taxes payable are the amount due to the government.
    C. Pretax income is income tax expense divided by one minus the statutory tax rate.

Use the following data to answer Questions 3 through 9.

-   A firm acquires an asset for $120,000 with a 4-year useful life and no salvage value.
-   The asset will generate $50,000 of cash flow for all four years.
-   The tax rate is 40% each year.
-   The firm will depreciate the asset over three years on a straight-line (SL) basis for tax purposes and over four years on a SL basis for financial reporting purposes.

3. Taxable income in year 1 is:
    A. $6,000.
    B. $10,000.
    C. $20,000.

4. Taxes payable in year 1 are:
    A. $4,000.
    B. $6,000.
    C. $8,000.

5. Pretax income in year 4 is:
    A. $6,000.
    B. $10,000.
    C. $20,000.

6. Income tax expense in year 4 is:
    A. $4,000.
    B. $6,000.
    C. $8,000.

7. Taxes payable in year 4 are:
    A. $4,000.
    B. $6,000.
    C. $20,000.

8.   At the end of year 2, the firm's balance sheet will report a deferred tax:
       A.   asset of $4,000.
       B.   asset of $8,000.
       C.   liability of $8,000.

9.   Suppose tax rates rise during year 2 to 50%. At the end of year 2, the firm's
       balance sheet will show a deferred tax liability of:
       A. $5,000.
       B. $6,000.
       C. $10,000.

10.   An increase in the tax rate causes the balance sheet value of a deferred tax asset
       to:
       A.   decrease.
       B.   increase.
       C.   remain unchanged.

11.   In its first year of operations, a firm produces taxable income of –$10,000. The
       prevailing tax rate is 40%. The firm's balance sheet will report a deferred tax:
       A.   asset of $4,000.
       B.   asset of $10,000.
       C.   liability of $4,000.

12.   An analyst is comparing a firm to its competitors. The firm has a deferred tax
       liability that results from accelerated depreciation for tax purposes. The firm is
       expected to continue to grow in the foreseeable future. How should the liability
       be treated for analysis purposes?
       A.   It should be treated as equity at its full value.
       B.   It should be treated as a liability at its full value.
       C.   The present value should be treated as a liability with the remainder being
            treated as equity.

13.   An analyst is comparing a firm to its competitors. The firm has a deferred tax
       liability and is expected to have capital expenditures decline in the future. How
       should the liability be treated for analysis purposes?
       A.   It should be treated as equity at its full value.
       B.   It should be treated as a liability at its full value.
       C.   The present value should be treated as a liability with the remainder being
            treated as equity.

14.   Which one of the following statements is *most accurate*? Under the liability
       method of accounting for deferred taxes, a decrease in the tax rate at the
       beginning of the accounting period will:
       A.   increase taxable income in the current period.
       B.   increase a deferred tax asset.
       C.   reduce a deferred tax liability.

15.   An analyst gathered the following information about a company:
- Taxable income is $40,000.
- Pretax income is $50,000.
- Current tax rate is 50%.
- Tax rate when the reversal occurs will be 40%.

What is the company's deferred tax liability at the end of year 1?
A. $3,500.
B. $4,000.
C. $5,000.

16.   While reviewing a company, an analyst identifies a permanent difference between taxable income and pretax income. Which of the following statements *most accurately* identifies the appropriate financial statement adjustment?
A. The amount of the tax implications of the difference should be added to the deferred tax liabilities.
B. The present value of the amount of the tax implications of the difference should be added to the deferred tax liabilities.
C. The effective tax rate for calculating tax expense should be adjusted.

17.   An analyst is reviewing a company with a large deferred tax asset on its balance sheet. She has determined that the firm has had cumulative losses for the last three years and has a large amount of inventory that can only be sold at sharply reduced prices. Which of the following adjustments should the analyst make to account for the deferred tax assets?
A. Record a deferred tax liability to offset the effect of the deferred tax asset on the firm's balance sheet.
B. Recognize a valuation allowance to reflect the fact that the deferred tax asset is unlikely to be realized.
C. Do nothing. The difference between taxable and pretax income that caused the deferred tax asset is likely to reverse in the future.

18.   If the tax base of an asset exceeds the asset's carrying value and a reversal is expected in the future:
A. a deferred tax asset is created.
B. a deferred tax liability is created.
C. neither a deferred tax asset nor a deferred tax liability is created.

19.   The author of a new textbook received a $100,000 advance from the publisher this year. $40,000 of income taxes were paid on the advance when received. The textbook will not be finished until next year. Determine the tax basis of the advance at the end of this year.
A. $0.
B. $40,000.
C. $100,000.

20.   According to IFRS, the deferred tax consequences of revaluing held-for-use equipment upward is reported on the balance sheet:
A. as an asset.
B. as a liability.
C. in stockholders' equity.

21.   KLH Company reported the following:
   - Gross DTA at the beginning of the year $10,500
   - Gross DTA at the end of the year $11,250
   - Valuation allowance at the beginning of the year $2,700
   - Valuation allowance at the end of the year $3,900

   Which of the following statements *best* describes the expected earnings of the firm? Earnings are expected to:
   A. increase.
   B. decrease.
   C. remain relatively stable.

ANSWERS – CONCEPT CHECKERS

1. **C** The difference between taxes payable for the period and the tax expense recognized on the financial statements results from differences between financial and tax accounting.

2. **C** Pretax income and income tax expense are not always linked because of temporary and permanent differences.

3. **B** Annual depreciation expense for tax purposes is ($120,000 cost – $0 salvage value) / 3 years = $40,000. Taxable income is $50,000 – $40,000 = $10,000.

4. **A** Taxes payable is taxable income × tax rate = $10,000 × 40% = $4,000. (The $10,000 was calculated in question #3).

5. **C** Annual depreciation expense for financial purposes is ($120,000 cost – $0 salvage value) / 4 years = $30,000. Pretax income is $50,000 – $30,000 = $20,000.

6. **C** Because there has been no change in the tax rate, income tax expense is pretax income × tax rate = $20,000 × 40% = $8,000. (The $20,000 was calculated in question #5).

7. **C** Note that the asset was fully depreciated for tax purposes after year 3, so taxable income is $50,000. Taxes payable for year 4 = taxable income × tax rate = $50,000 × 40% = $20,000.

8. **C** At the end of year 2, the tax base is $40,000 ($120,000 cost – $80,000 accumulated tax depreciation) and the carrying value is $60,000 ($120,000 cost – $60,000 accumulated financial depreciation). Since the carrying value exceeds the tax base, a DTL of $8,000 [($60,000 carrying value – $40,000 tax base) × 40%] is reported.

9. **C** The deferred tax liability is now $10,000 [($60,000 carrying value – $40,000 tax base) × 50%].

10. **B** If tax rates increase, the balance sheet value of a deferred tax asset will also increase.

11. **A** The tax loss carryforward results in a deferred tax asset equal to the loss multiplied by the tax rate.

12. **A** The DTL is not expected to reverse in the foreseeable future. The liability should be treated as equity at its full value.

13. **C** The present value of the portion of the DTL that is expected to reverse should be treated as a liability with the remainder being treated as equity.

14. **C** If the tax rate decreases, balance sheet DTL and DTA are both reduced. Taxable income is unaffected.

15. **B** The tax rate that should be used is the expected tax rate when the liability reverses. The deferred tax liability will be $10,000 × 40% = $4,000.

16. **C** If a permanent difference between taxable income and pretax income is identifiable, the effective tax rate for calculating tax expense should be adjusted.

17. **B**   A valuation allowance is used to offset deferred tax assets if it is unlikely that those assets will be realized. Because the company has a history of losses and inventory that is unlikely to generate future profits, it is unlikely the company will realize its deferred tax assets in full.

18. **A**   If the tax base of an asset exceeds the carrying value a deferred tax asset is created. Taxable income will be lower in the future when the reversal occurs.

19. **A**   For revenue received in advance, the tax base is equal to the carrying value minus any amounts that will *not* be taxed in the future. Since the advance has already been taxed, $100,000 will *not* be taxed in the future. Thus, the textbook advance liability has a tax base of $0 ($100,000 carrying value – $100,000 revenue not taxed in the future).

20. **C**   The deferred tax consequences of revaluing an asset upward under IFRS are reported in stockholders' equity.

21. **B**   The valuation allowance account increased from $2,700 to $3,900. The most likely explanation is the future earnings are expected to decrease, thereby reducing the value of the DTA.

The following is a review of the Financial Reporting and Analysis principles designed to address the learning outcome statements set forth by CFA Institute®. This topic is also covered in:

LONG-TERM LIABILITIES AND LEASES

EXAM FOCUS

Candidates should understand the difference between a coupon payment and interest expense and why market values of debt are more appropriate than book values for calculating leverage ratios and estimating firm value. Learn how the difference between current stock price and the conversion price for convertible bonds affects their treatment for analysis and how bonds with warrants are recorded on the balance sheet. You must know the financial statement and ratio effects of alternative accounting treatments, analyst adjustments, and the issuance of premium, par, and discount debt.

The effects on financial statements and ratios of treating a lease as a finance lease rather than as an operating lease are an important topic. Expect questions on how an analyst should adjust financial statements for off-balance-sheet financing activities such as take-or-pay contracts, throughput arrangements, and sales of receivables.

FINANCING LIABILITIES

A **bond** is a contractual promise between a borrower (the bond issuer) and a lender (the bondholder) that obligates the bond issuer to make payments to the bondholder over the term of the bond. Two types of payments are involved, periodic interest payments and repayment of principal at maturity.

Bond Terminology

- The **face value**, also known as the **maturity value** or **par value**, is the amount of principal that will be paid to the bondholder at maturity. The face value is used to calculate the coupon payments.
- The **coupon rate** is the interest rate stated in the bond that is used to calculate the coupon payments.
- The **coupon payments** are the periodic interest payments to the bondholders and are calculated by multiplying the face value by the coupon rate.
- The **market rate of interest** is the rate of return required by bondholders and depends on the bond's risks (e.g., default risk, liquidity risk, etc.), as well as the overall structure of interest rates. *Do not confuse the market rate of interest with the coupon rate.* The coupon rate is typically fixed for the term of the bond. The market rate of interest on a firm's bonds, however, will likely change over the bond's life, which changes the bond's market value as well.

- The **balance sheet liability** of a bond is equal to the present value of the remaining cash flows (coupon payments and face value), discounted at the market rate of interest *at issuance*. At maturity, the liability will equal the face value of the bond. The balance sheet liability is also known as the **book value** or **carrying value** of the bond liability.

- The **interest expense** reported in the income statement is calculated by multiplying the book value of the bond liability at the beginning of the period by the market rate of interest on the bond when it was issued.

[handwritten margin note: BS Liability PV of remain CF at mkt rate at issuance]

*[handwritten margin note: Int expense = BV * mkt rate]*

At the date of issuance, the market rate of interest may be equal to, less than, or greater than the coupon rate.

- When the market rate equals the coupon rate, the bond is a **par bond**.
- When the market rate is greater than the coupon rate, the bond is a **discount bond** (priced below par).
- When the market rate is less than the coupon rate, the bond is a **premium bond** (priced above par).

LOS 38.a: Compute the effects of debt issuance and amortization of bond discounts and premiums on financial statements and ratios.

Bonds Issued at Par

When a bond is issued at par, the market rate of interest at issuance is equal to the coupon rate. In this case, the present value of the coupon payments plus the present value of the face amount are equal to the par value. The effects on the financial statements are straightforward.

- On the balance sheet, assets and liabilities will increase by the bond proceeds (face value). The book value of the bond liability will not change over the term of the bond.
- On the income statement, interest expense for the period is equal to the coupon interest paid since the market rate and the coupon rate are the same.
- On the cash flow statement, the issue proceeds are reported as a cash inflow from financing activities and the coupon payments are reported as cash outflows from operating activities. At maturity, repayment of the face value is reported as a cash outflow from financing activities.

Bonds Issued at a Discount or Premium

When the market rate of interest at issuance is not equal to the coupon rate, the proceeds received (the present value of the coupon payments plus the present value of the face value) are not equal to par value. In this case, the bond is issued at a *premium* or a *discount*. The premium or discount at the issue date is usually relatively small for coupon bonds.

If the coupon rate is less than the market rate of interest, the proceeds received will be less than the face value. The difference is known as a discount. The coupon rate is lower than the coupon rate that would make the market price of the bond equal to its par value. Investors will pay less than face value because of the lower coupon rate. Such bonds are known as discount (from face value) bonds.

If the coupon rate is greater than the market rate, the bond price and the proceeds received will be greater than face value. We refer to such bonds as premium (above face value) bonds. In this case, investors will pay more for the above-market coupon payments.

Balance sheet impact

When a company issues a bond, assets and liabilities both initially increase by the bond proceeds. At any point in time, the book value of the bond liability will always equal the present value of the remaining future cash flows (coupon payments and maturity value) discounted at the market rate of interest at issuance.

 Professor's Note: Interest expense and the book value of a bond liability are calculated using the market rate of interest at <u>the time the bonds were issued</u>, not the market rate today. This is a crucial point.

Premium bonds are reported on the balance sheet at more than their face value. As the premium is amortized (reduced), the book value of the bond liability will decrease until it reaches its face value at maturity.

Discount bonds are reported on the balance sheet at less than their face value. As the discount is amortized, the book value of the bond liability will increase until it reaches face value at maturity.

Interest expense

For a bond issued at a premium or discount, interest expense and coupon interest paid in cash are *not* equal. Interest expense includes amortization of any discount or premium at issuance. Using the **effective interest rate method**, interest expense is equal to the book value of the bond liability at the beginning of the period, multiplied by the market rate of interest at issuance.

- For a premium bond, interest expense is less than the coupon payment (market rate < coupon rate). The difference between interest expense and the coupon interest payment is the amortization of the premium. The premium amortization is subtracted from the bond liability on the balance sheet. Thus, interest expense will decrease over time as the bond liability decreases and reduces periodic amortization of the remaining premium.
- For a discount bond, interest expense is greater than the coupon payment (market rate > coupon rate). The difference between interest expense and the coupon payment is the amortization of the discount. The amortization of the discount each period is added to the bond liability on the balance sheet. Therefore, interest expense will increase over time as the bond liability increases.

Professor's Note: In the case of a discount bond, the coupon is too low relative to the required rate of return of the market. The purpose of amortizing the discount is to (1) increase the book value of the bond liability over time and (2) increase interest expense so that the coupon payment plus discount amortization is approximately equal to the interest expense that would have prevailed had the bond been issued at par. This logic is reversed for premium bonds.

Cash flows

Coupon payments are an outflow of cash. Remember, interest expense and the coupon payment differ by the periodic amortization of any remaining discount or premium. Amortization is a non-cash item. So, when presenting the cash flow statement using the indirect method, any amortization of a discount or premium must be removed from net income in calculating cash flow from operations.

Firms that report under U.S. GAAP must report interest expense in the cash flow statement as an operating activity. Firms that report under IFRS can report interest expense as either an operating activity or a financing activity. Therefore, it may be necessary to reclassify the interest expense in order to compare firms that report under different standards.

Professor's Note: Some analysts believe that classifying interest expense as an operating activity is inconsistent with treating the bond proceeds as a financing activity. In addition, treating interest expense as an operating activity incorrectly describes the economics of a bond issued at a premium or discount. For example, for bonds issued at a discount, cash flow from operations is overstated. This is because the coupon payment is reported as an operating cash flow, while the discount, when paid (as part of a bond's maturity payment), is reported as a financing cash flow. Stated differently, had the firm issued the bond at par, the coupon payment would have been higher to match the market rate of interest. Reclassifying interest expense in the cash flow statement as a financing activity corrects the inconsistent treatment.

Example: Book values and cash flows

On December 31, 20X2, a company issued a 3-year, 10% annual coupon bond with a face value of $100,000.

Part A: Calculate the book value of the bond at year-end 20X2, 20X3, and 20X4, and the interest expense for 20X3, 20X4, and 20X5, assuming the bond was issued at a market rate of interest of (a.) 10%, (b.) 9%, and (c.) 11%.

Part B: The financial statements for 20X3 show that cash flow from operations was $50,000. Assuming that the market rate of interest was 9% when the bond was issued, how should this cash flow be analyzed when comparing it to other companies?

Answer: Part A

(a.) Bond issued at par. If the market rate of interest at issuance is 10%, the book value of the bonds will always be $100,000, and the interest expense will always be $10,000, which is equal to the coupon payment of $0.10 \times \$100,000$. There is no discount or premium to amortize.

(b.) Premium bond. If the market rate of interest is 9%, the present value of the cash payments (a 3-year annuity of $10,000 and a payment in three years of $100,000) is $102,531.

N = 3; PMT = 10,000; FV = 100,000; I/Y = 9; CPT → PV = $102,531

 Professor's Note: The present value computed in this manner will have a minus sign.

The following table shows the interest expense and book value at the end of each year.

Interest Expense and Book Value for a Premium Bond

Year	(1) Beginning Book Value	(2) Interest Expense (1) × 9%	(3) Coupon	(4) Ending Book Value (1) + (2) − (3)
20X3	$102,531	$9,228	$10,000	$101,759
20X4	101,759	9,158	10,000	100,917
20X5	100,917	9,083	10,000	100,000

The premium amortization for 20X3 is 10,000 − 9,228 = $772. For 20X4, the amortization is 10,000 − 9,158 = $842. Finally, for 20X5, premium amortization is $917. Note that the premium has been fully amortized upon maturity so that the book value of the bond equals par value.

(c.) Discount bond. If the market rate of interest is 11%, the present value of the cash payments (a 3-year annuity of $10,000 and a payment in three years of $100,000) is $97,556.

$$N = 3; PMT = 10,000; FV = 100,000; I/Y = 11; CPT \rightarrow PV = \$97,556$$

The following table shows the interest expense and book value at the end of each year.

Interest Expense and Book Value for a Discount Bond

Year	(1) Beginning Book Value	(2) Interest Expense (1) × 11%	(3) Coupon	(4) Ending Book Value (1) + (2) – (3)
20X3	$97,556	$10,731	$10,000	$98,287
20X4	98,287	10,812	10,000	99,099
20X5	99,099	10,901	10,000	100,000

Again, the pattern of discount amortization is such that the discount is fully amortized upon maturity, when the book value of the bond equals par value.

Answer: Part B

For the premium bond (9% market rate at issuance), the cash component of interest expense is overstated. CFO is understated in 20X3 because CFO is reduced by the coupon of $10,000 instead of by the true interest expense of $9,228. For analysis, cash flow from operations should be adjusted by adding $772 ($10,000 – $9,228). Note that since CFO is understated, CFF will be overstated over the life of a premium bond. While the proceeds of issuance are a positive CFF (+$102,531), the negative CFF at maturity is only the face value ($100,000). Over the life of the bond, net CFF (+2,531) is positive, by the same amount that CFO is understated.

Zero Coupon Bonds

Zero-coupon bonds make no periodic payments of interest. Zero-coupon bonds, also known as *pure discount bonds,* are issued at a discount from their par value and their annual interest expense is implied, not explicitly paid. The actual interest payment is included in the face value that is paid at maturity. The effects of zero-coupon bonds on the financial statements are qualitatively the same as any discount debt, but the impact is larger because the discount is larger.

Example: Effect of zero-coupon debt on CFO

Two companies have an identical value of $50,000 for cash sales less cash inputs and cash operating expenses. The only difference between the two companies is their financing. At the beginning of this year, Company A sold $1,000,000 face value of zero-coupon bonds maturing in three years. Company B sold $750,000 of 10% coupon bonds maturing in three years. Assume the market rate of interest on these bonds at issuance is 10%.

- How much did Company A receive for its bonds?
- What is interest expense for Company A over the three years of the bond's life?
- Compute the cash flow from operations for Company A and Company B for year 1 (ignore taxes).

Assume that both bonds are *annual pay* and are valued using annual-pay assumptions.

 Professor's Note: For the exam, know that most zero-coupon bonds in the United States are valued using a semiannual-pay convention.

Answer:

Company A receives the present value of $1,000,000 in three years:
$1,000,000 / (1.1)^3 = 751,315.$

or, N = 3; I/Y = 10; FV = 1,000,000; PMT = 0; CPT → PV = $751,315.

Interest expense in year 1 is $751,315 × 10% = $75,131.
Book value at the end of year 1 is $751,315 + $75,131 = $826,446.

Interest expense in year 2 is $826,446 × 10% = $82,645.
Book value at the end of year 2 is $826,446 + $82,645 = $909,091.

Interest expense in year 3 is $909,091 × 10% = $90,909.
Book value at the end of year 3 = $909,091 + $90,909 = $1,000,000.

Note that the "interest expense" for Company A is entirely composed of *discount amortization*. There is no cash interest component to Company A's interest expense.

CFO for Company A in year 1 is $50,000 because there is no cash interest expense.

CFO for Company B in year 1 is $50,000 – $75,000 = –$25,000. Company B's cash coupon payment reduces CFO significantly.

Without any adjustments, Company A's CFO appears significantly higher than Company B's CFO. An analyst should either adjust Company B's operating cash flow upward or Company A's downward when comparing the companies. Note that at issuance, CFF is approximately +$750,000 for both Company A and Company B ($751,315 for Company A), but at maturity CFF is –$750,000 for Company B and –$1,000,000 for Company A.

no CFO for zero coupon bond (handwritten margin note)

Amortization methods

Thus far, the amortization of the discount or premium was derived using the effective interest rate method. The effective interest rate method is required under IFRS. Under U.S. GAAP, the effective interest rate method is preferred, but the straight-line method is allowed if the results are not materially different. The straight-line method is similar to straight-line depreciation and the total discount or premium is allocated to the income statement equally each period over the term of the bond.

Issuance costs

Issuing a bond involves legal and accounting fees, printing costs, sales commissions, and other fees. Under IFRS, issuance costs are included in the measurement of the liability, thereby increasing the effective interest rate. Under U.S. GAAP, firms capitalize issuance costs as an asset (prepaid expense) and allocate the costs over the term of the bond.

Extinguishing debt

When bonds mature, no gain or loss is recognized by the issuer. At maturity, the original discount or premium has been fully amortized; thus, the book value of the bond liability and the face value are the same. The cash outflow to repay the bonds is reported in the cash flow statement as a financing activity.

A firm may choose to **redeem** bonds before maturity because interest rates have fallen, because the firm has generated surplus cash through operations, or because funds from the issuance of equity make it possible (and desirable).

When bonds are redeemed before maturity, a gain or loss is recognized by subtracting the redemption price from the book value of the bond liability at the reacquisition date. For example, assume a firm reacquired $1 million face amount of bonds at 102 percent of par when the book value of the bond liability was $995,000. The firm will recognize a loss of $25,000 ($995,000 book value – $1,020,000 redemption price). Had the book value been greater than the redemption price, a gain would have been recognized.

Under U.S. GAAP, any remaining (unamortized) bond issuance costs must also be written off and included in the gain or loss calculation. Writing off the cost of issuing the bond will reduce a gain or increase a loss. No write-off is necessary under IFRS since the issuance costs are already included in book value of the bond liability.

The gain or loss from extinguishing debt is reported in the income statement, usually as a part of continuing operations, and additional information is disclosed separately. Extinguishing debt is usually not a part of the firm's day-to-day operations; thus, analysts often eliminate the gain or loss from the income statement for analysis and forecasting purposes.

When presenting the cash flow statement using the indirect method, the gain or loss is eliminated from net income in arriving at cash flow from operations and the reacquisition price is reported as an outflow from financing activities.

Summary of Financial Statement Effects of Issuing a Bond

Figure 1: Cash Flow Impact of Issuing a Bond

	Cash Flow from Financing	Cash Flow from Operations
Issuance of debt	Increased by cash received (Present value of the bond at the market interest rate)	No effect
Periodic interest payments	No effect	Decreased by interest paid [(coupon rate) × (face or par value)]
Payment at maturity	Decreased by face (par) value	No effect

Figure 2: Economic or Analytic Perspective of Interest Payments

	Cash Flow from Financing	Cash Flow from Operations
Premium bonds	Overstated	Understated
Discount bonds	Understated	Overstated

Figure 3: Income Statement Impact of Issuing a Bond

$$\text{interest expense} = \begin{pmatrix} \text{market rate} \\ \text{at issue} \end{pmatrix} \times \begin{pmatrix} \text{balance sheet value} \\ \text{of liability at} \\ \text{beginning of period} \end{pmatrix}$$

Issued at Par	Issued at a Premium	Issued at a Discount
Market rate = coupon rate	Market rate < coupon rate	Market rate > coupon rate
Interest expense = coupon rate × face value = cash paid	Interest expense = cash paid − amortization of premium	Interest expense = cash paid + amortization of discount
Interest expense is constant	Interest expense decreases over time	Interest expense increases over time

Figure 4: Balance Sheet Impact of Issuing a Bond

Long-term debt is carried at the present value of the remaining cash payments discounted at the market rate prevailing when the debt was issued.

Issued at Par	Issued at a Premium	Issued at a Discount
Carried at face value	Carried at face value plus premium	Carried at face value less discount
	The liability decreases as the premium is amortized to interest expense	The liability increases as the discount is amortized to interest expense

LOS 38.b: Explain the role of debt covenants in protecting creditors by restricting a company's ability to invest, pay dividends, or make other operating and strategic decisions.

Debt covenants are restrictions imposed by the bondholders on the issuer to protect the bondholders' position. Debt covenants can decrease default risk and thus reduce borrowing costs. The bondholder can demand immediate repayment of the bond principal after a violation of any of the covenants (referred to as **technical default**). Analysis of the covenants is a necessary component of the credit analysis of a bond. Bond covenants are typically disclosed in the financial statement footnotes.

Examples of covenants include restrictions on:

- Dividend payments and share repurchases.
- Mergers and acquisitions.
- Sale, leaseback, and disposal of certain assets.
- Issuance of new debt in the future.
- Repayment patterns (e.g., sinking fund agreements and priority of claims).

Other covenants require the firm to maintain financial ratios such as the current ratio or debt-to-equity ratio, or financial statement items such as equity or net working capital, at certain levels. Covenants will specify whether GAAP or some other method is to be used when calculating the ratios.

Covenants protect bondholders from actions the firm may take that would harm the value of the bondholders' claims to firm assets and earnings (i.e., decrease credit quality). To the extent that covenants restrict, for example, the firm's ability to invest, take on additional debt, or pay dividends, analysis of covenants can be important for valuing the firm's equity (especially involving its growth prospects) as well as for analyzing and valuing its debt securities.

 Professor's Note: Bond covenants are described further in the Study Session on fixed income investments.

LOS 38.c: Describe the presentation of, and disclosures relating to, financing liabilities.

Firms will usually combine all of their long-term debt outstanding into one line on the balance sheet. The portion that is due within the next year is reported as a current liability. The firm separately discloses more detail about its long-term debt in the footnotes. The disclosure is useful in determining the timing and amount of future cash outflows. The footnote disclosure usually includes a discussion of:

- The nature of the liabilities.
- Maturity dates.
- Stated and effective interest rates.
- Call provisions and conversion privileges.
- Restrictions imposed by creditors.
- Assets pledged as security.
- The amount of debt maturing in each of the next five years.

A discussion of the firm's long-term liabilities is also found in the Management Discussion and Analysis section. This discussion is both quantitative, such as identifying obligations and commitments that are due in the future, and qualitative, such as discussing capital resource trends and material changes in the mix and cost of debt.

LOS 38.d: Determine the effects of changing interest rates on the market value of debt and on financial statements and ratios.

Recall that the book value of a bond liability is calculated based on the market rate of interest *at issuance*. So, as long as the market rate does not change, the bond liability represents fair (market) value. However, if the market rate changes, the balance sheet liability is no longer equal to market value.

An *increase* in the market rate of interest will result in a *decrease* in the fair value of the bond liability. Conversely, a *decrease* in the market rate *increases* the fair value. Changes in market interest rates result in a divergence between the book values of bonds and the market values or fair values of the economic liabilities. Recently issued IFRS and U.S. GAAP standards give companies the option to report more financial liabilities at fair value.

For purposes of analysis, the market value of the firm's debt may be more appropriate than book values. For example, a firm that issued a bond when interest rates were low is relatively better off when interest rates increase. This is because the firm could purchase the bond at its (now lower) market value. Decreasing the bond liability on the balance sheet to market value increases equity and decreases the debt-to-assets and debt-to-equity ratios. If interest rates have decreased since issuance, adjusting debt to its market value will have the opposite effects.

LOS 38.e: Describe two types of debt with equity features (convertible debt and debt with warrants) and calculate the effect of issuance of such instruments on a company's debt ratios.

Convertible Debt

Convertible bonds give the bondholder the right to exchange the bonds for stock for a specified time after issuance. The right is an **option** that has value to the bondholder. As a result of the option, the bondholder receives a lower rate of interest as compared to a bond that is not convertible, all else equal.

For firms following U.S. GAAP, the value of the conversion option is ignored when the bond is issued. None of the proceeds are reported as equity. The issuer simply reports the proceeds as a liability on the balance sheet. Just like a bond that is not convertible, the bond liability is equal to the present value of the remaining cash flows discounted at the market rate of interest at issuance. Similarly, any discount or premium at the issue date is amortized. The proceeds are reported in the cash flow statement as an inflow from financing activities.

If the bonds are converted into stock, the stock is recorded at the book value of the (extinguished) bond liability. The firm simply transfers the book value of the bond from liabilities to equity. No gain or loss is recognized. Obviously, transferring the liability to equity will result in lower leverage ratios. The conversion has no cash flow effects.

Under IFRS, the issuer separates the bond liability and the conversion option. The value of the bond without the conversion option is recorded as a liability. The value of the conversion option can be derived by subtracting the value of the bond without the option from the issue proceeds. The issuer records the value of the conversion option in stockholders' equity.

For analytical purposes, the equity feature of convertible bonds can be important. In general, when the stock price is significantly above the conversion price, the bonds are likely to be converted to stock and therefore should be treated as equity when calculating leverage ratios. Such treatment will decrease debt-to-equity, debt-to-assets, and debt-to-total-capital ratios. At the other extreme, when the stock price is significantly less than the conversion price, the convertible bond liability should be treated as debt when calculating ratios.

When the stock price is close to the conversion price, the classification is not as clear and the effect on leverage ratios is uncertain. The analyst should compute leverage ratios treating the convertible bonds alternatively as debt and as equity to gauge the impact of the choice of how the bond liability is treated. Choosing one treatment over the other should depend on the purpose of the analysis and the analyst's estimate of the probability of conversion over the relevant time horizon.

Debt with Warrants

Some bonds include **warrants** which give their owner the right to purchase shares of the issuer's stock at a specified price. Bonds with warrants are more commonly issued outside the U.S.

Like a conversion option, warrants have value. Thus, the bondholder receives a lower rate of interest compared to a bond issued without warrants included in the bond purchase. Bonds with warrants and convertible bonds do differ, however, in several respects.

- Unlike a conversion option, warrants can usually be detached (separated) from the bond at some point in the future.
- If the warrant is exercised, the bond remains outstanding and the bondholder owns both debt and equity.
- In order to exercise the warrant, the investor must pay the exercise price to the issuer. With convertible bonds, no payment is required when the bonds are converted.

[handwritten: Warrants recorded in SHE]

The accounting treatment of a bond issued with warrants is the same under both IFRS and U.S. GAAP. The issuer separately values the bond liability and the warrant. The value of the bond is determined without the warrant and is recorded as a liability. The value of the warrants can be derived by subtracting the value of the bond (without the warrant) from the issue proceeds. The issuer records the value of the warrants in stockholders' equity. Note that the treatment of issuing a bond with warrants is similar to the treatment of issuing a convertible bond under IFRS.

Because a portion of the proceeds of issuing a bond with warrants attached is classified as equity, both debt-to-equity and debt-to-total-capital will be *lower* than if a bond without warrants was issued for the same proceeds (market value) as the bond with warrants.

Convertible bonds and bonds issued with warrants are both potentially dilutive securities that must be considered when calculating diluted earnings per share.

Other Financial Instruments with Characteristics of Both Debt and Equity

Some financial instruments have characteristics of both debt and equity. Until recently, firms had some discretion in reporting these instruments on the balance sheet. By avoiding debt recognition, the issuing firm was able to report lower (better) leverage ratios.

Now, as a general rule, if a financial instrument requires the repayment of principal in the future, it must be reported as a liability on the balance sheet. One example is preferred stock that must be redeemed at some point in the future. This *mandatory redemption* feature is similar to the final principal payment (face value) of a bond. Thus, mandatory redeemable preferred stock must now be reported as debt on the issuer's balance sheet. In addition, the dividend payments on preferred stock with a mandatory redemption feature must be reported as interest expense in the income statement. If a firm has issued securities that require equity to be repurchased at a specific price in the future, the repurchase amount must be treated as a liability as well.

LOS 38.f: Discuss the motivations for leasing assets instead of purchasing them and the incentives for reporting the leases as operating leases rather than finance leases.

A **lease** is a contractual arrangement whereby the **lessor**, the owner of the asset, allows the **lessee** to use the asset for a specified period of time in return for periodic payments.

[margin note: lessor ↑owner]

Leases are classified as either **finance leases** or **operating leases**. In the U.S., a finance lease is known as a *capital lease*.

A finance lease is, in substance, a purchase of an asset that is financed with debt. Accordingly, at the inception of the lease, the lessee will add equal amounts to both assets and a liabilities on the balance sheet. Over the term of the lease, the lessee will recognize depreciation expense on the asset and interest expense on the liability.

[margin note: Finance/capital A I L recorded depr]

An operating lease is essentially a rental arrangement. No asset or liability is reported by the lessee and the periodic lease payments are simply recognized as rental expense in the income statement.

[margin note: Operating rental expense]

Leasing can have certain benefits:

- **Less costly financing.** Typically, a lease requires no initial payment. Thus, the lessee conserves cash.
- **Reduced risk of obsolescence.** At the end of the lease, the asset can be returned to the lessor.
- **Less restrictive provisions.** Leases can provide more flexibility than other forms of financing because the lease agreement can be negotiated to better suit the circumstances of each party.
- **Off-balance-sheet financing.** Operating leases do not require a liability to be entered on the balance sheet, improving leverage ratios compared to borrowing the funds to purchase the asset.
- **Tax reporting advantages.** In the U.S., firms can create a *synthetic lease* whereby the lease is treated as an ownership position for tax purposes. This allows the lessee to deduct depreciation expense and interest expense for tax purposes. For financial purposes, the lease is treated as a rental agreement and the lessee excludes the lease liability from the balance sheet.

[margin note: operating leases improve leverage ratios]

LOS 38.g: Determine the effects of finance and operating leases on the financial statements and ratios of the lessees and lessors.

 Professor's Note: Lease accounting by the lessor is covered in the next LOS.

Under U.S. GAAP, a lessee must classify a lease as a finance lease if *any one* of the following criteria is met:

- Title to the leased asset is transferred to the lessee at the end of the lease period.
- A *bargain purchase option* exists. A bargain purchase option is a provision that permits the lessee to purchase the leased asset for a price that is significantly lower than the fair market value of the asset at some future date.

- The lease period is 75% or more of the asset's economic life.
- The present value of the lease payments is 90% or more of the fair value of the leased asset.

A lease not meeting any of these criteria is classified as an operating lease.

> *Professor's Note: In a finance lease, the interest rate used by the lessee is the lower of the lessee's incremental borrowing rate and the lessor's implicit lease rate. However, the interest rate is not always disclosed in the lessee's financial statements. Thus, it may be necessary for the analyst to derive the interest rate from information disclosed in the footnotes to make adjustments for analytical purposes.*

Under IFRS, the lease criteria are not as clear-cut. Rather, classification of a lease is determined by examining the economic substance of the transaction.

Reporting by the Lessee

Operating lease: At the inception of the lease, no entry is made. During the term of the lease, *rent expense,* equal to the lease payment, is recognized in the lessee's income statement. In the cash flow statement, the lease payment is reported as an outflow from operating activities.

Finance lease: At the inception of the lease, the *present value* of future minimum lease payments is recognized as an asset and as a liability on the lessee's balance sheet. Over the term of the lease, the asset is *depreciated in* the income statement and *interest expense* is recognized. Interest expense is equal to the lease liability at the beginning of the period multiplied by the interest rate implicit in the lease.

In the cash flow statement, the lease payment is separated into interest expense and principal. Just like any amortizing loan, the principal portion of the lease payment is equal to the total payment minus the interest expense. Under U.S. GAAP, interest expense is reported in the cash flow statement as an outflow from operating activities and the principal payment is reported as an outflow from financing activities.

Example: Accounting for a finance lease

Affordable Leasing Company leases a machine for its own use for four years with annual payments of $10,000. At the end of the lease, the machine is returned to the lessor, who will sell it for its scrap value. The appropriate interest rate is 6%.

Calculate the impact of the lease on Affordable Leasing's balance sheet and income statement for each of the four years, including the immediate impact. Affordable Leasing depreciates all assets on a straight-line basis. Assume the lease payments are made at the end of the year.

Answer:

The lease is classified as a finance lease because the asset is being leased for 75% or more of its useful life (we know this because at the end of the lease term, the asset will be sold for scrap). The present value of the lease payments at 6% is $34,651.

N = 4; I/Y = 6; PMT = –10,000; FV = 0; CPT → PV = $34,651

This amount is immediately recorded as both an asset and a liability on the lessee's balance sheet.

 Professor's Note: Here we are assuming the payments are made at the end of the year. Watch out on the exam. Had the lease called for beginning of the year payments, it would have been necessary to change the payment mode on your calculator in order to compute the present value.

Over the next four years, depreciation will be $34,651 / 4 = $8,663 per year. The book value of the asset will decline each year by the depreciation expense.

The interest expense and liability values are shown in the following table. Note that the *principal repayment amount each period is* equal to the lease payment minus the interest expense for the period (6% times the liability at the beginning of the period).

Affordable Leasing Example: Finance Lease Calculations

Year	(1) Beginning Leasehold Value	(2) Interest Expense (1) × 6%	(3) Lease Payment	(4) Lease Liability (1) + (2) – (3)	(5) Book Value of the Asset
0				$34,651	$34,651
1	$34,651	$2,079	10,000	26,730	25,988
2	26,730	1,604	10,000	18,334	17,326
3	18,334	1,100	10,000	9,434	8,663
4	9,434	566	10,000	0	0

(handwritten note: original value less SL depr)

Column 5 shows the ending book value of the leased asset each year. Note that, initially, depreciation is greater than the amortization (principal repayment) of the loan, so the asset's book value declines more rapidly than the lease liability. In the later years of the lease term, annual interest expense is less and the amortization of the lease liability is greater. The book value of the leased asset and the lease liability are again equal (both are zero) at the end of the lease term.

Financial Statement and Ratio Effects of Operating and Finance Leases

Balance sheet. A finance lease results in an asset and a liability. Consequently, turnover ratios that use total or fixed assets in their denominator will be lower when a lease is treated as a finance lease rather than as an operating lease. Return on assets will also be

(handwritten note: Ratios turnover lower ROA lower leverage higher)

lower for finance leases. Most importantly, leverage ratios such as the debt-to-assets ratio and the debt-to-equity ratio will be higher with finance leases because of the recorded liability. The principal payment due within the next year is reported as a current liability on the lessee's balance sheet. This reduces the lessee's current ratio and working capital (current assets minus current liabilities).

Since the liability for an operating lease does not appear on the lessee's balance sheet, operating leases are sometimes referred to as *off-balance-sheet financing activities.*

Income statement. All else held constant, operating income (EBIT) will be higher for companies that use finance leases relative to companies that use operating leases. With an operating lease, the entire lease payment is an operating expense, while for a finance lease, only the depreciation of the leased asset (not the interest portion of the lease payment) is treated as an operating expense.

Let's assume Affordable Leasing can treat the lease in the previous example as either an operating lease or a finance lease. Figure 5 compares the income statement effects.

Figure 5: Affordable Leasing: Impact of the Choice of Lease Accounting Method on Income Statement

	Operating Lease	Finance Lease		
Year	*Rent Expense*	*Depreciation*	*Interest*	*Finance Lease Expense*
1	$10,000	$8,663	$2,079	$10,742
2	10,000	8,663	1,604	10,267
3	10,000	8,663	1,100	9,763
4	10,000	8,663	566	9,229
	$40,000			$40,000

Total expense over the life of the lease will be equal for a lease treated as an operating lease and for a lease treated as a finance lease because the sum of depreciation expense and interest expense will equal the total of the lease payments. In the early years of a lease, however, the interest expense is higher, so the sum of depreciation and lease interest expense is greater than the lease payment. Consequently, net income will be lower for finance leases in the early years of the lease and higher in the later years, when the interest expense is lower.

Cash flow. Total cash flow is unaffected by the accounting treatment of a lease as a finance lease or operating lease. In our example, the total cash outflow is $10,000 per year. If the lease is an operating lease (rent expense = $10,000), then the total cash payment reduces cash flow from operations. If the lease is a finance lease, then only the portion of the lease payment that is considered interest expense reduces cash flow from operations. The part of the lease payment considered repayment of principal reduces cash flow from financing activities. Figure 6 illustrates that for a finance lease, cash flow from operations (CFO) is higher and cash flow from financing (CFF) is lower, compared to an operating lease.

Figure 6: Affordable Leasing: Impact on Cash Flow

	Finance Lease		Operating Lease
Year	CF Operations	CF Financing	CF Operations
1	–$2,079	–$7,921	–$10,000
2	–1,604	–8,396	–10,000
3	–1,100	–8,900	–10,000
4	–566	–9,434	–10,000

Finance lease: higher CFO

If Affordable reports the lease as a finance lease, CFO is reduced by $2,079 in Year 1 and if it reports the lease as an operating lease, CFO is reduced by $10,000. Companies with finance leases will show higher CFO relative to firms that use operating leases (all else the same).

Figure 7 and Figure 8 summarize the differences between the effects of finance leases and operating leases on the financial statements of the lessee.

Figure 7: Financial Statement Impact of Lease Accounting

	Finance Lease	Operating Lease
Assets	Higher	Lower
Liabilities (current and long-term)	Higher	Lower
Net income (in the early years)	Lower	Higher
Net income (later years)	Higher	Lower
Total net income	Same	Same
EBIT (operating income)	Higher	Lower
Cash flow from operations	Higher	Lower
Cash flow from financing	Lower	Higher
Total cash flow	Same	Same

Figure 8: Ratio Impact of Lease Accounting

	Finance Lease	Operating Lease
Current ratio (CA / CL)	Lower	Higher
Working capital (CA – CL)	Lower	Higher
Asset turnover (Revenue / TA)	Lower	Higher
Return on assets* (NI / TA)	Lower	Higher
Return on equity* (NI / SE)	Lower	Higher
Debt / Assets	Higher	Lower
Debt / Equity	Higher	Lower

* In the early years of the lease.

In sum, all the ratios in Figure 8 are worse when the lease is capitalized. The only improvements from a finance lease are higher EBIT (because interest is not subtracted in calculating EBIT), higher CFO (because principal repayment is CFF), and higher net income in the later years of the lease (because interest plus depreciation is less than the lease payment in the later years).

Professor's Note: There are two points that candidates often find confusing here. First, interest payments are an operating cash flow but are not considered an operating expenditure. That is, they are not subtracted in calculating operating income (EBIT). Second, adding equal amounts to assets and liabilities will typically increase the debt-to-assets ratio. Since assets are typically larger than debt (liabilities), the numerator of the debt-to-assets ratio increases by a greater proportion than the denominator when equal amounts are added to each, so the ratio increases. With respect to the current ratio and working capital, the current year principal amortization for a finance lease is added to current liabilities, but there is no increase in current assets from accounting for the lease as a finance lease.

Required Disclosures

Lessees are required to disclose useful information about finance leases and operating leases in the financial statements or in the footnotes. For example, the lessee must disclose the lease payments that are due in each of the next five years. Lease payments due after five years can be aggregated.

Unfortunately, the interest rate used in the lessee's calculations is not always disclosed. Thus, it may be necessary for an analyst to derive the interest rate in order to make adjustments for analytical purposes. The interest rate is simply the internal rate of return (IRR) of the future lease payments; that is, the interest rate that equates the present value of the lease with the future lease payments.

Example: Lessee's Footnote Disclosure

Mustang Company conducts part of its operations from leased premises using various finance leases that expire in 10 years. In addition, Mustang leases equipment under non-cancelable operating leases. The future minimum lease payments are:

Years	Finance Leases	Operating Leases
1	$570	$125
2	570	110
3	530	90
4	290	70
5	260	65
Thereafter (evenly from Years 6 to 10)	1,000	250
Total minimum lease payments	$3,220	$710
Less interest portion	865	
Present value of future minimum lease payments	$2,355	

Part A. Calculate the implicit interest rate used by lessee.

Part B. Assume that Mustang reported debt of $2,950 and equity of $800 at the inception of the lease. If Mustang had treated the operating leases as finance leases, calculate the effects on the debt-to-equity ratio.

Answer:

Part A. Use the IRR function on your financial calculator to solve for the interest rate that will equate the present value of $2,355 with the future lease payments. The result is an IRR of 8.2%.

IRR = implicit interest rate

Year	Cash flow	Calculator Register
0	–$2,355	CF_0
1	570	CF_1
2	570	CF_2
3	530	CF_3
4	290	CF_4
5	260	CF_5
6	200	CF_6
7	200	CF_7
8	200	CF_8
9	200	CF_9
10	200	CF_{10}

The analyst can use the implicit lease rate to forecast lease interest expense and amortization of the lease liability when forecasting net income and balance sheet values for future periods. Analysts can also use the implicit lease rate to discount future operating lease payments to calculate the amount that operating leases would add to assets and liabilities if treated as finance leases (as we illustrate in Part B).

Part B. Use the NPV function on your financial calculator to compute the present value of the operating lease payments discounted at the implicit interest rate of 8.2%. The result is a PV of $509.

Year	Cash flow	Calculator Register
0	0	CF_0
1	125	CF_1
2	110	CF_2
3	90	CF_3
4	70	CF_4
5	65	CF_5
6	50	CF_6
7	50	CF_7
8	50	CF_8
9	50	CF_9
10	50	CF_{10}

Mustang's reported debt-to-equity ratio was 3.7 ($2,950 debt / $800 equity). Adjusting Mustang's debt for the operating lease results in a debt-to-equity ratio of 4.3 [($2,950 reported debt + $509 PV of operating lease) / $800 reported equity].

add PV of op lease to debt

Alternatively, an analyst can approximate the present value of the operating lease liability and asset by using the ratio of the present value of finance lease payments to the total finance lease payments. Here, that ratio is $2,355/$3,220 = 73.1%. Using this approximation, the present value of the operating lease is $720 × 73.1% = $519, which is close to the actual present value of the future minimum operating lease payments of $509 calculated in Part B.

LOS 38.h: Distinguish between a sales-type lease and a direct financing lease, and determine the effects on the financial statements and ratios of the lessors.

Under U.S. GAAP, if any one of the finance lease criteria for lessees is met, the collectibility of lease payments is reasonably certain, and the lessor has substantially completed performance, the lessor must treat the lease as a finance lease. Otherwise, the lessor will treat the lease as an operating lease.

From the lessor's perspective, a finance lease can be accounted for as either a **sales-type lease** or a **direct financing lease**.

Sales-type Lease

A sales-type lease is treated as if the lessor sold the asset and provided the financing to the buyer.

The lease is treated as a sales-type lease if the present value of the lease payments exceeds the carrying value of the asset. This will typically be the case when the lessor is a manufacturer or dealer because the cost of goods sold will be less than the fair market value of the leased asset.

At the inception of the lease, the lessor will recognize a sale equal to the present value of the lease payments, and cost of goods sold equal to the carrying value of the asset. Just as with a normal sales transaction, the difference between the sales price and cost of goods sold is gross profit. The asset is removed from the balance sheet and a lease receivable, equal to the present value of the lease payments, is created. As the lease payments are received, the principal portion of the payment reduces the lease receivable. It is as if the lessor sold the asset for its fair market value, and loaned the lessee that amount.

In addition to the gross profit, the lessor also recognizes interest revenue over the term of the lease. The interest revenue is equal to the lease receivable at the beginning of the period multiplied by the interest rate.

In the cash flow statement, the interest revenue portion of the lease payment is reported as an inflow from operating activities and the principal reduction is reported as an inflow from investing activities, just as with any amortizing loan the lessor may make.

Direct Financing Lease

In a direct financing lease, no gross profit is recognized by the lessor at the inception of the lease. The lessor is simply providing a financing function to the lessee. The lease is treated as a direct financing lease if the present value of the lease payments is equal to the carrying value of the leased asset.

PV pmt = carrying value no profit

At the inception of the lease, the lessor removes the asset from the balance sheet and a lease receivable is created in the same amount. As the lease payments are received, the principal portion of payment reduces the lease receivable.

In the income statement, the lessor recognizes interest income over the term of the lease. The interest portion of each lease payment is equal to the lease receivable at the beginning of the period multiplied by the interest rate.

In the cash flow statement, the interest portion of the lease payment is reported as an inflow from operating activities and the principal repayment portion of the lease payment is reported as an inflow from investing activities.

> **Example: Direct financing lease**
>
> Assume Johnson Company purchases an asset for $69,302 to lease to Carver, Inc. for four years with an annual lease payment of $20,000 at the end of each year. At the end of the lease, Carver will own the asset for no additional payment. The implied interest rate in the lease is 6% (N = 4, PV = –69,302, PMT = 20,000, FV = 0, CPT I/Y → 6). Determine how Johnson should account for the lease payments from Carver.
>
> **Answer:**
>
> Since the present value of lease payments of $69,302 is equal to the carrying value of the asset, Johnson treats the lease as a direct financing lease. Johnson removes the leased asset from the balance sheet and records a lease receivable of $69,302. The lease payments are recorded as follows:
>
> | Year | (1) Beginning Lease Receivable | (2) Interest Income (1) × 6% | (3) Lease Payment | (4) Ending Lease Receivable (1) +(2) – (3) |
> |------|------|------|------|------|
> | 0 | | | | $69,302 |
> | 1 | $69,302 | $4,158 | $20,000 | $53,460 |
> | 2 | 53,460 | 3,208 | 20,000 | 36,668 |
> | 3 | 36,668 | 2,200 | 20,000 | 18,868 |
> | 4 | 18,868 | 1,132 | 20,000 | 0 |
>
> Interest income received each year will increase earnings. In the cash flow statement, the interest income is reported as an inflow from operating activities. The principal reduction (column 3 – column 2) reduces the lease receivable and is treated in the cash flow statement as an inflow from investing activities.

Had Johnson manufactured the equipment with a cost of goods of $60,000, it would have recorded a gross profit of $69,302 – $60,000 = $9,302 at lease inception, put a lease receivable of $69,302 on its balance sheet, and then accounted for the interest income portion of the lease payments just as in the table above.

Operating Lease

If the lease is treated as an operating lease, the lessor simply recognizes the lease payment as rental income. In addition, the lessor will keep the leased asset on its balance sheet and recognize depreciation expense on the leased asset.

Returning to our example, if Johnson treats the lease as an operating lease, $20,000 of rental income is recognized each year. In addition, depreciation expense of $17,325.50 ($69,302 / 4 years) is also recognized. Figure 9 compares the income from a direct financing lease and an operating lease.

Figure 9: Income Comparison of a Direct Financing Lease and Operating Lease

	Direct Financing Lease	Operating Lease		
Year	Interest Income	Rental Income	Depreciation Expense	Operating Lease Income
1	$4,158	$20,000	$17,325	$2,675
2	3,208	20,000	17,326	2,674
3	2,200	20,000	17,325	2,675
4	1,132	20,000	17,326	2,674
	$10,698			$10,698

Total income over the life of the lease is the same for an operating lease and a direct financing lease. However, in the early years of the lease, the income reported from the direct financing lease is higher than the income reported from the operating lease. Just like an amortizing loan, the interest is higher in the early years. This situation reverses in the later years of the lease.

In the cash flow statement, the classifications result in significant differences in cash flow from operations, as seen in Figure 10.

Figure 10: Comparison of Cash Flows to the Lessor of a Direct Financing Lease and an Operating Lease

	Direct Financing Lease		Operating Lease
Year	CF Operations	CF Investing	CF Operations
1	$4,158	$15,842	$20,000
2	3,208	16,792	20,000
3	2,200	17,800	20,000
4	1,132	18,868	20,000

Total cash flow is the same for an operating lease and a direct financing lease. However, cash flow from operations is higher with the operating lease. With a direct financing lease, the lease payment is separated into the interest portion (CFO) and principal portion (CFI).

 Professor's Note: From the lessee's perspective, principal is a financing outflow. From the lessor's perspective, principal is a return of capital invested in the lease. Thus, the principal is reported as an investing inflow.

LOS 38.i: Describe the types and economic consequences of off-balance-sheet financing, and determine how take-or-pay contracts, throughput arrangements, and the sale of receivables affect financial statements and selected financial ratios.

Operating leases are just one example of many contractual obligations that are not recognized as liabilities on the balance sheet. Analysts should adjust financial statements to reflect the economic reality of off-balance-sheet financing activities.

Under a **take-or-pay contract** or **throughput arrangement**, the purchasing firm commits to buy a minimum quantity of an input (usually a raw material) over a specified period of time. As its name implies, a take-or-pay contract requires that payments be made even if the firm does not purchase the amount of the input stipulated in the contract. Prices may be fixed or related to market prices. Neither an asset nor a liability is recognized on the balance sheet. However, the purchaser must disclose the nature and minimum required payments in the footnotes to the financial statements and in the MD&A under U.S. reporting requirements. Details of commitments are typically reported in a section of the footnotes titled "Commitments and Contingencies."

The analyst should adjust the debt-to-total-capital ratio for these commitments by adding the sum of required purchase amounts to both debt and total capital. For a more accurate adjustment, the analyst can calculate the present value of these future purchase commitments and add it to debt and total capital to recalculate the debt-to-total-capital ratio.

Under a **sale of receivables with recourse**, a firm may sell its accounts receivable to an unrelated party, but the firm continues to service the original receivables and remits the collections to the buyer of the receivables. "With recourse" refers to the fact that the buyer of the receivables has not taken on the risk of non-payment. In this case, the seller of the receivables retains the credit risk and the transaction is, in essence, simply borrowing that is collateralized by the receivables. To the extent that the analyst determines that this is the case, the financial statements and ratios should be adjusted by treating the "sale" of receivables as collateralized borrowing.

Before computing ratios (e.g., the current ratio, receivables turnover, and leverage ratios), accounts receivable and current liabilities should be increased by the amount of receivables that were sold. Also, cash flow from operations should be adjusted by classifying the sale of the receivables as cash flow from financing (borrowing) instead of cash flow from operations (collection of accounts receivable).

Off-Balance-Sheet Financing and Financial Ratios

Because the debt on take-or-pay contracts and throughput arrangements is off-balance-sheet, it has the effect of lowering leverage ratios such as the debt ratio and the debt-to-equity ratio. That is why, for analytical purposes, the present value of the minimum purchase obligation should be added to both long-term liabilities and long-term assets before calculating leverage ratios.

The sale of receivables artificially reduces the accounts receivable balance and short-term borrowings. Consequently, leverage ratios are too low, receivables turnover is too high, and the current ratio (assuming it is greater than 1.0) is too high. That is why, for analytical purposes, the receivables and short-term debt should be added back to accounts receivable and current liabilities, respectively, on the balance sheet, and the ratios should be recalculated with these restated amounts.

Let's work through an example of the sale of receivables with recourse. Assume that a firm reports selling $170,000 of receivables, and footnote disclosures reveal the sale has not transferred the credit risk of the receivables (i.e., the receivables were sold with recourse). In addition, reported debt is $1,300,000, reported equity is $580,000, and the interest rate associated with the receivables sale is 9%.

For purposes of analysis, we should *treat the sale as a borrowing, reinstate the receivables, and treat the proceeds of the sale as debt.* We can adjust the end-of-period balance sheet as shown in Figure 11.

Figure 11: Balance Sheet Adjustments

	As Reported	Adjusted
Debt	$1,300,000	$1,470,000
Equity	$580,000	$580,000
Debt-to-equity ratio	2.24	2.53

We also need to make an adjustment to the income statement to include interest expense on the loan. We add interest on the receivables to both income and expense. (Assuming a 9% interest rate, interest expense would be $15,300). Hence, net income will not be affected, but the interest coverage ratio will be lower than reported (interest expense increased by a greater percentage than EBIT).

Figure 12: Income Statement Adjustments

	As Reported	Adjusted
EBIT	$265,000	$280,300
Interest expense	$102,000	$117,300
Coverage ratio	2.60	2.39

The cash flow statement also needs to be adjusted by reducing cash flow from operations and increasing cash flow from financing by the amount of the receivables sold. CFI and total cash flow are not affected.

KEY CONCEPTS

LOS 38.a

When debt is issued, a liability equal to the proceeds of the bond issue is recorded, so cash and liabilities initially both increase by the same amount. Interest expense each period is the coupon interest paid, plus the amortization of any discount below par value or minus the amortization of any premium above par value.

Proceeds of a debt issue and the repayment of principal amounts are financing cash flows. Cash interest paid is an operating cash outflow. Amortization of bond premiums and discounts do not affect cash flows as they are recognized.

LOS 38.b

Debt covenants are restrictions on the issuer that protect the bondholders' interests. Debt covenants can reduce default risk and decrease interest costs. Covenants can include restrictions on dividend payments and share repurchases; mergers and acquisitions; sale, leaseback, and disposal of certain assets; and issuance of new debt in the future. Other covenants require the firm to maintain ratios or financial statement items at specific levels.

LOS 38.c

Footnote disclosure concerning a borrower's financing liabilities usually includes the nature of the liabilities, maturity dates, stated and effective interest rates, call provisions and conversion privileges, restrictions imposed by creditors, assets pledged as security, and the amount of debt maturing in each of the next five years.

LOS 38.d

An *increase* in the market rate of interest will result in a *decrease* in the fair value of a bond liability. Conversely, a *decrease* in the market rate will result in an *increase* in the fair value. Historically, changes in market values did not affect balance sheet values of liabilities. Recent changes in both U.S. GAAP and IFRS provide for more disclosure of changes in the fair values of liabilities and for more liabilities to be reported on the balance sheet at fair value.

LOS 38.e

Under U.S. GAAP, the value of the conversion option is ignored when a convertible bond is issued and all of the bond proceeds are reported as a liability. Under IFRS, the issuer reports the pure bond liability as debt and the conversion option as part of stockholders' equity. Analysts should consider the likelihood that convertible bonds will be converted (compare the conversion price and market price of the firm's shares) and adjust the debt-to-equity ratio to determine the effect of conversion on the firm's leverage ratios.

For bonds with warrants attached, the issuer separately values the bond liability and the warrants. The value of the bond (without the warrants) is reported as a liability and the value of the warrants is reported in stockholders' equity.

LOS 38.f
Compared to purchasing an asset, leasing it may provide the lessee with less costly financing, reduce the risk of obsolescence, and include less restrictive provisions than a typical loan. Certain types of leases also provide tax advantages compared to purchasing the asset and keep the liability for payment off the balance sheet.

LOS 38.g
A finance (capital) lease requires that the present value of the lease payments be added to both assets and liabilities on the lessee's balance sheet. The lessee's income statement will reflect depreciation of the lease asset and interest expense on the lease liability. Cash lease payments are accounted for as interest (an operating cash outflow) and repayment of principal (a financing cash outflow).

An operating lease requires no balance sheet entries and is accounted for on the lessee's income statement as rental expense equal to the lease payment (an operating cash outflow).

Compared to an operating lease, a finance lease will increase assets, liabilities, leverage ratios, cash flows from operations, and operating income. It will decrease net income in the early years of the lease, financing cash flows, working capital, and the current ratio.

LOS 38.h
From the lessor's perspective, a finance lease is either a sales-type lease or a direct financing lease.

A lessor reports a lease as a direct financing lease when the present value of lease payments is equal to the asset's carrying value. The lessor reports a lease receivable at the inception of the lease and interest income over the life of the lease. The lease payment is treated as part interest income (CFO) and part principal reduction (CFI).

A lessor reports a lease as a sales-type lease when the present value of the lease payments exceeds the asset's carrying value, as it typically is for a manufacturer or dealer of the leased asset. The lessor reports gross profit as if the asset were sold for the fair value of the lease. The lessor reports a lease receivable at inception and interest income over the life of the lease. The lease payment is treated as part interest income (CFO) and part principal reduction (CFI).

LOS 38.i
Analysts should adjust the financial statements for off-balance-sheet activities such as operating leases, take-or-pay agreements, throughput agreements, and receivable sales with recourse. In each case, assets and liabilities are increased by the appropriate adjustment. It may also be necessary to reclassify some cash flows from operations to cash flows from financing.

CONCEPT CHECKERS

Use the following data to answer Questions 1 through 8.

A firm issues a $10 million bond with a 6% coupon rate, 4-year maturity, and annual interest payments when market interest rates are 7%.

1.   The bond can be classified as a:
A. discount bond.
B. par bond.
C. premium bond.

2.   The annual coupon payments will each be:
A. $600,000.
B. $676,290.
C. $700,000.

3.   Total of all cash payments to the bondholders is:
A. $12,400,000.
B. $12,738,721.
C. $12,800,000.

4.   The initial book value of the bonds is:
A. $9,400,000.
B. $9,661,279.
C. $10,000,000.

5.   For the first period the interest expense is:
A. $600,000.
B. $676,290.
C. $700,000.

6.   If the market rate changes to 8% and the bonds are carried at amortized cost, the book value of the bonds at the end of the first year will be:
A. $9,484,581.
B. $9,661,279.
C. $9,737,568.

7.   The total interest expense reported by the issuer over the life of the bond will be:
A. $2,400,000.
B. $2,738,721.
C. $2,800,000.

8.   For analytical purposes, what is the impact on the debt-to-equity ratio if the market rate of interest increases after the bond is issued?
A. An increase.
B. A decrease.
C. No change.

9.   According to U.S. GAAP, the coupon payment on a bond is:
     A. reported as an operating cash outflow.
     B. reported as a financing cash outflow.
     C. reported as part operating cash outflow and part financing cash outflow.

10. Wolfe Inc. has a capital structure consisting of $10 million of liabilities and $15 million of equity. Wolfe issues $0.7 million of preferred shares and $1.0 million of bonds with warrants attached (debt component comprises 80% of the value) for total cash proceeds of $1.7 million. Which of the following amounts is the *revised* debt-to-total capital ratio upon the issuance of the two new financial instruments?
     A. 0.404.
     B. 0.431.
     C. 0.679.

11. A company has convertible bonds on its books with a conversion price of $20 per share. The stock price is currently $40 per share. For analytical purposes, the bonds should be treated as:
     A. a combination of debt and common stock.
     B. debt.
     C. equity.

12. Which of the following is *least likely* to be disclosed in the financial statements of a bond issuer?
     A. The amount of debt that matures in each of the next five years.
     B. Collateral pledged as security in the event of default.
     C. The market rate of interest on the balance sheet date.

13. As compared to purchasing an asset, which of the following is *least likely* an incentive to structure a transaction as a finance lease?
     A. At the end of the lease, the asset is returned to the lessor.
     B. The terms of the lease terms can be negotiated to better meet each party's needs.
     C. The lease enhances the balance sheet by the lease liability.

14. For a lessee:

	Operating leases are accounted for like:	Operating lease payments are reported as:
A.	Rental agreements	Lease expense
B.	Asset purchases	Lease expense
C.	Rental agreements	Interest expense

15. For a lessor, a sales-type lease results in:
     A. rental income.
     B. gross profit.
     C. depreciation expense.

16. For a company that has sold receivables but retained the credit risk, which of the following is *least likely* to require adjustment by an analyst?
     A. Current ratio.
     B. Inventory turnover.
     C. Debt-to-equity.

17. Which of the following is *least likely* an off-balance-sheet financing method?
     A. Sale of receivables.
     B. Throughput arrangements.
     C. Convertible bonds.

18. Which of the following statements about direct financing leases and operating leases is *least accurate* for a lessor?
     A. Total cash flows are not affected by the accounting treatment of the lease.
     B. As compared to an operating lease, a direct financing lease will result in higher operating cash flows.
     C. An operating lease will result in lower earnings in the earlier years of the lease, while the direct financing lease will result in lower earnings in the later years.

19. A finance lease results in the following net income effects to a lessee as compared to an operating lease:

	Early years	Later years
A.	Lower	Lower
B.	Lower	Higher
C.	Higher	Lower

20. For a lessee, finance lease interest expense is equal to the:
     A. interest rate multiplied by the beginning lease liability.
     B. interest rate multiplied by the lease payment.
     C. lease payment.

COMPREHENSIVE PROBLEMS

A. Consider the effects on the following financial statement items and ratios of capitalizing a lease rather than treating it as an operating lease. Indicate the effect of capitalizing the lease on the following during the first year of the lease (circle one).

CFF	higher	lower	no change
CFO	higher	lower	no change
CFI	higher	lower	no change
Total cash flow	higher	lower	no change
EBIT	higher	lower	no change
Net income	higher	lower	no change
D/A	higher	lower	no change
D/E	higher	lower	no change
ROA	higher	lower	no change
ROE	higher	lower	no change
Total asset turnover	higher	lower	no change

B. Babson Corp. sold $550,000 of receivables during the most recent period. Meg Jones, CFA, is adjusting balance sheet items and ratios for this sale of receivables because significant credit risk on them remains with Babson. Indicate increase, decrease, or unchanged to reflect the effect of adjustment on the indicated items and ratios.

Debt	Cash	Current ratio (= 1)
Debt-to-equity	Receivables	Working capital
Receivables turnover	Cash conversion cycle	Interest coverage
CFO	CFF	CFI

ANSWERS – CONCEPT CHECKERS

1. **A** This bond is issued at a discount since the coupon rate < market rate.

2. **A** Coupon payment = (coupon rate × face value of bond) = 6% × $10,000,000 = $600,000.

3. **A** Four coupon payments and the face value = ($600,000 × 4) + $10,000,000 = $12,400,000.

4. **B** The present value of a 4-year annuity of $600,000 plus a 4-year lump sum of $10 million, all valued at a discount rate of 7%, equals $9,661,279. Choice C can be eliminated because the bond was issued at a discount.

5. **B** Market interest rate × book value = 7% × $9,661,279 = $676,290.

6. **C** The new book value = beginning book value + interest expense – coupon payment = $9,661,279 + $676,290 – $600,000 = $9,737,569. The interest expense was calculated in question 5. Alternatively, changing N from 4 to 3 and calculating the PV will yield the same result. The change in market rates will not affect amortized costs.

7. **B** Coupon payments + discount interest = coupon payments + (face value – issue value) = $2,400,000 + ($10,000,000 – $9,661,279) = $2,738,721.

8. **B** An increase in the market rate will decrease the price of a bond. For analytical purposes, adjusting the bond liability to its economic value will result in a lower debt-to-equity ratio (lower numerator and higher denominator).

9. **A** The actual coupon payment on a bond is reported as operating cash outflow.

10. **A** The $0.7 million of preferred shares are treated as equity. For the warrants, $0.8 million would be treated as debt and $0.2 million as equity. liabilities = $10 million + $0.8 million = $10.8 million equity = $15 million + $0.7 million + $0.2 million = $15.9 million debt-to-total capital ratio = liabilities / (liabilities + equity) = $10.8 million / ($10.8 million + $15.9 million) = 0.404

11. **C** The bonds should be treated as equity for analytical purposes because the stock price is significantly above the conversion price.

12. **C** The market rate on the balance sheet date is not typically disclosed. The amount of debt principal scheduled to be repaid over the next five years and collateral pledged (if any) are generally included in the footnotes to the financial statements.

13. **C** Operating leases enhance the balance sheet by excluding any lease liability. With a finance lease, an asset and a liability are reported on the balance sheet as with purchase made with debt.

14. **A** Operating leases are accounted for like rental agreements (finance leases are like purchases). Operating lease payments are reported as lease expense.

15. **B** In a sales-type lease, the lessor reports gross profit and interest income. In operating lease, the lessor reports rental income and depreciation expense.

16. **B** Selling receivables does not affect inventory; thus, inventory turnover does not require adjustment.

17. **C** Convertible bonds are reported on the balance sheet as a liability.

18. **B** For an operating lease, all of the lease payment is reported by the lessor as an operating inflow. With a direct financing lease, the payment is separated into interest revenue (operating inflow) and principal reduction (investing inflow). The accounting treatment of a lease affects the classification of cash flows but not the total cash flows.

19. **B** In the early years, a finance lease results in lower net income because interest plus depreciation expense is greater than rent expense under an operating lease. This effect reverses in the later years of the lease.

20. **A** Interest expense is calculated each year by multiplying the beginning balance of the lease liability by the interest rate of the lease.

ANSWERS – COMPREHENSIVE PROBLEMS

A. With a capital lease:
- CFF is lower.
- CFO is higher.
- CFI is unchanged.
- Total cash flow is unchanged.
- EBIT is higher.
- Net income is lower in the early years.
- D/A is higher.
- D/E is higher.
- ROA is lower.
- ROE is lower.
- Asset turnover is lower.

B. To adjust these items, we treat the sale of receivables as if it were a short-term borrowing and add back the amount of receivables sold. This will increase debt and the D/E ratio. Receivables increase and current liabilities increase by the same amounts, so working capital, the current ratio (because it is equal to 1), and cash position are unchanged by the adjustment. The receivables turnover ratio is decreased by adding back AR, so the cash conversion cycle is longer. The cash generated by the sale is CFF after adjustment rather than CFO, so CFF increases and CFO decreases. The increase in interest from adjusting debt upward will decrease the interest coverage ratio, assuming EBIT > interest expense. CFI is unaffected.

FINANCIAL ANALYSIS TECHNIQUES

Study Session 10

EXAM FOCUS

This topic review presents a "tool box" for an analyst. It would be nice if you could calculate all these ratios, but it is imperative that you understand what firm characteristic each one is measuring, and even more important, that you know whether a higher or lower ratio is better in each instance. Different analysts calculate some ratios differently. It would be helpful if analysts were always careful to distinguish between total liabilities, total interest-bearing debt, long-term debt, and creditor and trade debt, but they do not. Some analysts routinely add deferred tax liabilities to debt or exclude goodwill when calculating assets and equity; others do not. Statistical reporting services almost always disclose how each of the ratios they present was calculated. So do not get too tied up in the details of each ratio, but understand well what each one represents and what factors would likely lead to significant changes in a particular ratio. The DuPont formulas have been with us a long time and were on the test when I took it back in the 1980s. The extended form here is different that the one presented in the Study Session on Corporate Finance, making it less likely that you need to memorize it. Either way, decomposing ROE into its components is an important analytic technique and it should definitely be in your tool box.

LOS 39.a: Evaluate and compare companies using ratio analysis, common-size financial statements, and charts in financial analysis.

Common-size statements normalize balance sheets and income statements and allow the analyst to more easily compare performance across firms and for a single firm over time.

- A vertical common-size balance sheet expresses all balance sheet accounts as a percentage of total assets.
- A vertical common-size income statement expresses all income statement items as a percentage of sales.

In addition to the comparison of financial data across firms and time, common-size analysis is appropriate for quickly viewing certain financial ratios. For example, the gross profit margin, operating profit margin, and net profit margin are all clearly indicated within a common-size income statement.

- Vertical common-size income statement ratios are especially useful in studying trends in costs and profit margins.

$$\text{vertical common-size income statement ratios} = \frac{\text{income statement account}}{\text{sales}}$$

- Balance sheet accounts can also be converted to common-size ratios by dividing each balance sheet item by total assets.

$$\text{vertical common-size balance-sheet ratios} = \frac{\text{balance sheet account}}{\text{total assets}}$$

Example: Constructing common-size statements

The common-size statements in Figure 1 show balance sheet items as percentages of assets, and income statement items as percentages of sales.

- You can convert all asset and liability amounts to their actual values by multiplying the percentages listed below by their total assets of $57,100; $55,798; and $52,071, respectively for 20X6, 20X5, and 20X4 (data is USD millions).
- Also, all income statement items can be converted to their actual values by multiplying the given percentages by total sales, which were $29,723; $29,234; and $22,922, respectively, for 20X6, 20X5, and 20X4.

Figure 1: Vertical Common-Size Balance Sheet and Income Statement

Balance Sheet Fiscal year end	20X6	20X5	20X4
Assets			
Cash & cash equivalents	0.38%	0.29%	0.37%
Accounts receivable	5.46%	5.61%	6.20%
Inventories	5.92%	5.42%	5.84%
Deferred income taxes	0.89%	0.84%	0.97%
Other current assets	0.41%	0.40%	0.36%
Total current assets	13.06%	12.56%	13.74%
Gross fixed assets	25.31%	23.79%	25.05%
Accumulated depreciation	8.57%	7.46%	6.98%
Net gross fixed assets	16.74%	16.32%	18.06%
Other long term assets	70.20%	71.12%	68.20%
Total assets	100.00%	100.00%	100.00%
Liabilities			
Accounts payable	3.40%	3.40%	3.79%
Short term debt	1.00%	2.19%	1.65%
Other current liabilities	8.16%	10.32%	9.14%
Total current liabilities	12.56%	15.91%	14.58%
Long term debt	18.24%	14.58%	5.18%
Other long term liabilities	23.96%	27.44%	53.27%
Total liabilities	54.76%	57.92%	73.02%
Preferred equity	0.00%	0.00%	0.00%
Common equity	45.24%	42.08%	26.98%
Total liabilities & equity	100.00%	100.00%	100.00%

Income Statement Fiscal year end	20X6	20X5	20X4
Revenues	100.00%	100.00%	100.00%
Cost of goods sold	59.62%	60.09%	60.90%
Gross profit	40.38%	39.91%	39.10%
Selling, general & administrative	16.82%	17.34%	17.84%
Depreciation	2.39%	2.33%	2.18%
Amortization	0.02%	3.29%	2.33%
Other operating expenses	0.58%	0.25%	-0.75%
Operating income	20.57%	16.71%	17.50%
Interest and other debt expense	2.85%	4.92%	2.60%
Income before taxes	17.72%	11.79%	14.90%
Provision for income taxes	6.30%	5.35%	6.17%
Net income	11.42%	6.44%	8.73%

Even a cursory inspection of the income statement in Figure 1 can be quite instructive. Beginning at the bottom, we can see that the profitability of the company has increased nicely in 20X6 after falling slightly in 20X5. We can examine the 20X6 income statement values to find the source of this greatly improved profitability. Cost of goods sold seems to be stable, with an improvement (decrease) in 20X6 of only 0.48%. SG&A was down approximately one-half percent as well.

These improvements from (relative) cost reduction, however, only begin to explain the 5% increase in the net profit margin for 20X6. Improvements in two items, "amortization" and "interest and other debt expense," appear to be the most significant factors in the firm's improved profitability in 20X6. Clearly the analyst must investigate further in both areas to learn whether these improvements represent permanent improvements or whether these items can be expected to return to previous percentage-of-sales levels in the future.

We can also note that interest expense as a percentage of sales was approximately the same in 20X4 and 20X6. We must investigate the reasons for the higher interest costs in 20X5 to determine whether the current level of 2.85% can be expected to continue into the next period. In addition, over 3% of the 5% increase in net profit margin in 20X6 is due to a decrease in amortization expense. Since this is a noncash expense, the decrease may have no implications for cash flows looking forward.

This discussion should make clear that common-size analysis doesn't tell an analyst the whole story about this company, but can certainly point the analyst in the right direction to find out the circumstances that led to the increase in the net profit margin and to determine the effects, if any, on firm cash flow going forward.

Another way to present financial statement data that is quite useful when analyzing trends over time is a horizontal common-size balance sheet or income statement. The divisor here is the first-year values, so they are all standardized to 1.0 by construction. Figure 2 illustrates this approach.

Figure 2: Horizontal Common-Size Balance Sheet Data

	20X4	20X5	20X6
Inventory	1.0	1.1	1.4
Cash and marketable sec.	1.0	1.3	1.2
Long-term debt	1.0	1.6	1.8
PP&E (net of depreciation)	1.0	0.9	0.8

Trends in the values of these items as well as the relative growth in these items are readily apparent from a horizontal common-size balance sheet.

Professor's Note: We have presented data in Figure 1 with information for the most recent period on the left and in Figure 2 we have presented the historical values from left to right. Both presentation methods are common, and on the exam you should pay special attention to which method is used in the data presented for any question.

We can view the values in the common-size financial statements as ratios. Net income is shown on the common-size income statement as net income/revenues, which is the net profit margin, and tells the analyst the percentage of each dollar of sales that remains for shareholders after all expenses related to the generation of those sales are deducted. One measure of financial leverage, long-term debt to total assets, can be read directly from the vertical common-size financial statements. Specific ratios commonly used in financial analysis and interpretation of their values are covered in detail in this review.

A **stacked column graph** (also called a *stacked bar graph*) shows the changes in items from year to year in graphical form. Figure 3 presents such data for a hypothetical corporation.

Figure 3: Stacked Column (Stacked Bar) Graph

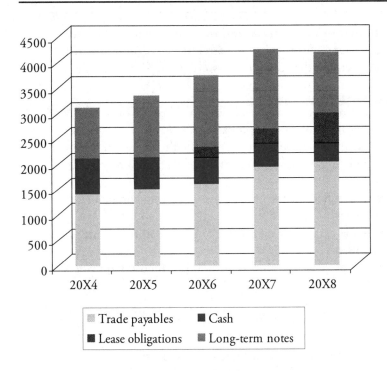

Another alternative for graphic presentation of data is a **line graph**. Figure 4 presents the same data as Figure 3, but as a line graph. The increase in trade payables and the decrease in cash are evident in either format and would alert the analyst to potential liquidity problems that require further investigation and analysis.

Figure 4: Line Graph

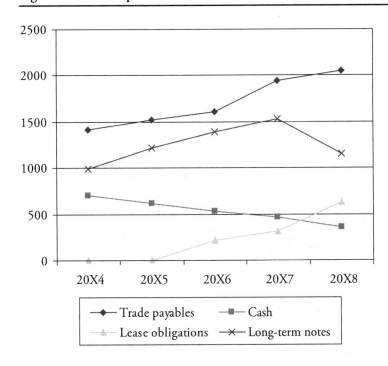

LOS 39.b: Describe the limitations of ratio analysis.

You must be aware of the **limitations of financial ratios.** Ratios are used for internal comparisons and comparisons across firms. They are often most useful in identifying questions that need to be answered rather than for answering questions directly. Their limitations are:

- Financial ratios are not useful when viewed in isolation. They are only valid when compared to those of other firms or to the company's historical performance.
- Comparisons with other companies are made more difficult because of different accounting treatments. This is particularly important when analyzing non-U.S. firms.
- It is difficult to find comparable industry ratios when analyzing companies that operate in multiple industries.
- Conclusions cannot be made from viewing one set of ratios. All ratios must be viewed relative to one another.
- Determining the target or comparison value for a ratio is difficult, requiring some range of acceptable values.

In conducting your analysis, you must always be aware of the limitations of ratios. Ask yourself these questions:

- Do the firms being compared have similar accounting practices?
- When comparing divisions within a firm, are the ratios comparable?
- Do the ratios being used give consistent readings?
- Do the ratios yield a reasonable figure for the industry?

LOS 39.c: Calculate, classify, and interpret activity, liquidity, solvency, profitability, and valuation ratios.

Financial ratios can be segregated into different classifications by the type of information about the company they provide. One such classification scheme is:

Activity ratios. This category includes several ratios also referred to asset utilization or turnover ratios (e.g., inventory turnover, receivables turnover, and total assets turnover). They often give indications of how well a firm utilizes various assets such as inventory and fixed assets.

Liquidity ratios. Liquidity here refers to the ability to pay cash expenses in the short term as they come due.

Solvency ratios. Solvency ratios give the analyst information on the firm's financial leverage and ability to meet its longer-term obligations.

Profitability ratios. Profitability ratios provide information on how well the company generates operating profits and net profits from its sales.

Valuation ratios. Sales per share, earnings per share, and price to cash flow per share are examples of ratios used in comparing the relative valuation of companies.

Professor's Note: We examine valuation ratios in another LOS concerning equity analysis later in this review.

It should be noted that these categories are not mutually exclusive. An activity ratio such as payables turnover may also provide information about the liquidity of a company, for example. There is no one standard set of ratios for financial analysis. Different analysts use different ratios and different calculation methods for similar ratios. Some ratios are so commonly used that there is very little variation in how they are defined and calculated. We will note some alternative treatments and alternative terms for single ratios as we detail the commonly used ratios in each category.

ACTIVITY RATIOS

* A measure of accounts receivable turnover is *receivables turnover:*

$$\text{receivables turnover} = \frac{\text{annual sales}}{\text{average receivables}}$$

 Professor's Note: In most cases when a ratio compares a balance sheet account (such as receivables) with an income or cash flow item (such as sales), the balance sheet item will be the average of the account instead of simply the end-of-year balance. Averages are calculated by adding the beginning-of-year account value to the end-of-year account value, then dividing the sum by two.

It is considered desirable to have a receivables turnover figure close to the industry norm.

* The inverse of the receivables turnover times 365 is the *average collection period*, or *days of sales outstanding*, which is the average number of days it takes for the company's customers to pay their bills:

$$\text{days of sales oustanding} = \frac{365}{\text{receivables turnover}}$$

It is considered desirable to have a collection period (and receivables turnover) close to the industry norm. The firm's credit terms are another important benchmark used to interpret this ratio. A collection period that is too high might mean that customers are too slow in paying their bills, which means too much capital is tied up in assets. A collection period that is too low might indicate that the firm's credit policy is too rigorous, which might be hampering sales.

- A measure of a firm's efficiency with respect to its processing and inventory management is *inventory turnover*:

$$\text{inventory turnover} = \frac{\text{cost of goods sold}}{\text{average inventory}}$$

 Professor's Note: Pay careful attention to the numerator in the turnover ratios. For inventory turnover, be sure to use cost of goods sold, not sales.

- The inverse of the inventory turnover times 365 is the *average inventory processing period, number of days of inventory,* or *days of inventory on hand*:

$$\text{days of inventory on hand} = \frac{365}{\text{inventory turnover}}$$

As is the case with accounts receivable, it is considered desirable to have days of inventory on hand (and inventory turnover) close to the industry norm. A processing period that is too high might mean that too much capital is tied up in inventory and could mean that the inventory is obsolete. A processing period that is too low might indicate that the firm has inadequate stock on hand, which could hurt sales.

- A measure of the use of trade credit by the firm is the *payables turnover* ratio:

$$\text{payables turnover} = \frac{\text{purchases}}{\text{average trade payables}}$$

- The inverse of the payables turnover ratio multiplied by 365 is the *payables payment period* or *number of days of payables*, which is the average amount of time it takes the company to pay its bills:

$$\text{number of days of payables} = \frac{365}{\text{payables turnover ratio}}$$

 Professor's Note: We have shown days calculations for payables, receivables, and inventory based on annual turnover and a 365-day year. If turnover ratios are for a quarter rather than a year, the number of days in the quarter should be divided by the quarterly turnover ratios in order to get the "days" form of these ratios.

- The effectiveness of the firm's use of its total assets to create revenue is measured by its *total asset turnover*:

$$\text{total asset turnover} = \frac{\text{revenue}}{\text{average total assets}}$$

Different types of industries might have considerably different turnover ratios. Manufacturing businesses that are capital-intensive might have asset turnover ratios near one, while retail businesses might have turnover ratios near 10. As was the case with the current asset turnover ratios discussed previously, it is desirable for the total asset turnover ratio to be close to the industry norm. Low asset turnover ratios might mean that the company has too much capital tied up in its asset base. A turnover ratio that is too high might imply that the firm has too few assets for potential sales, or that the asset base is outdated.

- The utilization of fixed assets is measured by the *fixed asset turnover* ratio:

$$\text{fixed asset turnover} = \frac{\text{revenue}}{\text{average net fixed assets}}$$

As was the case with the total asset turnover ratio, it is desirable to have a fixed asset turnover ratio close to the industry norm. Low fixed asset turnover might mean that the company has too much capital tied up in its asset base or is using the assets it has inefficiently. A turnover ratio that is too high might imply that the firm has obsolete equipment, or at a minimum, that the firm will probably have to incur capital expenditures in the near future to increase capacity to support growing revenues. Since "net" here refers to net of accumulated depreciation, firms with more recently acquired assets will typically have lower fixed asset turnover ratios.

- How effectively a company is using its working capital is measured by the *working capital turnover* ratio:

$$\text{working capital turnover} = \frac{\text{revenue}}{\text{average working capital}}$$

Working capital (sometimes called *net* working capital) is current assets minus current liabilities. The working capital turnover ratio gives us information about the utilization of working capital in terms of dollars of sales per dollar of working capital. Some firms may have very low working capital if outstanding payables equal or exceed inventory and receivables. In this case the working capital turnover ratio will be very large, may vary significantly from period to period, and is less informative about changes in the firm's operating efficiency.

LIQUIDITY RATIOS

Liquidity ratios are employed by analysts to determine the firm's ability to pay its short-term liabilities.

- The *current ratio* is the best-known measure of liquidity:

$$\text{current ratio} = \frac{\text{current assets}}{\text{current liabilities}}$$

The higher the current ratio, the more likely it is that the company will be able to pay its short-term bills. A current ratio of less than one means that the company has negative working capital and is probably facing a liquidity crisis. Working capital equals current assets minus current liabilities.

- The *quick ratio* is a more stringent measure of liquidity because it does not include inventories and other assets that might not be very liquid:

$$\text{quick ratio} = \frac{\text{cash + marketable securities + receivables}}{\text{current liabilities}}$$

The higher the quick ratio, the more likely it is that the company will be able to pay its short-term bills. Marketable securities are short-term debt instruments, typically liquid and of good credit quality.

- The most conservative liquidity measure is the *cash ratio:*

$$\text{cash ratio} = \frac{\text{cash + marketable securities}}{\text{current liabilities}}$$

The higher the cash ratio, the more likely it is that the company will be able to pay its short-term bills.

The current, quick, and cash ratios differ only in the assumed liquidity of the current assets that the analyst projects will be used to pay off current liabilities.

- The *defensive interval ratio* is another measure of liquidity that indicates the number of days of average cash expenditures the firm could pay with its current liquid assets:

$$\text{defensive interval} = \frac{\text{cash + marketable securities + receivables}}{\text{average daily expenditures}}$$

Expenditures here include cash expenses for costs of goods, SG&A, and research and development. If these items are taken from the income statement, noncash charges such as depreciation should be added back just as in the preparation of a statement of cash flows by the indirect method.

- The *cash conversion cycle* is the length of time it takes to turn the firm's cash investment in inventory back into cash, in the form of collections from the sales of that inventory. The cash conversion cycle is computed from days sales outstanding, days of inventory on hand, and number of days of payables:

$$\text{cash conversion cycle} = \left(\begin{array}{c}\text{days sales}\\\text{outstanding}\end{array}\right) + \left(\begin{array}{c}\text{days of inventory}\\\text{on hand}\end{array}\right) - \left(\begin{array}{c}\text{number of days}\\\text{of payables}\end{array}\right)$$

High cash conversion cycles are considered undesirable. A conversion cycle that is too high implies that the company has an excessive amount of capital investment in the sales process.

SOLVENCY RATIOS

- A measure of the firm's use of fixed-cost financing sources is the *debt-to-equity* ratio:

$$\text{debt-to-equity} = \frac{\text{total debt}}{\text{total shareholders' equity}}$$

Increases and decreases in this ratio suggest a greater or lesser reliance on debt as a source of financing.

Total debt is calculated differently by different analysts and different providers of financial information. Here, we will define it as long-term debt plus interest-bearing short-term debt.

Some analysts include the present value of lease obligations and/or non-interest-bearing current liabilities, such as trade payables.

- Another way of looking at the usage of debt is the *debt-to-capital* ratio:

$$\text{debt-to-capital} = \frac{\text{total debt}}{\text{total debt} + \text{total shareholders' equity}}$$

Capital equals all short-term and long-term debt plus preferred stock and equity. Increases and decreases in this ratio suggest a greater or lesser reliance on debt as a source of financing.

- A slightly different way of analyzing debt utilization is the *debt-to-assets* ratio:

$$\text{debt-to-assets} = \frac{\text{total debt}}{\text{total assets}}$$

Increases and decreases in this ratio suggest a greater or lesser reliance on debt as a source of financing.

- Another measure that is used as an indicator of a company's use of debt financing is the *financial leverage* ratio (or leverage ratio):

$$\text{financial leverage} = \frac{\text{average total assets}}{\text{average total equity}}$$

Average here means the average of the values at the beginning and at the end of the period. Greater use of debt financing increases financial leverage and, typically, risk to equity holders and bondholders alike.

- The remaining risk ratios help determine the firm's ability to repay its debt obligations. The first of these is the *interest coverage ratio:*

$$\text{interest coverage} = \frac{\text{earnings before interest and taxes}}{\text{interest payments}}$$

  The lower this ratio, the more likely it is that the firm will have difficulty meeting its debt payments.

- A second ratio that is an indicator of a company's ability to meet its obligations is the *fixed charge coverage* ratio:

$$\text{fixed charge coverage} = \frac{\text{earnings before interest and taxes} + \text{lease payments}}{\text{interest payments} + \text{lease payments}}$$

  Here, lease payments are added back to operating earnings in the numerator and also added to interest payments in the denominator. Significant lease obligations will reduce this ratio significantly compared to the interest coverage ratio. Fixed charge coverage is the more meaningful measure for companies that lease a large portion of their assets, such as some airlines.

PROFITABILITY RATIOS

- The *net profit margin* is the ratio of net income to revenue:

$$\text{net profit margin} = \frac{\text{net income}}{\text{revenue}}$$

  Analysts should be concerned if this ratio is too low. The net profit margin should be based on net income from continuing operations, because analysts should be primarily concerned about future expectations, and "below the line" items such as discontinued operations will not affect the company in the future.

Operating profitability ratios look at how good management is at turning their efforts into profits. Operating ratios compare the top of the income statement (sales) to profits. The different ratios are designed to isolate specific costs.

Know these terms:

gross profits	= net sales – COGS
operating profits	= earnings before interest and taxes = EBIT
net income	= earnings after taxes but before dividends
total capital	= long-term debt + short-term debt + common and preferred equity
total capital	= total assets

How they relate in the income statement:

	Net sales
−	Cost of goods sold
	Gross profit
−	Operating expenses
	Operating profit (EBIT)
−	Interest
	Earnings before taxes (EBT)
−	Taxes
	Earnings after taxes (EAT)
+/−	Below the line items adjusted for tax
	Net income
−	Preferred dividends
	Income available to common

The *gross profit margin* is the ratio of gross profit (sales less cost of goods sold) to sales:

$$\text{gross profit margin} = \frac{\text{gross profit}}{\text{revenue}}$$

An analyst should be concerned if this ratio is too low.

- The *operating profit margin* is the ratio of operating profit (gross profit less selling, general, and administrative expenses) to sales. Operating profit is also referred to as earnings before interest and taxes (EBIT):

$$\text{operating profit margin} = \frac{\text{operating income}}{\text{revenue}} \text{ or } \frac{\text{EBIT}}{\text{revenue}}$$

Strictly speaking, EBIT includes some nonoperating items, such as gains on investment. The analyst, as with other ratios with various formulations, must be consistent in his calculation method and know how published ratios are calculated. Analysts should be concerned if this ratio is too low. Some analysts prefer to calculate the operating profit margin by adding back depreciation and any amortization expense to arrive at earnings before interest, taxes, depreciation, and amortization (EBITDA).

Sometimes profitability is measured using earnings before tax (EBT), which can be calculated by subtracting interest from EBIT or from operating earnings. The *pretax margin* is calculated as:

$$\text{pretax margin} = \frac{\text{EBT}}{\text{revenue}}$$

Another set of profitability ratios measure profitability relative to funds invested in the company by common stockholders, preferred stockholders, and suppliers of debt financing.

The first of these measures is the *return on assets* (ROA). Typically, ROA is calculated using net income:

$$\text{return on assets (ROA)} = \frac{\text{net income}}{\text{average total assets}}$$

This measure is a bit misleading, however, because interest is excluded from net income but total assets include debt as well as equity. Adding interest adjusted for tax back to net income puts the returns to both equity and debt holders in the numerator. This results in an alternative calculation for ROA:

$$\text{return on assets (ROA)} = \frac{\text{net income} + \text{interest expense}\,(1 - \text{tax rate})}{\text{average total assets}}$$

A measure of return on assets that includes both taxes and interest in the numerator is the *operating return on assets*:

$$\text{operating return on assets} = \frac{\text{operating income}}{\text{average total assets}} \quad \text{or} \quad \frac{\text{EBIT}}{\text{average total assets}}$$

- The *return on total capital* (ROTC) is the ratio of net income before interest and taxes to total capital:

$$\text{return on total capital} = \frac{\text{EBIT}}{\text{average total capital}}$$

Total capital includes short- and long-term debt, preferred equity, and common equity. Analysts should be concerned if this ratio is too low. Total capital is the same as total assets. The interest expense that should be added back is gross interest expense, not net interest expense (which is gross interest expense less interest income).

An alternative method for computing ROTC is to include the present value of operating leases on the balance sheet as a fixed asset and as a long-term liability. This adjustment is especially important for firms that are dependent on operating leases as a major form of financing. Calculations related to leasing were discussed in an earlier Study Session.

- The *return on equity* (ROE) is the ratio of net income to average total equity (including preferred stock):

$$\text{return on equity} = \frac{\text{net income}}{\text{average total equity}}$$

Analysts should be concerned if this ratio is too low. It is sometimes called return on total equity.

- A similar ratio to the return on equity is the *return on common equity:*

$$\text{return on common equity} = \frac{\text{net income} - \text{preferred dividends}}{\text{average common equity}}$$

$$= \frac{\text{net income available to common}}{\text{average common equity}}$$

This ratio differs from the return on total equity in that it only measures the accounting profits available to, and the capital invested by, common stockholders, instead of common and preferred stockholders. That is why preferred dividends are deducted from net income in the numerator. Analysts should be concerned if this ratio is too low.

The return on common equity is often more thoroughly analyzed using the DuPont decomposition, which is described later in this topic review.

LOS 39.d: Demonstrate how ratios are related and how to evaluate a company using a combination of different ratios.

Example: Using ratios to evaluate a company

A balance sheet and income statement for a hypothetical company are shown below for this year and the previous year.

Using the company information provided, calculate the current year ratios. Discuss how these ratios compare with the company's performance last year and with the industry's performance.

Sample Balance Sheet

Year	Current year	Previous year
Assets		
Cash and marketable securities	$105	$95
Receivables	205	195
Inventories	310	290
Total current assets	620	580
Gross property, plant, and equipment	1,800	$1,700
Accumulated depreciation	360	340
Net property, plant, and equipment	1,440	1,360
Total assets	$2,060	$1,940
Liabilities		
Payables	$110	$90
Short-term debt	160	140
Current portion of long-term debt	55	45
Current liabilities	325	$275
Long-term debt	610	$690
Deferred taxes	105	95
Common stock	300	300
Additional paid in capital	400	400
Retained earnings	320	180
Common shareholders equity	1,020	880
Total liabilities and equity	$2,060	$1,940

Sample Income Statement

Year	Current year
Sales	$4,000
Cost of goods sold	3,000
Gross profit	1,000
Operating expenses	650
Operating profit	350
Interest expense	50
Earnings before taxes	300
Taxes	100
Net income	200
Common dividends	60

Financial Ratio Template

	Current Year	Last Year	Industry
Current ratio		2.1	1.5
Quick ratio		1.1	0.9
Days of sales outstanding		18.9	18.0
Inventory turnover		10.7	12.0
Total asset turnover		2.3	2.4
Working capital turnover		14.5	11.8
Gross profit margin		27.4%	29.3%
Net profit margin		5.8%	6.5%
Return on total capital		21.1%	22.4%
Return on common equity		24.1%	19.8%
Debt-to-equity		99.4%	35.7%
Interest coverage		5.9	9.2

Answer:

- current ratio = $\dfrac{\text{current assets}}{\text{current liabilities}}$

$$\text{current ratio} = \frac{620}{325} = 1.9$$

The current ratio indicates lower liquidity levels when compared to last year and more liquidity than the industry average.

- quick ratio = $\dfrac{\text{cash + receivables + marketable securities}}{\text{current liabilities}}$

$$\text{quick ratio} = \frac{(105 + 205)}{325} = 0.95$$

The quick ratio is lower than last year and is in line with the industry average.

- DSO (days of sales outstanding) = $\dfrac{365}{\text{revenue}/\text{average receivables}}$

$$\text{DSO} = \frac{365}{4{,}000/[(205+195)/2]} = 18.25$$

The DSO is a bit lower relative to the company's past performance but slightly higher than the industry average.

- inventory turnover = $\dfrac{\text{cost of goods sold}}{\text{average inventories}}$

  inventory turnover = $\dfrac{3{,}000}{(310 + 290) / 2} = 10.0$

Inventory turnover is much lower than last year and the industry average. This suggests that the company is not managing inventory efficiently and may have obsolete stock.

- total asset turnover = $\dfrac{\text{revenue}}{\text{average assets}}$

  total asset turnover = $\dfrac{4{,}000}{(2{,}060 + 1{,}940) / 2} = 2.0$

Total asset turnover is slightly lower than last year and the industry average.

- working capital turnover = $\dfrac{\text{revenue}}{\text{average working capital}}$

  beginning working capital = 580 − 275 = 305

  ending working capital = 620 − 325 = 295

  working capital turnover = $\dfrac{4{,}000}{(305 + 295) / 2} = 13.3$

Working capital turnover is lower than last year, but still above the industry average.

- gross profit margin = $\dfrac{\text{gross profit}}{\text{revenue}}$

  gross profit margin = $\dfrac{1{,}000}{4{,}000} = 25.0\%$

The gross profit margin is lower than last year and much lower than the industry average.

- net profit margin = $\dfrac{\text{net income}}{\text{revenue}}$

net profit margin = $\dfrac{200}{4,000}$ = 5.0%

The net profit margin is lower than last year and much lower than the industry average.

- return on total capital = $\dfrac{\text{EBIT}}{\text{short- and long-term debt + equity}}$

beginning total capital = 140 + 45 + 690 + 880 = 1,755

ending total capital = 160 + 55 + 610 + 1,020 = 1,845

return on total capital = $\dfrac{350}{(1,755 + 1,845)\,/\,2}$ = 19.4%

The return on total capital is below last year and below the industry average. This suggests a problem stemming from the low asset turnover and low profit margin.

- return on common equity = $\dfrac{\text{net income – preferred dividends}}{\text{average common equity}}$

return on common equity = $\dfrac{200}{(1,020 + 880)\,/\,2}$ = 21.1%

The return on equity is lower than last year but better than the industry average. The reason it is higher than the industry average is probably because of greater use of leverage.

- debt-to-equity ratio = $\dfrac{\text{total debt}}{\text{total equity}}$

debt-to-equity ratio = $\dfrac{610 + 160 + 55}{1,020}$ = 80.9%

Note that preferred equity would be included in the denominator if there were any, and that we have included short-term debt and the current portion of long-term debt in calculating total (interest-bearing) debt.

The debt-to-equity ratio is lower than last year but still much higher than the industry average. This suggests the company is trying to get its debt level more in line with the industry.

- interest coverage = $\dfrac{\text{EBIT}}{\text{interest payments}}$

  interest coverage = $\dfrac{350}{50} = 7.0$

The interest coverage is better than last year but still worse than the industry average. This, along with the slip in profit margin and return on assets, might cause some concern.

LOS 39.e: Demonstrate the application of and interpret changes in the component parts of the DuPont analysis (the decomposition of return on equity).

The **DuPont system of analysis** is an approach that can be used to analyze return on equity (ROE). It uses basic algebra to break down ROE into a function of different ratios, so an analyst can see the impact of leverage, profit margins, and turnover on shareholder returns. There are two variants of the DuPont system: The original three-part approach and the extended five-part system.

For the **original approach**, start with ROE defined as:

$$\text{return on equity} = \left(\frac{\text{net income}}{\text{equity}} \right)$$

Average or year-end values for equity can be used. Multiplying ROE by (revenue/revenue) and rearranging terms produces:

$$\text{return on equity} = \left(\frac{\text{net income}}{\text{revenue}} \right)\left(\frac{\text{revenue}}{\text{equity}} \right)$$

The first term is the profit margin and the second term is the equity turnover:

$$\text{return on equity} = \left(\frac{\text{net profit}}{\text{margin}} \right)\left(\frac{\text{equity}}{\text{turnover}} \right)$$

We can expand this further by multiplying these terms by (assets/assets), and rearranging terms:

$$\text{return on equity} = \left(\frac{\text{net income}}{\text{sales}} \right)\left(\frac{\text{sales}}{\text{assets}} \right)\left(\frac{\text{assets}}{\text{equity}} \right)$$

 Professor's Note: For the exam, remember that (net income / sales) × (sales / assets) = return on assets (ROA).

The first term is still the profit margin, the second term is now asset turnover, and the third term is a financial leverage ratio that will increase as the use of debt financing increases:

$$\text{return on equity} = \left(\begin{array}{c}\text{net profit} \\ \text{margin}\end{array}\right)\left(\begin{array}{c}\text{asset} \\ \text{turnover}\end{array}\right)\left(\begin{array}{c}\text{leverage} \\ \text{ratio}\end{array}\right)$$

This is the original DuPont equation. It is arguably the most important equation in ratio analysis, since it breaks down a very important ratio (ROE) into three key components. If ROE is relatively low, it must be that at least one of the following is true: The company has a poor profit margin, the company has poor asset turnover, or the firm has too little leverage.

Professor's Note: Often candidates get confused and think the DuPont method is a way to calculate ROE. While you can calculate ROE given the components of either the original or extended DuPont equations, this isn't necessary if you have the financial statements. If you have net income and equity, you can calculate ROE. The DuPont method is a way to decompose ROE, to better see what changes are driving the changes in ROE.

Example: Decomposition of ROE with original DuPont

Staret Inc. has maintained a stable and relatively high ROE of approximately 18% over the last three years. Use traditional DuPont analysis to decompose this ROE into its three components and comment on trends in company performance.

Staret Inc. Selected Balance Sheet and Income Statement Items (Millions)

Year	20X3	20X4	20X5
Net Income	21.5	22.3	21.9
Sales	305	350	410
Equity	119	124	126
Assets	230	290	350

Answer:

ROE 20X3: 21.5 / 119 = 18.1%

20X4: 22.3 / 124 = 18.0%

20X5: 21.9 / 126 = 17.4%

DuPont 20X3: 7.0% × 1.33 × 1.93

20X4: 6.4% × 1.21 × 2.34

20X5: 5.3% × 1.17 × 2.78

(some rounding in values)

While the ROE has dropped only slightly, both the total asset turnover and the net profit margin have declined. The effects of declining net margins and turnover on ROE have been offset by a significant increase in leverage. The analyst should be concerned about the net margin and find out what combination of pricing pressure and/or increasing expenses have caused this. Also, the analyst must note that the company has become more risky due to increased debt financing.

Example: Computing ROE using original DuPont

A company has a net profit margin of 4%, asset turnover of 2.0, and a debt-to-assets ratio of 60%. What is the ROE?

Answer:

Debt-to-assets = 60%, which means equity to assets is 40%; this implies assets to equity (the leverage ratio) is 1 / 0.4 = 2.5

$$\text{ROE} = \left(\frac{\text{net profit}}{\text{margin}}\right)\left(\frac{\text{total asset}}{\text{turnover}}\right)\left(\frac{\text{assets}}{\text{equity}}\right) = (0.04)(2.00)(2.50) = 0.20, \text{ or } 20\%$$

The **extended (5-way) DuPont equation** takes the net profit margin and breaks it down further.

$$\text{ROE} = \left(\frac{\text{net income}}{\text{EBT}}\right)\left(\frac{\text{EBT}}{\text{EBIT}}\right)\left(\frac{\text{EBIT}}{\text{revenue}}\right)\left(\frac{\text{revenue}}{\text{total assets}}\right)\left(\frac{\text{total assets}}{\text{total equity}}\right)$$

Note that the first term in the 3-part DuPont equation, net profit margin, has been decomposed into three terms:

$\dfrac{\text{net income}}{\text{EBT}}$ is called the *tax burden* and is equal to $(1 - \text{tax rate})$.

$\dfrac{\text{EBT}}{\text{EBIT}}$ is called the *interest burden.*

$\dfrac{\text{EBIT}}{\text{revenue}}$ is called the *EBIT margin.*

We then have:

$$\text{ROE} = \left(\begin{array}{c}\text{tax}\\\text{burden}\end{array}\right)\left(\begin{array}{c}\text{interest}\\\text{burden}\end{array}\right)\left(\begin{array}{c}\text{EBIT}\\\text{margin}\end{array}\right)\left(\begin{array}{c}\text{asset}\\\text{turnover}\end{array}\right)\left(\begin{array}{c}\text{financial}\\\text{leverage}\end{array}\right)$$

An increase in interest expense as proportion of EBIT will increase the interest burden. Increases in either the tax burden or the interest burden will tend to decrease ROE.

EBIT in the second two expressions can be replaced by operating earnings. In this case, we have the operating margin rather than the EBIT margin. The interest burden term would then show the effects of nonoperating income as well as the effect of interest expense.

Note that in general, high profit margins, leverage, and asset turnover will lead to high levels of ROE. However, this version of the formula shows that more leverage *does not always* lead to higher ROE. As leverage rises, so does the interest burden. Hence, the positive effects of leverage can be offset by the higher interest payments that accompany more debt. Note that higher taxes will always lead to lower levels of ROE.

Example: Extended DuPont analysis

An analyst has gathered data from two companies in the same industry. Calculate the ROE for both companies and use the extended DuPont analysis to explain the critical factors that account for the differences in the two companies' ROEs.

Selected Income and Balance Sheet Data

	Company A	Company B
Revenues	$500	$900
EBIT	35	100
Interest expense	5	0
EBT	30	100
Taxes	10	40
Net income	20	60
Total assets	250	300
Total debt	100	50
Owners' equity	$150	$250

Answer:

EBIT = EBIT / revenue

Company A: EBIT margin = 35 / 500 = 7.0%

Company B: EBIT margin = 100 / 900 = 11.1%

asset turnover = revenue / assets

Company A: asset turnover = 500 / 250 = 2.0

Company B: asset turnover = 900 / 300 = 3.0

interest burden = EBT / EBIT

Company A: interest burden = 30 / 35 = 85.7%

Company B: interest burden = 100 / 100 = 1

financial leverage = assets / equity

Company A: financial leverage = 250 / 150 = 1.67

Company B: financial leverage = 300 / 250 = 1.2

tax burden = net income / EBT

Company A: tax burden = 20 / 30 = 66.7%

Company B: tax burden = 60 / 100 = 60.0%

Company A: ROE = 0.667 × 0.857 × 0.07 × 2.0 × 1.67 = 13.4%

Company B: ROE = 0.608 × 1.0 × 0.111 × 3.0 × 1.2 = 24%

Company B has a higher tax burden but a lower interest burden (a lower ratio indicates a higher burden). Company B has better EBIT margins and better asset utilization (perhaps management of inventory, receivables, or payables, or a lower cost basis in its fixed assets due to their age), and less leverage. Its higher EBIT margins and asset turnover are the main factors leading to its significantly higher ROE, which it achieves with less leverage than Company A.

LOS 39.f: Calculate and interpret the ratios used in equity analysis, credit analysis, and segment analysis.

Valuation ratios are used in analysis for investment in common equity. The most widely used valuation ratio is the *price-to-earnings* (P/E) ratio, the ratio of the current market price of a share of stock divided by the company's earnings per share. Related measures based on price per share are the *price-to-cash flow*, the *price-to-sales*, and the *price-to-book value* ratios.

 Professor's Note: The use of the above valuation ratios is covered in detail in the review of price multiples in the Study Session on Equity Securities.

Per-share valuation measures include *earnings per share* (EPS). *Basic EPS* is net income available to common divided by the weighted average number of common shares outstanding.

Diluted EPS is a "what if" value. It is calculated to be the lowest possible EPS that could have been reported if all firm securities that can be converted into common stock, and that would decrease basic EPS if they had been, were converted. That is, if all dilutive securities had been converted. Potentially dilutive securities include convertible debt and convertible preferred stock, as well as options and warrants issued by the company. The numerator of diluted EPS is increased by the after-tax interest savings on any dilutive debt securities and by the dividends on any dilutive convertible preferred stock. The denominator is increased by the common shares that would result from conversion or exchange of dilutive securities into common shares.

 Professor's Note: Refer back to our topic review on Understanding the Income Statement for details and examples of how to calculate basic and diluted EPS.

Other per-share measures include: *cash flow per share, EBIT per share,* and *EBITDA per share.* Per-share measures for different companies cannot be compared. A firm with a $100 share price can be expected to generate much greater earnings, cash flow, EBITDA, and EBIT per share than a firm with a $10 share price.

Dividends

Dividends are declared on a per-common-share basis. Total dividends on a firm-wide basis are referred to as *dividends declared*. Neither EPS nor net income is reduced by the payment of common stock dividends. Net income minus dividends declared is retained earnings, the earnings that are used to grow the corporation rather than being distributed to equity holders. The proportion of a firm's net income that is retained to fund growth is an important determinant of the firm's *sustainable growth rate*.

To calculate the sustainable growth rate for a firm, the rate of return on resources is measured as the return on equity capital, or the ROE. The proportion of earnings reinvested is known as the retention rate (RR).

- The formula for the *sustainable growth rate*, which is how fast the firm can grow without additional external equity issues while holding leverage constant, is:

$$g = RR \times ROE$$

- The calculation of the *retention rate* (RR) is:

$$\text{retention rate} = \frac{\text{net income available to common} - \text{dividends declared}}{\text{net income available to common}}$$

$$= 1 - \text{dividend payout ratio}$$

where :

$$\text{dividend payout ratio} = \frac{\text{dividends declared}}{\text{net income available to common}}$$

Example: Calculating sustainable growth

The following figure provides data for three companies.

Growth Analysis Data

Company	A	B	C
Earnings per share	$3.00	$4.00	$5.00
Dividends per share	1.50	1.00	2.00
Return on equity	14%	12%	10%

Calculate the sustainable growth rate for each company.

Answer:

RR = 1 – (dividends / earnings)

Company A: RR = 1 – (1.50 / 3.00) = 0.500
Company B: RR = 1 – (1.00 / 4.00) = 0.750
Company C: RR = 1 – (2.00 / 5.00) = 0.600

g = RR × ROE

Company A: g = 0.500 × 14% = 7.0%
Company B: g = 0.750 × 12% = 9.0%
Company C: g = 0.600 × 10% = 6.0%

Some ratios have specific applications in certain industries.

Net income per employee and *sales per employee* are used in the analysis and valuation of service and consulting companies.

Growth in same-store sales is used in the restaurant and retail industries to indicate growth without the effects of new locations that have been opened. It is a measure of how well the firm is doing at attracting and keeping existing customers and, in the case of locations with overlapping markets, may indicate that new locations are taking customers from existing ones.

Sales per square foot is another metric commonly used in the retail industry.

Business Risk

The standard deviation of revenue, standard deviation of operating income, and the standard deviation of net income are all indicators of the variation in and the uncertainty about a firm's performance. Since they all depend on the size of the firm to a great extent, analysts employ a size-adjusted measure of variation. The **coefficient of variation** for a variable is its standard deviation divided by its expected value.

 Professor's Note: We saw this before as a measure of portfolio risk in Quantitative Methods.

Certainly, different industries have different levels of uncertainly about revenues, expenses, taxes, and nonoperating items. Comparing coefficients of variation for a firm across time, or among a firm and its peers, can aid the analyst is assessing both the relative and absolute degree of risk a firm faces in generating income for its investors.

$$CV \text{ sales} = \frac{\text{standard deviation of sales}}{\text{mean sales}}$$

$$CV \text{ operating income} = \frac{\text{standard deviation of operating income}}{\text{mean operating income}}$$

$$CV \text{ net income} = \frac{\text{standard deviation of net income}}{\text{mean net income}}$$

Banks, insurance companies, and other financial firms carry their own challenges for analysts. Part of the challenge is to understand the commonly used terms and the ratios they represent.

Capital adequacy typically refers to the ratio of some dollar measure of the risk, both operational and financial, of the firm to its equity capital. Other measures of capital are also used. A common measure of capital risk is *value-at-risk*, which is an estimate of the dollar size of the loss that a firm will exceed only some specific percent of the time, over a specific period of time.

Banks are subject to minimum *reserve requirements*. Their ratios of various liabilities to their central bank reserves must be above the minimums. The ratio of a bank's liquid assets to certain liabilities is called the *liquid asset requirement*.

The performance of financial companies that lend funds is often summarized as the *net interest margin*, which is simply interest income divided by the firm's interest-earning assets.

Credit Analysis

Credit analysis is based on many of the ratios that we have already covered in this review. In assessing a company's ability to service and repay its debt, analysts use interest coverage ratios (calculated with EBIT or EBITDA), return on capital, and debt-to-assets ratios. Other ratios focus on various measures of cash flow to total debt.

Ratios have been used to analyze and predict firm bankruptcies. Altman (2000)[1] developed a Z-score that is useful in predicting firm bankruptcies (a low score indicates high probability of failure). The predictive model was based on a firm's working capital to assets, retained earnings to assets, EBIT to assets, market to book value of a share of stock, and revenues to assets.

Segment Analysis

A **business segment** is a portion of a larger company that accounts for more than 10% of the company's revenues or assets, and is distinguishable from the company's other lines of business in terms of the risk and return characteristics of the segment. **Geographic segments** are also identified when they meet the size criterion above and the geographic unit has a business environment that is different from that of other segments or the remainder of the company's business.

Both U.S. GAAP and IFRS require companies to report segment data, but the required disclosure items are only a subset of the required disclosures for the company as a whole. Nonetheless, an analyst can prepare a more detailed analysis and forecast by examining the performance of business or geographic segments separately. Segment profit margins, asset utilization (turnover), and return on assets can be very useful in gaining a clear picture of a firm's overall operations. For forecasting, growth rates of segment revenues and profits can be used to estimate future sales and profits and to determine the changes in company characteristics over time.

Figure 5 illustrates how Boeing broke down its results into business segments in its 2006 annual report (source: Boeing.com).

---

1. Edward I. Altman, "Predicting Financial Distress of Companies: Revisiting the Z-Score and Zeta® Models," July 2000.

Figure 5: Boeing Inc. Segment Reporting

(Dollars in millions)

Year ended December 31	2006	2005	2004
Revenues:			
Commercial Airplanes	$28,465	21,365	19,925
Integrated Defense Systems:			
Precision Engagement and Mobility Systems	14,350	13,510	12,835
Network and Space Systems	11,980	12,254	13,023
Support Systems	6,109	5,342	4,881
Total Integrated Defense Systems	32,439	31,106	30,739
Boeing Capital Corporation	1,025	966	959
Other	299	657	275
Accounting differences/eliminations	(698)	(473)	(498)
Total revenues	$61,530	$53,621	$51,400
Earnings from operations:			
Commercial Airplanes	$2,733	$1,431	$745
Integrated Defense Systems:			
Precision Engagement and Mobility Systems	1,238	1,755	1,697
Network and Space Systems	958	1,399	577
Support Systems	836	765	662
Total Integrated Defense Systems	3,032	3,919	2,936
Boeing Capital Corporation	291	232	183
Other	(738)	(363)	(546)
Unallocated expense	(1,733)	(2,407)	(1,311)
Settlement with U.S. Department of Justice, net of accruals	(571)		
Earnings from operations	3,014	2,812	2,007
Other income, net	420	301	288
Interest and debt expense	(240)	(294)	(335)
Earnings before income taxes	3,194	2,819	1,960
Income tax expense	(988)	(257)	(140)
Net earnings from continuing operations	$2,206	$2,562	$1,820
Income from discontinued operations, net of taxes of $6			10
Net gain/(loss) on disposal of disposal of discontinued operations, net of taxes of $5, $(5) and $24	9	(7)	42
Cumulative effect of accounting change, net of taxes of $10		17	
Net earnings	$2,215	$2,572	$1,872

LOS 39.g: Describe how the results of common-size and ratio analysis can be used to model and forecast earnings.

Both common-size financial statements and ratio analysis can be used in preparing pro forma financial statements that provide estimates of financial statement items for one or more future periods. The preparation of pro forma financial statements and related forecasts is covered in some detail in the next Study Session, Corporate Finance. Here, some examples will suffice.

A forecast of financial results that begins with an estimate of a firm's next-period revenues might use the most recent COGS, or an average of COGS, from a common-size income statement. On a common-size income statement, COGS is calculated as a percentage of revenue. If the analyst has no reason to believe that COGS in relation to sales will change for the next period, the COGS percentage from a common-size income statement can be used in constructing a pro forma income statement for the next period based on the estimate of sales.

Similarly, the analyst may believe that certain ratios will remain the same or change in one direction or the other for the next period. In the absence of any information indicating a change, an analyst may choose to incorporate the operating profit margin from the prior period into a pro forma income statement for the next period. Beginning with an estimate of next-period sales, the estimated operating profit margin can be used to forecast operating profits for the next period.

Rather than point estimates of sales and net and operating margins, the analyst may examine possible changes in order to create a range of possible values for key financial variables.

Three methods of examining the variability of financial outcomes around point estimates are: *sensitivity analysis, scenario analysis*, and *simulation*. Sensitivity analysis is based on "what if" questions such as: What will be the effect on net income if sales increase by 3% rather than the estimated 5%? Scenario analysis is based on specific scenarios (a specific set of outcomes for key variables) and will also yield a range of values for financial statement items. Simulation is a technique in which probability distributions for key variables are selected and a computer is used to generate a distribution of values for outcomes based on repeated random selection of values for the key variables.

KEY CONCEPTS

LOS 39.a

Common-size financial statements allow an analyst to compare performance across firms, evaluate the performance of a firm over time, and quickly view certain financial ratios. Ratios are used to evaluate firm performance over time or to compare a company to another company or to industry average ratios.

Vertical common-size data are stated as a percentage of sales (for income statements) or as a percentage of total assets (for balance sheets). Horizontal common-size data present each item as a percentage of its value in a base year.

Stacked column graphs illustrate the composition of financial statement items. Line graphs are used to illustrate changes in financial statement values over time.

LOS 39.b

Ratio analysis has limitations. Ratios are not useful when viewed in isolation, different companies use different accounting treatments, comparable ratios can be hard to find for companies that operate in multiple industries, ratios must be analyzed relative to one another, and determining the range of acceptable values for a ratio can be difficult.

LOS 39.c

Activity ratios indicate how well a firm uses its assets. They include receivables turnover, days of sales outstanding, inventory turnover, days of inventory on hand, payables turnover, payables payment period, and turnover ratios for total assets, fixed assets, and working capital.

Liquidity ratios indicate a firm's ability to meet its short-term obligations. They include the current, quick, and cash ratios, the defensive interval, and the cash conversion cycle.

Solvency ratios indicate a firm's ability to meet its long-term obligations. They include the debt-to-equity, debt-to-capital, debt-to-assets, financial leverage, interest coverage, and fixed charge coverage ratios.

Profitability ratios indicate how well a firm generates operating income and net income. They include net, gross, and operating profit margins, pretax margin, return on assets, operating return on assets, return on total capital, return on total equity, and return on common equity.

Valuation ratios are used to compare the relative values of stocks. They include earnings per share and price-to-earnings, price-to-sales, price-to-book value, and price-to-cash-flow ratios.

LOS 39.d

An analyst should use an appropriate combination of different ratios to evaluate a company over time and relative to comparable companies. The interpretation of an increase in ROE, for example, may be quite different for a firm that has significantly increased its financial leverage compared to one that has maintained or decreased its financial leverage.

LOS 39.e

Basic DuPont equation:

$$ROE = \left(\frac{net\ income}{sales}\right)\left(\frac{sales}{assets}\right)\left(\frac{assets}{equity}\right)$$

Extended DuPont equation:

$$ROE = \left(\frac{net\ income}{EBT}\right)\left(\frac{EBT}{EBIT}\right)\left(\frac{EBIT}{revenue}\right)\left(\frac{revenue}{total\ assets}\right)\left(\frac{total\ assets}{total\ equity}\right)$$

LOS 39.f

Ratios used in equity analysis include price-to-earnings, price-to-cash flow, price-to-sales, and price-to-book value ratios, and basic and diluted earnings per share. Other ratios are relevant to specific industries such as retail and financial services.

Credit analysis emphasizes interest coverage ratios, return on capital, debt-to-assets ratios, and cash flow to total debt.

Firms are required to report some items for significant business and geographic segments. Profitability, leverage, and turnover ratios by segment can give the analyst a better understanding of the performance of the overall business.

LOS 39.g

Common-size financial statements and ratio analysis can be used to construct pro forma financial statements based on a forecast of sales growth and assumptions about the relation of changes in key income statement and balance sheet items to growth of sales.

CONCEPT CHECKERS

1. To study trends in a firm's cost of goods sold (COGS), the analyst should standardize the cost of goods sold numbers to a common-sized basis by dividing COGS by:
    A. assets.
    B. sales.
    C. net income.

2. Which of the following is *least likely* a limitation of financial ratios?
    A. Data on comparable firms are difficult to acquire.
    B. Determining the target or comparison value for a ratio requires judgment.
    C. Different accounting treatments require the analyst to adjust the data before comparing ratios.

3. An analyst who is interested in a company's long-term solvency would *most likely* examine the:
    A. return on total capital.
    B. defensive interval ratio.
    C. fixed charge coverage ratio.

4. RGB, Inc.'s purchases during the year were $100,000. The balance sheet shows an average accounts payable balance of $12,000. RGB's payables payment period is *closest* to:
    A. 37 days.
    B. 44 days.
    C. 52 days.

5. RGB, Inc. has a gross profit of $45,000 on sales of $150,000. The balance sheet shows average total assets of $75,000 with an average inventory balance of $15,000. RGB's total asset turnover and inventory turnover are *closest* to:

	Asset turnover	Inventory turnover
A.	7.00 times	2.00 times
B.	2.00 times	7.00 times
C.	0.50 times	0.33 times

6. If RGB, Inc. has annual sales of $100,000, average accounts payable of $30,000, and average accounts receivable of $25,000, RGB's receivables turnover and average collection period are *closest* to:

	Receivables turnover	Average collection period
A.	2.1 times	174 days
B.	3.3 times	111 days
C.	4.0 times	91 days

7. A company's current ratio is 1.9. If some of the accounts payable are paid off from the cash account, the:
    A. numerator would decrease by a greater percentage than the denominator, resulting in a lower current ratio.
    B. denominator would decrease by a greater percentage than the numerator, resulting in a higher current ratio.
    C. numerator and denominator would decrease proportionally, leaving the current ratio unchanged.

8. A company's quick ratio is 1.2. If inventory were purchased for cash, the:
    A. numerator would decrease more than the denominator, resulting in a lower quick ratio.
    B. denominator would decrease more than the numerator, resulting in a higher current ratio.
    C. numerator and denominator would decrease proportionally, leaving the current ratio unchanged.

9. All other things held constant, which of the following transactions will increase a firm's current ratio if the ratio is greater than one?
    A. Accounts receivable are collected and the funds received are deposited in the firm's cash account.
    B. Fixed assets are purchased from the cash account.
    C. Accounts payable are paid with funds from the cash account.

10. RGB, Inc.'s receivable turnover is ten times, the inventory turnover is five times, and the payables turnover is nine times. RGB's cash conversion cycle is *closest* to:
    A. 69 days.
    B. 104 days.
    C. 150 days.

11. RGB, Inc.'s income statement shows sales of $1,000, cost of goods sold of $400, pre-interest operating expense of $300, and interest expense of $100. RGB's interest coverage ratio is *closest* to:
    A. 2 times.
    B. 3 times.
    C. 4 times.

12. Return on equity using the traditional DuPont formula equals:
    A. (net profit margin) (interest component) (solvency ratio).
    B. (net profit margin) (total asset turnover) (tax retention rate).
    C. (net profit margin) (total asset turnover) (financial leverage multiplier).

13. RGB, Inc. has a net profit margin of 12%, a total asset turnover of 1.2 times, and a financial leverage multiplier of 1.2 times. RGB's return on equity is *closest* to:
    A. 12.0%.
    B. 14.2%.
    C. 17.3%.

14. Use the following information for RGB, Inc.:
     • EBIT/revenue = 10%
     • Tax retention rate = 60%
     • Revenue/assets = 1.8 times
     • Current ratio = 2 times
     • EBT/EBIT = 0.9 times
     • Assets/equity = 1.9 times

     RGB, Inc.'s return on equity is *closest* to:
     A. 10.5%.
     B. 14.0%.
     C. 18.5%.

15. Which of the following equations *least accurately* represents return on equity?
     A. (net profit margin)(equity turnover).
     B. (net profit margin)(total asset turnover)(assets/equity).
     C. (ROA)(interest burden)(tax retention rate).

16. Paragon Co. has an operating profit margin (EBIT/revenue) of 11%; an asset turnover ratio of 1.2; a financial leverage multiplier of 1.5 times; an average tax rate of 35%; and an interest burden of 0.7. Paragon's return on equity is *closest* to:
     A. 9%.
     B. 10%.
     C. 11%.

17. A firm has a dividend payout ratio of 40%, a net profit margin of 10%, an asset turnover of 0.9 times, and a financial leverage multiplier of 1.2 times. The firm's sustainable growth rate is *closest* to:
     A. 4.3%.
     B. 6.5%.
     C. 8.0%.

18. An analyst who needs to model and forecast a company's earnings for the next three years would be *least likely* to:
     A. assume that key financial ratios will remain unchanged for the forecast period.
     B. use common-size financial statements to estimate expenses as a percentage of net income.
     C. examine the variability of the predicted outcomes by performing a sensitivity or scenario analysis.

COMPREHENSIVE PROBLEMS

A. The following table lists partial financial statement data for Alpha Company:

Alpha Company

Sales	$5,000
Cost of goods sold	2,500
Average	
Inventories	$600
Accounts receivable	450
Working capital	750
Cash	200
Accounts payable	500
Fixed assets	4,750
Total assets	$6,000
Annual purchases	$2,400

Calculate the following ratios for Alpha Company:
- Inventory turnover.
- Days of inventory on hand.
- Receivables turnover.
- Days of sales outstanding.
- Payables turnover.
- Number of days of payables.
- Cash conversion cycle.

Use the following information for problems B through E.

Beta Co. has a loan covenant requiring it to maintain a current ratio of 1.5 or better. As Beta approaches year-end, current assets are $20 million ($1 million in cash, $9 million in accounts receivable, and $10 million in inventory) and current liabilities are $13.5 million.

B. Calculate Beta's current ratio and quick ratio.

C. Which of the following transactions would Beta Co. *most likely* enter to meet its loan covenant?
- Sell $1 million in inventory and deposit the proceeds in the company's checking account.
- Borrow $1 million short term and deposit the funds in their checking account.
- Sell $1 million in inventory and pay off some of its short-term creditors.

D.   If Beta sells $2 million in inventory on credit, how will this affect its current ratio?

E.   If Beta sells $1 million in inventory and pays off accounts payable, how will this affect its quick ratio?

ANSWERS – CONCEPT CHECKERS

1. **B**   With a vertical common-size income statement, all income statement accounts are divided by sales.

2. **A**   Company and industry data are widely available from numerous private and public sources. The other statements describe limitations of financial ratios.

3. **C**   Fixed charge coverage is a solvency ratio. Return on total capital is a measure of profitability and the defensive interval ratio is a liquidity measure.

4. **B**   Payables turnover = (purchases / avg. AP) = 100 / 12 = 8.33. Payables payment period = 365 / 8.33 = 43.8 days

5. **B**   total asset turnover = (sales / total assets) = 150 / 75 = 2 times

    inventory turnover = (COGS / avg. inventory) = (150 − 45) / 15 = 7 times

6. **C**   receivables turnover = (S / avg. AR) = 100 / 25 = 4

    average collection period = 365 / 4 = 91.25 days

7. **B**   Current ratio = (cash + AR + inv) / AP. If cash and AP decrease by the same amount and the current ratio is greater than 1, then the denominator falls faster (in percentage terms) than the numerator, and the current ratio increases.

8. **A**   Quick ratio = (cash + AR) / AP. If cash decreases, the quick ratio will also decrease. The denominator is unchanged.

9. **C**   Current ratio = current assets / current liabilities. If CR is > 1, then if CA and CL both fall, the overall ratio will increase.

10. **A**   (365 / 10 + 365 / 5 − 365 / 9) = 69 days

11. **B**   Interest coverage ratio = EBIT / I = (1,000 − 400 − 300) / 100 = 3 times

12. **C**   This is the correct formula for the three-ratio DuPont model for ROE.

13. **C** $\text{return on equity} = \left(\dfrac{\text{net income}}{\text{sales}}\right)\left(\dfrac{\text{sales}}{\text{assets}}\right)\left(\dfrac{\text{assets}}{\text{equity}}\right) = (0.12)(1.2)(1.2) = 0.1728 = 17.28\%$

14. **C**   Tax burden = (1 − tax rate) = tax retention rate = 0.6.

    ROE = 0.6 × 0.9 × 0.1 × 1.8 × 1.9 = 0.1847 = 18.47%.

15. **C**   (ROA)(interest burden)(tax retention rate) is not one of the DuPont models for calculating ROE.

16. **A**   Tax burden = 1 − 0.35 = 0.65.

    ROE = 0.65 × 0.7 × 0.11 × 1.2 × 1.5 = 0.0901.

17. **B** g = (retention rate)(ROE)

ROE = net profit margin × asset turnover × equity multiplier = (0.1)(0.9)(1.2) = 0.108

g = (1 − 0.4)(0.108) = 6.5%

18. **B** An earnings forecast model would typically estimate expenses as a percentage of sales.

ANSWERS – COMPREHENSIVE PROBLEMS

A. inventory turnover = COGS / avg. inventory = 2500 / 600 = 4.167 times

days of inventory on hand = 365 / inventory turnover = 365 / 4.167 = 87.6 days

receivables turnover = sales / avg. account receivable = 5,000 / 450 = 11.11 times

days of sales outstanding = 365 / receivables turnover = 365 / 11.11 = 32.85 days

payables turnover = purchases / avg. payables = 2,400 / 500 = 4.8 times

number of days of payables = 365 / payables turnover = 365 / 4.8 = 76 days

cash conversion cycle = days of inventory on hand + days of sales outstanding − number of days of payables

= 33 + 88 − 76 = 45 days

B. current ratio = current assets / current liabilities

= [(1 + 9 + 10) / 13.5] = 20 / 13.5 = 1.48 times

Quick ratio = (cash + marketable securities + receivables) / current liabilities

= (1 + 9) / 13.5 = 10 / 13.5 = 0.74 times

C. Selling $1 million in inventory and pay off some of its short-term creditors would increase the current ratio: (20 − 1) / (13.5 − 1) = 19 / 12.5 = 1.52.

Selling $1 million in inventory and depositing the proceeds in the company's checking account would leave the ratio unchanged: (20 + 1 − 1) / 13.5 = 1.48. Borrowing $1 million short term and depositing the funds in their checking account would decrease the current ratio: (20 + 1) / (13.5 + 1) = 21 / 14.5 = 1.45.

D. If inventory goes down and receivables rise by the same amount, current assets would be unchanged.

E. QR = (cash + AR) / AP. AP will decrease without any change to the numerator, thus increasing the overall ratio.

The following is a review of the Financial Reporting and Analysis principles designed to address the learning outcome statements set forth by CFA Institute®. This topic is also covered in:

FINANCIAL REPORTING QUALITY: RED FLAGS AND ACCOUNTING WARNING SIGNS

EXAM FOCUS

This review covers a broad array of methods to manipulate earnings through the choice of accounting methods and estimates. There are some long lists that you cannot be expected to replicate. You should, however, understand every point on every list, how income or balance sheet items are affected, and why the indicated warning sign suggests accounting manipulation. With this in mind, focus strongly on the warning signs of various accounting irregularities. Remember, firms may manipulate earnings to decrease or increase them. Firms may artificially decrease earnings in periods of good earnings growth in such a way that they can be "stored," only to reappear in a future period when results would have otherwise fallen short of expectations.

LOS 40.a: Describe incentives that might induce a company management to overreport or underreport earnings.

Firms are motivated to **manage earnings** because of the potential benefits.

Management may be motivated to *overstate net income* to:

- Meet earnings expectations.
- Remain in compliance with lending covenants.
- Receive higher incentive compensation.

Managing earnings can also involve *understating net income*. Management may be motivated to underreport earnings to:

- Obtain trade relief in the form of quotas or protective tariffs.
- Negotiate favorable terms from creditors.
- Negotiate favorable labor union contracts.

Firms may also be motivated to *manage the balance sheet*. For example, by overstating assets or understating liabilities, the firm appears more solvent. Conversely, a firm might understate assets or overstate liabilities to appear less solvent in order to negotiate concessions with creditors and other interested parties. A firm may also manage its balance sheet in order to enhance performance ratios. For example, lower assets will result in a higher return on assets ratio and a higher asset turnover ratio.

LOS 40.b: Describe activities that will result in a low quality of earnings.

Generally accepted accounting principles (GAAP) can be exploited by a firm to achieve a specific outcome while meeting the letter, but not the spirit, of the accounting standards; however, earnings quality will usually deteriorate. Low quality earnings are the result of:

- *Selecting acceptable accounting principles that misrepresent the economics of a transaction.* For example, a firm might choose the units-of-production method of depreciation in periods when the consumption of the asset is better measured by the straight-line or accelerated methods. If the units-of-production method results in lower depreciation than the straight-line method early in the asset's life, earnings will be accelerated to the early years of the asset's life.
- *Structuring transactions to achieve a desired outcome.* For example, a firm might structure the terms of a lease to avoid capital lease recognition, resulting in lower liabilities, lower leverage ratios, and lower fixed assets.
- *Using aggressive or unrealistic estimates and assumptions.* For example, lengthening the lives of depreciable assets or increasing the salvage value will result in lower depreciation expense and higher earnings.
- *Exploiting the intent of an accounting principle.* For example, some firms have applied a narrow rule regarding unconsolidated special purposes entities (SPE) to a broad range of transactions, because leverage is lower if the firm does not consolidate the SPE.

LOS 40.c: Describe the "fraud triangle."

Users of financial information should become familiar with the risk factors and warning signs of fraud. Statement on Auditing Standards No. 99, *Consideration of Fraud in a Financial Statement Audit* (SAS No. 99), issued by the American Institute of Certified Public Accountants (AICPA), identifies three conditions that are usually present when fraud occurs. These conditions, known as the **fraud triangle**, are illustrated in Figure 1. Note that not all of these conditions need to be present for fraud to occur.

Figure 1: "Fraud Triangle"

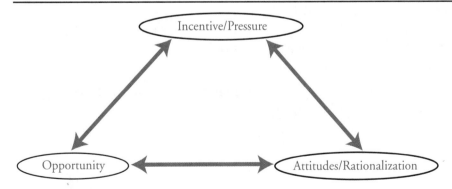

Fraud.
It
Oughta
Accelerate

I
O
A

- **Incentive or pressure** is the motive that exists to commit fraud. For example, management may want to meet earnings expectations because their compensation depends the firm's stock price.
- **Opportunity** exists when there is a weakness in internal controls.
- **Attitudes or rationalization** is a mindset that fraudulent behavior is justified.

LOS 40.d: Describe the risk factors related to incentives and pressures that may lead to fraudulent accounting.

SAS No. 99 identified four risk factors related to the incentives or pressures (motive) that may lead to fraudulent reporting.

1. *Threats to financial stability or profitability* as a result of economic, industry, or firm conditions such as:

   - Intense competition or market saturation, along with declining margins.
   - Vulnerability to rapid changes in technology, rates of product obsolescence, or interest rates.
   - Declining customer demand or increasing business failures.
   - Operating losses that may result in bankruptcy, foreclosure, or a hostile takeover.
   - Recurring negative operating cash flow or inability to generate positive cash flow while reporting earnings or earnings growth.
   - Rapid growth or unusual profitability.
   - New accounting standards, laws, or regulatory requirements.

2. *Excessive third party pressures* on management from:

   - Aggressive or unrealistic profitability or trend expectations.
   - Debt or equity financing requirements in order to stay competitive.
   - Stock exchange listing requirements.
   - Debt covenants and repayment requirements.
   - Impact of real or perceived effects of poor financial performance on a pending transaction, such as a business acquisition.

3. *Personal net worth of management or the board of directors is threatened* because of:

   - A significant financial interest in the firm.
   - A significant amount of contingent compensation based on achieving aggressive targets for stock price, operating profit, or cash flow.
   - Personal guarantees of the firm's debt.

4. *Excessive pressure on management or operating personnel to meet internal financial goals*, including sales and profitability targets.

LOS 40.e: Describe the risk factors related to opportunities that may lead to fraudulent accounting.

SAS No. 99 identified four risk factors related to the opportunities to commit fraud in financial reporting.

1. The *nature of the firm's industry or operations* might involve:
   - Significant related party transactions, particularly when those parties are unaudited, or audited by another firm.
   - Ability to dictate terms and conditions to suppliers and customers that may result in transactions that are not at arm's length.
   - Significant estimates and judgments in accounting for assets, liabilities, revenues, and expenses.
   - Unusual or complex transactions, especially near year-end, such as transactions that present "substance over form" issues.
   - Operations that exist or transactions that occur internationally where cultures and business practices may differ.
   - Bank accounts or operations located in tax-havens without clear business justification.

2. *Ineffective management monitoring* as a result of:
   - Management being dominated by a single person or small group.
   - Ineffective oversight by the board of directors or audit committee.

3. *A complex or unstable organizational structure* as evidenced by:
   - Difficulty in determining who is in control.
   - Organizational structure that involves unusual legal entities or unusual lines of authority.
   - High turnover among management, legal counsel, or board members.

4. *Deficient internal controls* that can result from:
   - Inadequate monitoring controls.
   - High turnover rates of accounting and information technology personnel.
   - Ineffective accounting and information systems.

> *Professor's Note: The last three factors relate to corporate governance. In firms with more effective corporate governance systems, the opportunities to commit fraud are limited. See the topic review of corporate governance in the Study Session on Corporate Finance for more details.*

LOS 40.f: Describe the risk factors related to attitudes and rationalizations that may lead to fraudulent accounting.

SAS No. 99 identified the following risk factors related to attitudes and rationalization to justify fraudulent behavior:

1. *Inappropriate ethical standards* or failure to effectively communicate or support a firm's ethical standards.

2. *Excessive participation by nonfinancial management in the selection of accounting standards* and the determination of estimates.

3. Known history or allegations of *violations of laws and regulations by management or board members*.

4. *A management obsession with maintaining or increasing the firm's stock price or earnings trend.*

5. *Making commitments to third parties to achieve aggressive results.*

6. *Failing to correct known reportable conditions* in a timely manner.

7. *Inappropriately minimizing earnings for tax purposes.*

8. Management's continued *use of materiality as a basis to justify inappropriate or questionable accounting methods*.

9. *A strained relationship between management and the current or previous auditor* as evidenced by any of the following:

   - Frequent disputes on accounting, auditing, and reporting issues.
   - Unreasonable demands on the auditor, such as unreasonable time constraints.
   - Restricting the auditor's access to people and information.
   - Limiting the auditor's ability to effectively communicate with the board of directors and audit committee.
   - Domineering management behavior toward the auditor.

LOS 40.g: Describe common accounting warning signs and methods of detecting each.

Aggressive revenue recognition. The most common earnings manipulation technique is recognizing revenue *too soon*. Recall that revenue is recognized in the income statement when it is earned and payment is reasonably assured. Usually revenue is recognized at delivery but, in some cases, revenue can be recognized before delivery takes place. Firms are required to report their revenue recognition policies in the financial statement footnotes. It is important to understand when revenue recognition takes place.

Some examples of aggressive recognition include:

- Bill-and-hold arrangements whereby revenue is recognized before the goods are shipped.
- Holding the accounting period open past year-end.
- Sales-type leases whereby the lessor recognizes a sale, and profit, at the inception of the lease, especially when the lessee does not capitalize the lease.
- Recognizing revenue before fulfilling all of the terms and conditions of sale.
- Recognizing revenue from swaps and barter transactions with third parties.

Different growth rates of operating cash flow and earnings. Over time, there should be a fairly stable relationship between the growth of operating cash flow and earnings. If

Study Session 10

Cross-Reference to CFA Institute Assigned Reading #40 – Financial Reporting Quality: Red Flags and Accounting Warning Signs

not, earnings manipulation may be occurring. A firm that is reporting growing earnings, but negative or declining operating cash flow, may be recognizing revenue too soon and/or delaying the recognition of expense.

The relationship of operating cash flow and earnings can be measured with the **cash flow earnings index** (operating cash flow/net income). An index that is consistently less than one or that is declining over time is suspect.

Abnormal sales growth as compared to the economy, industry, or peers. Abnormal growth may be the result of superior management or products, but may also indicate accounting irregularities. Receivables that are growing faster than sales, as indicated by an increasing average collection period, may be evidence of aggressive revenue recognition.

Abnormal inventory growth as compared to sales growth. Increasing inventory may be an indication of obsolete products or poor inventory management, but it could also result from overstating inventory, decreasing the cost of goods sold and thereby increasing gross profit and net profit. This can be detected by looking a declining inventory turnover ratio.

 Professor's Note: Recall that ending inventory is equal to beginning inventory plus purchases minus cost of goods sold (COGS). If ending inventory is too high, COGS will be too low, all else equal.

Boosting revenue with nonoperating income and nonrecurring gains. Some firms try to reclassify nonoperating income and nonrecurring gains as revenue, in effect, moving these items "up" the income statement. Net income is the same but revenue growth is higher.

Delaying expense recognition. By capitalizing operating expenditures, the firm delays expense recognition to future periods. Watch for an increase in assets with unusual sounding names such as "deferred marketing charges" or "deferred customer acquisition costs."

Abnormal use of operating leases by lessees. Operating leases are common in most firms. However, some firms use this off-balance-sheet financing technique to improve ratios and reduce perceived leverage. Analysts should compare the firm's use of leasing, as a financing source, to its industry peers. For analytical purposes, consider treating operating leases as capital leases.

Hiding expenses by classifying them as extraordinary or nonrecurring. The result is to move expenses "down" the income statement and boost income from continuing operations.

LIFO liquidations. When a LIFO firm sells more inventory than it purchases or produces during a period of rising prices, it reduces the cost of goods sold and increases profit, although taxes are higher as well. Such profits are not sustainable because the firm will eventually run out of inventory. A declining LIFO reserve is an indication of a LIFO liquidation. Firms should disclose the effects of a LIFO liquidation in the financial statement footnotes.

Abnormal gross margin and operating margin as compared to industry peers. Abnormal margins may be the result of superior management or cost controls; however, they may be an indication of accounting irregularities. Determine the firm's conservatism by comparing the firm's accounting principles, as disclosed in the footnotes, to those of its industry peers.

Extending the useful lives of long-term assets. Depreciating or amortizing the cost of an asset over more periods results in higher reported earnings. Compare the useful lives of the firm's assets with those of its industry peers.

Aggressive pension assumptions. Aggressive assumptions such as a high discount rate, low compensation growth rate, or high expected rate of return on pension assets will result in lower pension expense and higher reported earnings. Compare these assumptions with those of its industry peers.

Year-end surprises. Higher earnings in the fourth quarter that cannot be explained by seasonality may be an indication of manipulation.

Equity method investments and off-balance-sheet special purpose entities. Equity method investments are not consolidated. However, the pro-rata share of the investee's earnings are included in net income. Watch for frequent use of nonconsolidated special purpose entities.

Other off-balance-sheet financing arrangements including debt guarantees. Firms must disclose these arrangements in the financial statement footnotes. For analytical purposes, consider increasing balance sheet liabilities for these arrangements.

 Professor's Note: Keep in mind that these are warning signs of low quality earnings. They are not necessarily indications that fraud has occurred or will occur.

LOS 40.h: Describe the accounting warning signs related to the Enron accounting scandal.

A study of Enron indicates numerous warning signs to investors, analysts, and creditors. Following is a brief discussion of some of the red flags in Enron's financial statements for the fiscal year 2000.

- **Insufficient operating cash flow.** Although Enron's operating cash flow exceeded net income, certain transactions were classified as operating activities when, in substance, the transactions were more like financing activities. In addition, Enron did not generate sufficient operating cash flow to fund its investing activities. Financing activities made up the difference.
- **Pressure to support stock price and debt ratings.** If Enron's stock price declined by a certain amount, or if Enron's debt rating dropped below investment grade, additional collateral in the form of Enron stock was required by its lenders. These provisions provided an incentive for Enron to manipulate earnings in order to boost its stock price and debt ratings. Recall that one of the motivations for overreporting earnings is to remain in compliance with lending covenants.

- **Revenues reported using mark-to-market accounting.** Mark-to-market revenue accounting is allowed in very limited situations, mostly involving commodities. Enron applied this accounting method to a number of different types of contracts. In some cases, there were no established market prices to value the underlying contract; thus, market value was simply estimated by Enron. As a result, Enron could recognize revenue before the contracts were even operational.

- **Excessive revenues reported in the last half of the year.** Revenues reported in the third and fourth quarters were disproportionate with Enron's seasonal trend from previous years.

- **Inflated sales to SPEs.** Enron securitized assets and sold the securitizations at inflated values to special purposes entities. In some cases, Enron protected the SPE investors from the risks involved in the transactions.

- **Use of mark-to-market accounting for equity method investments.** Recall that equity method investments are not consolidated; rather, the pro-rata earnings of the investee are reported in net income. In some cases, Enron reported mark-to-market gains on equity investments, rather than simply their GAAP income.

- **Use of barter transactions.** In some cases, Enron would sell cable capacity to a party and simultaneously purchase capacity from the same party.

- **Significant use of related party transactions.** Probably the most egregious irregularities occurred using limited partnerships whereby an Enron employee served as general partner. The limited partnerships engaged in billions of dollars in derivatives transactions with Enron. The primary assets of the partnerships included receivables from Enron and Enron securities.

- **Senior management compensation and turnover.** Senior management's compensation was based mostly on bonus and stock awards. In addition, during the year 2001, several key top managers resigned.

LOS 40.i: Describe the accounting warning signs related to the Sunbeam accounting scandal.

As previously noted, the most common earnings manipulation technique is recognizing revenue too soon. Sunbeam Corporation's 1996 and 1997 financial statements provide an excellent case study in earnings manipulation through aggressive revenue recognition. Sunbeam was a financially distressed company and, as part of Sunbeam's turnaround, management engaged in a number of questionable transactions. Following is a brief discussion of some of the warning signs found in Sunbeam's financial statements:

- **Created "cookie jar" reserves.** As a part of its turnaround, Sunbeam recognized restructuring charges and created reserves by recognizing losses in its 1996 income statement. For example, writing off inventory results in a reported loss; however, this loss turns into a profit when the inventory is sold in subsequent periods.

- **Receivables increased faster than sales.** In 1997, Sunbeam's receivables increased faster than sales. Sales without collections may be an indication that both sales and receivables are of poor quality.

- **Generated negative operating cash flow.** In 1997, Sunbeam reported a record level of earnings but operating cash flow was negative. The negative cash flow was primarily the result of increasing inventories and receivables.

- **Engaged in bill-and-hold sale arrangements.** In 1997, Sunbeam changed its revenue recognition policy and began recognizing some sales under bill-and-hold arrangements, whereby revenue was recognized before the goods were shipped.

- **Inappropriately reduced bad debt expense**. In 1997, bad debt expense related to receivables decreased even though sales and receivables increased significantly.
- **Increased fourth quarter revenues**. The financial statement footnotes indicate that Sunbeam's products are not seasonal, yet the footnotes reveal that Sunbeam initiated an early buy program for certain products. Accordingly, the percentage of Sunbeam's total revenue was highest in the fourth quarter. An increase in fourth quarter revenue of a nonseasonal business is a red flag.

KEY CONCEPTS

LOS 40.a

Management may be motivated to overstate earnings to meet analyst expectations, remain in compliance with debt covenants, or because higher reported earnings will increase their compensation. Management may be motivated to understate earnings to obtain trade relief, renegotiate advantageous repayment terms with existing creditors, negotiate more advantageous union labor contracts, or "save" earnings to report in a future period.

LOS 40.b

Low earnings quality can result from selecting accounting principles that misrepresent the economics of transactions, structuring transactions primarily to achieve a desired effect on reported earnings, using aggressive or unrealistic estimates and assumptions, or exploiting the intent of an accounting standard.

LOS 40.c

The "fraud triangle" consists of:
- *Incentive / pressure*—the motive to commit fraud.
- *Opportunities*—the firm has a weak internal control system.
- *Attitude / rationalization*—the mindset that fraud is justified.

LOS 40.d

Risk factors related to incentives and pressures for fraud include:
- Threats to the firm's financial stability or profitability.
- Excessive third-party pressures on management.
- Threats to the personal net worth of management or board members.
- Excessive pressure on management and employees to meet internal targets.

LOS 40.e

Risk factors related to opportunities for fraud include:
- The nature of the industry or operations.
- Ineffective monitoring of management.
- Complex or unstable organizational structure.
- Deficient internal controls.

LOS 40.f

Risk factors related to attitudes and rationalizations for fraud include:
- Inappropriate or inadequately supported ethical standards.
- Excessive participation by nonfinancial management in selecting accounting methods.
- A history of legal and regulatory violations by management or board members.
- Obsessive attention to the stock price or earnings trend.
- Aggressive commitments to third parties.
- Failure to correct known compliance problems.
- Minimizing earnings inappropriately for tax reporting.
- Continued use of materiality to justify inappropriate accounting.
- A strained relationship with the current or previous auditor.

LOS 40.g
Common warning signs of earnings manipulation include:
- Aggressive revenue recognition.
- Different growth rates of operating cash flow and earnings.
- Abnormal comparative sales growth.
- Abnormal inventory growth as compared to sales.
- Moving non-operating income and nonrecurring gains up the income statement to boost revenue.
- Delaying expense recognition.
- Excessive use of off-balance-sheet financing arrangements including leases.
- Classifying expenses as extraordinary or nonrecurring and moving them down the income statement to boost income from continuing operations.
- LIFO liquidations.
- Abnormal comparative margin ratios.
- Aggressive assumptions and estimates.
- Year-end surprises.
- Equity method investments with little or no cash flow.

LOS 40.h
Accounting warning signs related to the Enron scandal included:
- Insufficient operating cash flow.
- Pressure to support the stock price and debt ratings.
- Mark-to-market accounting for equity method investments.
- Disproportionately high revenues in the third and fourth quarters.
- Inflated sales of financial assets to special purpose entities.
- Significant barter and related-party transactions.
- High senior management turnover.

LOS 40.i
Accounting warning signs related to the Sunbeam scandal included:
- "Cookie jar" reserves.
- Receivables increasing faster than sales.
- Negative operating cash flow.
- Inflating revenue with bill-and-hold sale arrangements.
- Lower bad debt expense despite growing receivables.
- Outsized fourth quarter revenue for a business described as non-seasonal.

Study Session 10

Cross-Reference to CFA Institute Assigned Reading #40 – Financial Reporting Quality: Red Flags and Accounting Warning Signs

CONCEPT CHECKERS

1. Which of the following is *least likely* to be a motivation to overreport net income?
   A. Meet earnings expectations.
   B. Negotiate labor union contracts.
   C. Remain in compliance with bond covenants.

2. Which of the following is *most likely* an example of accounting fraud?
   A. Using aggressive pension assumptions.
   B. Booking revenue from a fictitious customer.
   C. Selecting an acceptable depreciation method that misrepresents the economics of the transaction.

3. The "fraud triangle" consists of:
   A. incentive or pressure, opportunity, and attitudes or rationalization.
   B. ineffective management, unstable organizational structure, and deficient internal controls.
   C. inappropriate ethical standards, violations of laws or regulations, and failing to correct known reportable conditions.

4. Competitive threats to the profitability or financial stability of a firm are *best* categorized as an accounting fraud risk factor related to:
   A. opportunities.
   B. incentives and pressures.
   C. attitudes and rationalizations.

5. According to Statement on Auditing Standards No. 99, Consideration of Fraud in a Financial Statement Audit, which of the following is *least likely* to be a risk factor related to opportunities to commit fraudulent accounting?
   A. Significant related party transactions.
   B. High turnover among accounting and information systems personnel.
   C. Aggressive or unrealistic profitability expectations from third parties.

6. Accounting fraud risk factors related to attitudes and rationalizations are *least likely* to include:
   A. Management has a strained relationship with the current or previous auditor.
   B. The firm does not effectively communicate an appropriate set of ethical standards.
   C. A high proportion of management's compensation depends on the firm exceeding targets for earnings or the stock price.

7. Which of the following actions is *least likely* to immediately increase earnings?
   A. Selling more inventory than is purchased or produced.
   B. Lowering the salvage value of depreciable assets.
   C. Holding the accounting period open past year-end.

8.   Accounting warning signs related to the Enron scandal *least likely* include:
       A. cookie-jar reserves.
       B. related-party transactions.
       C. inflated sales to special purpose entities.

9.   Which of the following actions was *least likely* a warning sign of potential earnings manipulation disclosed in Sunbeam's financial statement footnotes?
       A. Significant use of barter transactions.
       B. Receivables were increasing, but bad debt expense was decreasing.
       C. A record level of earnings, yet operating cash flow was negative.

Study Session 10

Cross-Reference to CFA Institute Assigned Reading #40 – Financial Reporting Quality: Red Flags and Accounting Warning Signs

ANSWERS – CONCEPT CHECKERS

1. **B**   Negotiating labor union contracts would be a reason to underreport, not overreport, earnings. The other choices are motivations to overreport earnings.

2. **B**   Booking revenue from a fictitious customer is fraud.

3. **A**   The three components of the fraud triangle are incentive or pressure, opportunity, and attitudes or rationalization.

4. **B**   Risk factors related to incentives and pressures include threats to the firm's financial stability or profitability from economic, industry, or firm-specific operating conditions.

5. **C**   Unrealistic profitability expectations from third parties is a risk factor related to incentives and pressures. The other choices are risk factors related to management's opportunities to commit fraud.

6. **C**   Significant threats to the personal wealth of managers and board members due to the firm not meeting its financial targets are a risk factor related to incentives and pressures. The other choices are risk factors related to attitudes and rationalizations.

7. **B**   Lowering the salvage value will result in higher depreciation expense, and thus, lower earnings. The other choices will immediately increase earnings. Selling more inventory than is purchased or produced will increase revenue without increasing cost of goods sold, which will increase earnings. Holding the accounting period open past year-end is an aggressive revenue recognition method that will boost earnings.

8. **A**   Enron engaged in significant related party transactions and had high asset sales to special purpose entities. Cookie-jar reserves were used by Sunbeam, but not Enron.

9. **A**   Sunbeam was not involved in significant barter transactions. The other choices are warning signs related to Sunbeam's accounting scandal.

ACCOUNTING SHENANIGANS ON THE CASH FLOW STATEMENT

EXAM FOCUS

Management has several ways to manipulate operating cash flow, including deciding how to allocate cash flow between categories and changing the timing of receipt of cash flows. Lengthening the terms of accounts payable, financing accounts payable, securitizing accounts receivable, and repurchasing stock options to offset dilution can affect the categorization and timing of cash flows. Not all increases in cash flow are sustainable.

CASH FLOW MANIPULATION

Accrual accounting is easily manipulated because of the many estimates and judgments involved. Operating cash flow is usually unaffected by estimates and judgments. However, firms can still create the perception that sustainable operating cash flow is greater than it actually is.

One technique is to misrepresent a firm's cash generating ability by classifying financing activities as operating activities and vice-versa. Additionally, management has discretion over the timing of cash flows. An analyst should take care to investigate the quality of a company's cash flows and determine whether increases in operating cash flow are sustainable. Management also has discretion over where to report cash flows, and the analyst should be aware that the difference in treatment among companies may make comparisons of cash flow less useful, particularly for valuation.

LOS 41: Analyze and discuss the following ways to manipulate the cash flow statement: stretching out payables; financing of payables; securitization of receivables; and using stock buybacks to offset dilution of earnings.

Stretching Accounts Payable

Transactions with suppliers are usually reported as operating activities in the cash flow statement. A firm can temporarily increase operating cash flow by simply stretching accounts payable; that is, delaying payments to its suppliers. By delaying payment, the firm effectively receives no-cost financing. However, stretching payables is not a sustainable source of increased cash flows, since the firm's suppliers may eventually refuse to extend credit because of the slower payments.

One way to determine whether a firm is stretching its payables is to examine the number of days in accounts payable. **Days' sales in payables** is calculated by dividing accounts payable by COGS and multiplying the result by the number of days in the period.

$$\text{days' sales in accounts payable} = \left(\frac{\text{accounts payable}}{\text{COGS}}\right) \times \text{number of days}$$

 Professor's Note: Earlier, we calculated the number of days of payables by dividing 365 by accounts payable turnover. Recall that accounts payable turnover is equal to purchases divided by average accounts payable.

Example: Calculating days sales in accounts payable

At year-end, Silver Creek Company reported cost of goods sold of $250 million. Ending accounts payable is $50 million. Assuming there are 365 days in a year, calculate the number of days on average it takes Silver Creek to pay its suppliers.

Answer:

$$\text{days' sales in accounts payable} = \left(\frac{\$50}{\$250}\right) \times 365 = 73 \text{ days}$$

Financing Accounts Payable

Delaying the cash flows associated with payables can also be accomplished by entering into a financing arrangement with a third party, usually a financial institution. Such an arrangement allows the firm to manage the timing of the reported operating cash flows.

Consider a manufacturing firm's credit purchases of raw materials. In an indirect cash flow statement, the increase in inventory decreases operating cash flow and the increase in accounts payable increases operating cash flow. Total operating cash flow does not change.

When the account payable is due, a financial institution makes payment to the supplier on behalf of the firm, and the firm reclassifies the account payable to short-term debt. The decrease in accounts payable decreases operating cash flow, and the increase in short-term debt increases financing cash flow. At this point, operating cash flow is lower and financing cash flow is higher, but total cash flow is still unaffected. The firm might time the arrangement so that the lower operating cash flow is offset by higher operating cash flows from other sources, such as seasonal cash flows or cash flows from receivable sales or securitizations. In effect, the firm times the operating cash outflow to occur when other operating cash inflows are higher.

Finally, when the firm repays the financial institution, the firm reports the outflow of cash as a financing activity and not an operating activity. Ultimately, the firm has delayed the outflow of cash. Of course, the financial institution will charge a fee (interest) to handle the arrangement.

Securitizing Accounts Receivable

Firms can immediately convert accounts receivable to cash by borrowing against the receivables, or by selling or securitizing the receivables. When a firm borrows with its receivables as collateral, the inflow of cash is reported as a financing activity in the cash flow statement.

When receivables are securitized, they are usually transferred to a bankruptcy remote structure known as a special purpose entity (SPE). The SPE pools the receivables together and sells securities representing an interest in the pool. A securitization is treated just like a collection; that is, the inflow of cash is reported as an operating activity in the cash flow statement because the transaction is reported as a sale. So, by securitizing its accounts receivable, rather than waiting to collect from the customer, a firm can accelerate operating cash flow into the current period.

Accelerating operating cash flow by securitizing receivables is not sustainable because the firm only has a limited amount of accounts receivable.

Securitizing accounts receivable may also affect earnings. When the receivables are securitized, the firm can recognize a gain in some cases. This gain is the result of differences between the book value and fair value of the receivables at the time of securitization. The gain can be affected by a number of estimates including the expected default rate, the expected prepayment rate, and the discount rate used.

GAAP is silent on where the gains from securitizations should be reported in the income statement. Some firms take a more aggressive approach and include the gains as revenue. Other firms reduce operating expenses by the amount of the gains. Some firms report the gains as a part of nonoperating income.

Repurchasing Stock to Offset Dilution

When a firm's stock options are exercised, shares must be issued. The higher the stock price relative to the exercise price, the more shares that must be issued by the firm. As the shares are issued, earnings per share are diluted (reduced).

Firms often repurchase stock to offset the dilutive effects of stock option exercise. The cash received from the exercise of the option and the outflow of cash from the share repurchase are both reported as financing activities in the cash flow statement. Because there is a tax benefit when options are exercised, exercise increases operating cash flow.

For analytical purposes, the net cash outflow for share repurchases to avoid dilution should be reclassified from financing activities to operating activities to better reflect the substance of the transaction. Since employee stock options are part of compensation, an analyst should subtract the cash outflow from operating cash flow to recognize the true cash cost of options-based compensation.

KEY CONCEPTS

LOS 41

Stretching accounts payable by delaying payment is not a sustainable source of operating cash flow. Suppliers may refuse to extend additional credit because of the slower payments. Stretching accounts payable can be identified by increases in the number of days in payables.

Arranging for a third party to finance (pay) a firm's payables in one period, so that the firm can account for repayment as a financing (rather than operating) cash flow in a later period, is a method to decrease operating cash flows in a period of seasonally high CFO, and increase them in a subsequent period.

Securitizing accounts receivable accelerates operating cash flow into the current period, but this source of cash is not sustainable and artificially increases receivables turnover. Securitizing receivables may also allow the firm to immediately recognize gains in the income statement.

Some firms repurchase stock to offset the dilutive effect of the exercise of employee stock options. The analyst must determine whether the increase in operating cash flow resulting from the income tax benefits of the exercise of employee stock options is sustainable. For analysis, the net cash outflow to repurchase stock should be considered an operating activity instead of a financing activity, since it is essentially a compensation expense.

CONCEPT CHECKERS

1. Decreasing accounts payable turnover by delaying payments to suppliers is *most likely* to cause cash flow from financing activities to:
    A. increase.
    B. decrease.
    C. remain unchanged.

2. As part of its working capital management program, Rotan Corporation has an accounts payable financing arrangement with the First National Bank. The bank pays Rotan's vendors within 30 days of the invoice date. Rotan reimburses the bank 90 days after the invoice is due. Ignoring interest, what is the *most likely* effect on Rotan's operating cash flow and financing cash flow when the bank is repaid?
    A. Both will decrease.
    B. Neither will decrease.
    C. Only one will decrease.

3. In order to generate cash, Company A securitized its accounts receivable through a special purpose entity. Company B pledged its accounts receivable to a local bank in order to secure a short-term loan. Assuming Company A and Company B are identical in all other respects, which company has higher operating cash flow and which company has higher financing cash flow?

Higher operating cash flow	Higher financing cash flow
A. Company A	Company A
B. Company A	Company B
C. Company B	Company A

4. Over the past two years, a firm reported higher operating cash flow as a result of securitizing its accounts receivable and from increasing income tax benefits from employee stock options. The tax benefits are solely the result of higher tax rates. Should an analyst conclude that these two sources of operating cash flow are sustainable?
    A. Both sources are sustainable.
    B. Neither source is sustainable.
    C. Only one of these sources is sustainable.

ANSWERS – CONCEPT CHECKERS

1. **C** Decreasing accounts payable turnover by delaying payments to suppliers is a source of operating cash, not a source of financing cash. Decreasing accounts payable turnover is not a sustainable source of cash flow because suppliers may eventually refuse to extend credit because of the slower payments.

2. **C** When the bank is repaid, the cash outflow is reported as a financing activity. Operating cash flow is not affected when payment is made.

3. **B** The cash received from securitizing receivables is reported as an operating activity. The cash received from borrowing against accounts receivable is reported as a financing activity.

4. **B** Accelerating operating cash flow by securitizing receivables is not sustainable because the firm only has a limited amount of accounts receivable. An increase in tax benefits as a result higher of tax rates is not sustainable. Tax rates could also decrease in the future.

The following is a review of the Financial Reporting and Analysis principles designed to address the learning outcome statements set forth by CFA Institute®. This topic is also covered in:

FINANCIAL STATEMENT ANALYSIS: APPLICATIONS

EXAM FOCUS

A relatively short reading here, with applications of the analytic methods detailed in the previous topic review. Pay special attention to the method outlined for forecasting cash flows. Memorize the four types of items important in the determination of credit quality. Lastly, analyst adjustments to financial statements are covered one more time. Understand the reasons for all the adjustments covered and how the adjustments will affect financial ratios used for valuation and credit analysis.

LOS 42.a: Evaluate a company's past financial performance and explain how a company's strategy is reflected in past financial performance.

In the previous review, we introduced a number of financial ratios that can be used to assess a company's profitability, leverage, solvency, and operational efficiency. The analyst can evaluate trends in these ratios, as well as their levels, to evaluate how the company has performed in these areas.

Trends in financial ratios and differences between a firm's financial ratios and those of its competitors or industry averages can indicate important aspects of a firm's business strategy. Consider two firms in the personal computer business. One builds relatively high-end computers with cutting-edge features, and one competes primarily on price and produces computers with various configurations using readily available technology. What differences in their financial statements would we expect to find?

Premium products are usually sold at higher gross margins than less differentiated commodity-like products, so we should expect cost of goods sold to be a higher proportion of sales for the latter. We might also expect the company with cutting-edge features and high quality to spend a higher proportion of sales on research and development, which may be quite minimal for a firm purchasing improved components from suppliers rather than developing new features and capabilities in-house. The ratio of gross profits to operating profits will be larger for a firm that spends highly on research and development or on advertising.

In general, it is important for an analyst to understand a subject firm's business strategy. If the firm claims it is going to improve earnings per share by cutting costs, examination of operating ratios and gross margins over time will reveal whether the firm has actually been able to implement such a strategy and whether sales have suffered as a result.

LOS 42.b: Prepare a basic projection of a company's future net income and cash flow.

A forecast of future net income and cash flow often begins with a forecast of future sales. Over shorter horizons, the "top down" approach to forecasting sales is used. The analyst begins with a forecast of GDP growth, often supplied by outside research or an in-house economics group. Historical relationships can be used to estimate the relationship between GDP growth and the growth of industry sales. If the subject firm's market share is expected to remain the same, the growth of firm sales will be the same as the growth in industry sales. If the analyst has reason to believe the firm's market share will increase or decrease next period, the market share can be adjusted for this change and then multiplied by estimated industry sales for the next period to get the forecast of firm sales for the period.

In a simple forecasting model, some historical average or trend-adjusted measure of profitability (operating margin, EBT margin, or net margin) can be used to forecast earnings. In complex forecasting models, each item on an income statement and balance sheet can be estimated based on separate assumptions about its growth in relation to revenue growth. For multi-period forecasts, the analyst typically employs a single estimate of sales growth at some point that is expected to continue indefinitely.

To estimate cash flows, the analyst must make assumptions about future sources and uses of cash. The most important of these will be increases in working capital, capital expenditures on new fixed assets, issuance or repayments of debt, and issuance or repurchase of stock. A typical assumption is that noncash working capital as a percentage of sales remains constant. A first-pass model might indicate a need for cash in future periods, and these cash requirements can then be met by projecting necessary borrowing in future periods. For consistency, interest expense in future periods must also be adjusted for any increase in debt.

Figure 1 illustrates this method. This projection assumes the company's sales increase 5% per year, its cost of goods sold is 35% of sales, and operating expenses are 55% of sales. It also assumes noncash working capital stays constant at 85% of sales and fixed capital requirements will be 5% of sales in each year. Net income is projected to increase over the forecast period, but the analysis reveals that cash is expected to decrease, suggesting a need for financing.

Figure 1: Income and Cash Flow Projection

	20X0	20X1	20X2	20X3	20X4
Sales @ +5% per year	86,145	90,452	94,975	99,724	104,710
Cost of goods sold @ 35% of sales	30,151	31,658	33,241	34,903	36,648
Operating expenses @ 55% of sales	47,380	49,749	52,236	54,848	57,590
Pretax income	8,614	9,045	9,497	9,972	10,471
Taxes @ 35%	3,015	3,166	3,324	3,490	3,665
Net income	5,599	5,879	6,173	6,482	6,806
Cash (Borrowing)	8,615	6,311	3,891	1,350	(1,317)
Noncash working capital @ 85% of sales	73,223	76,884	80,729	84,765	89,003
Current assets	81,838	83,195	84,620	86,116	87,686
Net income	5,599	5,879	6,173	6,482	6,806
– Investment in working capital	3,478	3,661	3,844	4,036	4,238
– Investment in fixed capital @ 5% of sales	4,307	4,523	4,749	4,986	5,235
Change in cash	(2,186)	(2,304)	(2,420)	(2,541)	(2,668)
Beginning cash	10,801	8,615	6,311	3,891	1,350
Ending cash	8,615	6,311	3,891	1,350	(1,317)

LOS 42.c: Describe the role of financial statement analysis in assessing the credit quality of a potential debt investment.

[handwritten margin note: Character, collateral, capacity]

Traditionally, credit analysts have spoken of the "three C's," "four C's," or even the "five C's" of credit analysis. One version of the three C's includes: Character, Collateral, and Capacity to repay. Character refers to firm management's professional reputation and the firm's history of debt repayment. The ability to pledge specific collateral reduces lender risk. It is the third C, the capacity to repay, that requires close examination of a firm's financial statements and ratios. Since some debt is for periods of 30 years or longer, the credit analyst must take a very long-term view of the firm's prospects.

Credit rating agencies such as Moody's and Standard and Poor's employ formulas that are essentially weighted averages of several specific accounting ratios and business characteristics. The specific items used in the formula and their weights vary from industry to industry, but the types of items considered can be separated into four general categories:

1. *Scale and diversification.* Larger companies and those with more different product lines and greater geographic diversification are better credit risks.

2. *Operational efficiency.* Such items as operating ROA, operating margins, and EBITDA margins fall into this category. Along with greater vertical diversification, high operating efficiency is associated with better debt ratings.

3. *Margin stability.* Stability of the relevant profitability margins indicates a higher probability of repayment (leads to a better debt rating and a lower interest rate). Highly variable operating results make lenders nervous.

4. *Leverage.* Ratios of operating earnings, EBITDA, or some measure of free cash flow to interest expense or total debt make up the most important part of the credit rating formula. Firms with greater earnings in relation to their debt and in relation to their interest expense are better credit risks.

LOS 42.d: Discuss the use of financial statement analysis in screening for potential equity investments.

In many cases an analyst must select portfolio stocks from the large universe of potential equity investments. Whether the object is to select growth stocks, income stocks, or value stocks, accounting items and ratios can be used to identify a manageable subset of available stocks for further analysis.

Some investment strategies even have financial ratios in their names, such as low price/earnings and low price/sales investing. Multiple criteria are used because a screen based on a single factor can include firms with other undesirable characteristics. For example, a company with a low P/E may also have operating losses, declining sales prospects, or very high leverage.

Analysts should be aware that their equity screens will likely include and exclude many or all of the firms in particular industries. A screen to identify firms with low P/E ratios will likely exclude growth companies from the sample. A low price-to-book or high dividend screen will likely include an inordinate proportion of financial services companies.

Backtesting refers to using a specific set of criteria to screen historical data to determine how portfolios based on those criteria would have performed. There is, of course, no guarantee that screening criteria that have identified stocks that outperformed in the past will continue to do so. Analysts must also pay special attention to the potential effects of survivorship bias, data-mining bias, and look-ahead bias (see the topic review on Sampling and Estimation) when evaluating the results of backtesting.

LOS 42.e: Determine and justify appropriate analyst adjustments to a company's financial statements to facilitate comparison with another company.

Because different companies choose different accounting methods, an analyst must be prepared to adjust the financial statements of one company to make them comparable to those of another company or group of companies. Differences in accounting methods chosen by firms subject to the same standards, as well as differences in accounting methods due to differences in local accounting standards, can make comparisons between companies problematic.

Consider two companies in the same industry that have different depreciation schedules. One company has selected straight-line depreciation even though physical assets in its industry tend to lose most of their productive value early in their economic lives. The analyst would need to adjust the depreciation of that firm so that the net income figures for the firms are comparable. A change in a firm's financial statement depreciation would lead to changes in gross profit, operating profit, and so on down to net profit and earnings per share.

Differences between U.S. GAAP and IFRS require an analyst to adjust the financial statements of firms from different countries before comparing their financial results. Important differences between the two include their treatments of the effect of exchange rate changes, certain securities held by the firm, and inventory cost flows. Differences in accounting standards are covered in more detail in the next topic review.

We have already covered other adjustments for certain accounting methods and estimates. The analyst may need to convert financial statements for LIFO-based firms to FIFO, or vice-versa. Analysts would likely increase both liabilities and assets for a firm with significant operating leases, or for one with take-or-pay contracts.

KEY CONCEPTS

LOS 42.a
Trends in a company's financial ratios and differences between its financial ratios and those of its competitors or industry average ratios can reveal important aspects of its business strategy.

LOS 42.b
A company's future income and cash flows can be projected by forecasting sales growth and using estimates of profit margins and the increases in working capital and fixed assets necessary to support the forecast sales growth.

LOS 42.c
Credit analysis uses a firm's financial statements to assess its credit quality. Indicators of a firm's creditworthiness include its scale and diversification, operational efficiency, margin stability, and use of financial leverage.

LOS 42.d
Potentially attractive equity investments can be identified by screening a universe of stocks using minimum or maximum values of one or more ratios. Which (and how many) ratios to use, what minimum or maximum values to use, and how much importance to give each ratio all present challenges to the analyst.

LOS 42.e
When companies use different accounting methods or estimates relating to areas such as inventory accounting, depreciation, capitalization, and off-balance-sheet financing, analysts must adjust the financial statements for comparability.

CONCEPT CHECKERS

1. The table below shows selected data from a company's financial statements.

	20X6	20X7	20X8	20X9
Sales	8,614	9,217	9,862	10,553
COGS	5,304	5,622	6,072	6,679
Purchases	5,257	5,572	6,018	6,620
Inventory	2,525	2,475	2,421	2,362
Accounts receivable	3,491	3,728	3,928	4,352
Accounts payable	1,913	2,102	2,311	2,539

Based on these results, what was this company's *most likely* strategy for improving its operating activity during this period?
A. Improve its inventory management.
B. Change its credit and collections policies with its customers.
C. Change the degree to which it uses trade credit from suppliers.

2. An analyst who is projecting a company's net income and cash flows is *least likely* to assume a constant relationship between the company's sales and its:
A. interest expenses.
B. cost of goods sold.
C. noncash working capital.

3. Credit analysts are likely to consider a company's credit quality to be improving if the company reduces its:
A. scale and diversification.
B. margin stability.
C. leverage.

4. Which of the following stock screens is *most likely* to identify stocks with high earnings growth rates?
A. Dividend payout ratio > 30%.
B. Price to cash flow per share ratio < 12.
C. Book value to market value ratio < 25%.

5. An analyst needs to compare the financial statements of Firm X and Firm Y. Which of the following differences in the two firms' financial reporting is *least likely* to require the analyst to make an adjustment?

	Firm X	Firm Y
A.	Straight line depreciation	Accelerated depreciation
B.	Direct method cash flows	Indirect method cash flows
C.	IFRS financial reporting	U.S. GAAP financial reporting

©2008 Kaplan Schweser

ANSWERS – CONCEPT CHECKERS

1. **A**   To analyze this company's operating strategy, calculate its activity ratios:

	20X7	20X8	20X9
Inventory turnover	2.25	2.48	2.79
Receivables turnover	2.55	2.58	2.55
Payables turnover	2.78	2.73	2.73
Days of inventory on hand	162	147	131
Days of sales outstanding	143	142	143
Number of days of payables	132	134	134

The ratios that have changed most significantly are the ones related to inventory. Receivables and payables performance has remained steady, suggesting no change in the company's use of supplier credit or extension of customer credit.

2. **A**   Projections of net income and cash flows are typically based on assumptions that cost of goods sold, operating expenses, and noncash working capital remain a constant percentage of sales. The projections then show whether additional borrowing is needed during the forecast period. If so, the analyst will adjust the interest expense to reflect the additional debt.

3. **C**   Lower leverage improves a company's creditworthiness. Larger scale, more diversification, higher operating efficiency, and more stable margins also tend to indicate better credit quality.

4. **C**   Firms with high growth rates will tend to have high market values relative to the book value of their equity. Low price to cash flow ratios would tend to identify value stocks rather than growth stocks. Screening for high dividend payout ratios would tend to identify mature firms with relatively few growth opportunities.

5. **B**   Cash flows are the same under either method. Differences in depreciation methods and IFRS versus U.S. GAAP reporting can require an analyst to adjust financial statements to make them comparable.

The following is a review of the Financial Reporting and Analysis principles designed to address the learning outcome statements set forth by CFA Institute®. This topic is also covered in:

INTERNATIONAL STANDARDS CONVERGENCE

EXAM FOCUS

The convergence of U.S. GAAP and international accounting standards is an ongoing process. The exact differences between the two can be expected to change over time as the governing bodies work toward convergence. Here you should gain an understanding of the key differences, including upward revaluations and the prohibition of LIFO inventory accounting under international standards. The process of restating a company's financials to make them comparable with another company's or those of a group of peer companies is the important lesson here, along with the effects of restatement on key financial ratios.

LOS 43.a: Identify and explain the major international accounting standards for each asset and liability category on the balance sheet and the key differences from U.S. generally accepted accounting principles (GAAP).

The elements of the balance sheet (assets, liabilities, and equity) are defined in the IASB's conceptual framework. According to the framework, for an item to be recognized on the balance sheet as an asset (liability), it must be probable that a future economic benefit (expense) will flow to or from the firm *and* the item's cost can be reliably measured. Conceptually, equity is simply assets minus liabilities.

Marketable Investment Securities

Marketable investment securities are initially recorded on the balance sheet at cost; that is, the fair value at the date of acquisition. The main issue involves whether to adjust the balance sheet to reflect subsequent changes in fair value. The adjustments depend on the classification of the securities.

As discussed in the topic review on understanding the balance sheet, marketable investment securities are classified as either held-to-maturity, trading, or available-for-sale under SFAS No. 115. Under IFRS, the accounting for marketable investment securities is virtually the same. One difference is that trading securities are known as "held-for-trading" securities under IFRS.

Held-to-maturity securities are debt securities acquired with the intent and ability to own them until they mature. Held-to-maturity securities are reported on the balance sheet at amortized cost. Amortized cost is equal to the face (par) value less any unamortized discount or plus any unamortized premium. Subsequent changes in fair value are ignored unless the security is sold or otherwise disposed of.

Held-for-trading securities are debt and equity securities, including derivatives, acquired with the intent to profit from near-term price fluctuations. Held-for-trading securities are reported on the balance sheet at fair value. Unrealized gains and losses (changes in market value before the securities are sold) are recognized in the income statement.

Available-for-sale securities are debt and equity securities that a firm does not expect to hold until maturity nor expect to trade in the near term. Like held-for-trading securities, available-for-sale securities are reported on the balance sheet at fair value. However, any unrealized gains or losses are not recognized in the income statement. Rather, any unrealized gains or losses are reported as other comprehensive income.

Regardless of a security's classification, dividend income, interest income, and any realized gains and losses (actual gains or losses relative to carrying values realized when securities are sold) are recognized in the income statement.

Figure 1 summarizes the differences among the treatments of the three categories of marketable securities on the balance sheet and income statement.

Figure 1: Summary of Marketable Investment Security Classifications

	Held-for-trading	Available-for-sale	Held-to-maturity
Balance sheet	Fair value	Fair value	Amortized cost
Income statement	Unrealized G/L	No effect	No effect

Example: Classification of investment securities

Triple D Corporation purchased a 6% bond, at par, for $1,000,000 at the beginning of the year. Interest rates have recently increased, and the market value of the bond declined $20,000. Determine the bond's treatment on the financial statements under each classification of securities.

Answer:

If the bond is classified as a *held-to-maturity* security, the bond is reported on the balance sheet at $1,000,000 and interest income of $60,000 [$1,000,000 × 6%] is reported in the income statement.

If the bond is classified as a *held-for-trading* security, the bond is reported on the balance sheet at $980,000 and the $20,000 unrealized loss and $60,000 of interest income are both recognized in the income statement.

If the bond is classified as an *available-for-sale* security, the bond is reported on the balance sheet at $980,000 and $60,000 of interest income is recognized in the income statement. The $20,000 unrealized loss is not recognized in the income statement; rather, it is reported as other comprehensive income and decreases stockholders' equity.

The performance of held-for-trading securities is more transparent since both unrealized gains and unrealized losses are recognized in the income statement. Conversely, there is asymmetric treatment with available-for-sale securities since the unrealized gains and losses bypass the income statement and are reported as a direct adjustment to equity. By bypassing the income statement, the performance of available-for-sale securities can be misinterpreted by analysts. If a firm owns an equity security classified as available-for-sale, continuing decreases in share prices do not affect the income statement as long as the security is not sold.

Firms that follow IFRS are required to make qualitative and quantitative disclosures about credit risk, liquidity risk, and market risk. Qualitative disclosures provide information about managing the risks and quantitative disclosures deal with the amount of risk.

Inventory

Under IFRS, the choice of inventory method is based on the physical flow of the inventory; that is, whether the inventory that is purchased or produced first, is sold first. Two acceptable methods are the first-in, first-out (FIFO) method and the average cost method. Recall in the topic review on understanding the income statement that the last-in, first-out (LIFO) method is allowed under U.S. GAAP but is not permitted under IFRS.

Under IFRS and U.S. GAAP, inventory is reported on the balance sheet at the lower of cost or net realizable value. In the United States, once an inventory write-down occurs, any subsequent recovery of value is ignored. Under IFRS, subsequent recovery in the value of inventory can be included in inventory values.

Property and Equipment

Under IFRS and U.S. GAAP, property and equipment, sometimes referred to as fixed assets, are reported on the balance sheet at original cost less accumulated depreciation. U.S. GAAP does not permit upward revaluations of property and equipment.

Under IFRS, property and equipment can be revalued upward. In this case, the property and equipment are reported at fair value at the revaluation date less the accumulated depreciation since revaluation.

The increase in value is reported in the income statement to the extent that a previous downward valuation was *included in net income*. Otherwise, any increase in value is reported as a *direct adjustment to equity*. This results in consistent treatment in the income statement. Similarly, a decrease in value is reported as a loss on the income statement unless it reverses a previous upward revaluation taken directly to equity.

Intercorporate Investments

When a firm makes an equity investment in another firm, the accounting treatment depends on the firm's ability to influence or control the policies and actions of the investee. The classification of marketable equity securities as held-for-trading and available-for-sale only applies to **passive investments**. An investment is considered passive if the investor cannot significantly influence or control the investee. As a practical guideline, an ownership interest of less than 20% is considered passive.

If an ownership interest is between 20% and 50%, the investor can usually significantly influence the investee. Under IFRS, **significant influence** is defined as the power to participate in the financial and operating policy decisions of the investee without control or joint control over those policies.[1]

For investments over which they have significant influence, firms must use the **equity method** of accounting. Under the equity method, a pro-rata share of the investee's net income is reported as investment income and increases the reported value of the firm's equity investment. Dividends received from the equity investment decrease the reported value of the investment (but increase cash).

If an ownership interest is greater than 50%, the investor can usually control the investee. In this case, the **consolidation method** must be used, and the firm reports *all* of the assets and liabilities, as well as the net income, of the investee in its own financial statement items.

In the case of joint control of an investee, such as an ownership interest in a joint venture, IFRS recommends the use of the **proportionate consolidation method.** Under proportionate consolidation, the investor reports its pro-rata share of the assets, liabilities, and net income of the investee. Alternatively, the equity method can be used, but proportionate consolidation is preferred.

Under U.S. GAAP, the equity method is usually required for joint ventures. Proportionate consolidation is permitted under IFRS only.

Figure 2 summarizes the accounting treatment for intercorporate investments.

---

1. International Accounting Standard No. 31.

Figure 2: Accounting Treatment for Intercorporate Investments

Method	Ownership	Degree of Influence
Market	Less than 20%	No significant influence
Equity	20% – 50%	Significant influence
Consolidation	More than 50%	Control
Proportionate Consolidation (IFRS only)	Shared	Joint control (venture)

Goodwill

Recall from the topic review on understanding the balance sheet that goodwill is the excess of purchase price over the fair value of the identifiable assets and liabilities acquired in a business acquisition. Goodwill is an unidentifiable intangible asset that cannot be separated from the firm.

Goodwill is not systematically amortized in the income statement but is tested at least annually for impairment. If impaired, goodwill is written down on the balance sheet and the consequent loss is recognized on the income statement. The impairment of goodwill does not affect cash flows, but does affect certain financial ratios. In periods after a write-down, ratios such as ROA, ROE, and asset turnover will improve because the denominator of each is reduced.

Judgment is involved in determining whether goodwill is impaired. Of course, when judgment is involved, there are opportunities for the firm to manipulate earnings.

For comparability, analysts often make the following adjustments:

- Completely eliminate goodwill when computing ratios.
- Exclude goodwill impairment charges from the income statement when analyzing trends.
- Evaluate future acquisitions in terms of the price paid relative to the earning power of the acquired assets.

Two other issues affect the comparability of the financial statements of the acquiring firm in a business acquisition.

1. The assets and liabilities of the acquired firm are recorded at fair value at the date of acquisition. As a result, the acquiring firm reports assets and liabilities with a mixture of bases for valuation; old assets continue to be reported at historical cost while acquired assets are carried at their fair value.

2. The revenues and expenses of the acquired firm are included in the acquiring firm's income statement *from* the acquisition date. There is no restatement of prior-period income statements. Without restatement, acquisitions may create an illusion of growth.

Identifiable Intangible Assets

Under U.S. GAAP and IFRS, purchased intangible assets are reported on the balance sheet at their cost less accumulated amortization. The costs of internally developed intangibles are generally expensed as incurred. U.S. GAAP does not permit upward revaluations of intangible assets.

As with property and equipment, IFRS does allow upward revaluations of identifiable intangible assets. Intangible assets are then reported at their fair value as of the revaluation date, less the accumulated amortization since revaluation.

As with property and equipment, any increase in value is reported in the income statement to the extent that a previous downward revaluation reduced net income. Any upward revaluation in excess of prior downward revaluation is reported as a direct adjustment to equity. Under the same principle, a decrease in value is reported in the income statement to the extent that a previous upward revaluation was included in net income, and any decrease in value in excess of prior upward revaluation is reported as a direct adjustment to equity.

Analysts must be aware that not all intangible assets are reported on the balance sheet. Some intangibles are expensed as incurred. These unrecorded assets must still be considered when valuing a firm. A valuable brand name such as Coke®, the software developed by Microsoft Corporation, or the patents and manufacturing expertise of a large pharmaceutical firm may not be recorded as firm assets.

Provisions

Provisions are nonfinancial liabilities that are uncertain as to their timing or amount. Examples include warranty obligations and contingencies. According to IAS No. 37, a firm should recognize a liability when it has a present obligation that is a result of a past event and the firm can reliably estimate the cost to settle the obligation.

U.S. GAAP does not use the term "provisions." Under U.S. GAAP, if a contingency is probable and can be reasonably estimated, a loss is recognized in the income statement and a liability is recorded on the balance sheet.

LOS 43.b: Identify and explain the major international accounting standards for major revenue and expense categories on the income statement, and the key differences from U.S. GAAP.

The definitions of revenue and the criteria for revenue recognition under U.S. GAAP and IFRS differ slightly. The main principles are the same but U.S. GAAP provides more industry-specific guidance than IFRS.

Construction Contracts

Under U.S. GAAP, the percentage-of-completion method of revenue recognition is appropriate for contracts that extend beyond one accounting period if the outcome of the project can be reasonably estimated. Accordingly, revenue, expense, and therefore profit are recognized as the work is performed. If the outcome of project cannot be reasonably estimated, the completed-contract method is required.

Under IFRS, if the firm cannot reliably measure the outcome of the project, revenue is recognized to the extent of contract costs and profit is only recognized at project completion.

Cost of Goods Sold

IFRS does not permit LIFO inventory accounting. LIFO firms that follow U.S. GAAP must disclose the LIFO reserve in the footnotes to their financial statements. The change in the LIFO reserve over a period of time is equal to the difference between COGS calculated under LIFO and COGS calculated under FIFO. Disclosure of the LIFO reserve allows users to adjust the LIFO COGS to FIFO COGS. This adjustment enhances the comparability U.S. and IFRS firms.

Operating Expenses

U.S. GAAP differentiates between expenses and losses, but IFRS does not. Under IFRS, losses not related to a firm's primary business operations are included in operating expenses.

Depreciation

Tangible assets (excluding land) are depreciated, intangible assets (except goodwill) are amortized, and natural resources are depleted. All three terms describe the allocation of an asset's cost over its useful life. The allocation process requires the use of estimates such as useful life and salvage value. Estimates often change as new information is acquired. A change in an estimate is put into effect prospectively; that is, no cumulative adjustment is made for prior period depreciation, just as with U.S. GAAP.

In choosing an appropriate allocation method (e.g., straight-line, accelerated), IFRS requires that the method reflect the pattern of expected consumption and the allocation must be made on a systematic basis over the asset's useful life.

Interest Expense

Borrowing costs are generally expensed in the year incurred. Under IFRS, firms can *choose* to capitalize interest that is related to the acquisition, construction, or production of an asset that will take a substantial time to complete. The capitalized interest is simply added to the cost of the asset and is eventually recognized in the income statement as the asset is depreciated.

Firms that follow U.S. GAAP *must* capitalize construction interest.

Income Taxes

Both U.S. GAAP and IFRS require firms to recognize temporary differences between financial reporting standards and tax reporting standards. These differences can create both deferred tax assets and deferred tax liabilities.

The differences between IFRS and U.S. GAAP in accounting for income taxes relate primarily to differences and exceptions in financial accounting principles between U.S. GAAP and IFRS.

Nonrecurring Items

Analysts often ignore nonrecurring items when forecasting future earnings because recurring earnings are usually viewed as more sustainable. Over the past several years, there has been convergence between U.S. GAAP and IFRS in reporting discontinued operations and changes in accounting principles. However, their treatments of extraordinary items still differ.

Under U.S. GAAP, an extraordinary item is a material transaction that is both unusual in nature and infrequent in occurrence. Extraordinary items are reported in the income statement, net of tax, below income from continuing operations.

IFRS does not permit firms to treat items as "extraordinary" in the income statement. The analyst, however, can use required IFRS disclosures to separate recurring and non-recurring earnings.

LOS 43.c: Identify and explain the major differences between international and U.S. GAAP accounting standards concerning the treatment of interest and dividends on the cash flow statement.

Under U.S. GAAP, dividends paid to the firm's shareholders are reported as CFF and interest paid is reported as CFO. Interest received and dividends received from investments are also reported as CFO.

IFRS allows more flexibility in the classification of interest and dividend cash flows. Under IFRS, interest and dividends received may be classified as either operating *or* investing activities (CFO or CFI). Dividends paid to the firm's shareholders and interest paid on the firm's debt may be classified as either CFO or CFF.

LOS 43.d: Interpret the effect of differences between international and U.S. GAAP accounting standards on the balance sheet, income statement, and the statement of changes in equity for some commonly used financial ratios.

When comparing firms that follow different accounting standards, the analyst must make adjustments to the specific balance sheet and income statement accounts that differ. This is done by recasting the financial statements of one of the firms so that the financial statements of both firms can be compared.

As an example, consider a U.S. firm that reports its inventory under LIFO and an IFRS firm that reports its inventory under FIFO. The income statements and balance sheets of the two firms cannot be compared without recasting the IFRS firm's financial statements to U.S. GAAP or vice versa. Because LIFO firms are required to disclose the LIFO reserve in the financial statement footnotes, it is usually easier to convert the LIFO firm statements to a FIFO basis.

In an inflationary environment, a LIFO firm will report higher COGS and lower inventory as compared to a FIFO firm. Higher COGS will result in lower profitability (gross profit, operating profit, taxable profit, and net profit). Lower taxable profit will result in lower income taxes. Lower net profit will also result in lower equity (lower retained earnings).

The LIFO reserve is the difference between LIFO and FIFO inventory. By adding the LIFO reserve to the U.S. firm's inventory balance, the analyst can state the U.S. firm's inventory on a FIFO basis to make it comparable with the IFRS firm.

In addition, it is necessary to convert LIFO COGS to FIFO COGS. This can be accomplished by subtracting the increase in the LIFO reserve over the period from LIFO COGS.

Example: LIFO adjustments for comparison purposes

Brownfield Company is a LIFO firm. At the end of last year, Brownfield reported inventory of $2 million and cost of goods sold of $6.4 million. Brownfield's LIFO reserve was $600,000 at the beginning of the year and $900,000 at year-end. Calculate Brownfield's COGS and ending inventory on a FIFO basis.

Answer:

The LIFO reserve increased $300,000 over the year [$900,000 – $600,000]. By subtracting the increase in the LIFO reserve from LIFO COGS, COGS on a FIFO basis is $6.1 million [$6.4 million – $300,000].

By adding the LIFO reserve of $900,000 to Brownfield's LIFO inventory of $2 million, inventory on a FIFO basis is $2.9 million [$2 million + $900,000].

Adjustments to LIFO inventory and LIFO COGS (in an inflationary environment) to their FIFO equivalents will result in:

- Higher gross profit margin [(revenue – COGS) / revenue] because of lower COGS.
- Higher operating profit margin [operating profit / revenue] because of higher gross profit.
- Higher net profit margin [net income / revenue] because of higher operating profit.
- Higher current ratio [current asset / current liabilities] because of higher current assets (inventory).
- Lower total asset turnover ratio [revenue / average total assets] because of higher total assets (inventory).
- Lower inventory turnover ratio [COGS / average inventory] because of lower COGS and higher inventory.
- Lower debt-to-equity ratio because of higher equity.

KEY CONCEPTS

LOS 43.a

Held-for-trading securities are reported at fair value on the balance sheet and any unrealized gains and losses are recognized in the income statement.

The equity method is used for business combinations when the investor can significantly influence the investee (between 20% and 50% ownership interest). The consolidation method is used when the investor can control the investee (greater than 50% ownership interest). In the case of joint control, proportionate consolidation is preferred under IFRS, but the equity method is required under U.S. GAAP.

Inventory is reported on the balance sheet at the lower of cost or net realizable value under IFRS and at the lower of cost or market under U.S. GAAP. A recovery of value subsequent to a writedown can be recognized under IFRS but not under U.S. GAAP.

Under IFRS, the value of property and equipment and identifiable intangible assets can be revalued upward, but under U.S. GAAP, they cannot.

LOS 43.b

When the firm cannot reliably estimate the outcome of a project, it recognizes costs as revenue to the extent they are likely recoverable, but firms reporting under U.S. GAAP must use the completed contract method.

The LIFO inventory cost method is permitted by U.S. GAAP but is prohibited under IFRS.

IFRS requires the depreciation method to allocate an asset's cost systematically over its useful life and reflect the pattern of asset consumption.

IFRS does not permit firms to treat items as "extraordinary items" on the income statement as they can under U.S. GAAP.

LOS 43.c

Under U.S. GAAP, dividends paid are financing activities while interest paid or received and dividends received are operating activities. Under IFRS, dividends and interest paid can be reported as either operating activities or financing activities. Interest received and dividends received can be reported as either operating activities or investing activities.

LOS 43.d

To compare financial statement ratios of firms reporting under U.S. GAAP and IFRS, an analyst must adjust the data for one of the firms to make the financial statements comparable.

CONCEPT CHECKERS

1. Are held-for-trading securities and influential securities reported on the balance sheet at fair value?

	Held-for-trading	Influential
A.	Yes	No
B.	Yes	Yes
C.	No	Yes

2. According to the International Accounting Standards Board, should the costs of developing goodwill and the costs of acquiring goodwill be capitalized?

	Developing goodwill	Acquiring goodwill
A.	Yes	No
B.	No	Yes
C.	No	No

3. At the end of 20X6, Toreador Inc. owned equipment that became impaired. At the time of impairment, the market value of the equipment was $150,000 and a $25,000 expense was recognized. At the end of 20X7, the market value of the equipment increased $40,000. Which of the following *best* describes the effect of the recovery on Toreador's 20X7 financial statements according to the International Accounting Standards Board?
   A. Neither net income nor shareholders' equity are affected.
   B. Net income increases $25,000 and shareholder's equity increases $40,000.
   C. Net income increases $25,000 and shareholders' equity increases $15,000.

4. Bledsoe Construction Company is in the second year of a 3-year contract to build a new hotel. Due to a labor strike, Bledsoe is unable to reliably estimate the total cost of the project. Can Bledsoe recognize revenue in the first year of the project according to U.S. accounting standards and international accounting standards?

	U.S. accounting standards	International accounting standards
A.	Yes	Yes
B.	No	Yes
C.	No	No

5. According to the International Accounting Standards Board, where should a firm report interest received and dividends received in the cash flow statement?
   A. Operating activities or investing activities.
   B. Operating activities only.
   C. Neither operating activities nor investing activities.

6. At the end of the year, a firm reported LIFO inventory of $100,000 and cost of goods sold of $320,000. If the LIFO reserve was $30,000 at the beginning of the year and $80,000 at year-end, how much was FIFO COGS?
   A. $220,000.
   B. $240,000.
   C. $270,000.

7. An analyst wants to compare the financial results of a U.S. firm and a European firm. The accounting standards followed by both firms are the same except that the European firm revalues its real property upward to reflect fair value. The U.S. firm's real property is reported at historical cost. The analyst decides to restate the European firm's real property by eliminating the unrealized gains. What effect will the restatement have on the European firm's total asset turnover and debt-to-equity ratios?

	Total asset turnover	Debt-to-equity
A.	Lower	Higher
B.	Higher	Higher
C.	Higher	Lower

ANSWERS – CONCEPT CHECKERS

1. **A**   A held-for-trading security is reported on the balance sheet at fair value. An influential security is accounted for using the equity method. Under the equity method, the balance sheet account is not reported at fair value.

2. **B**   The costs associated with developing goodwill should be expensed as incurred. The cost of goodwill acquired in a business acquisition is capitalized.

3. **B**   The impairment loss of $25,000 was reported in 20X6 net income. Therefore, $25,000 of the $40,000 increase in market value is reported in 20X7 net income. The remainder of $15,000 is reported as a direct adjustment to shareholders' equity. Total shareholders' equity increases $40,000; $25,000 from net income (increases retained earnings) and $15,000 from the direct adjustment.

4. **B**   Since Bledsoe cannot reasonably estimate cost, the completed-contract method is required under U.S. GAAP and no revenues are recognized until project completion. Bledsoe can use the percentage-of-completion method under IFRS; however, revenue is recognized only to the extent that costs are incurred. No profit can be recognized until the project is complete.

5. **A**   Under IFRS, interest received and dividends received can be reported as either operating activities or investing activities. Under U.S. GAAP, interest received and dividends received are reported as operating activities in the cash flow statement.

6. **C** $320,000 LIFO COGS – ($80,000 ending reserve – $30,000 beginning reserve) = $270,000 FIFO COGS.

7. **B**   Removing the unrealized gain from assets will increase the total asset turnover ratio (lower assets). Removing the unrealized gain from equity will increase the debt-to-equity ratio (lower equity).

1. Which of the following would *least likely* be included in the Management Discussion and Analysis (MD&A) portion of the financial statements?
   A. Outlook for future results based on known trends.
   B. Discussion of depreciation methods or changes in method.
   C. Information about expected capital expenditures and events with liquidity implications.

2. Contractors, Inc. has contracted to build a stadium for the City of Waston. The contract price is $100 million, costs are estimated to be $60 million, and the time to completion is three years. Compared to the completed contract method, what effect will using the percentage-of-completion method *most likely* have on a year 2 leverage ratio and year 3 cash flow from operations?
   A. Both will be the same using either method.
   B. Both will lower using percentage-of-completion.
   C. Only one will be lower using percentage-of-completion.

3. Two firms are identical except that the first pays higher interest charges and lower dividends, while the second pays higher dividends and lower interest charges. Both prepare their financial statements under U.S. GAAP. Compared to the first, the second will have cash flow from financing (CFF) and earnings per share (EPS) that are:

	CFF	EPS
A.	The same	Higher
B.	Lower	Higher
C.	Lower	The same

4. Which of the following is an analyst *least likely* to be able to find on or calculate from either a common-size income statement or a common-size balance sheet?
   A. Inventory turnover.
   B. Operating profit margin.
   C. Debt to equity ratio.

5. If a firm's inventory turnover and number of days of payables both increase, the effect on a firm's cash conversion cycle is:
   A. to shorten it.
   B. to lengthen it.
   C. uncertain.

6. The following information is summarized from Famous, Inc.'s financial statements for the year ended December 31, 20X0:
   - Sales were $800,000.
   - Net profit margin was 20%.
   - Sales to assets was 50%.
   - Equity multiplier is 1.6.
   - Interest Expense was $30,000.
   - Dividends declared were $32,000.

   Famous, Inc.'s sustainable growth rate based on results from this period is *closest* to:
   A. 3.2%.
   B. 8.0%.
   C. 12.8%.

7. On January 1, Orange Computers issued employee stock options for 400,000 shares. Options on 200,000 shares have an exercise price of $18, and options on the other 200,000 shares have an exercise price of $22. The year-end stock price was $24, and the average stock price over the year was $20. The change in the number of shares used to calculate diluted earnings per share for the year due to these options is *closest* to:
   A. 20,000 shares.
   B. 67,000 shares.
   C. 100,000 shares.

8. Premier Corp.'s year-end LIFO reserve was $2,500,000 in 20X6 and $2,300,000 in 20X7. Premier's $200,000 decline in the LIFO reserve is *least likely* a result of:
   A. a LIFO liquidation.
   B. declining purchase prices.
   C. amortization of the LIFO reserve.

9. If a firm issues par bonds with warrants attached rather than issuing an equal amount of par convertible bonds with the same coupon rate, it will tend to:
   A. improve the firm's leverage ratios.
   B. decrease ROA prior to conversion or warrant exercise.
   C. decrease income variability prior to conversion or warrant exercise.

10. Train paid $8 million to acquire a franchise at the beginning of 20X5 that was expensed in 20X5. If Train had elected to capitalize the franchise as an intangible asset and amortize the cost of the franchise over eight years, what effect would this decision have on Train's 20X5 cash flow from operations (CFO) and 20X6 debt-to-assets-ratio?
    A. Both would be higher with capitalization.
    B. Both would be lower with capitalization.
    C. One would be higher and one would be lower with capitalization.

11. Graphics, Inc. has a deferred tax asset of $4,000,000 on its books. As of December 31, it is probable that $2,000,000 of the deferred tax asset's value will never be realized because of the uncertainty about future income. Graphics, Inc. should:
    A. reduce the deferred tax asset account by $2,000,000.
    B. establish a valuation allowance of $2,000,000.
    C. establish an offsetting deferred tax liability of $2,000,000.

12. Which of the following was *least likely* a financial reporting quality warning sign related to the Sunbeam accounting scandal?
    A. Improper bill-and-hold transactions.
    B. Creating excessive reserves in a period of poor earnings.
    C. Investing cash flows much higher than operating cash flows.

13. If Lizard Inc., a lessee, treats a 5-year lease as a finance lease with straight line depreciation rather than as an operating lease:
    A. it will have greater equity at lease inception.
    B. its operating income will be less in the first year of the lease.
    C. its CFO will be greater and CFF will be less in the second year of the lease.

14. Compared to a long-lived asset with no costs of disposal, an otherwise identical asset that has significant expected environmental remediation costs at the end of its useful life will have which of the following effects on the financial statements?
    A. Equity will be lower at asset acquisition.
    B. Interest coverage ratios will be lower during each year of the asset's life.
    C. Net income will be unaffected over the asset's life.

15. Taking an impairment charge due to a decrease in the value of a long-lived depreciable asset is *least likely*, in the period the impairment is recognized, to reduce a firm's:
    A. net income.
    B. operating income.
    C. taxes payable.

16. Under U.S. GAAP, firms are required to capitalize:
    A. any asset with a useful economic life of more than one year.
    B. interest paid on loans to finance construction of a long-lived asset.
    C. research and development costs for a drug that will almost certainly provide a revenue stream of five years or more.

17. With regard to the exercise of employee stock options, which of the following is *least likely* a concern to the analyst?
    A. Increased operating cash flow from the tax benefits of exercise of the options.
    B. Effects of exercise on investing cash flows.
    C. Classification of the cash flow to repurchase shares.

18. During a period of falling prices and stable inventory quantities, what are the effects on net income and cash flow of using FIFO inventory accounting (for financial and tax reporting) as compared to LIFO for a firm reporting under U.S. GAAP?
    A. Both are higher using FIFO.
    B. Both are lower using FIFO.
    C. One is higher and one is lower using FIFO.

19. Over the last year, ArtGraphics saw its accumulated depreciation increase from $340,000 to $370,000. It purchased no capital assets during the period, but had plant, property, equipment with a book value of $400,000 at the end of the year. The average useful life of the firm's depreciable assets as of year-end is *closest* to:
    A. 6 years
    B. 12 years
    C. 26 years

20. Victory Corp. received interest income from federally tax exempt bonds of $40,000 in the year 20X0. Its statutory tax rate is 40%. The effect of this difference between taxable and pre-tax income is *most likely* a(n):
    A. decrease in its effective tax rate to below 40%.
    B. increase in its deferred tax asset of $16,000.
    C. increase in its deferred tax liability of $16,000.

21. The effects of treating a sale of receivables with recourse as a borrowing against receivables are *least likely* to include:
    A. increasing the total debt ratio.
    B. decreasing the receivables turnover ratio.
    C. reducing the value of cash and marketable securities.

22. A firm based in Germany that prepares its financial statements under IFRS but issues publicly traded securities in the United States:
    A. is required by the SEC to prepare financial statements in accordance with U.S. GAAP.
    B. must prepare separate financial statements, one under IFRS and one under U.S. GAAP.
    C. can either prepare a set of financial statements under U.S. GAAP or include a reconciliation of IFRS statement items with their GAAP equivalents and related disclosures.

23. An analyst is comparing two firms, one that reports under IFRS and one that reports under FASB standards. An analyst is *least likely* to do which of the following to facilitate comparison of the companies?
    A. Add the LIFO reserve to inventory for a U.S.-based firm that uses LIFO.
    B. Add the present values of each firm's future minimum operating lease payments to both assets and liabilities.
    C. Adjust the income statement of one of the firms if both have significant unrealized gains or losses from changes in the fair values of trading securities.

24. An analyst wants to compare the cash flows of two U.S. companies, one that reports cash flow using the direct method and one that reports it using the indirect method. The analyst is *most likely* to:
   A. convert the indirect statement to the direct method to compare the firms' cash expenditures.
   B. adjust the reported CFO of the firm that reports under the direct method for depreciation and amortization expense.
   C. increase CFI for any dividends reported as investing cash flows by the firm reporting cash flow by the direct method.

SELF-TEST ANSWERS: FINANCIAL REPORTING AND ANALYSIS

1. **B** The MD&A is required to contain information on trends in sales and expenses, expected capital expenditures and other events affecting liquidity, and the outlook for the future based on known trends. Details of depreciation methods are contained in the footnotes to the financial statements.

2. **C** The percentage-of-completion method recognizes a proportion of estimated project profits, which will increase net income, retained earnings, and equity and assets relative to the completed contract method. With increased equity and assets, both the debt/assets and debt/equity ratios are decreased. Cash flows are unaffected by the method selected to account for the project on the financial statements.

3. **B** Interest paid is an operating cash flow, and dividends paid are a financing cash flow, so the firm that pays higher dividends will have lower CFF. The firm with lower interest expense will have higher EPS.

4. **A** Inventory turnover involves sales (from the income statement) and average inventory (from the balance sheet) so it cannot be calculated from common-size statements. Debt to equity is debt/assets divided by equity/assets. Operating profits/sales can be read directly from the common-size income statement.

5. **A** Cash conversion cycle = collection period + inventory period – payables period.

   An increase in inventory turnover will decrease the inventory period and shorten the cash conversion cycle. An increase in the payables period will also shorten the cash conversion cycle.

6. **C** Famous, Inc.'s sustainable growth rate = (retention rate)(ROE).

   ROE = 0.20(800,000) / [(800,000/0.5)(1/1.6)] = 160,000/1,000,000 = 16%.

   Alternatively:

   ROE = (0.20)(0.50)(1.6) = 0.16 = 16%

   Retention rate = (1 – Dividend Payout Ratio) = 1 – {32,000/[(0.20)(800,000)]} = 0.80.

   Sustainable growth = 0.80 (16%) = 12.8%.

7. **A** Based on the average stock price, only the options at 18 are in the money (and therefore dilutive). Using the treasury stock method, the average shares outstanding for calculating diluted EPS would increase by [(20 – 18)/20] 200,000 = 20,000 shares.

8. **C** LIFO reserves are not amortized. A decline in the LIFO reserve occurs when the increasing prices that created the reserve begin declining or when inventory is liquidated (i.e., fewer units in inventory at the end of the year than at the beginning).

9. **A** With convertible bonds, the proceeds at issuance represent a balance sheet liability. For a bond with warrants attached, the fair market value of the warrants is recorded as equity, and the remainder of the proceeds is recorded as a liability, so liabilities to assets and liabilities to equity are both lower (improved). With interest expense the same on both issues, there is no effect on net income or ROA.

10. **C**   If the cost were amortized rather than expensed, the $8 million cost of the franchise would be classified as an investing cash flow rather than an operating cash flow, so CFO would increase (and CFI decrease). The asset created by capitalizing the cost would increase assets, so the debt-to-assets ratio would decrease.

11. **B**   If it becomes probable that a portion of a deferred tax asset will not be realized, a valuation allowance should be established. A valuation allowance serves to reduce the value of a deferred tax asset for the probability that it will not be realized (the difference between tax payable and income tax expense will not reverse in future periods).

12. **C**   Investing cash flows were much higher than operating cash flows for Enron, indicating a need for a great deal of financing. The other two choices were both warning signs related to the Sunbeam accounting scandal.

13. **C**   With a finance lease, only the interest portion of the lease payment is classified as CFO, so CFO will be greater than it would be with an equivalent operating lease. CFF will be less for a finance lease because the principal portion of each lease payment is classified as a financing cash outflow. Operating income, EBIT, will be reduced only by the (equal) annual depreciation expense with a finance lease, so operating income will be greater for a finance lease than for an operating lease (for which the entire lease payment will be an operating expense). At inception, a finance lease will increase assets and liabilities by the same amount so there is no effect on equity.

14. **B**   At asset acquisition, a liability equal to the present value of the asset disposal costs is created and an asset of equal value is created, so there is no initial effect on equity. The increase in the liability (accretion) each year is recorded as interest expense, so interest coverage ratios are lower each year when there are asset disposal costs. With asset disposal costs, net income will be reduced each year by both the interest expense on the liability and by depreciation of the offsetting asset that is created.

15. **C**   Impairment charges reduce operating income and net income in the period of the charge. Taxes are not affected because any loss in asset value will reduce taxes only when the asset is disposed of and the loss is actually realized. The debt to equity ratio increases in the period of the charge because equity is reduced.

16. **B**   Interest on loans that specifically fund construction of long-lived assets must be capitalized under U.S. GAAP. Assets of insignificant value (e.g., metal waste basket) are typically expensed even when their useful lives are many years. R&D costs are expensed under U.S. GAAP.

17. **B**   There are no effects on investing cash flows from the exercise of employee stock options. Option exercise results in a tax deduction that reduces taxes and increases operating cash flow. Since employee incentive stock options are properly part of compensation expense, cash expenditures to repurchase shares and avoid dilution are properly classified as operating cash flows rather than as financing cash flows (their classification under accounting standards).

18. **C**   With falling prices, FIFO inventory accounting will result in higher COGS, lower net income, and higher cash flow because of lower taxes on the lower net income.

19. **C**   Annual depreciation is 370,000 − 340,000 = 30,000.

Average depreciable life is gross fixed assets/annual depreciation = (400,000 + 370,000)/30,000 = 25.66 years.

20. **A** The receipt of the tax-exempt interest income will create a permanent difference between pretax income and taxable income. Since the tax-free interest increases pre-tax income, but not income tax expense, the effective tax rate will be less than 40%. No deferred tax liability is created because the difference between pretax and taxable income will never reverse.

21. **C** The analyst should treat the "sale" of receivables as a loan secured by the receivables. This means the receivables should be added back to accounts receivable, decreasing receivables turnover. A current liability equal to the value of the loan should be added to the balance sheet, which will increase the total debt ratio. The cash received remains on the balance sheet so there is no reduction in the value of cash and marketable securities.

22. **C** Foreign issuers in U.S. markets must either submit U.S. GAAP compliant financial statements or separately provide a reconciliation of their IFRS statements with U.S. GAAP, including related disclosures that will aid financial statement users in the United States.

23. **C** Unrealized gains and losses on trading securities are reported in the income statement under both U.S. and IFRS standards. Since LIFO is not permitted under IFRS, adjusting the inventory amount for a LIFO firm is a likely adjustment. To account for differences in how companies report leases, adding the present value of future minimum operating lease payments to both the assets and liabilities of a firm will remove the effects of lease reporting methods from solvency and leverage ratios.

24. **A** By converting a cash flow statement to the direct method, an analyst can view cash expenses and receipts by category, which will facilitate a comparison of two firms' cash outlays and receipts. CFO is correct under either method and requires no adjustment. Neither dividends received nor dividends paid are classified as CFI under U.S. GAAP.

FORMULAS

Activity Ratios:

$$\text{receivables turnover} = \frac{\text{annual sales}}{\text{average receivables}}$$

$$\text{days of sales oustanding} = \frac{365}{\text{receivables turnover}}$$

$$\text{inventory turnover} = \frac{\text{cost of goods sold}}{\text{average inventory}}$$

$$\text{days of inventory on hand} = \frac{365}{\text{inventory turnover}}$$

$$\text{payables turnover} = \frac{\text{purchases}}{\text{average trade payables}}$$

$$\text{number of days of payables} = \frac{365}{\text{payables turnover ratio}}$$

$$\text{total asset turnover} = \frac{\text{revenue}}{\text{average total assets}}$$

$$\text{fixed asset turnover} = \frac{\text{revenue}}{\text{average net fixed assets}}$$

$$\text{working capital turnover} = \frac{\text{revenue}}{\text{average working capital}}$$

Liquidity Ratios:

$$\text{current ratio} = \frac{\text{current assets}}{\text{current liabilities}}$$

$$\text{quick ratio} = \frac{\text{cash + marketable securities + receivables}}{\text{current liabilities}}$$

$$\text{cash ratio} = \frac{\text{cash + marketable securities}}{\text{current liabilities}}$$

$$\text{defensive interval} = \frac{\text{cash + marketable securities + receivables}}{\text{average daily expenditures}}$$

$$\text{cash conversion cycle} = \left(\begin{array}{c}\text{days sales}\\\text{outstanding}\end{array}\right) + \left(\begin{array}{c}\text{days of inventory}\\\text{on hand}\end{array}\right) - \left(\begin{array}{c}\text{number of days}\\\text{of payables}\end{array}\right)$$

Solvency Ratios:

$$\text{debt-to-equity} = \frac{\text{total debt}}{\text{total shareholders' equity}}$$

$$\text{debt-to-capital} = \frac{\text{total debt}}{\text{total debt} + \text{total shareholders' equity}}$$

$$\text{debt-to-assets} = \frac{\text{total debt}}{\text{total assets}}$$

$$\text{financial leverage} = \frac{\text{average total assets}}{\text{average total equity}}$$

$$\text{interest coverage} = \frac{\text{earnings before interest and taxes}}{\text{interest payments}}$$

$$\text{fixed charge coverage} = \frac{\text{earnings before interest and taxes} + \text{lease payments}}{\text{interest payments} + \text{lease payments}}$$

Profitability Ratios:

$$\text{net profit margin} = \frac{\text{net income}}{\text{revenue}}$$

$$\text{gross profit margin} = \frac{\text{gross profit}}{\text{revenue}}$$

$$\text{operating profit margin} = \frac{\text{operating income}}{\text{revenue}} \text{ or } \frac{\text{EBIT}}{\text{revenue}}$$

$$\text{pretax margin} = \frac{\text{EBT}}{\text{revenue}}$$

$$\text{return on assets (ROA)} = \frac{\text{net income}}{\text{average total assets}}$$

$$\text{return on assets (ROA)} = \frac{\text{net income} + \text{interest expense} (1 - \text{tax rate})}{\text{average total assets}}$$

$$\text{operating return on assets} = \frac{\text{operating income}}{\text{average total assets}} \text{ or } \frac{\text{EBIT}}{\text{average total assets}}$$

$$\text{return on total capital} = \frac{\text{EBIT}}{\text{average total capital}}$$

$$\text{return on equity} = \frac{\text{net income}}{\text{average total equity}}$$

$$\text{return on common equity} = \frac{\text{net income} - \text{preferred dividends}}{\text{average common equity}}$$

$$= \frac{\text{net income available to common}}{\text{average common equity}}$$

Free Cash Flow to the Firm:

FCFF = net income + noncash charges + [interest expense × (1 – tax rate)] – fixed capital investment – working capital investment

FCFF = cash flow from operations + [interest expense × (1 – tax rate)] – fixed capital investment

Free Cash Flow to Equity:

FCFE = cash flow from operations – fixed capital investment + net borrowing

$$\text{common-size income statement ratios} = \frac{\text{income statement account}}{\text{sales}}$$

$$\text{common-size balance sheet ratios} = \frac{\text{balance sheet account}}{\text{total assets}}$$

$$\text{common-size cash flow ratios} = \frac{\text{cash flow statement account}}{\text{revenues}}$$

original DuPont equation: $\text{ROE} = \left(\dfrac{\text{net profit}}{\text{margin}}\right)\left(\dfrac{\text{asset}}{\text{turnover}}\right)\left(\dfrac{\text{leverage}}{\text{ratio}}\right)$

extended DuPont equation:

$$\text{ROE} = \left(\frac{\text{net income}}{\text{EBT}}\right)\left(\frac{\text{EBT}}{\text{EBIT}}\right)\left(\frac{\text{EBIT}}{\text{revenue}}\right)\left(\frac{\text{revenue}}{\text{total assets}}\right)\left(\frac{\text{total assets}}{\text{total equity}}\right)$$

$$\text{basic EPS} = \frac{\text{net income} - \text{preferred dividends}}{\text{weighted average number of common shares outstanding}}$$

$$\text{diluted EPS} = \frac{\left[\text{net income} - \dfrac{\text{preferred}}{\text{dividends}}\right] + \begin{bmatrix}\text{convertible}\\ \text{preferred}\\ \text{dividends}\end{bmatrix} + \left(\begin{matrix}\text{convertible}\\ \text{debt}\\ \text{interest}\end{matrix}\right)(1-t)}{\left(\begin{matrix}\text{weighted}\\ \text{average}\\ \text{shares}\end{matrix}\right) + \left(\begin{matrix}\text{shares from}\\ \text{conversion of}\\ \text{conv. pfd. shares}\end{matrix}\right) + \left(\begin{matrix}\text{shares from}\\ \text{conversion of}\\ \text{conv. debt}\end{matrix}\right) + \left(\begin{matrix}\text{shares}\\ \text{issuable from}\\ \text{stock options}\end{matrix}\right)}$$

Coefficients of Variation:

$$\text{CV sales} = \frac{\text{standard deviation of sales}}{\text{mean sales}}$$

$$\text{CV operating income} = \frac{\text{standard deviation of operating income}}{\text{mean operating income}}$$

$$\text{CV net income} = \frac{\text{standard deviation of net income}}{\text{mean net income}}$$

Inventories:

$$\text{ending inventory} = \text{beginning inventory} + \text{purchases} - \text{COGS}$$

$$\text{current cost of inventory (FIFO)} = \text{LIFO inventory} + \text{LIFO reserve}$$

$$\text{COGS}_{\text{FIFO}} = \text{COGS}_{\text{LIFO}} - (\text{ending LIFO reserve} - \text{beginning LIFO reserve})$$

Long-Lived Assets:

$$\text{straight-line depreciation} = \frac{\text{cost} - \text{salvage value}}{\text{useful life}}$$

$$\text{DDB depreciation} = \left(\frac{2}{\text{useful life}}\right)(\text{cost} - \text{accumulated depreciation})$$

$$\text{average age in years} = \frac{\text{accumulated depreciation}}{\text{annual depreciation expense}}$$

$$\text{average age as a percentage} = \frac{\text{accumulated depreciation}}{\text{ending gross investment}}$$

$$\text{average depreciable life} = \frac{\text{ending gross investment}}{\text{annual depreciation expense}}$$

$$\text{remaining useful life} = \frac{\text{ending net investment}}{\text{annual depreciation expense}}$$

Deferred Taxes:

$$\text{income tax expense} = \text{taxes payable} + \Delta\text{DTL} - \Delta\text{DTA}$$

Debt Liabilities:

$$\text{interest expense} = \begin{pmatrix} \text{the market rate} \\ \text{at issue} \end{pmatrix} \times \begin{pmatrix} \text{the balance sheet value} \\ \text{of the liability at} \\ \text{the beginning of the period} \end{pmatrix}$$

Performance Ratios

$$\text{Cash flow-to-revenue} = \frac{\text{CFO}}{\text{net revenue}}$$

$$\text{Cash return-on-assets} = \frac{\text{CFO}}{\text{average total assets}}$$

$$\text{Cash return-on-equity} = \frac{\text{CFO}}{\text{average total equity}}$$

$$\text{Cash-to-income} = \frac{\text{CFO}}{\text{operating income}}$$

$$\text{Cash flow per share} = \frac{\text{CFO} - \text{preferred dividends}}{\text{weighted average number of common shares}}$$

Coverage Ratios

$$\text{Debt coverage} = \frac{\text{CFO}}{\text{total debt}}$$

$$\text{Interest coverage} = \frac{\text{CFO} + \text{interest paid} + \text{taxes paid}}{\text{interest paid}}$$

$$\text{Reinvestment} = \frac{\text{CFO}}{\text{cash paid for long-term assets}}$$

$$\text{Debt payment} = \frac{\text{CFO}}{\text{cash long-term debt repayment}}$$

$$\text{Dividend payment} = \frac{\text{CFO}}{\text{dividends paid}}$$

$$\text{Investing and financing} = \frac{\text{CFO}}{\text{cash outflows from investing and financing activities}}$$

INDEX